Inclusive Leadership

INCLUSIVE LEADERSHIP: EQUITY AND BELONGING IN OUR COMMUNITIES

EDITED BY

JOANNE BARNES
Indiana Wesleyan University, USA

MICHAEL J. STEVENS
Weber State University, USA

BJØRN ZAKARIAS EKELUND
Human Factors AS, Norway

AND

KAREN PERHAM-LIPPMAN
Jensen Hughes, USA

emerald PUBLISHING

United Kingdom – North America – Japan – India – Malaysia – China

Emerald Publishing Limited
Emerald Publishing, Floor 5, Northspring, 21-23 Wellington Street, Leeds LS1 4DL

First edition 2023

Reprints and permissions service
Contact: www.copyright.com

British Library Cataloguing in Publication Data
A catalogue record for this book is available from the British Library

ISBN: 978-1-83797-441-2 (Print)
ISBN: 978-1-83797-438-2 (Online)
ISBN: 978-1-83797-440-5 (Epub)

ISSN: 2058-8801 (Series)

INVESTOR IN PEOPLE

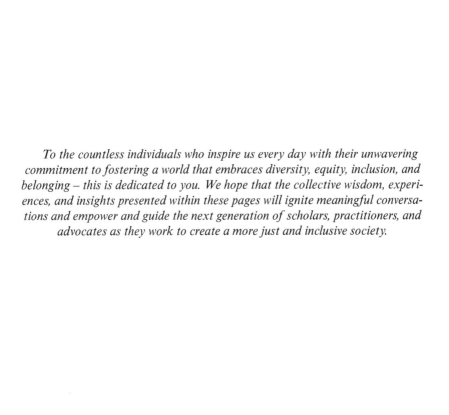

To the countless individuals who inspire us every day with their unwavering commitment to fostering a world that embraces diversity, equity, inclusion, and belonging – this is dedicated to you. We hope that the collective wisdom, experiences, and insights presented within these pages will ignite meaningful conversations and empower and guide the next generation of scholars, practitioners, and advocates as they work to create a more just and inclusive society.

Contents

Part Two: Diversity, Equity, Inclusion, Belonging, and Education

Part Three: The Application and Practice of Diversity, Equity, Inclusion, and Belonging/Accessibility

About the Editors

Joanne Barnes, Ed.D., is a Professor in the Ph.D. in Organizational Leadership program at Indiana Wesleyan University and Senior Consultant with Kozai Group focusing on diversity, equity, inclusion, and belonging (DEIB). She serves on the board of Houghton University and the International Leadership Association. She was a Master Coach for the 2019/2020 United Nations (UN) WE Empower winners and Coach for the 2018 UN WE Empower winners. She presents at top conferences on leadership and has publications on women and leadership, cultural intelligence, and global leadership. She is the Lead Editor for *SAGE DEIB Business Skills* and serves on editorial review boards. She is an active member of Alpha Kappa Alpha Sorority, Inc.

Michael J. Stevens, Ph.D., is a Distinguished Presidential Professor at Weber State University and consults widely with businesses and nonprofits. His expertise includes leadership and organizational culture; leveraging people and culture for competitive advantage; intercultural effectiveness for diverse and inclusive workplaces; and leadership assessment, selection, and development. His award-winning research includes the creation and validation of assessments that measure a person's competencies to work successfully in self-managed teams and culturally diverse environments. To date, his assessments have been taken by 275,000+ people in over 130 countries. He is a Founding Partner of the Kozai Group, Inc., a global leadership development and assessment consultancy. He has held leadership and board positions in industry, government, education, and not-for-profit enterprises.

Bjørn Zakarias Ekelund, Psychologist (Norway), M.B.A. (UK). In 1993, he established Human Factors, an organizational psychology consulting company where he now works as a Chairman and Senior Consultant. The company and he himself are most known for the development in 1995 of Diversity Icebreaker®, a concept that has been used by multiple facilitators in more than 75 countries and is presented in his book *Unleashing the Power of Diversity. How to Open Minds for Good* (2019). In 2008, he was awarded "Consultant of the Year" in Norway. He has published 6 books and over 30 scientific articles.

Karen Perham-Lippman, CDP, CAGS, has over a decade of experience implementing diversity, equity, inclusion; environmental, social and governance; and corporate social responsibility strategies globally. Karen is Jensen Hughes'

Diversity, Equity and Inclusion Director and an adjunct professor in the Business Center at Community College of Denver, which serves Colorado's most diverse student population. In 2021, she received a governor's appointment to Colorado's Business Experiential Learning Commission. She has been recognized with awards for leadership and service, is a Certified Diversity Professional and is ACUE-certified for designing learner centered and equitable courses. She has been published with Emerald, SAGE Publishing, Merits International Journal, and Ethics International Press and is a Ph.D. candidate in Organizational Leadership at Eastern University.

About the Contributors

Wendi L. Adair, Ph.D., is Professor of Organizational Psychology and Director of the Culture-as-Work Lab at University of Waterloo in Ontario, Canada. Her research examines the impact of culture on communication, for example, what is said and what is not said, and interdependent work outcomes, such as conflict resolution, trust, and team performance. She is an active contributor to Indigenous Workways, a collaborative research project bringing Indigenous voices to the mainstream Canadian workplace and icEdge, an assessment and training tool for effective communication in diverse workplaces.

Niels Agger-Gupta, Ph.D., is Acting-Director and Associate Professor in the School of Leadership Studies at Royal Roads University in Victoria, BC, Canada. He has consulted, researched, published, and teaches reconciliation, diversity, appreciative inquiry, world cafe as research, and inclusive leadership and change. He is the Co-author (with Brigitte Harris) of Chapter 17: Dialogic change and the practice of inclusive leadership in A. Boitano & H. E. Schockman (Eds.), *Breaking the zero-sum game: Transforming societies through inclusive leadership* (2017). Among other publications, he co-authored and edited the *Cultural and Linguistic Competency Standards*, Los Angeles County Department of Health Services, Office of Diversity (2003).

Jennifer Aranda, Ed.D., Leadership and Civic Engagement Educator for the University of Minnesota Extension, is an Intercultural Development Inventory (IDI) Qualified Administrator and Gallup Strengths Coach. Her background includes service/community-building with a focus on marginalized populations, particularly in rural and satellite cities. She has partnered with multiple sectors exploring social equity and justice by facilitating dialogue that shapes pathways toward change. With a former antiques/vintage small business, she values historical perspectives and honors the individual stories that are foundations of the collective. With previous residences in multiple states, her cultural agility combines with advocacy for holistic community transformation.

Nikki Bade, M.A.-L., Doctor of Social Sciences candidate, in the College of Interdisciplinary Studies, Royal Roads University, and a full-time Human Resources (HR) Practitioner. Her current research is on how non-Indigenous

Canadian organizations may foster a culturally safe workplace where Indigenous employees feel both a sense of inclusion and belonging. She is also a full-time HR leader with a mid-sized energy company in Calgary, AB. She has published articles and conference papers on the topics of front-line employee retention, employee engagement, and the application of arts-based methodologies in an organizational setting.

Allan Bird, Ph.D., is Senior Professor at Goa Institute of Management, India. He has authored, co-authored, or edited 9 books, over 40 book chapters, and more than 60 journal articles. He is a Reviewing Editor for the *Journal of International Business Studies*. He is a Fellow of the Academy of International Business and served as President of the Association of Japanese Business Studies, and Chair of the Careers Division in the Academy of Management. He was a key Architect of the International Organization Network and inaugural President of the Consortium for Undergraduate International Business Education which he helped found.

Julia Bott, M.Ed., has been an Educator in the Boston Public Schools for over 20 years and is deeply committed to inclusive education. She is currently Executive Director of Inclusive Education working with school leaders and educators across the district to build the capacity of schools to effectively educate all learners within the least restrictive learning environment. In 2001, she was named Thomas C. Passios Massachusetts Elementary Principal of the Year and a National Elementary Principal of the Year. She is a doctoral student in Educational Leadership at Boston College and is licensed to serve students with moderate special needs.

Tamarah Danielle Brownlee, M.P.H., has spent the last 22 years as a human resources executive across several industries cultivating cultures of excellence which embody an inclusive and diverse work environment that promotes belonging in the workplace through programmatic and leadership efforts. She is currently pursuing her doctoral degree in Organizational Leadership and is a sought-after speaker, coach, and life strategist helping people discover the purpose within to achieve personal leadership success. She is an avid believer in purpose as she completes her first book *The Key* on leadership and spiritual formation.

Ethan d'Ablemont Burnes serves in the new position of Assistant Superintendent of Inclusive Education in the Boston Public Schools, where he works to bring the systemic changes needed to make the district more deeply inclusive. Before this, he was Assistant Superintendent of Special Education. Prior, he served as the principal of the Manning School in Jamaica Plain for 11 years where he focused on building an inclusion model for students with emotional impairments and increasing the academic challenge in the classroom. The school was recognized as a School of Distinction by the Massachusetts Department of Elementary and Secondary Education.

Yolanda Caldwell, M. A. is a consultant, coach, award-winning facilitator, international speaker, and independent trustee. She specializes in creating and implementing customized solutions for organizational improvement, community development, and personal development. She is the founder and owner of Titus Enterprises, LLC and Chief Diversity Officer, inaugural Director of the Women's Leadership Institute, and the BOLD Women's Leadership Network at the College of Saint Rose in Albany, NY. A doctoral student at Fairleigh Dickinson University, she is pursuing an Ed.D in Higher Education. In 2020, Yolanda was recognized by the International Leadership Association with the Women and Leadership Outstanding Practice with Broad Impact Award.

Scott Chazdon, Ph.D., is an evaluation and research specialist with the University of Minnesota Extension Department of Community Development. Trained as a sociologist, he has professional experience in evaluation project management, grant writing, research, public policy analysis, as well as community development and organizing. He has become a national leader in the use of Ripple Effect Mapping as an evaluation tool for exploring the impacts of community development programming, as well as in the development of readiness assessments for long-term, issue-based work in communities.

Rosalind F. Cohen, Ph.D., Senior Professional in Human Resources, has over 25 years of experience as a Senior Leader in Human Resources, Inclusion and Belonging. She is the Founder and President of Socius Strategies, a San Francisco-based advisory firm that combines a pragmatic approach with social and industrial psychology and mentorship to build cultures of connectedness. She earned her Ph.D. in Leadership and Change from Antioch University, where her research explored the relationships between dimensions of inclusive leadership, employee engagement, and identity. Her latest book on employee engagement, inclusive leadership, and organizational success is forthcoming in 2024. She has bold ideas and a vision of radical connectedness that create better workplaces.

Valerie J. Davis, Ph.D., Professional Certified Coach as per the International Coaching Federation, is President, Lysistrata Incorporated, a firm that specializes in executive coaching, leadership development, and coach education. Prior to her consulting career, she served in executive roles in global organizations. She received her doctorate in Human Development with an emphasis on leadership from Fielding Graduate University. She believes strongly in service to her community and in capacity building. She is currently the Board Chair for The Peel Learning Foundation, a community-based, charitable organization that raises funds to enable students to achieve personal excellence by providing resources that help them overcome barriers due to poverty.

Nurcan Ensari, Ph.D., is a social and organizational psychologist who teaches and conducts research in the area of intergroup relations, leadership, and diversity management. She conducts multicultural research with international collaborators from England, India, Turkey, Thailand, Greece, and Hong Kong. She is a reviewer and editor for several journals, and a recipient of academic awards. She is currently a Professor in the Organizational Psychology Program in Alliant International University. She has a M.A. and Ph.D. in Social Psychology, University of Southern California, and a M.A. in Social Psychology and B.S. in Mathematics from Bogazici University in Istanbul, Turkey.

Valencia Gabay, M.Ed., works to design inclusive learning environments that support equal access to financial knowledge and promotes financial well-being as part of personal well-being. She is an instructional designer, organizational leadership scholar, international presenter, and co-author of *Group Coaching and Mentoring: A Framework for Fostering Organizational Change*. She is currently the Program Director for Financial Education and Wellbeing at the American College of Financial Services and is working on her Ph.D. in Organizational Leadership.

Trisha Gott, Ed.D., is an Assistant Professor and Associate Dean of Academics at the Staley School of Leadership at Kansas State University. She teaches undergraduate and professional coursework related to considering the ethical dimensions of leadership and leadership development. She focuses on practice-based leadership education and development for professionals. Since 2016, she has served as Co-principal Investigator and Co-director for the Mandela Washington Fellowship Civic Engagement and Leadership Institute at Kansas State since 2016. She is particularly interested in understanding how leadership interventions sustain, translate, and advance community leadership in a global setting.

Brad Grubb, Ed.D., M.A., M.S., has devoted over 30 years to the fields of higher education and organizational/employee development. He is a consultant and coach in the field of diversity, equity, inclusion, and belonging, with an emphasis on cultural humility. He currently serves as an adjunct Professor at Indiana Wesleyan University in the Ph.D. in Organizational Leadership program. His research is in unconscious bias and inclusion, multicultural, and global leadership. He has presented the above topics at multiple conferences and is currently serving as a Co-editor for *SAGE Business Skills on DEIB*.

Jacqueline N. Gustafson, Ed.D., is the Dean of the College of Behavioral and Social Sciences, Professor of Psychology, and Fellow at the Dr Paul and Annie Kienel Leadership Institute at California Baptist University, and the Founder and Chief Executive Officer of the Abeba Collection, a social enterprise lifestyle brand. She has conducted fieldwork on four continents, is a sought-after national speaker, author of numerous articles and book chapters, and is the co-author of the book *Pursuing Wisdom: A Primer for Leaders and Learners*. She has been recognized with several awards for her innovation in community engagement and work to advance equity.

Janice Branch Hall, Ph.D., is the first Associate Dean for diversity, equity, inclusion, and belonging (DEIB) in the Pamplin College of Business at Virginia Tech. She is responsible for envisioning, reimagining, and translating strategic directions into concrete goals and plans that promote the success of all stakeholders, including efforts to enhance the visibility and lived experiences of underrepresented and underserved populations. A Richmond, Virginia, native, Hall received a bachelor's in Psychology from the College of William and Mary, a master's in Management from Wake Forest University, and a Ph.D. in Higher Education Administration from the University of Tennessee, Knoxville.

Yael Hellman, Ed.D. (Institutional Management), M.A. (Creative Arts Therapy), repurposes her professorial experience as Educational Development Administrator of the Los Angeles County Sheriff's Department, overseeing academic, vocational, and therapeutic instruction for incarcerated persons and diversity-enrichment training for staff. Author of *Learning for Leadership: A Facilitative Approach for Training Leaders*, she guides private- and public-sector executives, instructors, and advancement candidates through experiential exercises that create workspaces embracing – not just tolerating – cultural, social, and individual diversities. Her worldwide travels confirm that introspective, relational leadership links persons globally as well as within business and service organizations.

Jocelyn I. Hernandez-Swanson, M.P.S., is a former Leadership and Civic Engagement Educator with the University of Minnesota Extension, passionate about supporting community leaders in fostering equitable and inclusive cities and organizations. Her background is in leading racial equity changemaking in higher education and local government, with a focus on civic engagement and inclusive participation. As a formerly undocumented immigrant and bilingual Mexicana, she brings systems thinking and courageous imagination to create spaces where power is acknowledged and racial equity is a priority, resulting in strengthened diverse leadership.

Elizabeth Holcombe, Ph.D., is a Senior Postdoctoral Research Associate in the Pullias Center for Higher Education at the USC Rossier School of Education. Her current work involves a qualitative study of equity-minded leadership teams in higher education in partnership with the American Council on Education. Her research uses an organizational lens to understand various policies and practices that affect student success, including undergraduate teaching and assessment, faculty workforce and development issues, and leadership in higher education. She has published papers in the *Journal of Student Affairs Research and Practice, Educational Policy, Higher Education*, and *American Behavioral Scientist*, among others.

Lea Hubbard, Ph.D., is a Professor in the School of Leadership and Education Sciences at the University of San Diego. She earned her Ph.D. in Sociology from the University of California San Diego. Her work focuses on educational reform and educational leadership as well as educational inequities across ethnicity, class, and gender. Working nationally and internationally, she has co-authored several books and written articles on school reform and leadership. Her most recent articles include "School Reform from a Constructivist Perspective" in the *International Encyclopedia of Education 4th Edition* and "Responsible School Leadership in Crisis" in the *Journal of School Leadership*.

Antonio Jimenez-Luque, Ph.D., is an Assistant Professor of Leadership at the University of San Diego. His work explores how cultural, social, and historical perspectives influence conceptualizations and practice of leadership. At the intersection of critical theory and intercultural studies, his research topics are (1) organizational culture and identity development, (2) social movements and leadership, and (3) critical interculturality and global social justice. He is the author of *Leadership, Diversity, and Social Justice: Culture as a System for Resistance and Emancipation* and has published in different journals such as *Leadership, Voluntary Sector Review*, and the *International Journal of Servant Leadership*.

Adrianna Kezar, Ph.D., is Dean's Professor of Leadership, Wilbur-Kieffer Professor of Higher Education, at the University of Southern California and Director of the Pullias Center for Higher Education within the Rossier School of Education. She is a national expert on leadership, equity and diversity, change, student success, the changing faculty, and governance in higher education. She is well published with 20 books/monographs, over 100 journal articles, and over 100 book chapters and reports. Recent books include *Shared Leadership in Higher Education* (2021, Stylus), *Administration for Social Justice and Equity* (2019, Routledge), and *How Colleges Change 2nd Ed.* (2018, Routledge).

Aashna Khurana is a Ph.D. student in the Lynch School of Education and Human Development at Boston College. She is also a Professional Special Educator and has worked as an Assessment Associate at ASER Centre, Pratham Education Foundation. She worked on development of Assessment for All Tool, focused on including children with special needs in large-scale assessments in India, and ASER 2019 Early Years tool to assess skills of children aged 4–8 years. Currently, she is one of the lead researchers on the Boston Public Schools Inclusion Initiative that aims to reform the inclusive education service delivery system.

Linda Kligman, Ph.D., serves as President of the International Institute for Restorative Practices Graduate School. Dedicated to inclusive learning and decision-making, she recently co-authored a chapter with Razwana Begum Abdul Rahim, Ph.D., titled "Democratizing leadership-followership: Restorative practices in the age of disruption" in Springer's *Handbook of Global Leadership and Followership: Integrating the Best Leadership Theory and Practice*. In 2020, her research in workplace leadership received two honors from Union Institute and University for its interdisciplinarity and social relevance. The praxis of this work is featured in her forthcoming book, *Heart Strong Work: Improving Workplace Culture*.

Catherine T. Kwantes, Ph.D., is a Full Professor of Industrial Organizational Psychology at the University of Windsor in Ontario, Canada. She is a cross-cultural psychologist who researches the role social culture plays in workplace culture and interactions. Specifically, her work focuses on trust, trustworthiness, and social justice in the workplace. She is a member of the Indigenous Workways project, which is funded by SSHRC is the Social Sciences and Humanities Research Council of Canada (SSHRC) and Ontario Research Fund: Research Excellence (ORF-RE) and seeks to provide tools for organizations to increase employment outcomes for Indigenous employees.

Charles Lee-Johnson, D.Min., is the Pastor of The Life Church in Riverside, California; Associate Dean for the Division of Social Work at California Baptist University; and the Chief Executive Officer of National Family Life and Education Center, providing consultation and training services for organizations serving vulnerable families. He is co-author of the new book, *Healing Conversations on Race: Four Key Practices From Scripture and Psychology.* His commitment to diversity, equity, and inclusion has made him one of the most dynamic and inspirational social workers in America.

Cornelis Johannes (Kees) Matthijssen is Lieutenant General in the Netherlands Armed Forces. He served as Force Commander for the UN Mission MINUSMA in Mali from January 2022 to January 2023. His 42 years of military service include deployments to Bosnia and Herzegovina, Iraq, and Afghanistan, each in a command position at a different level. He holds a master's degree of Strategic Studies (MSS). He was awarded the French "Legion of Honour" and the German "Bundeswehr Cross of Honour" for his outstanding cooperation with both nations. He is known for his excellent leadership. Cycling is his preferred sport.

Henry L. McClendon, Jr, is the Director for Community Engagement at the International Institute for Restorative Practices. A lifelong resident of Detroit, Michigan, He served as the Education and Community Leadership Program Officer for the Detroit-based Skillman Foundation. His career includes appointments as Executive Assistant to Detroit Mayor Coleman A. Young, Sr, and leadership roles for Prison Fellowship Ministries and New Detroit, one of the nation's oldest race relations coalitions. In 2017, he co-designed the Detroit Police Community Summit with Bishop Daryl Harris, Total Life Christian Ministries, and fifth Precinct Commander (now Assistant Chief), Eric Ewing, Detroit Police Department.

Flor García Mencos is founder and Executive Director of Circula Center for Restorative Leadership, an organization that supports civil society leaders in Central America through training in restorative leadership. She is a clinical psychologist, an Executive Coach graduate from INCAE Business School, and is Trainer Certified in Restorative Practices and Certified in Nonviolent Communication. She has collaborated with the government of Guatemala and international cooperation agencies to develop and implement projects aimed at psychosocial care in natural disasters, reincorporation of the migrant population, and programs with war survivors in transitional justice processes.

Stacy Menezes, Ph.D. candidate at the Goa Institute of Management, India. She has a master's in Industrial and Organizational Psychology and worked in the People Department in organizations in India. She has presented a paper on inclusion at the Indian Academy of Management Conference and continues to publish her work in relevant academic journals. Her research interests are in the critical areas of inclusive talent identification, competency development, and developmental interventions. With her passion for organizational psychology and a strong research background, she is dedicated to contributing to the field and making a meaningful impact in promoting inclusive workplaces.

Justin Mui is the Executive Director of Lutheran Community Care Services Ltd. in Singapore. He has an M.A. in Tri-Sector Collaboration from Singapore Management University and a Graduate Diploma in Social Work from the National University of Singapore. He is a frequent guest speaker on podcasts. Believing that entrenched mindsets perpetuate similar solutions and that relationships are the conduit for transformation, he has created safe spaces for stakeholders to have the "missing conversation." These include peacemaking among residents-in-conflict in public housing, rebuilding communities of care for ex-offenders, and addressing school bullying by widening the circle of support.

Sarah Smith Orr, Ph.D., M.B.A., is teaching faculty with courses in Advanced Leadership at University of California, Los Angeles, Extension and Leading Social Entrepreneurial Ventures courses at University of Nevada, Reno. She owns a consultancy with research and work in the United States and internationally focused on system-changing social entrepreneurs. Selected published works: "The Twenty-First Century: The Century of the Social Sector" featuring Drucker's philosophies and frameworks in *The Drucker Difference* (McGraw Hill, 2009), and "The Social Entrepreneur: Tackling the World's Toughest Problems Through Innovation," *The Role of Entrepreneurs in the Political Economy of the Pacific Rim* (Nanjing University Press, 2015).

Shauneen Pete, Ph.D., is from Little Pine First Nation (Treaty 6) and Cowessess First Nation (Treaty 4). Chair of the Emerging Indigenous Scholars Circle at Royal Roads University, her research focuses on the Indigenization and decolonization of Canadian higher education. She also examines the experiences of Indigenous faculty, in particular, since the publication of the Truth and Reconciliation Commission of Canada's final report in 2015. She is a co-editor on the forthcoming publication, *Decolonizing Educational Relationships* with Fatima Pirbhai-Illich and Fran Martin. She also published "Decolonizing Equity Praxis" in Billie Allan and Rhonda Hackett's *Decolonizing Equity* (2022, Fernwood Publishing).

Tissa Richards is a TedX and keynote speaker, leadership expert, and corporate facilitator who works with F1000 and growth-stage organizations, guiding them to create blueprints for individual and organizational success, develop high-performance cultures, and diversify C-suites and corporate boardrooms. As a repeat software founder and CEO, she sits at the intersection of entrepreneurship, fundraising, and executive leadership. She has raised millions of dollars for her companies, won awards for innovation and products, and holds multiple software patents. She helps clients secure public board roles and guides executives in increasing their compensation packages by articulating their compelling value propositions.

Ronald E. Riggio, Ph.D., is the Henry R. Kravis Professor of Leadership and Organizational Psychology at Claremont McKenna College. He is a social/personality psychologist and leadership scholar with more than two dozen authored or edited books and more than 250 articles/book chapters. His research interests are in leadership, team processes, I-O Psychology, and organizational and nonverbal communication. He is part of the Fullerton Longitudinal Study, examining leadership development across the lifespan (from one year of age and through middle adulthood). Besides research on leadership development, he has been actively involved in training young (and not so young) leaders.

Katrina S. Rogers, Ph.D., Masters of Environmental Law and Policy, is the seventh President of Fielding Graduate University in Santa Barbara, CA, and Washington, D.C. Fielding offers a doctoral concentration in Inclusive Leadership and Social Justice in their Human and Organizational Development programs. She led the European campus for Thunderbird School of Global Management in Geneva, Switzerland, for a decade, working with international organizations. In addition to many books and articles, she is the author of *Democracy, Civic Engagement, and Citizenship in Higher Education: Reclaiming Our Civic Purpose.* She received a Presidential postdoctoral fellowship from the Humboldt Foundation and was a Fulbright scholar to Germany.

Martin Scanlan, Ph.D., is an Associate Professor in the Lynch School of Education and Human Development at Boston College. His scholarship examines systemic transformation of school systems toward integrated service delivery and on asset-oriented approaches to educating culturally and linguistically diverse students. In particular, he supports communities of practice helping adults advance toward these ends, and he continues to work closely with building- and district-level administrators to bridge research and practice. Before moving to the academy, he spent over a decade working in teaching and administration in urban elementary and middle schools in Washington, D.C., Berkeley, CA, and Madison, WI.

Birgit Schreiber, Ph.D., is a Senior Associate for HELM, South Africa, and a senior expert for the international higher education sector, has served in senior leadership positions, with expertise sub-Saharan Africa and Europe higher education. She has over 90 publications on various themes around social justice, student affairs, student engagement, and higher education. She was the founding editor and is the editorial executive of the *Journal for Student Affairs in Africa* (JSAA). After being the Africa Chair, she is the Vice-President for the International Association of Student Affairs and Services. ORCid: 0000-0003-2469-0504.

Keyhan Shams, M.Sc., is an Iranian doctoral candidate in Leadership Communication at the Staley School of Leadership at Kansas State University. He has worked as a Consultant for the United Nations Human Settlements Program in Iran, for the Iranian government, and as a leadership coach in Iranian communities. He is the author of *The City Iranians Need* (2016), which was launched at the United Nations Habitat III conference. As a former urban planner, his main research interests revolve around how leadership emerges in the public sphere.

Carolyn M. Shields, Ph.D., University of Saskatchewan, is President of The Commonwealth Council for Educational Administration and Management and Professor of Educational Leadership at Wayne State University, Detroit. After years of teaching in high school, she has focused on the creation of inclusive, equitable, excellent, and socially just environments and societies. For her work on *transformative leadership theory* – which includes 14 books, over 100 articles and chapters, and numerous international keynote addresses – she has received many honors and international recognition, including lifetime achievement awards from The University Council for Educational Administration and The Canadian Association for Studies in Educational Administration and an honorary doctorate from Laval University, Quebec.

Bryanne Smart, M.P.Ed., is the Associate Director, Indigenous Relations, Co-operative and Experiential Education at the University of Waterloo in Ontario, Canada. She has a master's degree in Professional Education and Aboriginal Leadership from Western University in Canada. She has worked with and for Indigenous people and communities for nearly two decades and centralizes her work in community-led approaches. This work is demonstrated throughout her ongoing contributions to CEE and with the Indigenous Workways project.

Cary Snow is a university educator and a celebrated chef who has been featured in magazines such as *Better Homes and Garden* and *Restaurant Start-Up and Growth*. He is a motivated, experienced change agent who builds diverse, culturally rich, and collaborative environments. With over 20 years of experience in higher education and culinary arts, he has focused his doctoral studies on organizational leadership. He uses his research in areas such as social justice's effect on recruitment and retention to work with organizations and businesses, assisting them in building and establishing sustainable DEIB practices.

Tobias Spanier, M.A., is an Extension Educator in Leadership and Civic Engagement with the University of Minnesota. In his educator role, he has over 25 years of providing leadership development research and education to individuals, organizations, and communities. He is passionate about connecting community needs and university resources to address critical issues in Minnesota and the world. He is a Qualified Administrator for the IDI. He is a past graduate and facilitator with LEAD21, a leadership development program for faculty, specialists, program and team leaders, and others in land grant universities' colleges of agricultural, environmental, and human sciences.

Anne-Marij Strikwerda-Verbeek is Lieutenant Colonel in the Netherlands Armed Forces. She studied International and European Law before joining the army as a Military Legal Advisor (LEGAD) in 2006. She was deployed to Afghanistan as LEGAD and to Mali as Personal Assistant to the Force Commander. She was also Military Assistant to the Deputy Commander of the Royal Netherlands Army from 2018 to 2019. She holds an executive master's degree in Security and Defense. She has a particular interest in psychological safety and just culture, gender, and diversity. Her favorite sport is horseback riding.

Trenae Thomas has served the Indianapolis area to improve outcomes for marginalized groups. She has been a leader in adult education where she worked to create pathways to quality jobs. Currently, she is a Manager of workforce equity with the Markle Foundation supporting the ReWork America Alliance initiative. The initiative is focused on providing skills and resources to improve employment outcomes for people of color. She has an M.S. in Strategic Management from Indiana Wesleyan University and is currently working on completing her Ph.D. in Organizational Leadership.

Natsumi Ueda is Graduate Research Assistant at Pullias Center for Higher Education and Ph.D. candidate at Rossier School of Education, University of Southern California. Her research focuses on higher education leadership, organizational change, diversity, equity, and inclusion, and intergroup relations. For her dissertation, she explores college students from diverse cultural backgrounds and identities working together on equity and social justice initiatives on campus with the purpose of uncovering promising practices of intercultural collaboration to create equitable campuses.

Donald Williams, Jr, Ph.D., is a strategist, researcher, and consultant. He was a 2019–2020 Fellow in the White House Fellows Program and served as a Speechwriter and Senior Advisor to the Secretary of the Department of Housing and Urban Development. He has completed community-building events in over 10 countries and has led more than 9,000 volunteers in 10 years. He created an orphanage volunteer partnership in the Netherlands Antilles, taught Math and English in Ghana, led global disaster relief efforts, and founded and directed an outreach organization in Japan.

Ellen Wolter, M.P.H., M.P.A., is a Leadership and Civic Engagement Extension educator with the University of Minnesota Extension Department of Community Development. She has over 20 years of experience working with nonprofits, state and local governments, and higher education institutions conducting community-engaged research projects and facilitating conversations that support data-informed decision-making. Before joining Extension, she worked for Wilder Research, where she collaborated with Minnesota organizations to identify community-level trends to address challenges facing rural communities. She has also held positions with Hennepin County and the University of Minnesota's Office of Community Engagement for Health.

Denise Zinn, Ed.D., is the Senior Associate at USAf HELM, South Africa. She was the Deputy Vice-Chancellor: Teaching and Learning at Nelson Mandela

Foreword

It is often tempting to proclaim, "We've come a long way," but the persistent challenges faced by historically underrepresented and marginalized individuals tell a different story. In a world where not everyone is granted equal opportunities and the "just keep trying" mantra persists, there remains an urgent need to practice and understand diversity, equity, inclusion, and belonging (DEIB).

Some may argue that in our globalized world, we already champion and comprehend diversity. They may further note that women lead countries, as exemplified in *Time*'s 2022 publication featuring 13 accomplished female leaders. However, we must also confront the harsh reality of those facing exclusion and a lack of opportunity and belonging in their chosen professions. It is disheartening that despite Juneteenth being recognized as a federal holiday in the United States, numerous institutions of higher learning and businesses fail to grasp the significance of this date. This raises the question we fear facing: Are we all truly free?

We must not only acknowledge the multiple ethnic and racial groups that enrich our cultures but also wholeheartedly seek to understand and embrace the diversity of identities, generations, sexual orientations, religious beliefs, and more across our communities, workplaces, and learning institutions. Each individual brings immeasurable value to the workforce and society, and we must actively listen to their stories and unite to find meaningful solutions to the world's pressing challenges.

This book you hold in your hands, *Inclusive Leadership: Equity and Belonging in Our Communities*, serves as a guide to what it means and looks like to be an ally and advocate for DEIB. Divided into four parts – (a) Understanding Diversity, Equity, Inclusion, and Belonging, (b) Diversity, Equity, Inclusion, Belonging, and Education, (c) The Application and Practice of Diversity, Equity, Inclusion, and Belonging/Accessibility, and (d) Diversity, Equity, Inclusion, Belonging/Accessibility: A Community and Global Perspective – this book offers readers a roadmap toward fostering inclusivity and fairness.

I know that the editors and authors of this book sincerely hope that the chapters contained within illuminate the path for you, your leadership, and all who seek to prioritize and implement DEIB principles for the betterment of society as a whole. We can collectively build a more just and harmonious world by embracing DEIB. Let us embark on this transformative journey together.

— Daisy Auger-Domínguez
Author of *Inclusion Revolution: The Essential Guide to Dismantling Racial Inequity in the Workplace* and Chief People Officer at Vice Media

Acknowledgments

This book was created from an outpouring of passion from the many individuals who recognize the importance of diversity, equity, inclusion, and belonging. We greatly appreciate each person and admire those who shared research and practice and who live a life of advocacy striving for social equity and justice.

The editorial team thanks Debra DeRuyver for tireless efforts in coordination, organization, and communication on behalf of the International Leadership Association (ILA) and in partnership with the editorial team. We are truly grateful for her commitment to our collective mission and the invaluable role she has played in the realization of this project. A special thank you to Dr. Cynthia Cherry, President and CEO of the ILA. We thank her for her vision for this project and the passion and advocacy she displays daily to create a more inclusive and equitable world. Thank you to the entire ILA staff for being on this journey with us. The power of the collective allows this book to become a reality.

Finally, we wish to acknowledge everyone who responded to our request for chapter proposals for being willing to share their experiences and best ideas. Regardless of whether their chapters were included, these individuals represent an illustration of the larger, worldwide group of dedicated and generous people who are engaged in this important work.

Introduction

The Multifaceted World of Leading Diversity, Equity, Inclusion, Belonging, and Accessibility

Joanne Barnes, Michael J. Stevens, Bjørn Zakarias Ekelund and Karen Perham-Lippman

> "Our ability to reach unity in diversity will be the beauty and the test of our civilization."
>
> —Mahatma Gandhi

It seems we can find, almost daily, increasing calls in public life to minimize – and even unwind – the hard-fought gains that have been achieved by fostering greater diversity, equity, inclusion, belonging, and accessibility (DEIBA). The need for a more thoughtful, nuanced, and insightful approach to inclusive leadership thus appears to grow more urgent by the day. By pulling together a broad and comprehensive collection of perspectives, this book is our attempt to address this need. Expanding on two successful International Leadership Association (ILA) Diversity, Equity, Inclusion, and Belonging Virtual Summits, this book answers the call for greater awareness, advocacy, action, and transformation for inclusive leadership, while bringing a global perspective to bear on the intersectionality of the different components of the DEIBA space.

Through the results of a rigorous and competitive review process, we share the final selected chapters in this book, which come from an array of academic researchers, educators, organizational leaders, nonprofit scholars, development and consulting professionals, and others. If the number of submissions we received in response to our call for proposed chapters is an indication of the enthusiasm for this work, we are filled with optimism.

The chapters in this book are organized into four parts, each dedicated to helping leaders better understand and advance DEIBA initiatives and applications. Our goal in presenting this collection is to provide a practical book that helps improve not only how we conceptualize and think about the DEIBA space but also to provide tools and case studies to help guide the practice of inclusive leadership.

When authentic and mutually respectful DEIBA are leveraged to advance a shared common purpose, we can see amazing things happen – everyone connected to an enterprise is far more likely to wrap their "hearts, minds, and souls" around a shared mission and vision. Though not an easy task, we have seen firsthand that it is possible to leverage our collective differences to build creativity, innovation, and enduring organizations – not despite but precisely because of our differences. As the editors of this volume, we are committed to developing a robust and rigorous DEIBA mindset that can both inform our core values and self-identity as leaders, while also serve as the foundation for a steadfast commitment to strengthening "our universal web of interconnected human dignity" (Martin Luther King Jr, Letter from Birmingham Jail). We invite readers to join us on this journey.

— Joanne Barnes
— Michael J. Stevens
— Bjørn Zakarias Ekelund
— Karen Perham-Lippman

Part One

Understanding Diversity, Equity, Inclusion, and Belonging

Chapter 1

Shared Equity Leadership: A New Model for Making Inclusion and Equity Part of Organizational Culture

Natsumi Ueda, Adrianna Kezar and Elizabeth Holcombe

University of Southern California, USA

Abstract

This chapter describes a new leadership model called shared equity leadership (SEL). The goal of SEL is to create culture change that embeds shared values of diversity, equity, and inclusion (DEI) into the core of an organization. SEL emerged from a qualitative multiple-case study of leaders who were committed to establishing an equitable organization at eight colleges and universities that had seen success in their equity efforts. We reviewed over 1,000 pages of documents and interviewed 126 leaders, including cabinet-level executives, mid-level leaders, and group-level leaders. While we identified this model on college campuses, it has relevance for any organizational context. SEL entails three elements: (1) a personal journey toward critical consciousness in which leaders solidify their commitment to equity, (2) a set of values that center equity and guide the work, and (3) a set of practices that leaders enact collectively to change inequitable structures. Distinct from traditional leadership models, SEL encompasses both personal and organizational processes of leadership and emphasizes collaborative, relational, personal, and emotional aspects of leadership. This change starts with transforming awareness and behaviors of individuals, who engage in personal journeys toward critical consciousness and develop an urgent sense of responsibility for creating change. Organizations can facilitate their personal journeys and begin structuring SEL by forming a diverse team and socializing

Inclusive Leadership: Equity and Belonging in Our Communities
Building Leadership Bridges, Volume 9, 3–13
Copyright © 2023 by Emerald Publishing Limited
All rights of reproduction in any form reserved
ISSN: 2058-8801/doi:10.1108/S2058-880120230000009001

them into SEL expectations. With a concerted effort of leaders committed to SEL values and practices, an organization can be transformed so that equity is everyone's work.

Keywords: Equity; leadership; organizational change; organizational culture; systemic inequities; higher education

DEI is an increasing priority for organizational leaders. Responding to the concerns of the historically marginalized groups related to systemic inequities, corporations, public sectors, colleges, and universities Have been trying to create more inclusive and equitable work environments and outcomes for employees and those whom they serve. These efforts include making public statements to denounce violence and discrimination, developing DEI strategic plans and goals, and implementing identity-conscious recruitment, hiring, and promotion practices. To advance DEI goals, an organization typically assigns DEI responsibility to a single office or a specific person responsible for all DEI-related programs. However, such a DEI office or manager is often isolated from other parts of an organization and mainstream operation (Dobbin & Kalev, 2007). Being siloed from day-to-day work of employees and organizational decision-making, the DEI office and manager have limited influence and authority to implement DEI strategies. Under the structure, employees and organizational leaders tend to think that DEI is not their responsibility and continue working "as usual" without noticing how the "usual" is creating inequity. Isolating DEI initiatives does not seem to work well. How, then, can DEI initiatives be implemented more comprehensively across an organization? What does it take for organizational leaders to make it possible? In this chapter, we propose a new leadership model called SEL, which answers those questions.

SEL emerged from our recent research of leaders at eight colleges and universities in the United States who were committed to establishing an equitable organization. The goal of SEL is to create culture change that embeds shared values of equity into the core of an organization. SEL dismantles inequitable organizational structures and creates equitable conditions and outcomes for minoritized groups of people. We define SEL as *a collaborative process where leaders work together to instantiate both personal and organizational transformation, contributing to a change in organizational culture in which equity becomes everyone's work rather than siloed in a single office or leader's purview.* While we identified this model on college campuses, it has relevance for any organizational context. This chapter is organized as follows. First, we describe the research project that leads to the SEL model development. Second, we describe the model and its three main elements: personal journey toward critical consciousness, values, and practices. Finally, we provide important considerations for implementing SEL.

SEL Research Project

A team of researchers at the Pullias Center for Higher Education (Pullias) and American Council on Education (ACE) jointly launched the SEL project in 2019.

The Pullias and ACE leaders met to discuss current DEI issues on college campuses, in particular, the sluggish changes toward equity and how many ineffective DEI efforts are siloed in a single office and disconnected from broader organizational priorities. Brainstorming possible approaches that might shift this trend by reviewing literature (Kezar & Holcombe, 2017) and talking to campus leaders, the team theorized that *culture change* is necessary to dismantle inequitable structures, and leadership is crucial in driving this change.

This project was a qualitative multiple-case study featuring 126 leaders at eight institutions engaging in DEI efforts. We selected participating institutions that met two criteria: (1) an institution had strong evidence of advancing a DEI agenda and (2) a wide range of campus stakeholders were participating in a shared form of leadership. The selected institutions were Foothill College, Montana State University, Penn State–Abington, Rutgers University–Newark, Texas A&M University–San Antonio, University of Michigan, University of Richmond, and Westchester Community College. These institutions vary in their institutional types (public and private, research universities, regional comprehensive institutions, community colleges, liberal arts colleges, and minority serving institutions), location (rural, urban, and suburban), state-level political contexts, and presence/absence of race-conscious policies. Despite the variance in institutional characteristics, we found consistent patterns that defined the SEL model across institutions.

Within the selected institutions, we reviewed over 1,000 pages of documents and conducted 126 interviews. Documents included strategic plans, reports, summaries of key meetings, presidential communications about DEI work, and other publicly unavailable information that we obtained from a campus liaison at each site. Interviewees included cabinet-level executives, such as provosts and presidents, and mid-level leaders, such as department chairs, associate deans, unit heads, as well as ground-level leaders, such as faculty members and staff. The large amount of qualitative data helped paint a rich picture of why these campuses had seen success in their equity efforts and how they were doing it – an approach we termed SEL.

SEL Model

In the SEL model, a greater number of individuals in various roles and positions are involved in leadership to advance equity, share the responsibilities of contributing to organizational change, and work together across organizational divisions and varying personal backgrounds. In our multiple-case study, we found examples of leaders working collaboratively across departments and levels of the hierarchy, from front-line staff to mid-level leaders to senior-level leaders. The model also brings together leaders' diverse perspectives, experiences, and expertise. A shared leadership approach taps into the collective capacity latent within an organization and maximizes the breadth and depth of its impact to advance equity.

SEL involves personal and organizational transformation, which are both essential for promoting lasting cultural change. Personal transformation involves the process of individuals learning to understand the structural nature of inequity, deepening their own personal commitment to equity, and taking actions to create changes. By organizational transformation, we mean that an organization transforms its long-existing norms, structures, processes, practices, and policies that privilege certain groups over others and maintain the inequitable status quo. New structures that center equity help instantiate new norms and values across the organization. Personal and organizational transformation reinforces each other. As more leaders grow to be equity-minded and learn to work collectively, the force for change toward equity increases, which drives organizational transformation. As organizations transform to establish new policies and practices that support equity work, individuals gain more resources and opportunities to increase understanding of systemic inequity, develop capacity to create change, and feel supported to do equity work.

The SEL model (Fig. 1.1) entails three main elements: (1) a *personal journey toward critical consciousness* in which leaders solidify their commitment to equity, (2) a set of *values* that center equity and guide the work, and (3) a set of *practices* that leaders enact collectively to change inequitable structures (Kezar et al., 2021). There are 8 values and 17 practices. However, every individual does not have to have every value and practice. In fact, few of the leaders we interviewed possess skills in all areas. Rather, we want to bring a range of expertise or skills from diverse individuals by distributing leadership throughout an organization. With a wider range of skills, experiences, knowledge, and perspectives, we can enact more of the SEL values and practices, which can create a broader and deeper organizational change.

Personal Journey Toward Critical Consciousness

A *personal journey toward critical consciousness* is at the heart of SEL. Leaders must first turn inward to turn outward and commit to transform their organizations. This internal effort involves learning about systemic and historical inequities, reflecting on how one's own identity and experience are related to the inequities, and contemplating one's own role in creating change. This journey could occur in different ways depending on leaders' identities and backgrounds. For example, leaders with marginalized identities develop personal commitment to equity work

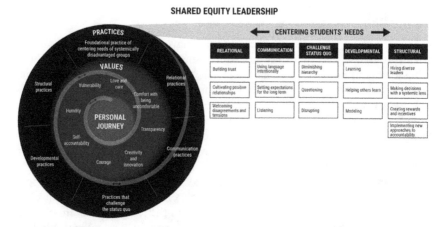

Fig. 1.1.   SEL Model. *Source*: Personal Journey Toward Critical Consciousness, © The ACE and Pullias Center for Higher Education.

because they have experienced discrimination in the past. For others with a dominant identity (i.e., White), equity work becomes personal when they experience exclusion based on one of their marginalized identities (i.e., sexual minority). Those who do not recall any experiences of discrimination come to personally commit to equity work through learning about the history or others' lived experiences.

While equity leaders can have different courses of journeys, what is common is that they develop critical understanding of systemic inequities and realize their own role in creating change. They become more aware of how they are negatively impacted by the system and, at the same time, contributing to inequity and injustice. With that realization, DEI issues become personal to them, and they develop a greater sense of responsibility and commitment to creating a new and equitable structure. When the number of leaders who are awakened to such a responsibility reaches a critical mass, it becomes possible to set an organizational priority for equity. In such an organization, a group of equity-minded leaders comes together to implement a new set of SEL values and practices that transforms an organization to be a more equitable place.

Values

The second element of the SEL model is *values*, which are the beliefs and ideals shared among leaders. The values represent a way of being, showing up, and relating to others as a leader. Individual leaders learn to embody the values of SEL through leaders' personal commitment to equity and working collaboratively with others. Some of the SEL values are markedly different from traditional notions of leadership that emphasize hierarchy, authority, and individual traits and abilities. In contrast to the values underlying traditional leadership approaches, SEL values emphasize collaborative and relational processes, such as transparency and comfort with being uncomfortable, as well as personal, emotional aspects of leadership, such as love and care, courage, humility, and vulnerability. Table 1.1 presents descriptions of all nine SEL values. These values guide the SEL practices.

Practices

SEL *practices* represent new ways of acting that are oriented toward challenging inequities and creating new structures and policies. By practices, we mean the ongoing, regular activities that leaders perform both individually and collectively to advance an equity agenda. We identified 17 practices and categorized them into 6 domains, including fundamental practices of centering the needs of systematically marginalized communities, relational practices, communication practices, developmental practices, practices that challenge the status quo, and structural practices. Relational and communication practices suggest effective ways of working with others and across differences. Developmental practices build knowledge and skills and foster people's capacity to do equity work. Practices that challenge the status quo guide leaders to call out the entrenched policies and practices that reproduce inequities, while actively working to dismantle them. Structural practices support leaders in implementing concrete changes to organizational structures and culture. Table 1.2 presents the descriptions of all the SEL practices.

Table 1.1.   Descriptions of SEL Values.

Love and care	An ethos of love and care underscores the personal nature of SEL. Leaders feel and display love and care for those with whom they are working. They approach any relationship with a deep sense of caring and compassion, even if they tend to disagree or have had contrasting experiences
Comfort with being uncomfortable	Equity work sometimes requires leaders to sit with the emotions and pains of others uncomfortably rather than immediately finding solutions. It is important for leaders to be comfortable with such feelings of discomfort
Transparency	A value of transparency means that leaders are honest, clear, and open about decision-making, successes, failures, and challenges of their work
Creativity and imagination	Creativity and imagination are necessary because there are no universally agreed-upon ways of doing equity work
Courage	Courage for shared equity leaders means standing up for equity even when it's not popular or easy and remaining dedicated in the face of resistance or skepticism
Self-accountability	Leaders who have self-accountability hold themselves accountable for doing the work, getting results, learning about equity, and challenging their preconceived notions. They are also willing to change their beliefs and practices as they continue to learn and grow.
Humility	Humility for shared equity leaders means to admit when they have done something wrong or when something has not worked well. They understand that they do not have all the answers or solutions, their experience isn't everyone's experience, and they have things to learn from other people
Vulnerability	Vulnerability in SEL means being able to be open about difficult personal experiences or being willing to risk exposing their true selves, even without knowing exactly how they will be received. These vulnerable experiences are often related to race or other aspects of identity and can be painful to share. Being vulnerable helps leaders build connections, trust one another, and better understand others' perspectives and experiences

Table 1.2.   Descriptions of SEL Practices.

Foundational practice	Centering the needs of systematically marginalized communities	The foundational SEL practice is centering the needs of systematically marginalized communities when making decisions by considering all the different ways the decisions might affect people of those communities
Relational practices	Building trust	Leaders need to build trust among members of the leadership team to lead effectively in a collaborative manner
	Cultivating positive relationships	Leaders can learn to trust each other by cultivating positive relationships in more informal settings, such as having a potluck party outside of formal, professional settings
	Welcoming disagreements and tensions	Disagreements and tensions are an inevitable part of doing equity work; therefore, it is important to normalize them. By welcoming and respectfully managing disagreements and tensions, the leadership team creates a safe place where diverse perspectives are valued and rewarded
Communication practices	Using language intentionally	The practice of using language intentionally includes explicitly naming equity challenges, frequently and publicly talking about equity to emphasize its importance, choosing asset-focused rather than deficit-focused languages, and framing their work for different audiences to garner support
	Setting expectations	Equity work takes time. Leaders need to set expectations for the long term so that stakeholders understand that the larger systemic changes take time to enact
	Listening	Listening authentically and actively to others' perspectives, and experiences is crucial for equity leaders to collaborate effectively

(*Continued*)

Table 1.2.   (*Continued*)

Developmental practices	Learning	Leaders learn about equity and leadership in four different ways: Listening, specifically to others' stories Looking at data, facts, and figures, such as racially disaggregated data on student outcomes Learning formally through professional development sessions on equity topics or leadership Learning informally through reading or discussions with colleagues
	Helping others learn	Leaders help others learn by using the inverse of the four aforementioned strategies that they used to learn: Sharing personal stories Marshaling data to draw colleagues' attention to inequity Facilitating professional development sessions about equity or leadership Creating environments where colleagues can learn informally from one another
	Modeling	Leaders model SEL values and practices by exercising them, which helps others to see how they work and gain confidence that equitable change is possible
Practices that challenge the status quo	Diminishing hierarchy	Diminishing organizational hierarchy enables all perspectives to be heard. Minimizing hierarchy helps leaders without positional authority feel comfortable challenging senior leaders
	Questioning	Leaders need to ask questions about taken-for-granted policies and practices, their deeply held assumptions, and any outstanding or unresolved issues
	Disrupting	Leaders can take this practice a step further by intentionally disrupting traditional norms or ways of thinking and operating by pointing out inequities

Table 1.2. (*Continued*)

Structural practices	Hiring diverse leaders (or composing diverse teams)	Hiring leaders from marginalized backgrounds makes a leadership team better represent the diversity and complexity of organizational members. Diverse perspective brought to the table helps solve complex equity challenges
	Systemic decision-making	When practicing systemic decision-making, leaders make sure to have a cohesive approach across an organization. They embed equity in every facet of an organization to make it unavoidable
	Creating rewards and incentives	Leaders can reward/incentivize equity work by tying budgets to equity efforts, acknowledging equity work in the review and promotion, providing grants/credits for an equity-oriented project or participation in equity-related professional development opportunities
	Implementing new approaches to accountability	New accountability approaches are informal (e.g., holding colleagues accountable in a respectful, professional way) and others more formal (e.g., explicit and measurable DEI goals or holistic and qualitative approaches)

Implementation of SEL

How can organizational leaders implement SEL? Here, we provide some recommendations of how to start up and maintain SEL to create change in your organization.

Starting Up

To start up SEL, it is important for organizational leaders to scrutinize and reflect on an organizational context that is relevant to current DEI work. In particular, leaders might need to ask the following questions: What is the historic trauma that the organization took part in against marginalized communities and is the organization transparent and honest about it? What are the current organizational context and practices that may still systematically disadvantage certain communities and does the organization acknowledge that? Does the organization provide accessible ways for leaders and employees to learn about such an organizational history and context?

The next consideration is forming a team to start the culture change efforts toward equity. Thinking about who should be constructing a SEL team, it is important to thoughtfully select diverse leaders to participate in SEL. Leaders need to be recruited from a broad cross-section of offices, divisions, and positions within the organizational hierarchy and a pool of individuals from diverse racial, ethnic, gender, sexuality, and religious backgrounds. Once a SEL team is formed, the team members need to be thoroughly socialized into SEL so that they have shared expectations for SEL values and practices. It is also important to provide space where each leader can engage in personal journeys and deepen their understanding and commitment to equity work.

Maintaining

To maintain SEL, organizations need to provide capacity building that enables various people to enact SEL, which includes professional development, modeling SEL, and providing resources and support spaces (Holcombe et al., 2023). An organization must provide ongoing training and professional development that addresses topics of implicit bias, racism, power, or privilege and helps leaders learn how to work together and share leadership. When experienced leaders help new ones learn, they can teach by modeling SEL values and practices. It is also important for an organization to recognize that equity work is inherently personal and emotion-laden that often causes severe stress and burnout. Understanding the risk, an organization needs to provide resources and support for leaders, such as safe space to share their emotions with others and feel validated.

To sustain SEL, organizations also need to reward and incentivize equity work by incorporating SEL into part of annual reviews, merit increases, and promotional criteria. Furthermore, accountability systems need to be put in place to measure progress and identify areas for improvement, which is crucial to advance equity sustainably (Kezar et al., 2022). In the context of SEL, however, leaders need to rethink what success means and how to measure it so that it can capture the SEL work and its goal of culture change.

Summary

SEL represents a collaborative process of leadership shared across many leaders to change culture toward equity in an organization. Distinct from traditional leadership models, SEL encompasses both personal and organizational processes of leadership and emphasizes collaborative, relational, personal, and emotional aspects of leadership, which are inevitable to drive culture change. This change starts with transforming awareness and behaviors of individuals, who engage in personal journeys toward critical consciousness and develop an urgent sense of responsibility for creating change. Organizations can facilitate their personal journeys and begin structuring SEL by forming a diverse team and socializing them into SEL expectations. With a concerted effort of leaders committed to SEL values and practices, an organization can be transformed so that equity is everyone's work.

References

Dobbin, F., & Kalev, A. (2007). The architecture of inclusion: Evidence from corporate diversity programs. *Harvard Journal of Law & Gender*, *30*(2), 279–301.

Holcombe, E., Harper, J., Ueda, N., Kezar, A., Dizon, J. P. M., & Vigil, D. (2023). *Capacity building for shared equity leadership: Approaches and considerations for the work.* American Council on Education. https://www.acenet.edu/Documents/Shared-Equity-Leadership-Capacity.pdf

Kezar, A. J., & Holcombe, E. M. (2017). *Shared leadership in higher education.* American Council on Education. https://www.vumc.org/faculty/sites/default/files/Shared-Leadership-in-Higher-Education.pdf

Kezar, A., Holcombe, E., & Vigil, D. (2022). *Shared responsibility means shared accountability: Rethinking accountability within shared equity leadership.* American Council on Education. https://www.acenet.edu/Documents/Shared-Equity-Leadership-Accountability.pdf

Kezar, A., Holcombe, E., Vigil, D., & Dizon, J. P. M. (2021). *Shared equity leadership: Making equity everyone's work. American Council on Education.* https://www.acenet.edu/Documents/Shared-Equity-Leadership-Work.pdf

Chapter 2

Inclusive Leadership and Power

Valerie J. Davis[a] and Katrina S. Rogers[b]

[a]*Lysistrata Incorporated, Canada*
[b]*Fielding Graduate University, USA*

Abstract

The study of power is essential to any study of leadership, as power is fundamental to human organization and is understood to be a driving force of leadership. Power is typically thought of in terms of having dominance over others from a hierarchically higher position. In this chapter, we explore how power is typically defined in the literature and propose that mutualism represents an expanded definition of power and one that more closely aligns with the concept of inclusive leadership. We make a case for viewing power as a capacity that can be developed in others rather than a commodity that can be obtained, horded, or doled out. With this in mind, we explore how these two phenomena intersect from the perspectives of powerdistance, hierarchy, and empowerment. We argue that power expressed as dominance creates distance between leaders and employees, while mutualistic expressions reduce such distance, and that hierarchy and power have been erroneously conflated and when disaggregated can serve a useful purpose in a low-power-distance culture. Finally, through empowerment, we consider approaches to the development of power in others, which is a topic that is rarely considered in the leadership literature. Inclusive leadership offers an important pathway for moving organizations and society toward justice through the creation of cultures characterized by cooperation, unity, and diversity where greater numbers of people step into their capacity for power and begin to address the challenges facing humanity. This is realizable in cultures that promote mutualistic power.

Keywords: Leadership; power; dominance; mutualism; capacity; development

Inclusive Leadership: Equity and Belonging in Our Communities
Building Leadership Bridges, Volume 9, 15–23
Copyright © 2023 by Emerald Publishing Limited
All rights of reproduction in any form reserved
ISSN: 2058-8801/doi:10.1108/S2058-880120230000009002

> The power of leadership is the power of integrating. This is the
> power which creates community .... The person who influences
> me most is not he who does great deeds but he who makes me feel
> I can do great deeds. (Follett, 1918, p. 78)

The study of inclusive leadership is incomplete without considering its relationship to power, as power is a fundamental aspect of human organization and a driving force of leadership (Northouse, 2010; Yukl, 2013). While power is typically equated with dominance, this chapter offers a broader definition that more closely aligns with inclusivity. First, we propose definitions for inclusive leadership and power, followed by an exploration of the intersection of these two phenomena from the perspectives of power-distance, hierarchy, and empowerment. Finally, we consider both the importance of and approach to developing the capacity in others to exercise power that aligns with inclusive leadership.

Defining Inclusive Leadership

Inclusive leadership is a relatively nascent concept which represents a significant shift in our thinking about the practice of leadership. A litmus test of its effectiveness is the experience by everyone of feeling included. Leaders are fundamental to that experience (Nishii & Hannes, 2022). As such, it is imperative for inclusive leaders to prioritize building cultures that embrace diversity and collaboration (Kugelmass, 2003) and to strive to "[build] relationships that foster learning, engagement, and creativity" (Gallegos, 2014, p. 184). Other important measures of effectiveness are building psychological safety (Shore & Chung, 2021) and courageously challenging the status quo (Dillon & Bourke, 2016), thereby providing the opportunity for everyone to reach their full potential. Inclusive leaders embrace diversity because they understand the value that it brings, both culturally and economically (Dillon & Bourke, 2016; Hunt et al., 2020).

Inclusive leadership is characterized by leaders who actively seek greater participation and representation in decision-making and who create an environment where unique perspectives and contributions are valued, respected, and incorporated (Morgan, 2017). In a study of collaborative leaders who embrace similar leadership values and goals when compared to those of inclusive leaders, participants explained that power-as-dominance used to control others can be experienced as an abuse of power (Davis, 2016). Thus, inclusive leaders need to be consciously aware of and reflective of how they exercise power and explore expressions that align with the goal of inclusivity.

Defining Power

Defining power can be a challenging task, as there is a clear lack of consensus about definitions, particularly in the political science literature where power is frequently debated (Lukes, 2005; Morriss, 2002; Wartenberg, 1990). Wartenberg observes that "... theories have no common point of agreement ... almost every assertion that is made about power seems grounds for further controversy" (p. 10). There appears to be no debate about power representing the degree of influence that an individual or organization has among their peers. However, debates continue about whether it can be exercised solely as a form of dominance and whether power is a capacity or is something that can be possessed.

Weber's (1964) view that power is a means of achieving dominance has had an enduring influence on the leadership literature to the extent that power-as-dominance expressed by those in hierarchically elevated positions has served to overshadow other important discourses that have played a role in human history (Karlberg, 2005). For example, consider the collective power being exercised in public squares around the globe in recent history as a growing number of movements demand equity and social justice, from Tiananmen Square to the Arab Spring to the Black Lives Matter protests, among others. The notion that power can have a positive expression has been eschewed by some theorists, and acknowledged by others, but considered inconsequential because it is not reflective of our social worlds (Morriss, 2002).

Mutualistic Power

One such positive expression of power is mutualistic power, also known as power-with. This refers to a dynamic that is grounded in reciprocal benefit and collaboration between two or more parties. Where there is an inequality in a relationship, leaders can employ mutualistic power to support the empowerment of others and create greater equity. They do this by providing opportunities for others to release their capacities to express power. Where the relationship is more equal, power can be shared, thereby allowing all parties to work together to achieve common goals (Karlberg, 2005).

Mutualistic power is not a new concept. Follett (1918) introduced the notion of power-with more than a century ago. She promotes egalitarian approaches to leadership that utilize collaborative and participatory decision-making as opposed to domination and control. Follett proposes that leaders need to consult with employees on complex problems and on problem-solving implementation, evaluation, and revisions. She believes this would not only benefit the organization by offering diverse perspectives, but it would also provide opportunities to develop employees through their engagement with and taking a lead in situations that align with both their realized and latent capacities. Later leadership theorists such as Lippitt (1982), Drucker (1995), Kanter (1995), and McGregor (2006) acknowledge, build on, and promulgate Follett's theories of leadership and the use of power-with. Despite these contributions, the exploration of mutualistic forms of power has failed to gain a foothold in mainstream literature.

We are not proposing that one dimension of power is better than another. Such a position would only serve to reinforce a tendency in Western cultures to view the world in dichotomous terms. Power is not inherently good or bad; rather, it is made manifest by the intentions of the person exercising power. Power-as-dominance can fulfill an important purpose. For example, crime; aggressive acts on the part of individuals, groups, or nations; and corruption continue to plague humanity. There are times when power-as-dominance in response to major and/or imminent challenges or crises may be appropriate, particularly when it is expressed in the best interests of everyone. When it is used in the context of a political democracy, constituents may or may not accept the actions of the leaders and can exercise their right to vote them out of office. While we propose that mutualistic power aligns with inclusive leadership, we also suggest that inclusive leaders would not be precluded from using dominance where appropriate.

Power as Capacity

Power-to is a third expression of power explored in the literature. Pitkin (1972) introduced this concept to mean that individuals have the power to accomplish actions independently. Karlberg (2005) goes further and asserts that power-to represents an overarching concept of the exercise of power which can be applied in concert with other expressions of power. For example, an individual may have the power to exercise power with another. In this way, power can be understood to represent a capacity.

This argument aligns with theorists who have proposed that power has more than one expression, and that it is a pervasive social force that can be expressed by anyone with the capacity to do so (Arendt, 1969; Karlberg, 2005). In the leadership literature, power is typically treated as a capacity. Gardner (1990) expresses it as "the capacity to bring about certain intended consequences in the behavior of others" (p. 55). Bennis and Nanus (2003) define power as "the capacity to translate intention into reality and sustain it" (p. 16). Yukl (2013) describes power as "the capacity to influence the attitudes and behavior of other people in the desired direction" (p. 218). Capacity is frequently presented as an inherent and relatively enduring aspect of a person's personality (Morriss, 2002). However, the developmental literature indicates that personality is as much an acquired aspect as it is inherent to the individual and evolves through engagement with the environment (Csikszentmihalyi, 1993; Hatcher, 1982; Kegan, 1994).

Research also indicates that we are born into this world hardwired for goodness and altruism (Bloom, 2013; Keltner, 2009), suggesting that negative behaviors are therefore learned. And power-as-dominance used to constrain or oppress others when not warranted can be classified as a negative behavior. From these perspectives, it is possible to state that how one exercises power is something that can be learned. If this is the case, it would also follow that individuals have a choice in how they exercise power (Lukes, 2005; Morriss, 2002). Thus, individuals can choose to exercise mutualistic power as easily as power-as-dominance.

The Intersection of Inclusive Leadership and Power

Power-distance

We have argued that the use of power-as-dominance or power-over has monopolized our understanding of leadership until recently, that power can be expressed in broader terms, and that mutualistic power or power-with is one such expression that appears to align more closely with our understanding of inclusive leadership than does power-as-dominance. Examining the use of power through the lens of *power-distance* reinforces this argument.

The use of power-as-dominance promotes what Hofstede et al. (1997/2010) refer to as a high-power-distance culture. They describe high power-distance as

> the extent to which the less powerful members of institutions and organizations within a country expect and accept that power is distributed unequally .... The way power is distributed is usually explained from the behavior of the more powerful members, the leaders rather than those led. (Hofstede et al., 1997/2010, p. 61)

In his review of empirical studies examining organizations manifesting high power-distance, Khatri (2009) found that managers tend to micromanage employees, and that they are able to exercise unlimited power and control. Communication is mostly downward vertically, thereby creating the potential for significant communication gaps. Employees are inclined to demonstrate a lack of willingness to participate in the decision-making process and prefer to passively follow instructions. In essence, they can be described as disempowered. Because decisions are typically made at the top of the hierarchy, where there are gaps in information, the quality of decisions is generally of a lower quality, and a fertile ground for breaches in ethics emerges.

The cultures created by inclusive leaders are in direct contrast to those of high power-distance and can be described as low-power-distance cultures. Leaders in high-power-distance cultures would favor exercising power-as-dominance or power-over. Based on our understanding of inclusive leadership, leaders in inclusive cultures would prefer to express power in mutualistic terms or as power-with, which manifests as a low-power-distance culture. As indicated earlier, leaders who exercise mutualistic power value collaboration and participatory decision-making and seek to grow the capacities of their employees to exercise power such that the employees can contribute at their highest potential.

Hierarchy

In an inclusive culture, hierarchy is transformed. Like power and dominance, power and hierarchy are also frequently conflated in the leadership literature. Hierarchy represents a stratum of positions ranked one upon the other. Each level is understood to be subordinate to the one above bringing increasing power and generally more status and prestige to the holder of a leadership role. Hierarchy itself is not at odds with inclusive leadership or mutualistic expressions of power as it can serve a valuable purpose (Karlberg, 2005). If we disaggregate hierarchy from power and consider it within the context of a culture of inclusion, it is not the successive levels that present a problem; it is the power, status, and privilege that are out of place. Hierarchy can be helpful to leaders at progressively higher levels who are called upon to address an ever-expanding scope of responsibility with increasing levels of complexity. It enables them to focus on the issues that align with their capacities and allows those who occupy positions in lower stratums to do the same. Importantly, any abuse of the responsibility that comes with hierarchy can erode the very trust that inclusive leaders seek to build (Davis, 2016) and thereby undermine the entire inclusivity project. Thus, the fertile ground for breaches of ethics found in high-power-distance organizations would be anathema to a culture of inclusivity.

Inclusive leaders also need to strive toward creating and maintaining equity across the organization. By equity we mean recognizing everyone's unique capacities, "treating everyone differently dependent on need" (Shore & Chung, 2021, p. 21), and being aware of and actively working to remove barriers to equal opportunity (Nishii & Hannes, 2022). It could be said that inclusive leaders seek to create a culture of unity where the diversity of the individual members is valued and promoted. When equity is largely achieved, other forms of organizing structures become possible.

Stark (2001) suggests that when leaders promote equity, they are also moving toward heterarchical structures. He stated that heterarchical structures "are characterized ... by distributed intelligence and the organization of diversity" (p. 1). Distributed intelligence is a term found in network theory used to describe the distribution of information and decision-making across a structure described as equitable. Stark (2001) explained that heterarchical structures enable greater adaptability to changing conditions because they allow for a diversity of perspectives. Adaptability is thought to be an important capacity for dealing with complexity. Uhl-Bien et al. (2007) made similar observations in their discussion of complexity leadership. Inclusive leadership and power align with both hierarchical as well as heterarchical structures, so long as the predominant expression of power is mutualistic. As we have discussed, mutualistic power aligns with organizations that promote equity.

Empowerment

We have proposed that a critical role of an inclusive leader in creating and sustaining a low-power-distance culture is to animate the potential within individuals and/or groups to exercise their own power, which we are defining as the act of empowerment. In the power-as-dominance orthodoxy, empowerment is typically thought to represent a process of gifting power to less powerful others. However, if power is a capacity, this raises the question as to how empowerment can be accomplished. We propose that it requires an educational process that is rarely found in high-power-distance cultures and, while not exclusive to inclusive leaders, aligns well with a culture of inclusivity.

Consider the analogy of walking with inexperienced employees. In a hierarchical culture characterized by power-as-dominance, a leader might walk ahead of or behind individuals to act as a role model and/or overseer. An inclusive leader who employs mutualistic power will walk beside or accompany less experienced colleagues on their learning journey, to serve as a coach, mentor, and collaborator. Practices used in other paradigms of leadership, such as the delegation of increasingly more challenging assignments remain useful, but the methods around delegation may need to change. Decisions about what the employees will work on to develop their capacity and the actions they will take need to be made jointly. This will ensure that the employees share ownership for their own development.

Development will also need to be transformed in cases of experienced employees who have already developed their capacity for expressing power. The leader now has potential partners who can shoulder increasing responsibilities and assume the role of the leader in less complex situations. In this case, the more appropriate term for the dynamics of the situation may be *shared power*. The focus of development becomes one of growing the capacity of the employees for managing issues of increasing responsibility and complexity, nurturing their ability to take initiatives, and releasing their capacity for creativity and innovation.

The approach to learning in the case of both inexperience and experienced employees is built on the same foundation. The leader ensures that employees have adequate knowledge for the task ahead, confers with them to determine appropriate actions and outcomes, provides opportunities for self-reflection, and jointly reflects with the individuals or groups to clarify what is being learned and to decide what next steps need to be taken to build on this learning. Through time and experience, the leader will be able to play a lesser role, allowing more junior employees to step into progressively larger roles.

Learning to Exercise Power

While the approach above provides important scaffolding for developing others, it does not specifically address building capacity for exercising power. This is a subject that is not generally part of educational curricula (Sutherland et al., 2015). However, there are examples we can learn from. These include conceptual classroom learning and experiential exercises through both simulation and in real-life contexts (Sutherland et al., 2015). As Sutherland et al. (2015) observe, classroom or rational/technical learning offers only cognitive growth. It is through engaging in an experience of exercising power that people can gain knowledge of both the visceral and the performative aspects and the impact the exercise of power has on both the actor and the recipient. Simulations provide the opportunity for learning about feeling, thinking, and doing power. Sutherland et al. (2015) suggest a few examples of simulations that offer a starting point for those wishing to explore this avenue, including their own exercise of conducting a choral choir. Our view is that real-life experiences provide the greatest learning, particularly when leaders simultaneously engage in their own learning and reflection in partnership with their employees.

When Hope and History Rhyme

Inclusive leadership offers the possibility of addressing many current and emerging needs of society. Our social worlds are becoming increasingly complex alongside heightened threats from seemingly intractable challenges such as climate change, economic inequality, racial injustice, and pandemics, to name a few. At the same time, there are growing numbers of movements demanding equity and justice for all. These include, but are not limited to, the recent demonstrations in Iran, the #MeToo, and the 2SLGBTQIA+ movements. How can we address both these challenges and the need for equity and justice for everyone? Inclusive leadership offers an important pathway for moving society in the direction of justice through the creation of organizations and communities characterized by cooperation, unity, diversity, and equity where greater numbers of people are invited to step into their capacity for exercising power and begin to address the challenges facing humanity.

In this chapter, we have considered broader definitions of power including mutualism or power-with and some of the ways that inclusive leadership and power intersect. This exploration suggests that inclusive leadership may represent a paradigm shift in our thinking about both leadership and empowerment of others, and that it may also represent a significant pathway toward justice. For the understanding and practice of leadership to evolve, it is essential to broaden our constructions of power, enabling us to consider diverse ways in which it can be exercised and ultimately lead to more inclusive and effective leadership practices. How power is defined and exercised within the context of inclusive leadership and the inclusive cultures leaders endeavor to create will have an indelible impact and is therefore a critical topic that deserves ongoing exploration.

One might well ask if the transformations in thinking and acting suggested in this chapter are possible for the generality of the population. If we look to power in nature, we have recently witnessed a paradigm shift in our thinking about power in the natural world, moving from the idea that power is generated, used, and then dissipated to the reality that atomic fusion generates more power than the sum of two fused atoms. Our hope for the future is that atomic fusion will become our mental model for the exercise of power in our social worlds and that the exercise of mutualistic power will assume a place of importance in the practice of leadership.

References

Arendt, H. (1969). *On violence*. Harcourt Brace Jovanovich.

Bennis, W., & Nanus, B. (2003). *Leaders: The strategies for taking charge* (2nd ed.). HarperCollins.

Bloom, P. (2013). *Just babies: The origins of good and evil*. Crown Publishers.

Csikszentmihalyi, M. (1993). *The evolving self: A psychology for the third millennium*. Harper Perennial.

Davis, V. J. (2016). *How collaborative leaders construct power: Exploring a new leadership discourse* (Order No. 1842260067). Doctoral Dissertation. Fielding Graduate University.

Dillon, B., & Bourke, J. (2016). *The six signature traits of inclusive leadership: Thriving in a diverse new world*. https://www2.deloitte.com/us/en/insights/topics/talent/six-signature-traits-of-inclusive-leadership.html

Drucker, P. F. (1995). Introduction. In P. Graham (Ed.), *Mary Parker Follett: Prophet of management* (pp. 1–9). Beard Books.

Follett, M. P. (1918). *The new state – Group organization the solution for popular government*. Longman, Green.

Gallegos, P. V. (2014). The work of inclusive leadership: Fostering authentic relationships, modeling courage and humility. In B. M. Ferdman & B. R. Deane (Eds.), *Diversity at work: The practice of inclusion* (pp. 177–202). Jossey-Bass.

Gardner, J. W. (1990). *On leadership*. The Free Press.

Hatcher, W. S. (1982). *The concept of spirituality: Baha'i studies 11*. https://bahai-library.com/pdf/h/hatcher_concept_spirituality_bsn11.pdf

Hofstede, G., Hofstede, G. J., & Minkov, M. (2010). *Culture and organizations: Software of the mind* (3rd ed.). McGraw Hill (Original work published 1997).

Hunt, D. V., Dixon-Fyle, S., Prince, S., & Dola, K. (2020). *Diversity wins: How inclusion matters*. https://www.mckinsey.com/featured-insights/diversity-and-inclusion/diversity-wins-how-inclusion-matters

Kanter, R. M. (1995). Preface. In P. Graham (Ed.), *Mary Parker Follett: Prophet of management* (pp. xiii–xix). Beard Books.

Karlberg, M. (2005). The power of discourse and the discourse of power: Pursuing peace through discourse intervention. *International Journal of Peace Studies, 10*(1), 1–23. http://www.gmu.edu/programs/icar/ijps/vol10_1/Karlberg_101IJPS.pdf

Kegan, R. (1994). *In over our heads: The mental demands of modern life*. Harvard University Press.

Keltner, D. (2009). *Forget survival of the fittest: It is kindness that counts /Interviewer: D. DiSalvo*. Scientific American. Retrieved from http://www.scientificamerican.com / article/forget-survival-of-the-fittest/.

Khatri, N. (2009). Consequences of power distance orientation in organizations. *The Journal of Business Perspective, 13*(1), 1–9. https://doi.org/10.1177/097226290901300101

Kugelmass, J. W. (2003). *Inclusive leadership: Leadership for inclusion*. National College for School Leadership. https://dera.ioe.ac.uk/5081/1/kugelmass-inclusive-leadership-full.pdf

Lippitt, R. (1982). The changing leader–follower relationships of the 1980s. *The Journal of Applied Behavioral Science, 18*, 395–403.

Lukes, S. (2005). *Power: A radical view* (2nd ed.). Palgrave Macmillan.

McGregor, D. (2006). *The human side of enterprise: Annotated edition*. McGraw Hill.

Morgan, E. (2017). Breaking the zero-sum game: Transforming societies through inclusive leadership. In A. Boitano, R. L. Dutra, & H. E. Schockman (Eds.), *Breaking the zero-sum game: Transforming societies through inclusive leadership* (pp. 5–27). Emerald Publishing Limited.

Morriss, P. (2002). *Power: A philosophical analysis*. Manchester University Press.

Nishii, L. H., & Hannes, L. (2022). A multi-level framework of inclusive leadership in organizations. *Group & Organization Management, 47*(4), 683–722. https://doi.org/10.1177/10596011221111505

Northouse, P. G. (2010). *Leadership: Theory and practice* (5th ed.). Sage.

Pitkin, H. F. (1972). *Wittgenstein and justice: On the significance of Ludwig Wittgenstein for social and political thought*. University of California Press.

Shore, L. M., & Chung, B. G. (2021). Inclusive leadership: How leaders sustain or discourage work group inclusion. *Group & Organization Management, 47*(4), 723–754. https://doi.org/10.1177/1059601121999580

Stark, D. (2001). Heterarchy: Exploiting ambiguity and organizational diversity. *Brazilian Journal of Political Economy, 21*(1), 21–39.

Sutherland, I., Gosling, J. R., & Jelinek, J. (2015). Aesthetics of power: Why teaching about power is easier than learning for power, and what business schools could do about it. *Academy of Management Learning & Education, 14*(4), 607–624. https://doi.org/10.5465/amle.2014.0179

Uhl-Bien, M., Marion, R., & McKelvey, B. (2007). Complexity leadership theory: Shifting leadership from the industrial age to the knowledge era. *The Leadership Quarterly, 18*(4), 298–318. https://doi.org/10.1016/j.leaqua.2007.04.002

Wartenberg, T. E. (1990). *The forms of power: From domination to transformation*. Temple University Press.

Weber, M. (1964). *The theory of social and economic organizations*. The Free Press.

Yukl, G. (2013). *Leadership in organizations* (8th ed.). Pearson.

Chapter 3

Cultural Humility and Inclusion: Transformation to a Culture of Belonging

Joanne Barnes[a,b], Janice Branch Hall[c] and Brad Grubb[a]

[a]*Indiana Wesleyan University, USA*
[b]*Kozai Group, USA*
[c]*Pamplin College of Business, USA*

Abstract

In a world that represents a diverse genre of individuals ranging from age to sexual orientation and beyond, organizations struggle to create a culture of belonging. A culture where an individual feels comfortable and empowered to bring her authentic self to the workplace. We argue that a culture of belonging happens when leaders practice cultural humility and inclusion competencies and work together with their diverse populations to transform the existing culture. Creating a culture of belonging requires all leaders of the organization to assess their inclusion competencies, understand power dynamics that exist within the organization, and be constantly aware that belonging is a continual process. We found that when leaders of an organization engage in cultural humility training, inclusion competencies assessments, and personal development plans (PDPs), the outcome resulted in a greater awareness of self and others along with a recognition of the existing power dynamics that can result in employees feeling they are a part of the organization. We opined that cultures of belonging exist when organizational leaders ensure each members' psychological well-being and safety. We conclude that transparency in today's organization consists of leaders finding practical ways to connect diverse groups of members. Transparency is also about having open doors where people of all ethnic, racial, sexual, and religious statuses are welcome to enter. Our study supports the findings of Katz and Miller (2016) that a culture of belonging is where trust is built, the thoughts and ideas of others are respected, and safety exists for all members.

Keywords: Belonging; culture of belonging; cultural humility; inclusion; positive transformation; psychological safety and well-being

Inclusive Leadership: Equity and Belonging in Our Communities
Building Leadership Bridges, Volume 9, 25–38
Copyright © 2023 by Emerald Publishing Limited
All rights of reproduction in any form reserved
ISSN: 2058-8801/doi:10.1108/S2058-880120230000009003

In a more complex and diverse world than ever, one may question why the literature on diversity, equity, inclusion, and belonging (DEIB) has yet to be explored more deeply within the scholarly literature and implemented across business organizations. In the past 50 years, according to Nkomo et al. (2019), diversity has taken on various trajectories to the extent that individuals compartmentalize to represent just one group (e.g., women, Black, Indigenous, people of color [BIPOC], LGBTQ+). However, throughout the abundance of research on diversity, leadership literature has an opportunity to equip leaders better to change an organizational culture that is inclusive and based on cultural humility. Creating a culture of cultural humility, belonging, and inclusion must occur at every level of the organization (Nishii & Leroy, 2021). In this chapter, the authors provide research results from three unique organizational sectors that have used the Inclusion Competency Inventory (ICI) and cultural humility training to further move toward an organizational culture that advocates belonging. We present a model (see Fig. 3.1) that allows leaders to create a culture of belonging in today's diverse organizations by using inclusion competencies, cultural humility, and transformative behaviors, which include listening to act and continuous change.

Creating a culture of belonging begins with the individual, but organizations must invest in leader development to ensure leaders understand cultural humility and inclusion competencies. We present an intersection between the cultural humility and inclusion competencies that lead leaders and organizations into a transformative state that results in a culture of belonging. Self-awareness, both cultural humility and inclusion competencies, goes beyond understanding one's strengths and weaknesses but also includes the *other*-focused self-awareness that considers how the leader's behaviors affect others. Open leaders understand the power dynamics that exist in the organization and work toward bridging differences. We found that these leaders are egoless, listen to act, and spend time in self-reflection. Self-awareness, self-reflection, and critique lead to individual, group,

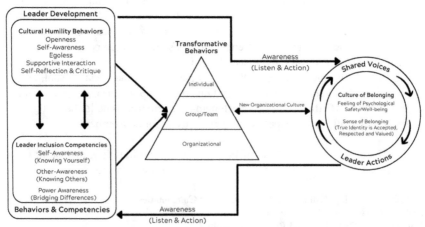

Fig. 3.1.   Conceptual Model: Cultural Humility and Inclusion Leadership Competencies Resulting in a Culture of Belonging.

and organizational transformation. We concur with Fowers and Davidov (2006), who argued transformation of character of the leader allows for respect and support of others. Therefore, we predict that positive transformation at all levels results from developing cultural humility and inclusion competencies.

Hook et al. (2013) defined cultural humility as having a relational attitude focused on others and understanding cultural identity. Similarly, inclusion competencies focus on one's ability for self-awareness, bridging power divides, and creating a culture that fosters belonging and psychological safety (Carmeli et al., 2010; Kozai Group, 2021; Shore et al., 2011). We argue that providing leaders with the abilities and behaviors to employ cultural humility and inclusion competencies will create a culture of belonging where employees feel a sense of psychological safety and well-being.

Failure to Be Inclusive

Often historical organizational culture is the catalyst that creates silos for its members. Bernstein et al. (2020) argued: "culture for inclusion implies a set of sustained practices at the group and organizational levels" (p. 397). As reported by McLean and Company©, an alarming trend is that organizations have not increased their diversity, equity, and inclusion (DEI) strategies since 2021. Between 2021 and 2023 of organizations surveyed by McLean and Company©, 63% had no documented DEI strategy (McLean & Company, 2023). Organizations cannot continue to operate without a strategic business plan that gives attention and resources to DEIB. Furthermore, leaders must be trained in diversity and changing a culture using inclusion competencies and cultural humility (see Fig. 3.1).

The Need for More Inclusive Organizations

The global coronavirus disease 2019 pandemic (COVID-19) shattered every sense of normalcy, shocking social systems and institutions, and its impacts are still relevant as of the writing of this book. Statista (2022, December 7) reported a 3.3% loss (roughly 1.1. million) of employees worldwide, likely due to the economic disruption caused by COVID-19. This loss is attributable to several factors, including layoffs, resignations, health, childcare responsibilities, and more (Osofsky et al., 2020). Following almost two years of disruption and uncertainty, businesses have difficulty in filling positions, while the economy still recovers (Maurer, 2021). Workers globally continue to leave their jobs, searching for roles that suit their values and work-life balance. Called "the Great Reshuffle" (Christian, 2021), employees are shifting to new industries and careers, offering greater work-life satisfaction. "There's now a greater ability for people to fit work into their lives, instead of having lives that squeeze into their work," Christian (2021, para. 4) explained. The future of work is evolving, resulting from these *pandemic epiphanies* (Christian, 2021). As the world began to recover, organizations were reintroduced to workers with a renewed mindset – If this employer cannot meet my needs for inclusion, I will find another that will!

Due to changes in leadership, employee composition, and organizational operating structures, leaders need to be aware of these changing demographics and know how to embrace them. Adejumo (2021) ascertained the importance of belonging as leaders strive to create a culture that welcomes all stakeholders. Nicholson (2022) further argued that inclusive leadership can be the catalyst to bridging organization-wide gaps of DEIB if leaders are engaged and held accountable. As opined by Gallegos (2014):

> Inclusive leadership and cultures of inclusion hold great promise for new ways of relating, sense-making, and creativity. The shift from cultures of individuality to collectivism, from isolation to collaboration, and from competition to mutuality can tap resources and energy needed to address the challenges to come. (pp. 197–198)

Benefits of an Inclusive Organization

Beneficial to organizations, a diversified workforce has produced positive outcomes such as increased productivity and revenue, more significant innovation, and engagement with a broader customer base (Ely & Thomas, 2020; Robinson & Dechant, 1997). Mor Barak and Daya (2014) argued that an inclusive workplace acknowledges and embraces all diverse members of the organization, thus ensuring each person feels a sense of belonging. Brimhall (2019) explored the literature on the benefits of inclusion by examining 17 empirical studies. An inclusive organization's benefits include improved employee self-esteem, increased job satisfaction and organizational commitment, and retention (Brimhall, 2019; McLeod & Herrington, 2017).

Cultural Humility and Inclusion Competencies

Researchers and practitioners have long explored methods and models to understand and address the conditions and human attributes that create organizational dynamics of difference in various contexts and settings, including healthcare, nursing, social work, psychology, education, and engineering (Buchanan & Wiklund, 2020; Morey, 2000; Purnell, 2016; Wells, 2000). Organizational culture manifests as a combination of interpersonal and intergroup cultural differences (Pagès, 2021), and adverse issues could arise if not appropriately managed, affirming Lee and Yang's (2013) assertion "the unconscious reference" to one's own cultural values is the root of most international business problems" (p. 1).

Cultural Humility

Coined by Tervalon and Murray-Garcia (1998), cultural humility was first used to encourage nursing and other healthcare educators to acknowledge patients' diversity and the inevitable power imbalance when considering actors in a healthcare relationship.

Since the turn of the 21st century, cultural humility definitions and general themes have emerged across professional and educational settings. We conceptualize cultural humility using the three main principles presented by Gottlieb (2021):

> (1) committing oneself to an ongoing process of compassionate self-awareness and inquiry, supported by a community of trusted and cognitively-diverse colleagues; (2) being open and teachable, striving

to see cultures as [others] see them, rather than as we have come to know or define them; and (3) continually considering the social systems – and their attendant assignations of power and privilege – that have helped shape reality as both we and [others] experience it. (p. 465)

Furthermore, we affirm the cultural humility assumptions presented by Foronda as (a) humans are diverse, (b) humans are inherently altruistic, (c) humans have equal value, (d) cultural conflict is a normal and expected part of life, and (e) humans are lifelong learners (Foronda, 2020, p. 8).

Inclusion Leadership Competencies

As cultural backgrounds become more diverse and unpredictable, leaders need to understand and cultivate inclusive competencies to meet social interaction challenges and reduce multicultural bias. Gundling (2017) defined inclusive leadership as a bridge-building process involving careful listening, reaching out to people with different perspectives, and persistence in finding common ground. Bernstein et al. (2020) captured the relevance of the inclusion study as involving everyday actions consequentially that produce the structure of social life. Shore and Chung (2022) acknowledged the expansion of literature on diversity and inclusion, noting the need to develop a clear and compelling framework to help determine what leader inclusion is and the needed inclusive leadership competencies.

Gundling and Williams (2021) stated that inclusive organizations look to transform employees into becoming insiders, regardless of their cultural upbringing, lived experience, or social backgrounds, and to feel a sense of belonging. The idea of transformation connects an individual who feels a sense of belonging and is valued for his/her uniqueness. Inclusion is a fundamental practice that seeks to gain the benefits of diversity through one's sense of being appreciated, valued, and safe while engaging in opportunities to contribute to the collective (Ferdman, 2021). Bernstein et al. (2020) implied that sustained practices at the individual, group, and organizational levels are vital in creating a culture that implements repetitious behaviors that promote inclusiveness, equity, and social justice. Gundling and Williams (2021) proffered, "Inclusion has the most powerful impact when it is not just an initiative, a corporate principle, or a required training program" (p. 6).

Organizations today are more complex, turbulent, and unpredictable as they face the challenges of a diverse and global workforce. As diversity increases in organizations, there is also a realization that promoting inclusion involves an equal opportunity for socially marginalized people (Shore et al., 2018). Inclusive behaviors result from leaders staying committed to building organizations that remove racial and cultural barriers while honoring individual differences and uniqueness. Zeng et al. (2020) stated that leaders who practice inclusive behaviors encourage employees to work independently and that inclusive leaders allow employees to be involved in decision-making while recognizing and supporting their contributions.

Inclusion Competency Inventory

While there are many perspectives on the required competencies for inclusion, for this research, the authors used the ICI to explore how leaders use inclusion to improve the organizational culture. The ICI includes three primary competencies focused on the individual level: (a) knowing yourself, (b) knowing others, and (c) bridging differences. Each competency contains subdimensions that drive the competency from awareness to action. For example, knowing yourself requires questions that reflect the individual's openness to change and adaptability to unfamiliar and diverse settings. When individuals commit to knowing themselves, continuous self-learning, and self-awareness of how one's behaviors impact others, will occur and shape new habits.

Inclusion and Belonging

For inclusion to occur in organizations, leaders must enforce inclusive competencies that promote a sense of belongingness and psychological safety among group members. Leaders willing to expand their diversity initiatives and exercise feelings of support with ongoing commitment can generate competencies that express empathy, be perceptive about cultural differences, and build lasting respect for the legacy of multiple histories (Gundling & Williams, 2019). Examples of inclusion competencies must center around awareness of oneself and communication with others.

Three core indicators surface when exploring the experience of inclusion. Those three indicators are equality, transparency, and belongingness (Hunt et al., 2020). The inclusive workplace involves equal opportunity for those who represent socially marginalized groups and non-marginalized groups to respect and engage equally (Shore et al., 2018).

Psychological Safety

Creating a sense of psychological safety is a primary mover in helping an individual feel a sense of belonging. Clark (2020) proffered that psychological or inclusion safety is created and sustained as individuals gain admittance to a group and repeated specification of acceptance. Clark added, "Giving inclusion safety is a moral imperative" (p. 8). Building individual competencies involves a growing knowledge of oneself, including regularly examining personal biases and balancing cultural knowledge with an openness to learning and change. The competency of knowing oneself is part of an integrated trilogy that includes the cultural skills of knowing others and bridging differences (Kozai Group, 2021). These three competencies provide a catalyst for creating a more inclusive environment.

When individuals seek out and develop positive relationships with people from diverse cultures, there is a wealth of understanding that can reduce prejudice and cultural conflict (Kozai Group, 2021). Non-verbal cues and observations create a capacity to identify disconnects and relational patterns that relate to human feelings and words. The construct of bridging differences includes the competencies of valuing different perspectives with an understanding of power sensitivity. Hearing and respecting other voices, especially marginalized voices, can lead to empathy and compassion for others' behaviors and circumstances (Kozai Group, 2021). Inclusion, therefore, has the seed to grow and prosper.

Results and Discussion

All organization types must consider culturally humble leaders who practice inclusion competencies to be successful in the 21st century and beyond. In our study, we interviewed business leaders and working professionals in business and leadership programs after completing the ICI (Kozai Group, 2021) and participated in cultural humility training and creating PDPs. Inclusion competencies consisted of knowing yourself (self-awareness), knowing others (other awareness), and bridging differences (power awareness).

Each organization's results used ranked factoring to determine the importance of the three factors associated with inclusion competencies. Once the data were analyzed for ranking, the results from the qualitative interviews were compared to the quantitative data to determine the association between cultural humility training, PDPs, and inclusion competency training. Specific themes emerged, indicated in Figs. 3.5 and 3.6. All groups demonstrated a need to better understand the dynamics of power sensitivity within their organizational structure. After the cultural humility training and completion of the PDPs, all participants found that their actions and behaviors related to the above skills improved.

The first group, Group A, consisted of leaders working in a for-profit healthcare organization. As shown in Fig. 3.2, the group member score indicated an opportunity for improvement in Bridging Differences associated with power sensitivity. Percentage distributions in the for-profit healthcare sector were $N = 75$; the ranked factors in descending order were as follows: (1) knowing others, (2) bridging differences, and (3) knowing yourself. Group A showed strengths in reading others and openness to change; however, the combined growth areas were adaptability, power sensitivity, and connecting with others.

In the second group, Group B, the participants represented members of various graduate school programs at one institution. As shown in Fig. 3.3, Group B had results similar to Group A, whereas the need to develop the inclusion skill of

	Low		Moderate			High	
	1	2	3	4	5	6	7
Knowing Yourself	13.3%	9.3%	16.0%	17.3%	14.7%	10.7%	18.7%
Openness to Change	4.0%	8.0%	14.7%	10.7%	17.3%	29.3%	16.0%
Adaptability	12.0%	18.7%	14.7%	21.3%	6.7%	12.0%	14.7%
Knowing Others	5.3%	12.0%	13.3%	10.7%	12.0%	22.7%	24.0%
Connecting With Others	14.7%	4.0%	14.7%	16.0%	21.3%	16.0%	13.3%
Reading Others	4.0%	5.3%	14.7%	14.7%	20.0%	18.7%	22.7%
Bridging Differences	5.3%	13.3%	20.0%	17.3%	12.0%	18.7%	13.3%
Valuing Different Perspectives	8.0%	12.0%	10.7%	17.3%	24.0%	18.7%	9.3%
Power Sensitivity	10.7%	16.0%	12.0%	21.3%	13.3%	12.0%	14.7%
ICI Total Score	6.7%	12.0%	12.0%	21.3%	12.0%	16.0%	20.0%

Fig. 3.2. Group A Inclusion Competency Scores and Areas for Growth.

Bridging Differences and Power Sensitivity was evident. The group member score indicated an opportunity for improvement in Bridging Differences associated with Power Sensitivity, Knowing Yourself, and Adaptability. Percentage distributions for the academic sector were $N = 100$, and the ranked factors in descending order were as follows: (1) knowing others, (2) knowing yourself, and (3) bridging differences.

The final population studied was members of a nonprofit Christian organization. While the sample size was relatively small, insights on the versatility of combining cultural humility behaviors with inclusion behaviors across sectors proved helpful. They will be discussed later in this chapter. Group C, as shown in Fig. 3.4, revealed a development need to understand better openness to change and valuing different perspectives. However, Group C did demonstrate areas of strength for reading others and adaptability. The percentage distribution for the Christian organization sector was $N = 10$; the ranked factors in descending order were as

	Low		Moderate			High	
	1	2	3	4	5	6	7
Knowing Yourself	20%	18%	15%	11%	21%	5%	10%
Openness to Change	25%	4%	12%	16%	15%	10%	18%
Adaptability	10%	13%	29%	18%	8%	9%	13%
Knowing Others	13%	17%	12%	17%	14%	15%	12%
Connecting With Others	22%	15%	11%	21%	19%	6%	6%
Reading Others	8%	9%	16%	18%	17%	12%	20%
Bridging Differences	20%	17%	13%	21%	11%	9%	9%
Valuing Different Perspectives	20%	15%	10%	23%	11%	8%	13%
Power Sensitivity	17%	12%	22%	20%	17%	5%	7%
ICI Total Score	19%	15%	13%	19%	10%	13%	11%

Fig. 3.3.   Group B Inclusion Competency Scores and Areas for Growth.

	Low		Moderate			High	
	1	2	3	4	5	6	7
Knowing Yourself	10%	20%	20%		40%		10%
Openness to Change	1	2	2	1	2	1	
Adaptability		2	2	2	2	2	
Knowing Others	10%	20%		50%		10%	10%
Connecting With Others		3	2	1	2	2	
Reading Others		2	3	2		2	1
Bridging Differences		20%	50%	10%		20%	
Valuing Different Perspectives	2	1	2	2	1		2
Power Sensitivity		2	3	3		1	1
ICI Total Score	10%	20%	10%	40%	10%	0%	10%

Fig. 3.4.   Group C Inclusion Competency Scores and Areas for Growth.

follows: (1) knowing yourself, (2) knowing others, and (3) bridging differences. The hierarchical nature of Group C illustrated that decision-making was from the top-down, and leaders sometimes listened to different perspectives.

All group members participated in completing PDPs, cultural humility training, and debrief sessions with the researchers. The following themes emerged from combined groups. The overarching questions guiding the interviews were as follows: *RQ1: What impact did understanding cultural humility and inclusion competencies have on your leadership behaviors?* (See Fig. 3.5.) Followed by *RQ2: In what ways has your leadership and organizational culture changed since implementing inclusion competencies and cultural humility behaviors?* (See Fig. 3.6.)

RQ1 combined analysis of all sectors and revealed that leaders had a greater acknowledgment of their internal biases and self-awareness, which often guided decision-making. Leaders were unaware of the power imbalances permeating

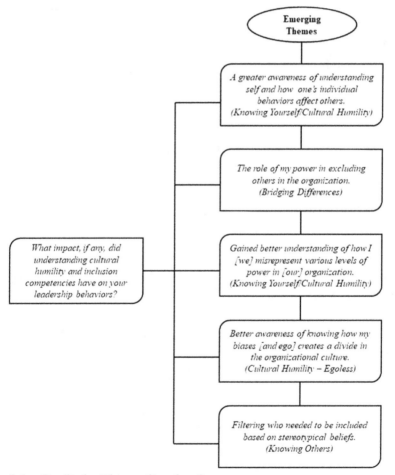

Fig. 3.5.   Qualitative Themes Question One.

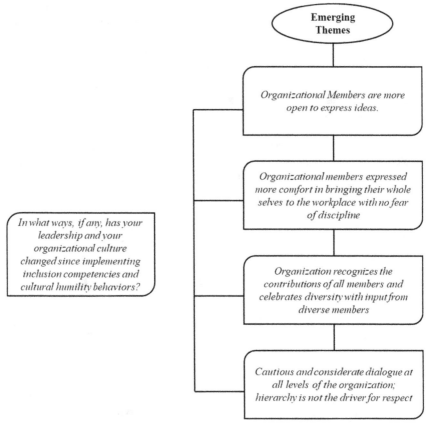

Fig. 3.6.   Qualitative Themes Question 2.

through multiple levels of the organization. The debrief sessions, creation of PDPs, and cultural humility training offered participants of the research insights about what behaviors needed to change or be improved and how they could utilize their collective strengths to improve their leadership to be more inclusive. Participants were able to make a connection between culturally humble practices and inclusion to become more self-aware. Self-awareness, egoless, and power sensitivity allowed leaders to become better at bridging differences, especially differences based on cultural and racial divides.

Inclusion is more than just policies and procedures. It is a change in the attitudes and behaviors of all organizational members to create a culture of belonging. The study participants who discussed organizational change noted that members became more open about bringing their whole identity to the workplace, which was often guarded prior to the leadership intervention of the ICI and cultural humility training. A sense of belonging was created by incorporating recognition of the diverse population and allowing them to lead initiatives based on talents, not just cultural backgrounds. Diverse individuals were not singled out as representatives for the entire group but rewarded for their contributions along with the majority population. These changes in organizational practices allowed members to feel comfortable with bringing their voices to the table, knowing their input was valued. Minority organizational members noted a change in the hierarchy and layers of the organization. As a result, individuals were promoted based on talents.

Conclusions

Throughout our research and practice of inclusion competencies and cultural humility, we have found that these two elements must function in tandem with each other and work together if organizations desire to create cultures of belonging for all stakeholders. The cycle presented in our conceptual model (see Fig. 3.1) demonstrates that cultural humility and inclusion competencies are an intricate part of leader transformation at all levels of the organization. Recognizing that a culture of belonging must begin from the top levels of leadership, it can only flourish with all members promoting inclusion and acting with cultural humility. To reduce failed inclusion attempts by organizations, we argue it is paramount that training for inclusion and cultural humility begins before one enters the workforce and continues at all levels of the organization. Organizational leaders must change their mindset from a one-and-done process, project, or policy to the realization that "inclusion is not ever done" (Ferdman & Deane, 2014, p. 595). Even though inclusion and belonging are different (Slepian & Jacoby-Senghor, 2021), creating a culture where one can bring their identity into the workplace without bias, ridicule, and negative stereotypical perceptions provides the foundation for our model that connects cultural humility, inclusion competencies, and psychological safety. Leaders must be transparent.

Transparency in today's organization consists of leaders finding practical ways to connect diverse groups of members. Sensemaking, a term coined by Karl Weick in the mid-1990s, is a process of a deeper understanding of problems requiring leaders to facilitate discussions among people and groups with different beliefs (Mrig & Sanaghan, 2017). Transparency is also about having open doors where people of all ethnic, racial, sexual, and religious statuses are welcome to enter. One feels a sense of belonging when organizations faithfully practice the following intentions: (a) build trust: do what you say you will do and honor confidentiality; (b) link to others' ideas, thoughts, and feelings; give the energy back; (c) speak up when people are excluded or made to feel small; and (d) create a sense of safety for your team members and yourself (Katz & Miller, 2016). While there is still much work to do in creating a culture of belonging, we proffer that cultural humility and inclusion competencies create the foundation for positive transformative actions.

References

Adejumo, V. (2021). Beyond diversity, inclusion, and belonging. *Leadership*, *17*(1), 62–73. https://doi.org/10.1177/1742715020976202

Bernstein, R. S., Bulger, M., Salipante, P., & Weisinger, J. Y. (2020). From diversity to inclusion to equity: A theory of generative interactions. *Journal of Business Ethics*, *167*(3), 395–410. https://doi.org/10.1007/s10551-019-04180-1

Buchanan, N. T., & Wiklund, L. O. (2020). Why clinical science must change or die: Integrating intersectionality and social justice. *Women & Therapy*, *43*(3–4), 309–329. https://doi.org/10.1080/02703149.2020.1729470

Brimhall, K. C. (2019). Inclusion and commitment as key pathways between leadership and nonprofit performance. *Nonprofit Management & Leadership*, *30*(1), 31–49. https://doi.org/10.1002/nml.21368

Carmeli, A., Reiter-Palmon, R., & Ziv, E. (2010). Inclusive leadership and employment involvement in creative tasks in the workplace: The mediating role of psychological safety. *Creativity Research Journal*, *22*(3), 250–260. https://doi.org/10.1080/10400419. 2010.504654

Christian, A. (2021, December 14). How the great resignation is turning into the great reshuffle. *BBC Worklife*. https://www.bbc.com/worklife/article/20211214-great-resignation-into-great-reshuffle

Clark, T. R. (2020). *The four stages of psychological safety: Defining the path to inclusion and innovation*. Berrett-Koehler Publishers.

Ely, R. J., & Thomas, D. A. (2020). Getting serious about diversity: Enough already with the business case. *Harvard Business Review*, *98*(6), 114–122.

Ferdman, B. M. (2021). Inclusive leadership: The fulcrum of inclusion. In B. M. Ferdman, J. Prime, J., & R. E. Riggio (Eds.), *Inclusive leadership: Transforming diverse lives, workplaces, and societies* (pp. 3–24). Routledge.

Ferdman, B. M., & Deane, B. R. (2014). Practicing inclusion: Looking back and looking ahead. In B. M. Ferdman & B. R. Deane (Eds.), *Diversity at work: The practice of inclusion* (pp. 593–600). Jossey-Bass.

Foronda, C. (2020). A theory of cultural humility. *Journal of Transcultural Nursing*, *31*(1), 7–12. https://doi.org/10.1177/1043659619875184

Fowers, B. J., & Davidov, B. J. (2006). The virtue of multiculturalism: Personal transformation, character, and openness to the other. *American Psychologist*, *61*(6), 581–594. https://doi.org/10.1037/0003-066X.61.6.581

Gallegos, P. V. (2014). The work of inclusive leadership: Fostering authentic relationships, modeling courage and humility. In B. M. Ferdman & B. R. Deane (Eds.), *Diversity at work: The practice of inclusion* (pp. 177–202). Jossey-Bass.

Gottlieb, M. (2021). The case for a cultural humility framework in social work practice. *Journal of Ethnic & Cultural Diversity in Social Work*, *30*(6), 463–481. https://doi.org /10.1080/15313204.2020.1753615

Gundling, E. (2017). *Inclusive leadership: Now more than ever*. Aperian Global.

Gundling, E. & Williams, C. (2019). *Inclusive leadership: From awareness to action*. Aperian Global.

Gundling, E., & Williams, C. (2021). *Inclusive leadership, global impact*. Aperian Global.

Hook, J. N., Davis, D. E., Owen, J., Worthington, E. L., Jr, & Utsey, S. O. (2013). Cultural humility: Measuring openness to culturally diverse clients. *Journal of Counseling Psychology*, *60*(3), 353–366. https://doi.org/10.1037/a0032595

Hunt, V., Dixon-Fyle, S., Dolan, K., & Prince, S. (2020). *Diversity wins: How inclusion matters*. McKinsey & Company.

Katz, J. H., & Miller, F. A. (2016). Defining diversity and adapting inclusion strategies on a global scale. *OD Practitioner*, *48*(3), 42–46.

Kozai Group. (2021). *Inclusion competencies*. https://www.kozaigroup.com/inclusion-competencies/

Lee, S., & Yang, Y. C. (2013). *How do multinational corporations creatively address D&I initiatives through corporate social responsibility?* https://ecommons.cornell.edu/bitstream/ handle/1813/74420/How_do_multinational_corporations_creatively_address_D_I_ initiatives_through_corporate_social_responsibility.pdf?sequence=1&isAllowed=y

Maurer, R. (2021, August 4). *Labor shortages: The disconnect and possible solutions.* Society for Human Resource Management (SHRM). https://www.shrm.org/resourcesand-tools/hr-topics/talent-acquisition/pages/labor-shortages-the-disconnect-solutions-unemployment-benefits-childcare-covid-fear.aspx

McLean & Company. (2023). *HR trends report 2023: Leading HR into the future of work.* McLean & Company. https://www.hr_2023_HR_Trends_Report.pdf

McLeod, A., & Herrington, V. (2017). Valuing different shades of blue: From diversity to inclusion and the challenge of harnessing difference. *International Journal of Emergency Services, 6*(3), 177–187. https://doi.org/10.1108/IJES-04-2017-0021

Mor Barak, M. E., & Daya, P. (2014). Fostering inclusion from the inside out to create an inclusive workplace. In B. M. Ferdman & B. R. Deane (Eds.), *Diversity at work: The practice of inclusion* (pp. 391–412). John Wiley & Sons.

Morey, A. I. (2000). Changing higher education curricula for a global and multicultural world. *Higher Education in Europe, 25*(1), 25–39. https://doi.org/10.1080/037977 20050002170

Mrig, M., & Sanaghan, P. (2017). *The skills future higher-ed leaders need to succeed.* Academic Impressions.

Nicholson, N. (2022). The missing DEI strategy: Cultivating inclusive leadership: The impact of leadership on DEI. *Leadership Excellence, 29*(6), 18–22.

Nishii, L. H., & Leroy, H. L. (2021). Inclusive leadership: Leaders as architects of inclusive workgroup climates. In B. M. Ferdman, J. Prime, & R. E. Riggio (Eds.), *Inclusive leadership: Transforming diverse lives, workplaces, and societies* (pp. 162–178). Routledge/Taylor & Francis Group.

Nkomo, S. M., Bell, M. P., Roberts, L. M., Joshi, A., & Thatcher, S. M. B. (2019). Diversity at a critical juncture: New theories for a complex phenomenon. *Academy of Management Review, 44*(3), 498–517. https://doi.org/10.5465/amr.2019.0103

Osofsky, J. D., Osofsky, H. J., & Mamon, L. Y. (2020). Psychological and social impact of COVID-19. *Psychological Trauma: Theory, Research, Practice, and Policy, 12*(5), 468–469. https://doi.org/10.1037/tra0000656

Pagès, A. (Ed.). (2021). *A history of Western philosophy of education in the contemporary landscape.* Bloomsbury Publishing.

Purnell, L. D. (2016). The Purnell model for cultural competence. In L. D. Purnell (Ed.), *Intervention in mental health-substance use* (pp. 57–78). CRC Press.

Robinson, G., & Dechant, K. (1997). Building a business case for diversity. *Academy of Management Perspectives, 11*(3), 21–31. https://doi.org/10.5465/ame.1997.9709231661

Shore, L. M., & Chung, B. G. (2022). Inclusive leadership: How leaders sustain or discourage work group inclusion. *Group & Organizational Management, 47*(4), 723–754. https://doi.org/10.1177/1059601121999580

Shore, L. M., Cleveland, J. N., & Sanchez, D. (2018). Inclusive workplaces: A review and model. *Human Resource Management Review, 28*(2), 176–189. https://doi.org/10.1016/j.hrmr.2017.07.003

Shore, L. M., Randel, A. E., Chung, B. G., Dean, M. A., Ehrhart, K. H., & Singh, G. (2011). Inclusion and diversity in work groups: A review and model for future research. *Journal of Management, 37*(4), 1262–1289. https://doi.org/10.1177/0149206310385943

Slepian, M. L., & Jacoby-Senghor, D. S. (2021). Identity threats in everyday life: Distinguishing belonging from inclusion. *Social Psychological and Personality Science, 12*(3), 392–406. https://doi.org/10.1177/1948550619895008

Statista. (2022, December 7). *Number of employees worldwide 1991–2022.* https://www.statista.com/statistics/1258612/global-employment-figures/

Tervalon, M., & Murray-Garcia, J. (1998). Cultural humility versus cultural competence: A critical distinction in defining physician training outcomes in multicultural education. *Journal of Health Care for the Poor and Underserved, 9*(2), 117–125. https://doi.org/10.1353/hpu.2010.0233

Wells, M. I. (2000). Beyond cultural competence: A model for individual and institutional cultural development. *Journal of Community Health Nursing, 17*(4), 189–199. https://doi.org/10.1207/S15327655JCHN1704_1

Zeng, H., Zhao, L., & Zhao, Y. (2020). Inclusive leadership and taking-charge behavior: Roles of psychological safety and thriving at work. *Frontiers in Psychology, 11*(Article 62), 1–11. https://doi.org/10.3389/fpsyg-2020.00062

Chapter 4

The Impact of Colonialism on Inclusion and Belonging in Organizations

Catherine T. Kwantes[a], Bryanne Smart[b] and Wendi L. Adair[b]

[a]*University of Windsor, Canada*
[b]*University of Waterloo, Canada*

Abstract

While diversity, equity, inclusion, and belonging (DEIB) in the workplace means making space for all employees, it has unique implications for Indigenous employees who live and work in countries built on colonialism. Indigenous peoples represent diverse groups with unique and rich cultures that in general share values that are more holistic, spiritual, traditional, egalitarian, and other-oriented than non-Indigenous populations. Such distinct worldviews help explain why non-Indigenous organizations struggle to understand and accommodate Indigenous employees' priorities and goal-oriented behavior. Creating equity, inclusivity, and belonging in the workplace for Indigenous employees requires more than implementing existing organizational practices with a new cultural awareness, it requires rethinking, reframing, and recreating organizational to facilitate a culture of trust. Re-examining organizational norms and assumptions with the ideas of relationship and responsibility that allow collaborative approaches to collective well-being and inclusivity is required. Creating inclusive workspaces requires that attention must be paid to both organizational (group-level) factors, such as organizational cultures of trust, and interpersonal (individual-level) factors, such as interpersonal trust. However, to build foundations of high-functioning and supportive organizational cultures and interpersonal trust that are sustainable, time and resources are necessary. Without this, the ability to reach the crucial result of engaging Indigenous employees and creating

Inclusive Leadership: Equity and Belonging in Our Communities
Building Leadership Bridges, Volume 9, 39–49
ISSN: 2058-8801/doi:10.1108/S2058-880120230000009004

safe workplaces serves only to be performative and not meaningful in terms of action, longevity, and the overall well-being of Indigenous people in the workplace.

Keywords: Indigenous; cultures of trust; organizational culture; organizational relationships; interpersonal trust; decolonization

Inclusion and belonging have particular meanings in settings with colonial histories. While DEIB in the workplace means making space for all employees, it has unique implications for Indigenous employees who live and work in countries built on colonialism. The legacy of colonialism is one that resonates globally, from the Ainu in Japan to the Sami in Norway to the Māori in New Zealand to First Nations in Canada and many, many more. Colonialism reflects a people taking control of another peoples' land, subjugating and dominating the original inhabitants. It is an expression of power that can range from outright genocide to subversive microaggressions and social discrimination, leaving a legacy of pain and mistrust that brings justice to the forefront (United Nations General Assembly, 2007). To engage Indigenous employees, organizations must shed intercultural barriers that foster marginalization and mistrust and replace them with cultures of trust while working to understand and repair past injustices.

In undertaking this project, the authors wish to recognize their own positionality and the perspectives that they bring to the discussion and suggestions in this chapter.

The first author is a female scholar of Western European descent who grew up in Asia and currently lives in North America on lands that were colonized by Europeans. Her research focuses on how societal culture impacts employee attitudes and behaviors and especially how that impact can relate to injustice and the development of greater social justice in the workplace. She recognizes the extent to which membership in various societal groups can impart vastly different degrees of privilege to members of those groups. In learning from Indigenous voices, she has come to understand how deeply the colonial past still pervades current interactions among peoples, groups, and organizations on the lands where she lives and works.

The second author is an Indigenous woman and member of Six Nations of the Grand River. With her mother being from the Seneca Nation and of the turtle clan, she has followed that matrilineal lineage. It is important to note that she is also of a mixed background, with her father being a second-generation English settler. She acknowledges as a White presenting individual the immense privilege held in this space and approaches her work from that lens and with the awareness and understanding of that privilege. She values the importance of foregrounding Indigenous voices and building foundational relationships in her work where she has spent two decades interviewing, listening, and working with Indigenous people and communities.

The third author grew up in a White, middle-class neighborhood on lands originally inhabited by the Lenape and Delaware Peoples. She began her academic career working at the intersection of national culture, communication, negotiation, and teamwork. Along with a graduate student in 2015, she began exploring how Indigenous employees experience identity conflict in Canadian organizations. Through ongoing consultation and partnership with Indigenous employees and students, she continues to learn about the history and contemporary experiences of Indigenous peoples. She recognizes the privilege that has brought her to this space as she works to bring Indigenous voices, worldviews, and methodologies to organizational psychology research and organizational practice.

Colonialism and DEIB Context

Indigenous peoples represent diverse groups with unique and rich cultures that in general share values that are more holistic, spiritual, traditional, egalitarian, and other-oriented than non-Indigenous populations (Julien et al., 2017; Stonefish & Kwantes, 2017; Verbos et al., 2011). Holistic values assist in understanding the meaning of work and workplace experiences of Indigenous employees (Tessier et al., 2023). Indigenous peoples strive for balanced achievement across intellectual, spiritual, physical, and emotional states, as well as equilibrium in their relationships with the self, family, community, and creator (Archibald, 2008; Chenoweth, 2016; Spiller et al., 2011; Wilson, 2008). In contrast, individuals and organizations of Western European heritage emphasize material achievement and accumulation of capital wealth (Brayboy, 2005). Gutierrez (2018), comparing her culture to Western wealth-building values, noted that for the Lakota,

> the goal is not materialistic things, but helping, giving, and taking care of one another. Our wealth is measured in our ability to care for our people and to provide a strong foundation for future generations. (p. 14)

Such distinct worldviews help explain why non-Indigenous organizations struggle to understand and accommodate Indigenous employees' priorities and goal-oriented behavior (Verbos et al., 2011).

Societal cultures are often mirrored by organizational cultures (Kwantes & Dickson, 2011, chapter 28), and while cultures may vary greatly, they all result from efforts at understanding and making sense of human experiences, reflecting an underlying agreement on what is real and what is valued (Weick, 1995). When organizations strongly reflect a single worldview and its associated values, the result is societal discrimination, exclusions, and marginalization being brought into the workplace. Ultimately, it is the interaction between societal and organizational cultures that define workplace values and norms (Dickson et al., 2014, chapter 15).

While this is generally true, the imbalance of power created by colonial histories and perpetuated by societal biases creates a unique context for Indigenous employees who are a part of the Western workforce today despite colonial efforts at cultural genocide and assimilation and despite the invisibility conferred on them through contemporary forms of racism (Leavitt et al., 2015). Indigenous employees (and those from other marginalized cultures) who have finished postsecondary education and attained careers are surrounded by ongoing race-related workplace challenges and the need to support family and communities in poverty, often making them less likely than their White counterparts to succeed and grow in the mainstream corporate landscape (Leavitt et al., 2015; Roberts & Mayo, 2019). Educational programs on the history and cultures of Indigenous peoples and the legacy of colonialism are essential tools for creating awareness and context. But such training programs do not address the psychological experience of Indigenous employees who report identity conflict, suppressing their core cultural identity at work and in many cases feeling forced to assimilate or exit (Adair et al., 2017; Hunt, 2022; Julien et al., 2017; Racine, 2016).

Indigenous people have an inherently different worldview than that of settler populations. Linda Tuhiwai Smith (2021) explains that Indigenous epistemological traditions frame the way in which Indigenous peoples see the world and interact within it and further speaks to the questions and solutions on how to be and operate within it. This concept transfers into the workplace as part of an Indigenous employee's holistic self. Add to this a history of societal exclusion and discriminatory policies affecting Indigenous people, and the divide in the workplace continues to grow. Due to this divide, Indigenous individuals within the workplace and beyond are constantly living in a duality to maintain connection in their role as an employee that is often misaligned to their true self (Fairbanks, 2005).

Prior to colonization, Indigenous people led lives full of culture and tradition, and intrinsically tied to those were work, responsibility, family, and community. These were not separate entities but once again tied to the holistic part of oneself. The modern way of work is far from these original values and worldviews, often having employees remove themselves from family, or community to attend work, furthering that disconnect. This intercultural workplace has been described as a "complex environment" that creates psychosocial barriers for Indigenous employees to be able to succeed and thrive in non-Indigenous workplaces (Steel & Heritage, 2020).

When societal cultures discriminate against members of particular groups, mistrust is created. It then requires active attention from organizations with concerted efforts to create organizational cultures that welcome and support employees from marginalized groups, ensuring equitable conditions for them to flourish and develop their careers (United Nations General Assembly, 2007). Cultural mistrust that exists for members of societally marginalized groups due to past and present experiences with racism and oppression has been described as "simply an individual's trust of own-group members over out-group members" (Bell & Tracey, 2006, p. 11). Nevertheless, organizations need not perpetuate societal inequities. When Indigenous employees are free to bring Indigenous values to the workplace and act in ways consistent with those values, improved mental health results (Brougham & Haar, 2013).

Fundamental to creating inclusion and belongingness is a critical examination of, and eradication of, both explicit and implicit power differentials as prejudice and power are inextricably linked (Turner, 2005). Bias in a society that provides power and privileges to one group over another is reinforced in many ways, from the obvious, such as unequal access to healthcare or education, to the subtle, such as the use of environments and symbols (Evans & Gaddie, 2021). Organizations and institutions often perpetuate these power differentials, and it requires deliberate and determined efforts to make real and lasting changes, given that "system-supporting inaction and the intergroup dynamic it produces is a central and highly effective technique used by dominant group members to hinder processes of change and preserve their power" (Täuber & Moughalian, 2022, p. 1128).

Indigenization of the workplace requires more than implementing existing organizational practices with a new cultural awareness; it requires rethinking, reframing, and recreating organizational practices (Newhouse, 2004; Newhouse & Chapman, 1996) to facilitate a culture of trust. It is re-examining organizational norms and assumptions with the ideas of relationship and responsibility that allow collaborative approaches to collective well-being and inclusivity (Pio & Waddock, 2021). Any examination of organizational constructs inherently requires a multi-level approach (Kozlowski & Klein, 2000). Group-level factors may emerge from individual interactions in the workplace and then, once emerged, have an influence on future individual interactions (LeBreton et al., 2022). Creating inclusive workspaces, therefore, requires that attention must be paid to both organizational (group-level) factors, such as organizational cultures of trust, and interpersonal (individual-level) factors, such as interpersonal trust.

Organizational Culture

An organizational culture of trust is key to creating inclusive workplaces where Indigenous employees have a sense of belonging (Adair et al., 2017). Creating organizational cultures of trust can be especially challenging in non-Indigenous-led organizations where trust may be a scarce commodity due to ongoing trauma from both historical factors and continuing societal discrimination.

Organizational cultures often, but not always, mimic the societal culture they are embedded in (Kwantes & Dickson, 2011, chapter 28). Organizational cultures can therefore perpetuate inequities or can intentionally make changes that help both the organization and its employees. Organizations benefit from the knowledge and perspectives of a diverse workforce – most notably when they develop a climate of diversity, that is, a workplace with fairness and inclusivity for all employees (Reinwald et al., 2019). Workplaces with diversity climates tend to have greater input from employees on practices and processes as well as better teamwork (Jiang et al., 2022). Employees also benefit from a climate of diversity, tending to have lower turnover intentions when the climate is strong (Kaplan et al., 2011). Indigenous employees who believe their organization values Indigenous ways of knowing and being are more loyal to their organization and go out of their way to be proactively helpful (Haar & Brougham, 2011).

Organizational cultures reflect the values of an organization (Hofstede, 1997) and also norms for employee behavior (Cooke & Szumal, 1993). Cultures of trust in an organization are characterized by ubiquitous, bidirectional, and unconsciously exhibited trusting behaviors representing the normative mode of interaction between coworkers (Talaei & Kwantes, 2020). Further, organizational cultures of trust are ones where individual employees feel that they trust decision-making in the organization – that organizational policies and practices will be fairly developed and equitably undertaken. An organizational culture of trust engenders a sense of psychological safety for employees – a sense that people are comfortable to be themselves and express themselves in the workplace (Edmondson, 2004). Psychological safety is "embedded in the way people interact with one another on a daily basis" (Mental Health Commission of Canada, 2013, p. 1).

Indigenous employees have highlighted the importance of voice, and of being heard, in experiencing psychological safety in the workplace (Jacobs et al., 2022). Another important aspect of psychological safety is cultural safety, or the sense of being able to bring one's culture into the workplace and have it respected (Kwantes et al., 2023). Cultural safety for Indigenous employees is an approach to inclusivity that "moves beyond the concept of cultural sensitivity to analyzing power imbalances, institutional discrimination, colonization and relationships with colonizers" (p. 1, National Aboriginal Health Organization, 2006). Key to a culture of trust for Indigenous employees, then, is a perception that one is free to be oneself in the workplace, that one's culture is respected and that Indigenous ways of knowing and being are acknowledged and valued in the same way that other ways of knowing and being are valued. Thus, organizations should ensure that psychological safety is something that is provided to all employees, and that cultural values and practices are recognized and respected.

Interpersonal Behaviors

Interpersonal trust for employees is a willingness to be vulnerable with coworkers and a confidence that coworkers will behave in a trustworthy manner (Mayer et al., 1995). Trust "is created through social processes of interaction and conversation" (Wright & Ehnert, 2010, p. 114). Interpersonal trust between employees creates an environment of collaboration, disclosure, and socio-emotional support (McAllister et al., 2006), all of which are consistent with Indigenous values for respectful and reciprocal relationships (McPhee et al., 2017).

The relationality inherent across Indigenous worldviews emphasizes interconnectedness of all beings and individual responsibility for respectful and responsible relations with all other beings (Kovach, 2010; Redpath & Nielsen, 1997; Wilson, 2008). In a workplace, all employees carry responsibility to make decisions that benefit everyone, including all their relations, the environment, and themselves (Chapman et al., 1991). Conflict is managed holistically, with community, voice, responsibility, and relationship repair (Gaywish, 2000). Thus, interpersonal trust is a natural consequence of relationality, and the bonds of relationality nurture inclusion and belongingness.

In cultures that value relationality, forming strong interpersonal bonds requires time and attention to socio-emotional and relational processes (Fehr & Gelfand, 2012). The Western workplace culture is low context, meaning people rely on words to say what they mean, have a transactional focus, and work according to clock time. In high-context, holistic Indigenous cultures, most information is contained in the context surrounding a verbal message, interactions are more relational than transactional, and time is fluid and flexible (Adair et al., 2017; Hall, 1976, 1994; Verbos et al., 2011). Low context communication norms do not accommodate relationality and socio-emotional awareness that can help build trust and inclusion.

Shawn Wilson notes in *Research Is Ceremony* (2008) that conversations create relational accountability and build trust. Jaydum Hunt (2022) writes of an Indigenous employee who shared that they cultivate trust by being open and having meaningful conversations. Another Indigenous employee described a trusting relationship characterized by openness, responsibility, and reciprocity with another racialized employee (Hunt, 2022). Building relationships takes time, patience, listening, and bidirectional learning, as Hunt describes in her relational conversation approach to research with Indigenous employees.

To build inclusive workplaces for Indigenous employees, organizational communication practices must recognize and understand relational forms of communication, holistic approaches to conflict management and decision-making that tie the self to coworkers, organization, and community. The path to interpersonal trust is through relational communication processes.

Implications and Recommendations

Colonialism has a deep, insidious, and pervasive influence on societies and therefore organizations. Creating cultures of trust for Indigenous employees means an intentional interruption of the link between societal and organizational cultures. Implicit bias training alone does not last (Lai et al., 2016) – rather, inclusive workspaces require long-term efforts to enact real culture change. Making meaningful changes to create workspaces that are more inclusive for Indigenous employees is therefore a long-term effort that must be thoughtfully sustained and nourished. Leaders play a key role in this, as relational leadership is important for trust in the workplace (Carmeli et al., 2012). Organizational cultures of trust develop over time, based on interactional patterns set by leaders and reinforced in daily interactions (Farnese et al., 2022) and through organizational artifacts and symbols.

Organizational cultures of trust can only develop in the context of employees knowing that their contributions, and they themselves, are valued by the organization. Organizations that visibly recognize the traditional peoples of the land where the organization is located through land acknowledgments and local artwork send a message related to the value the organization places on inclusivity and connections with Indigenous peoples and Indigenous employees. Further, organizations that are familiar with, and support, local businesses such as caterers and other suppliers indicate an openness and inclusivity to both employees and the community. Community connection is important for Indigenous inclusion in the workplace, and efforts to bring in externally paid Indigenous leaders for workshops, conflict resolution, and consultation are critical for creating an environment that truly recognizes and respects Indigenous worldviews.

While implementing the above is critical for organizations to recognize within their workplaces, it is equally important to ensure that the changes do not only happen or take place on the surface. The work needs to be demonstrated within organizations and throughout all levels, including leadership. By doing so, this creates a foundation for the development of a holistic organizational culture that not only supports the whole Indigenous employee, including cultural identity and development, but takes it a step further to ensure that Indigenous voices, practices, and worldviews begin to be woven throughout the fabric of the organization. A holistic organizational culture prioritizes values that align with Indigenous ways of being and knowing (Hunt, 2022). Leaders must initiate the activities that develop trusting, inclusive workplaces, but must also work to sustain such cultures. Thus, while organizational culture and interpersonal behaviors are key factors in creating and developing workplaces that are safe and welcoming to Indigenous people, a further step to consider is how those changes or modifications are being reflected, implemented, and ultimately measured. A key component of reconciliation as discussed through the findings and recommendations from Canada's Truth and Reconciliation Commission is twofold: the ability to speak and hear the truth but to further that with real and concrete action. One without the other can create systems or workplaces that end up reifying colonial practices that result in causing more harm than good toward Indigenous people in these settings (Tuck & Yang, 2012).

It is important that cultures and behaviors are not only implemented within organizational structures, but that Indigenous people are truly engaged throughout the process and free to be themselves in their places of work. To further ensure true and meaningful action, this needs to be taken a step further by challenging those who are non-Indigenous in these settings to act, choose, think, and feel what is being shared by Indigenous people and to truly consider what that means in the context of their respective organizations. By doing so, settler populations can begin to understand from listening and participating in systems that are familiar to Indigenous populations and begin to implement those within opposing colonial structures.

To build foundations of high-functioning and supportive organizational cultures and interpersonal trust that are sustainable, time and resources are necessary. Without this, the ability to reach the crucial result of engaging Indigenous employees and creating safe workplaces serves only to be performative and not meaningful in terms of action, longevity, and the overall well-being of Indigenous people in the workplace.

References

Adair, W., Kwantes, C. T., Stonefish, T., Badea, R., & Weir, W. (2017). Conversations about Aboriginal work experiences: Reflections for community members, organizations, and the academy. *Journal of Aboriginal Economic Development, 10*(2), 52–70.

Archibald, J. (2008). *Indigenous storywork: Educating the heart, mind, body, and spirit.* UBC Press.

Bell, T. J., & Tracey, T. J. G. (2006). The relation of cultural mistrust and psychological health. *Journal of Multicultural Counseling & Development, 34*(1), 2–14.

Brayboy, B. M. J. (2005). Toward a tribal critical race theory in education. *The Urban Review, 37,* 425–446.

Brougham, D., & Haar, J. M. (2013). Collectivism, cultural identity and employee mental health: A study of New Zealand Māori. *Social Indicators Research, 114*(3), 1143–1160.

Carmeli, A., Tishler, A., & Edmondson, A. C. (2012). CEO relational leadership and strategic decision quality in top management teams: The role of team trust and learning from failure. *Strategic Organization, 10*(1), 31–54.

Chapman, I., Newhouse, D., & McCaskill, D. (1991). Management in contemporary Aboriginal organizations. *The Canadian Journal of Native Studies, 11*(2), 333–349.

Chenoweth, J. (2016, June 7–8). *Finding QWEMQWƏMT – Balance and regeneration* [Paper presentation]. Sharing Knowledge and Building Relationships: Aboriginal Experience in the Cross-cultural Workplace workshop. Vancouver Island University, Cowichan Campus.

Cooke, R. A., & Szumal, J. L. (1993). Measuring normative beliefs and shared behavioral expectations in organizations. *Psychological Reports, 72*(3), 1299.

Dickson, M., Kwantes, C. T., & Magomaeva, A. B. (2014). Societal and organizational culture: Connections and a future agenda. In B. Schneider & K. Barbera (Eds.), *The Oxford handbook of organizational climate and culture* (pp. 276–296). Oxford University Press.

Edmondson, A. C. (2004). Psychological safety, trust, and learning in organizations: A group-level lens. In R. M. Kramer & K. S. Cook (Eds.), *Trust and distrust in organizations: Dilemmas and approaches* (Vol. 7, pp. 239–272). Russell Sage Foundation (Series on Trust).

Evans, J. J., & Gaddie, K. (2021). The systemic affect of culture, power, and terror in the southern public space. *Social Science Quarterly, 102*(3), 1151–1166.

Fairbanks, A. R. (2005). *Walking in two worlds: Making professional transitions between Native and non-Native worlds* [Doctoral dissertation]. University of Minnesota, Minneapolis.

Farnese, M. L., Benevene, P. L., & Barbieri, B. (2022). Learning to trust in social enterprises: The contribution of organisational culture to trust dynamics. *Journal of Trust Research, 12*(2), 153–178.

Fehr, R., & Gelfand, M. J. (2012). The forgiving organization: A multilevel model of forgiveness at work. *Academy of Management Review, 37*(4), 664–688.

Gaywish, R. (2000). Aboriginal people and mainstream dispute resolution: Cultural implications of use. In J. Oakes, R. Riewe, S. Koolage, L. Simpson, & N. Schuster (Eds.), *Aboriginal health, identity and resources* (pp. 113–124). Native Studies Press.

Gutierrez, S. (2018). *An Indigenous approach to community wealth building: A Lakota translation*. Democracy Collaborative. Retrieved February 21, 2023, from https://community-wealth.org/sites/clone.community-wealth.org/files/downloads/CommunityWealthBuildingALakotaTranslation-final-web.pdf

Haar, J. M., & Brougham, D. (2011). Consequences of cultural satisfaction at work: A study of New Zealand Māori. *Asia Pacific Journal of Human Resources, 49*(4), 461–475.

Hall, E. T. (1976). *Beyond culture*. Anchor.

Hall, E. T. (1994). *West of the thirties: Discoveries among the Navajo and Hopi*. Doubleday Books.

Hofstede, G. (1997). *Cultures and organizations: Software of the mind*. McGraw Hill.

Hunt, J. (2022). *Bringing Indigenous voices to the workplace* [Master's thesis]. University of Waterloo.

Jacobs, A., MacIntyre, M., Rhee, S., Lanoue, N., & Kwantes, C. T. (2022). *It must exist somewhere? The search for psychological safety in the Indigenous workforce* [Paper presentation]. Midwestern Psychological Association annual conference, Chicago, IL.

Jiang, Z., DeHart-Davis, L., & Borry, E. L. (2022). Managerial practice and diversity climate: The roles of workplace voice, centralization, and teamwork. *Public Administration Review, 82*(3), 459–472.

Julien, M., Somerville, K., & Brant, J. (2017). Indigenous perspectives on work-life enrichment and conflict in Canada. *Equality, Diversity and Inclusion: An International Journal, 36*(2), 165–181.

Kaplan, D. M., Wiley, J. W., & Maertz, C. P. (2011). The role of calculative attachment in the relationship between diversity climate and retention. *Human Resource Management, 50*(2), 271–287.

Kovach, M. (2010). *Indigenous methodologies: Characteristics, conversations, and contexts.* University of Toronto Press.

Kozlowski, S. W. J., & Klein, K. J. (2000). A multilevel approach to theory and research in organizations: Contextual, temporal, and emergent processes. In K. J. Klein & S. W. J. Kozlowski (Eds.), *Multilevel theory, research, and methods in organizations: Foundations, extensions, and new directions* (pp. 3–90). Jossey-Bass.

Kwantes, C. T., & Dickson, M. W. (2011). Organizational culture in a societal context: Lessons from globe and beyond. In N. N. Ashkanasy, C. Wilderom, & M. F. Peterson (Eds.), *The Handbook of organizational culture and climate* (2nd ed., pp. 494–514). Sage.

Kwantes, C. T., Jacobs, A., & MacIntyre, M. M. (2023, June). *Cultural safety in the workplace for Indigenous employees* [Paper presentation]. 84th annual national convention of the Canadian Psychological Association, Toronto, ON.

Lai, C. K., Skinner, A. L., Cooley, E., Murrar, S., Brauer, M., Devos, T., Calanchini, J., Xiao, Y. J., Pedram, C., Marshburn, C. K., Simon, S., Blanchar, J. C., Joy-Gaba, J. A., Conway, J., Redford, L., Klein, R. A., Roussos, G., Schellhaas, F. M. H., Burns, M., & Hu, X. (2016). Reducing implicit racial preferences: II. Intervention effectiveness across time. *Journal of Experimental Psychology. General, 145*(8), 1001–1016.

Leavitt, P. A., Covarrubias, R., Perez, Y. A., & Fryberg, S. A. (2015). "Frozen in time": The impact of Native American media representations on identity and self-understanding. *Journal of Social Issues, 71*(1), 39–53.

LeBreton, J. M., Moeller, A. N., & Wittmer, J. L. S. (2022). Data aggregation in multilevel research: Best practice recommendations and tools for moving forward. *Journal of Business and Psychology, 38*, 1–20.

Mayer, R. C., Davis, J. H., & Schoorman, F. D. (1995). An integrative model of organizational trust. *Academy of Management Review, 20*(3), 709–734.

McAllister, D. J., Lewicki, R. J., & Chaturvedi, S. (2006, August). Trust in developing relationships: From theory to measurement. *Academy of Management Annual Meeting Proceedings, 2006*(1), G1–G6.

McPhee, D., Julien, M., Miller, D., & Wright, B. (2017). Smudging, connecting, and dual identities: A case study of an aboriginal ERG. *Personnel Review, 46*(6), 1104–1119.

Mental Health Commission of Canada. (2013). *Psychological health and safety in the workplace.* CAN/CSA-Z1003-13/BNQ 9700-803/2013. http://shop.csa.ca/en/canada/occupational-health-and-safety-management/cancsa-z1003-13bnq-9700-8032013/invt/z10032013

National Aboriginal Health Organization (NAHO). (2006). *Fact sheet: Cultural safety.* Retrieved February 28, 2023, from https://fnim.sehc.com/getmedia/c1ef783b-520a-44cf-a7b8-d40df5e406e7/Cultural-Safety-Fact-Sheet.pdf.aspx?ext=.pdf

Newhouse, D. (2004). The challenges of Aboriginal economic development in the shadow of the Borg. *Journal of Aboriginal Economic Development, 4*(1), 36–37.

Newhouse, D., & Chapman, I. D. (1996). Organizational transformation: A case study of 2 Aboriginal organizations. *Human Relations, 49*(7), 995–1101.

Pio, E., & Waddock, S. (2021). Invoking indigenous wisdom for management learning. *Management Learning, 52*(3), 328–346.

Racine, A. A. (2016). *Bicultural identity integration at work: Effects of identity conflict on role conflict perceptions and exhaustion* [Master's thesis]. University of Waterloo.

Redpath, L., & Nielsen, M. O. (1997). A comparison of native culture, non-native culture and new management ideology. *Canadian Journal of Administrative Sciences/Revue Canadienne des Sciences de l'Administration ,14*(3), 327–339.

Reinwald, M., Huettermann, H., & Bruch, H. (2019). Beyond the mean: Understanding firm-level consequences of variability in diversity climate perceptions. *Journal of Organizational Behavior, 40*(4), 472–491.

Roberts, L. M., & Mayo, A. J. (2019). Toward a racially just workplace. *Harvard Business Review*. Retrieved September 10, 2020, from https://hbr. org/cover-story/2019/11/toward-a-racially-just-workplace

Smith, L. T. (2021). *Decolonizing methodologies: Research and indigenous peoples.* Bloomsbury Publishing.

Spiller, C., Erakovic, L., Henare, M., & Pio, E. (2011). Relational well-being and wealth: Maori businesses and an ethic of care. *Journal of Business Ethics, 98*(1), 153–169.

Steel, L., & Heritage, B. (2020). Inter-cultural contexts: Exploring the experience of indigenous employees in mainstream Australian organisations. *Australian Journal of Psychology, 72*(3), 248–256.

Stonefish, T., & Kwantes, C. T. (2017). Values and acculturation: A First Nations exploration. *International Journal of Intercultural Relations, 61*, 63–76. https://doi.org/10.1016/j.ijintrel.2017.09.005

Talaei, A., & Kwantes, C. T. (2020, July). Towards a conceptualization of cultures of trust. In O. Tararukhina (Chair), *Multilevel relationships within organizations.* Symposium accepted to "Psychology in the 21st Century: Open Minds, Societies & World, the 32nd International Congress of Psychology, Prague," Czech Republic, 2020/2021202120.

Täuber, S., & Moughalian, C. (2022). Collective system-supporting inaction: A conceptual framework of privilege maintenance. *European Journal of Social Psychology, 52*(7), 1128–1142.

Tessier, S. Kwantes, C. T., Buchanan, L., & Rangan, C. (2023, June). *Worldviews and the meaning of work: Indigenous and non-Indigenous perspectives* [Paper presentation]. 84th Annual National Convention of the Canadian Psychological Association, Toronto, ON.

Tuck, E., & Yang, K. W. (2012). Decolonization is not a metaphor. Decolonization: *Indigeneity, Education & Society, 1*(1), 1–40.

Turner, J. C. (2005). Explaining the nature of power: A three-process theory. *European Journal of Social Psychology, 35*, 1–22.

United Nations General Assembly. (2007). *United Nations Declaration on the Rights of Indigenous Peoples (UNDRIP)* https://social.desa.un.org/issues/indigenous-peoples/united-nations-declaration-on-the-rights-of-indigenous-peoples.

Verbos, A. K., Gladstone, J. S., & Kennedy, D. M. (2011). Native American values and management education: Envisioning an inclusive virtuous circle. *Journal of Management Education, 35*(1), 10–26.

Weick, K. E. (1995). *Sensemaking in organizations*. Sage.

Wilson, S. (2008). *Research is ceremony: Indigenous research methods*. Fernwood.

Wright, A., & Ehnert, I. (2010). Making sense of trust across cultural contexts. Organizational trust: A cultural perspective. In B. Fairbairn & N. Russell (Eds.), *Co-operative Canada: Empowering communities and sustainable businesses* (pp. 107–126). UBC Press.

Part Two

Diversity, Equity, Inclusion, Belonging, and Education

Chapter 5

The Development of Future Leaders' Inclusive Competencies: Lessons From a Business Management Course

Stacy Menezes[a], Allan Bird[a] and Michael J. Stevens[b]

[a]*Goa Institute of Management, India*
[b]*Weber State University, USA*

Abstract

The development of upcoming inclusive leaders requires not just knowledge of inclusion competencies but also knowledge of how to develop them and when to use them. This chapter examines the effectiveness of combining a psychometric assessment tool – the *Inclusion Competencies Inventory* (ICI) – and an improvement approach that places developmental responsibility in the hands of the student, not the instructor. The increased need for inclusivity in organizations requires business school graduates, who will soon be taking on the role of organizational leaders, to develop inclusion competencies. We seek to enhance inclusion competencies through a model based on reflective development and cognitive behavioral therapy (CBT). There are several implications for academicians and practitioners who may choose to adopt this unique, participant-driven approach to developing inclusion leadership competencies.

Keywords: Inclusion; business schools; *Inclusion Competencies Inventory*; personal development plan; leadership competencies; intercultural competence

Introduction

The rise of diversity in the workplace and in higher education settings has led to a greater need for inclusion competencies (Shore et al., 2018). The need is especially

Inclusive Leadership: Equity and Belonging in Our Communities
Building Leadership Bridges, Volume 9, 53–63
Copyright © 2023 by Emerald Publishing Limited
All rights of reproduction in any form reserved
ISSN: 2058-8801/doi:10.1108/S2058-880120230000009005

magnified for business students on the cusp of becoming future leaders. "Am I born inclusive, or can I develop inclusivity?" The answer to this question has implications for both students in academia and businesspeople.

If inclusion competencies can be developed, then a follow-on question focuses on the most effective ways to do it. Oddou and Mendenhall (2018) suggest that effective adult learning comes 10% from formal classroom instruction (lectures and seminars), 20% from developmental activities (most often in relationships with peers and through mentoring and coaching), and 70% through experiential avenues (involving applications and direct business interactions). This suggests that the most effective way to develop inclusion competencies will be through experiential approaches. Prior research has found that courses incorporating continuous assessment, heightened self-awareness, self-directed personal development plans (PDPs), feedback, and reflection are effective in developing global leadership intercultural competencies (Mendenhall et al., 2020). We hypothesize that it is possible to achieve comparable gains in the development of inclusion competencies through a similar approach. We aim to advance an understanding of individual-level inclusion competency acquisition in a management education context.

There can often be a gap between what management students are taught and what is valued and sought after by industry. Because graduating MBA students will soon take on roles as organizational leaders in implementing policies and practices requiring inclusion, it seems pivotal that they possess not only knowledge but capability (Nishii & Leroy, 2022). This chapter also answers the call for more studies on eastern cultures and how practicing inclusion behaviors can impact individuals themselves (Korkmaz et al., 2022), thereby enhancing their inclusion competencies in an expansive multicultural setting.

This chapter also extends research on inclusion competency in the following ways. First, it examines two complementary developmental theories to the specific context of inclusion competencies. Second, by examining competency development in business students about to enter a highly competitive labor market (characterized by, among other things, an emphasis on intercultural inclusion skills), it also focuses on a population that is likely to pursue leadership opportunities. Third, it addresses the role of PDPs as a tool in facilitating individual inclusion competence development.

Our objective is to understand whether individuals can develop inclusion competencies in an educational context that provides a short timeframe for doing so. In this chapter, we report on preliminary results from an ongoing multi-year, multi-round research project. Our research questions are:

RQ1. Can a learning intervention improve future leaders' inclusion competencies?
RQ2. Can future leaders' inclusion competencies be taught and developed by students?

In the next section, we consider the theoretical underpinning of competency development from the context of inclusion competencies. This is followed by a presentation of what we did. We conclude with a discussion of our preliminary findings of our ongoing study and their implications for theory and practice.

Thinking About Inclusion

Though the terms "diversity" and "inclusion" are often used interconnectedly, each has a distinct meaning (Roberson, 2006). Diversity is "the representation, in one social system, of people with distinctly different group affiliations of cultural significance" (Cox, 1993, p. 5), whereas inclusion is defined as "the degree to which an employee perceives that [they are] an esteemed member of the work group through experiencing treatment that satisfies [their] needs for belongingness and uniqueness" (Shore et al., 2011, p. 1265). "Inclusion differs from diversity in focusing not only on the compositional mix of people, but also on every employee's incorporation into organizational processes and culture" (Bernstein et al., 2020, p. 396).

Though research on diversity has grown exponentially, the distinction between the positive and negative consequences of diversity can be ambiguous (Qu et al., 2021). Diversity is often classified as being of two types: (1) surface-level diversity, which is categorized as more observable demographic differences such as gender, nationality, ethnicity, and so forth; and (2) deep-level diversity, which focuses on less observable differences, such as cognitive diversity (e.g., perspective-taking, neurodiversity, etc.; Schubert & Tavassoli, 2020). Diversity can also be a double-edged sword wherein divergence in thinking could result in more effective brainstorming of ideas, knowledge, perspectives, and so on but also lead to increased conflict and poor decision-making (Schubert & Tavassoli, 2020). A focus on inclusion practices can leverage the benefits of diversity (Shore et al., 2018) while reducing the costs.

While organizations can promote inclusive policies, actual inclusion arises from the voluntary behaviors of persons and as such individual competencies are thus requisite for organizational effectiveness. Korkmaz et al. (2022) propose an inclusion leadership model comprised of fostering employee uniqueness, strengthening belongingness within a team, showing appreciation, and supporting organizational efforts. Given these components of inclusive leadership, the question remains as to how one can develop these competencies so as to enact them. Perhaps paradoxically, there is substantial literature focused on inclusion at the organizational level, with a paucity of research focused on inclusion behaviors at the individual level (Davidson & Ferdman, 2002).

There has also been an evolution in management education fostered by the development of business management knowledge, which is seen in an increase in the number of business schools in India and across the globe (Mishra, Mahapatra & Dagar, 2022). Diversity and inclusion initiatives that are primarily focused on promoting these values and ideals in the classroom would help students foster the same in their future leadership roles (Hawkins & Staats, 2020).

Competency

McClelland (1973) first developed the concept of "competency" in contrast to the aptitude and intelligence tests used to assess and predict academic and other performance. Competencies "are more generally useful in clusters of life outcomes, including not only occupational outcomes but social ones as well, such as leadership, interpersonal skills, etc." (McClelland, 1973, p. 9). Competencies models are combinations of knowledge, skills, abilities, and other characteristics (KSAOs) necessary for expertise and are often used in human resource management processes of recruitment, selection, promotion, training, and development (Campion et al., 2011). A central characteristic of competencies is that they are malleable and can be enhanced through training and development (McClelland, 1973). A competency can thus be defined as

> an underlying characteristic of an employee (i.e., motive, trait, skill, aspects of one's self-image, social role, or a body of knowledge) which results in effective and/or superior performance in a job. (Boyatzis, 1982, p. 20)

Our focus is on inclusion competencies – that is, those traits, abilities, skills, and knowledge that underlie behaviors that help foster an environment where others feel like esteemed members of the work group and experience treatment that satisfies their needs for belonging and uniqueness. More specifically, our interest is in understanding the mechanisms by which inclusion competencies can be developed. For this, we consider two complementary theories.

Reflective Learning Theory

Reflective learning, defined as a process of continuous learning by looking back at one's actions or experiences and critically analyzing them (Schon, 1987), is pivotal in encouraging self-learning and critical thinking based on personal experience (Kolb & Kolb, 2005). Reflective learning requires that individuals consistently and deliberately describe, analyze, examine, and present personal experiences (Rodgers, 2002). A critical reflection is one that challenges individual assumptions, beliefs, and values. Reflective learning theory argues that individuals who engage in this process will then have a clearer sense of the world around them and learn from their experience for future applications (Hedberg, 2009). Reflection can provide individuals with a rich understanding (Rodgers, 2002), which facilitates learning through self-understanding, self-awareness, and self-discovery (Hedberg, 2009). Thus, "transformative growth comes through reflection on experience where such ideas and practices illuminate teachers' practice rather than usurp it" (Rodgers, 2002, p. 232).

The reflective model for developing inclusion competencies has the following developmental stages: awareness, experience, reflection, and assessment. Competency development is more easily achieved when triggered in an individual's cognition, often by an experience that compels them to confront a discrepancy in their self-concept, thoughts, attitudes, and actions (Mendenhall et al., 2013). Once aware of the discrepancy, individuals then pursue experiences to explore them. These experiences become a basis for reflection, the third stage, during which they may examine their motives, compare their actions to others, consider other perspectives, seek to understand behaviors and norms, and search for appropriate actions (Morris et al., 2014). In the final stage, individuals use what they learned in the reflection stage to modify their actions, thereby completing a learning cycle.

Cognitive Behavior Therapy

The development of inclusion competencies can also be considered from a CBT perspective. CBT is most widely used in clinical therapy settings but is also used in instructional and coaching settings (Butler et al., 2006; Macrodimitris et al., 2010). CBT methods are transparent, behavioral, and results oriented (Ducharme, 2004), focusing on the "cognition-affect-behavior-consequences chain" (Meichenbaum, 1986). It relies on individual accountability rather than outside figures for change (Mendenhall et al., 2020). Bandura (2005) argues that having knowledge is not enough, and that corrective feedback and self-regulation are essential to convert knowledge into performance. According to Meichenbaum (1986, pp. 347–349), the CBT methods:

> facilitate self-awareness about cognitive schema that influence how individuals appraise and process events, empower people to discover for themselves, where they become their own "personal scientist," how they can best create cognitive and behavioral changes to enhance their well-being, encourage individuals to view their cognitions and accompanying feelings as hypotheses worthy of testing rather than as facts or truth, and deploy people to perform "personal experiments" and review the consequences of their actions to learn new behavioral, interpersonal, cognitive, and emotional regulation skills.

Core characteristics of CBT methods are:

> (1) operate within a clear, limited time frame; (2) place the responsibility for developing self-awareness regarding cognitions and behavior and subsequent competency development on the individual; and (3) clearly state that the main goal is for people to learn new behavioral, interpersonal, cognitive and emotional-regulation skills. (Meichenbaum, 1986, p. 347)

Its pragmatic nature and inherent simplicity of structure have led to CBT being adopted in a range of non-clinical settings. In particular, CBT has been applied to develop competencies in business students over an academic term with only slight levels of directed coaching (Mendenhall et al., 2013). We adopt this approach here since it is well-suited as customized competency development, accountability, and development goals can change (Mendenhall et al., 2020).

What We Did

Following Feng (2016), who investigated an attempt to improve intercultural competence in a classroom setting by applying a model of reflective learning, we integrated reflective learning theory (Hedberg, 2009; Rodgers, 2002) and the use of a psychometric assessment – the *ICI* (Kozai Group, 2021) – into a course-based experience to foster the development of inclusion competencies.

Research Context

The selected site for our investigation was a business school in India focused on transforming and improving management education. The campus has over 900 students from different states of India and abroad and is diverse in terms of gender, education, work background, ethnicity, and linguistics, having over 25 student clubs and associations. Student body audits have identified a clear need and desire for greater inclusion. All students had prior work experience and had just completed a two-month full-time internship in the prior six-month period. In addition, the within-classroom environment can be considered competitive due to the use of relative grading in all courses. Students are also in competition with one another for job placement and future employment.

Sample

Our sample consisted of 52 students enrolled in a course on managing workplace diversity, with 27 male and 25 female students and reported age range between 20 and 29 years.

Inclusion Competencies

Inclusion competencies were measured using the inclusion competencies iventory (ICI), a psychometric self-report instrument developed by the Kozai Group (2021). It is composed of three broad facets and six subdimensions, as well as an overall score, which reflects a total single total composite for the assessment. The dimensions and subdimensions are described in greater detail below. The instrument consists of 45 items measuring the various targeted dimensions, along with 15 additional items to collect demographic information. There is also a social desirability check composed of five items. The Kozai Group reports that all of the various ICI scales and subscales have coefficient alpha reliabilities ranging from 0.78 to 0.91.

Knowing yourself (KY) is the first of the ICI's three facets and assesses the extent to which individuals are aware of "who you are," how open they are to change, and the likelihood they will adapt to challenging contexts or situations. It has two subdimensions: *Openness to change* (OC), which measures awareness of one's interest in continuous learning and developing, and *Adaptability* (AD), which measures the likelihood that one will be able to maintain a stable emotional self when challenged by difficult problems and interpersonal issues.

Knowing others (KO) is the second ICI facet and assesses the extent to which individuals have an interest in, and will act to develop, relationships with people who are different from them, as well as the ability to understand them. It has two subdimensions: *Connecting with others* (CO), which measures genuine interest in and desire to develop relationships with people who are different, and *Reading others* (RO), which measures the ability to decipher others' verbal and non-verbal cues accurately.

Bridging differences (BD) is the third ICI facet and assesses the extent to which individuals have an interest in multiple perspectives, an ability to see and value differing perspectives, and is sensitive to power dynamics. It has two subdimensions: *Valuing different perspectives* (VP), which measures openness to diverse perspectives and effort to appreciate and understand them, and *Power sensitivity* (PS), which measures one's awareness of power dynamics in organizational structures and individual relationships.

Personal Development Plan

In addition to pre- and post-administration of the ICI (i.e., initial baseline and post-treatment after three months), the treatment itself was primarily through the creation and implementation of a PDP, which is a development and tracking process that documents information on the competencies an individual has been working on (looking back) and is planning to develop further (looking forward; Beausaert et al., 2011). Data on student plans and performance were gathered via a set of PDP documents consisting of a one-page PDP, a weekly check-in report, and a PDP reflection report. Each of these elements is described in greater detail below.

Data Collection

Inclusion competency development was an integral element of the course. Students completed the ICI and, following debriefing and instruction sessions, were given one week to identify and then learn about the specific competency they chose to work on. They then submitted a one-page PDP that identified the competency they chose, their specific and measurable goal for working on it, and their detailed plan for accomplishing their goal.

The time period set for working on the PDP was five weeks. Beginning in the first week, students submitted a weekly check-in report that focused on three elements: (1) their efforts during the previous week to implement their plan, (2) the outcomes of their actions, and (3) their plan for the coming week, including any adjustments or revisions they felt necessary. The weekly reports served as a guided reflection on students' actions and experiences in implementing their PDP and growing their inclusion competencies.

At the end of the designated period, students completed a comprehensive reflection essay in which they addressed what they had accomplished, what effect their actions had on their development, and what they would do differently going forward. Reflection is required for effective leadership, both in-action (during the course) and on-action (after the course) (Roberts & Westville, 2008). The reflection was an occasion for them to also take stock of the entire experience and not just focusing on the development of an inclusion competency but considering its impact.

Part of the treatment also had students complete readings and participate in class sessions that included a mixture of thought-provoking discussions, brief presentations, relevant videos, simulations, and practical exercises. The course thus provided a holistic learning experience beyond textbooks and the classroom.

What We Found

Our preliminary analysis of the plans, weekly reports, and reflection papers point to significant growth in the inclusion competencies. Specifically, students exhibited greater self-knowledge, greater interest in and concern for others, improved ability to identify and value differing perspectives, and a greater sensitivity to the impact of power dynamics in settings characterized by greater diversity.

Our preliminary analysis of the statistical analysis in pre- and post-ICI scores (Menezes & Bird, 2023) found a negative change in some competencies which was unanticipated. This was explained by our review of students' PDP reflection reports that found a response shift bias (Howard & Dailey, 1979), something often seen in self-report pre- and post-tests involving assessment of one's own orientations or capability and particularly likely when considering matters with which one has little familiarity. In this case, the lack of familiarity was with concepts and behaviors surrounding inclusion. The phenomenon occurs when the participant's pre- and post-test scores are based on different understanding or interpretation of the dimensions and results in an ascending level of sophistication in comprehending the dimension. For example, many participants wrote about how they initially overestimated their inclusion competencies. Through the course and undertaking the PDP, their understanding of the dimensions grew and evolved, and their scores in the post-ICI were clarified and more self-critically honest and accurate, which provided an explanation for the unexpected negative changes. As one participant wrote in their reflection report:

> I could not believe the results at first, but after working through the Personal Development Plan, I find merit in the results and can see how it accurately portrayed my self-image and my need to develop my "connecting with others" competency. When I took the initial measurement, I could have overestimated my social skills and ability to understand others. Because of improved self-awareness through the exercise, I gained a better understanding of my capabilities and limitations. I can think more realistically about myself.

This phenomenon, known as the Dunning–Kruger effect (Dunning, 2011), offers a reasonable explanation. The central thesis of the effect is that people lacking knowledge of a subject of skill often overestimate their expertise or competence. However, this can result not only in erroneous decision-making but also lack of identification of their mistakes (Dunning, 2011). As they become more knowledgeable, particularly through experience, most people will incline toward reassessment. Thus, a positive impact can be seen in participants' recalibration of self-awareness closer to reality. A deeper understanding of the inclusion competencies would thus facilitate greater ongoing individual growth and relations with others.

What It Means

Our preliminary analysis found an improvement following the implementation of the PDP exercise, and even though some results were negative, they can be understood in a cautiously optimistic light. Specifically, there were positive changes in inclusion competencies, either by raising competency levels or in increased awareness and understanding of what inclusion means. Nevertheless, our study is just an incremental step forward in understanding how inclusion competencies might be developed.

The research has practical implications for educational institutions, specifically management programs. Business schools are professional schools in that, as with medical, dental, law, and engineering schools, they teach a body of knowledge and support the acquisition of a set of skills. This study supports the conclusion that among the capabilities business schools can help their students acquire are inclusion competencies, thereby aiding them to accept, respect, and value others in the workplace as future leaders.

There are also implications at the individual level with regard to the impact of changes deriving from the PDP experience. Though not a focus of this study, there is an obvious imperative to understand the impact of these changes as they relate to inclusive behaviors in both educational and workplace settings. This is yet another avenue for future research.

The modest nature of this study begs for further research. There are myriad directions research could go; we offer several. First, there is an obvious need for a more rigorous quasi-experimental design that would include a control group. The limited nature of our study precludes viewing the PDP experience as the primary causal force behind the changes identified. Second, a related line of inquiry should examine the process by which these changes occur. We adopted two complementary theoretical approaches – reflective learning and CBT – as a basis for the design of the PDP experience. However, the constrained nature of our research design (which was a consequence of serendipitous events) foreclosed the possibility of examining the causal process.

Future research should also utilize a retrospective pre-test to control for response-shift bias (Howard & Dailey, 1979) and dampen the possibility of a Dunning–Kruger effect. Additionally, because development is an ongoing process, a longer follow-up (e.g., 6–12 months) could help in identifying whether the changes we identified are enduring. Qualitative methods, such as in-depth interviews or cognitive task analysis, could explore which activities aid most in developing specific inclusion competencies.

Conclusion

We see an urgent need for educators and industry to work in collaboration to ensure individuals become self-aware, reflect on, and develop their inclusion competencies. This chapter provides an in-depth account of a management course intervention and its effectiveness in doing so. The results reported here show how educators may be able to help students' professional developmental journey while enhancing awareness of essential inclusion competencies. Though modest, this case study helps to lay a foundation for future inclusive leadership development.

References

Bandura, A. (2005). The evolution of social cognitive theory. In K. G. Smith & M. A. Hitt (Eds.), *Great minds in management: The process of theory development* (pp. 9–35). Oxford University Press.

Beausaert, S., Segers, M., & Gijselaers, W. (2011). The *Personal Development Plan Practice Questionnaire*: The development and validation of an instrument to assess the employee's perception of personal development plan practice. *International Journal of Training and Development, 15*(4), 249–270.

Bernstein, R. S., Bulger, M., Salipante, P., & Weisinger, J. Y. (2020). From diversity to inclusion to equity: A theory of generative interactions. *Journal of Business Ethics, 167*(3), 395–410.

Boyatzis, R. E. (1982). *The competent manager: A model for effective performance.* John Wiley & Sons.

Butler, A. C., Chapman, J. E., Forman, E. M., & Beck, A. T. (2006). The empirical status of cognitive-behavioral therapy: A review of meta-analyses. *Clinical Psychology Review, 26*(1), 17–31.

Campion, M. A., Fink, A. A., Ruggeberg, B. J., Carr, L., Phillips, G. M., & Odman, R. B. (2011). Doing competencies well: Best practices in competency modelling. *Personnel Psychology, 64*(1), 225–262.

Cox, T. (1993). *Cultural diversity in organizations: Theory, research and practice.* Berrett-Koehler Publishers.

Davidson, M. N., & Ferdman, B. M. (2002). Inclusion: What can I and my organization do about it. *The Industrial-Organizational Psychologist, 39*(4), 80–85.

Ducharme, M. J. (2004). The cognitive-behavioral approach to executive coaching. *Consulting Psychology Journal: Practice and Research, 56*(4), 214.

Dunning, D. (2011). The Dunning–Kruger effect: On being ignorant of one's own ignorance. In J. M. Olson & M. P. Zanna (Eds.), *Advances in experimental social psychology* (Vol. 44, pp. 247–296). Academic Press.

Feng, J. B. (2016). Improving intercultural competence in the classroom: A reflective development model. *Journal of Teaching in International Business, 27*(1), 4–22.

Hawkins, N., & Staats, B. (2020, July 31). *Toward a more inclusive business school.* Harvard Business Publishing Education. https://hbsp.harvard.edu/inspiring-minds/what-administrators-and-educators-can-do-now-to-drive-progress-on-diversity

Hedberg, P. R. (2009). Learning through reflective classroom practice: Applications to educate the reflective manager. *Journal of Management Education, 33*(1), 10–36.

Howard, G. S., & Dailey, P. R. (1979). Response-shift bias: A source of contamination of self-report measures. *Journal of Applied Psychology, 64*(2), 144.

Kolb, A. Y., & Kolb, D. A. (2005). Learning styles and learning spaces: Enhancing experiential learning in higher education. *Academy of Management Learning & Education, 4*(2), 193–212.

Korkmaz, A. V., van Engen, M. L., Knappert, L., & Schalk, R. (2022). About and beyond leading uniqueness and belongingness: A systematic review of inclusive leadership research. *Human Resource Management Review, 32*(4), 100894.

Kozai Group. (2021). *The Inclusion Competencies Inventory.* https://www.kozaigroup.com/inclusion-competencies

Macrodimitris, S. D., Hamilton, K. E., Backs-Dermott, B. J., & Mothersill, K. J. (2010). CBT basics: A group approach to teaching fundamental cognitive-behavioral skills. *Journal of Cognitive Psychotherapy, 24*(2), 132–146.

McClelland, D. C. (1973). Testing for competence rather than for "intelligence." *American Psychologist, 28*(1), 1–14.

Meichenbaum, D. (1986). Cognitive-behavior modification. In F. H. Kanfer & A. P. Goldstein (Eds.), *Helping people change* (3rd ed., pp. 346–380). Pergamon.

Mendenhall, M. E., Arnardottir, A. A., Oddou, G. R., & Burke, L. A. (2013). Developing cross-cultural competencies in management education via cognitive-behavior therapy. *Academy of Management Learning & Education, 12*(3), 436–451.

Mendenhall, M. E., Burke-Smalley, L. A., Arnardottir, A. A., Oddou, G. R., & Osland, J. S. (2020). Making a difference in the classroom: Developing global leadership competencies in business school students. In *Research handbook of global leadership.* Edward Elgar Publishing.

Menezes, S., & Bird, A. (2023, January 6–8). *Developing inclusion competencies: Competency development in an Indian business school* [Conference presentation]. Indian Academy of Management Conference, Mumbai, India.

Mishra, S. K., Mahapatra, G. P., & Dagar, C. (2022). Innovative practices in management education in India. In Pandey, A. Budhwar, P. & Bhawuk, D. P. (Eds.), *Indigenous Indian management: Conceptualization, practical applications and pedagogical initiatives* (pp. 493–522). Cham: Springer International Publishing.

Morris, M. W., Savani, K., & Roberts, R. D. (2014). Intercultural training and assessment: Implications for organizational and public policies. *Policy Insights from the Behavioral and Brain Sciences, 1*(1), 63–71.

Nishii, L. H., & Leroy, H. (2022). A multi-level framework of inclusive leadership in organizations. *Group & Organization Management, 47*(4), 683–722.

Oddou, G. R., & Mendenhall, M. E. (2018). Global leadership development: Processes and practices. In M. E. Mendenhall, J. S. Osland, A. Bird, G. R. Oddou, M. L. Maznevski, M. J. Stevens, & G. K. Stahl (Eds.), *Global leadership: Research, practice, and development* (3rd ed., pp. 229–270). Routledge.

Qu, J., Liu, M., & Cao, X. (2021). Team cognitive diversity and creativity: The role of team intellectual capital and inclusive climate. In *Academy of Management Proceedings* (Vol. 2021, No. 1, p. 15321). Academy of Management.

Roberson, Q. M. (2006). Disentangling the meanings of diversity and inclusion in organizations. *Group & Organization Management, 31*(2), 212–236.

Roberts, C., & Westville, I. N. (2008). Developing future leaders: The role of reflection in the classroom. *Journal of Leadership Education, 7*(1), 116–130.

Rodgers, C. R. (2002). Seeing student learning: Teacher change and the role of reflection. *Harvard Educational Review, 72*(2), 230.

Schon, D. A. (1987). *Educating the reflective practitioner: Toward a new design for teaching and learning in the professions.* Jossey-Bass.

Schubert, T., & Tavassoli, S. (2020). Product innovation and educational diversity in top and middle management teams. *Academy of Management Journal, 63*(1), 272–294.

Shore, L. M., Cleveland, J. N., & Sanchez, D. (2018). Inclusive workplaces: A review and model. *Human Resource Management Review, 28*(2), 176–189.

Shore, L. M., Randel, A. E., Chung, B. G., Dean, M. A., Holcombe Ehrhart, K., & Singh, G. (2011). Inclusion and diversity in work groups: A review and model for future research. *Journal of Management, 37*(4), 1262–1289.

Chapter 6

Advancing Gender Equality in Higher Education in South Africa: Emboldening Women Leaders in Complex Contexts

Birgit Schreiber[a] and Denise Zinn[b]

[a]HELM, South Africa
[b]USAf HELM, South Africa

Abstract

Change in higher education across the globe is taking place at an unprecedented pace. Various groups, especially women, are impacted differently by these changes. Women remain underrepresented in leadership at universities across the globe, and South African higher education is no different. For women to take up senior leadership roles more potently in universities, particularly in the Global South, it is essential that they not only cope with and compete in the patriarchal systems that characterize this sector but are also emboldened to contribute to changing patriarchal hegemony. There are shifts needed in prevailing management styles and leadership discourses toward a pluralistic and inclusive culture, where transformational and equitable leadership cultures become the norm and praxis. Given this context, we assessed the needs of women leaders in the South African higher education sector and designed a program to help shift their experience of themselves and their contexts. This chapter discusses this national executive development program – the Women in Leadership (WiL) program – which was developed and implemented with the aim to advance gender equality and inclusivity in higher education leadership in South Africa. This program aimed to embolden the women leaders in their ability to recognize, address, and impact barriers to gender equality.

Keywords: Women in Leadership; Global South; South Africa; patriarchal hegemony; gender; executive development

Inclusive Leadership: Equity and Belonging in Our Communities
Building Leadership Bridges, Volume 9, 65–73
Copyright © 2023 by Emerald Publishing Limited
All rights of reproduction in any form reserved
ISSN: 2058-8801/doi:10.1108/S2058-880120230000009006

Change in higher education across the globe is taking place at an unprecedented pace. Various groups, especially women,[1] are impacted differently by these changes as these impact higher education leadership, particularly at senior leadership levels (Gmelch & Buller, 2015; Seale & Cross, 2017). Women remain underrepresented in leadership at universities across the globe, and South African higher education is no different.

For women to take up senior leadership roles more potently in universities, particularly in the Global South, it is essential that they not only cope with and compete in the patriarchal systems that characterize this sector but more so are emboldened to contribute to changing patriarchal hegemony. There are shifts needed in prevailing management styles and leadership discourses toward a pluralistic and inclusive culture, where transformational and equitable leadership cultures become the norm and praxis.

Given this context, we assessed the needs of women leaders in the South African higher education sector and designed a program to help shift their experience of themselves and their contexts. This chapter discusses this national executive development program – the WiL program – which was developed and implemented with the aim to advance gender equality and inclusivity in higher education leadership in South Africa. This program aimed to embolden the women leaders in their ability to recognize, address, and impact barriers to gender equality. An evaluation of the program and its impact on the participants was undertaken, and in this chapter, we provide an overview of the program's components and the findings on its impact on the first cohort of participants.

Women in Higher Education Leadership

Women in higher education leadership often experience the practices around power and its implicit and explicit distribution, and overt or veiled sexism, that maintain prevalent patriarchal hegemony in "micro arrangements within a university space" (Fish, 2019, p. 31). Women, often part of the minority in leadership spaces, experience themselves "misaligned with hegemonic culture and need to face these alienating and exclusionary institutional cultures and practices" (HET, 2019, p. 31). These experiences within patriarchal leadership cultures contribute toward the asymmetries of gender balances in leadership, reflecting "the higher the fewer" (Diezmann & Grieshaber, 2019, n.p.) which applies across the higher education sector.

Women leaders in universities remain underrepresented in the global higher education sector despite several key initiatives that seek to advance gender equality in leadership in higher education via bespoke programs (Jarboe, 2016; Johnson, 2017; www.advance-he.ac.uk; www.acu.ac.uk/get-involved/gender/). South Africa also has several initiatives that seek to address the gender asymmetries in leadership in higher education (for instance, Higher Education Resource Services-South Africa (HERS-SA) and others, see Seale et al., 2021). Under the

---

[1]The terms "men" and "women" do not imply a denial of gender spectrum but are used in this binary form for this chapter.

auspices of Universities South Africa (USAf), a national umbrella body comprising all 26 public universities in South Africa, one such initiative called the WiL program has been undertaken by a strategic unit called Higher Education Leadership and Management (HELM). As its name implies, HELM is mandated to build and support leadership capacity in the sector, including for women in higher education.

Preparation for the WiL Program

The WiL program is based on a training needs analysis (TNA) which explored the needs of women leaders in higher education in South Africa. The TNA focused on women's experience in higher education leadership at 26 public universities in South Africa. A web-based survey recorded demographic data and explored the (1) skills considered already in place and (2) further training and development needs. The questions were closed- and open-ended and asked the participants to either list certain items, themes, or key terms and then to rank these. Open-ended responses were thematically analyzed.

This TNA generated "many interesting but not surprising aspects" (Seale et al., 2021, p. 8) and confirmed that women leaders in South African higher education experience a gendered leadership context. Furthermore, it revealed that women leaders want to understand their challenges and address the systemic barriers that maintain these challenges. Women leaders expressed that they seek to be part of programs that equip them to boldly impact their context to advance their leadership and to promote a more gender-fair higher education leadership culture. These findings are aligned with Mouton and Wildschut's (2015) study that found that middle and senior leadership in South Africa has an "acute" need for training and development programs, including gender awareness programs (p. 8).

Pedagogy and Approach to the WiL Program

Research on initiatives that aim to advance women leaders and gender equality often focuses on extended programs, many with a "collective learning approach" (Garavan & McCarthy, 2008; McCarthy & Garavan, 2008; Yemiscigil et al., 2023). The collective learning approach includes a relational aspect (Garavan & McCarthy, 2008; McCarthy & Garavan, 2008; Yemiscigil et al., 2023) and includes reflection, learning, and development that occur in the context of dyads, groups, and communities. This kind of learning involves learning in a peer context, learning from each other by engaging in discussion, sharing, reflecting, and challenging each other's experiences, in a way that normalizes, explores, and challenges experiences and interpretations of these (Jones et al., 2006; Yemiscigil et al., 2023). The WiL program described in this chapter utilizes a collective learning approach and has a strong emphasis on the relational aspect. In addition, we have employed a humanizing pedagogy, which seeks to restore dignity, worth, and confidence, to reverse the dehumanization, with all its negative consequences, to those who have had to live and work in inequitable and often overtly oppressive contexts. In this regard, the pedagogical approach and philosophy of radical Brazilian educator Paulo Freire have provided inspiration and guidance (Freire, 1970; Freire & Freire, 1994, 1997).

Besides the focus on humanizing pedagogies incorporated into the conceptualization of the program's architecture, content, and methodologies, there is also a recognition that institutional cultures require a re-examination if we are to advance a more gender-balanced leadership in our higher education sector.

The WiL Program

In response to the TNA (Seale et al., 2021) described above, the research undertaken on programs with similar goals, and drawing on the professional "lived" experience of the program team (who had themselves held leadership positions as women in higher education in South Africa), a senior-level leadership program was developed and implemented by USAf HELM in 2020, and since then annually. The WiL program as conceptualized by USAf HELM focuses on engaging professional women in middle and senior management and leadership in public universities in South Africa to advance their leadership and embolden their impact on the higher education context. The context is characterized by patriarchal management cultures; paradoxical demands; strident student, staff, and public voices; conflicting global and local imperatives; demands for sustainability and social justice; and fiscal challenges and shifts from massification to universification of higher education in a competitive local–global climate.

The WiL program has two specific aims: first, to embolden women leaders to take up more senior leadership positions and advance their leadership trajectory; and second, to embolden women leaders to recognize and challenge practices and structures in their institutional context that create barriers toward a more equitable and transformational leadership culture in which everyone, and especially women leaders, can thrive. The program focuses on women leaders to recognize power asymmetries, navigate patriarchal institutional cultures, and advance gender equity. The program is informed by principles of humanizing pedagogy (Freire, 1970; Keet et al., 2009; Salazar, 2013; Zinn & Rodgers, 2012) which foreground social justice, transformation, critical theory, and personal agency. The pedagogy centers the experience of the subject (in this case women in the contexts of work, home, and society), is interactive (drawing on their own knowledge and lived experiences) utilizing creative tools and activities, is cognizant and critical of the contexts and conditions in which the participants are embedded, and engages peer and collaborative learning from and with each other.

The focus of humanizing pedagogy foregrounds the acknowledgment and development of the self within context; values the self as a critical agent in the learning and development process; and emphasizes the relationships of learners with each other, with their communities, and with their context, situating them and contextualizing them and the facilitators or teachers (Keet et al., 2009). An underpinning approach is to provide participants with an *experience* of leadership, rather than only foregrounding skills or competencies development. The program focuses on the development of the self in context, self in relation to the collective and others, and the self in relation to one's own leadership path. The emerging transformation is at a personal level and emphasizes human agency that allows space for thinking and exploration on how change can be affected.

The WiL program is premised on the idea that the development of leadership capacity and confidence emboldens women to advocate for themselves and others like them, while they navigate and excel in leading diverse teams to shape change within the complex higher education context. WiL's goal is to contribute to a more equitable, diverse, and representative higher education environment, in which multiple perspectives and ways of thinking, doing, and being create an enabling environment in which all who work and live in it can thrive. The program includes acquisition and development of relevant knowledge about self and leadership in higher education institutions, a platform to engage with peers and experienced leaders, opportunities to form professional networks, and opportunities to develop skills. There is a focus on enabling women to envision and create environments in which creativity and diversity are encouraged and thrive.

The curriculum has several components. The core of the program includes 10 scheduled "sessions" focusing on relevant leadership topics and important skillsets required of leaders in South African universities. Most of these sessions are offered online in three-hour sessions every fortnight. At least two "in-person"/hybrid multi-day retreats are included in the program. These sessions were co-presented by two HELM facilitators and include a distinguished leader, most of whom are senior women leaders within the university sector, present their insights on the topic of that session. In addition, peer learning groups are set up, and these are met between sessions. We set up four individual coaching sessions for each participant with an experienced qualified coach, familiar with higher education contexts. The coaching sessions aimed to provide participants with an opportunity to experience individual support regarding their growth and personal development journey. All the coaches utilized an integral coaching approach.

Reflective assignments followed most sessions, and some involved practical tasks and engagements to encourage participants to think about how session content could be applied or implemented in their own institutional contexts. Participants were encouraged to keep a journal to record their private thoughts and reflections during the program. Asynchronous engagement with the material of the program, readings, and the production of a portfolio of learning including a reflective essay and learning portfolio were required to complete the program.

The topics of the sessions included an introductory orientation session, followed by the following topics: the self in context, paradigms, and purposes, leading in times of crisis and challenge, leading the higher education missions, leading and working with people, working with finances, career planning and advancement, and building networks (including global, regional, and national). Finally, in the wrap-up session, the focus was on reflection and review of their learning and preparation of the portfolio of learning.

Program Evaluation

The 2020 program was evaluated by a professional monitoring and evaluation company (Franklin, 2020) to investigate its impact on the participants and their ability to have an impact on their context. The evaluation aimed to explore the WiL program's relevance, implementation, and impact on the participants.

Methodology of the Evaluation

The data collection employed a mixed-methods approach that included interviews with program staff and facilitators and a series of engagements with participants in a variety of ways. In efforts to maximize the engagements with and feedback from participation, they were invited to engage in some or all the following, depending on their preference and availability: an electronic questionnaire, individual interviews, and/or focus group discussions. Participants' feedback was anonymized to preserve confidentiality. All 37 staff, facilitators, administrators, and participants of this 2020 program were contacted to provide feedback via any one or more of the channels offered to them.

Findings

Relevance

WiL's relevance in response to the challenges that women leaders are facing within the higher education context was confirmed by all interviewed participants. The motivation cited by many participants for their interest in the participant in WiL aligned well with the program's understanding of the challenges that women needed to face. Many participants were grappling with gender- and race-related issues within their workspaces and felt they needed support in understanding these and dealing skillfully with them.

Conceptualization

The humanizing pedagogy informing the way in which WiL was conceptualized and presented, the foregrounding of the relational approach, together with the practice of self-reflection, was woven into all aspects of the program. Participants reflected on how these opportunities for relating deepened their experience and that they felt safe to share of themselves in the process.

Coaching and Peer Group Learning

The coaching component was highlighted as an important part of the program, particularly in terms of being a mechanism for self-reflection. Similarly, the peer learning groups were also reported to be of high impact in terms of being a space that enabled participants to share, to test and normalize their experience, and to explore new ways of being and doing. The long-term benefits of access to a network of female leaders were recognized and highly valued by the participants.

Personal and Professional Changes

The evaluation revealed that WiL catalyzed significant personal and professional change and transformation for participants.

Each of the interviewed participants reported that the program added value to their personal and professional development. Specific themes that emerged relate to strengthening their leadership capacity and skills through understanding of themselves as agent and role-player in the context; enhancing self-reflection and self-awareness; establishing solidarity through networks and relationships; enhanced understanding of the Higher Education (HE) context and its impact on women; recognizing the value of self-care; and reflecting on their career trajectories.

Participants shared examples of how specific sessions contributed toward increased levels of leadership awareness, knowledge, and skills and a deeper understanding of their agency, their impact, and their responsibility in shaping their experience. Participants reported that WiL provided a space to explore the competencies and characteristics required when taking up leadership positions.

Almost all participants spoke of gaining significant insight through the opportunities for self-reflection in WiL, and examples were cited of how self-reflection has led to an enhanced sense of self. The emphasis on reflective thinking and the sharing of experiences was highly valued by the participants, who explained that this had provided a space to think about themselves in new and different ways. The significance of self-awareness became clear as participants shared how leadership styles were employed and were related to their personal sense of self. Participants spoke of how the various components of the program contributed to enhancing their self-reflection and self-awareness and many noted their appreciation of, and often surprise at, the impact of reflection during the journaling exercises.

The establishment of a network through WiL was appreciated as a significant outcome for participants. Many formed close relationships with other women via the peer learning groups or the broader group and valued the personal component of these relationships and the support they received. Participants shared how feeling part of a collective that shares similar experiences normalized their experiences and reduced a sense of loneliness and "being the only one" in certain perceptions.

There was an overarching theme that participants largely prioritized work at the expense of self-care. Participants indicated that the program raised awareness about this aspect and underscored the necessity of taking time for oneself to be better equipped to deal with daily challenges.

WiL provided an opportunity for participants to explore their potential and desire to advance further in leadership positions within their institutions. WiL inspired some to strive toward expanded career goals, and speak about their ambitions. Several participants highlighted that due to WiL, they have realized the importance of being clear and intentional about their professional goals and taking practical steps toward achieving these professional goals. This intentionality comes from making conscious career decisions, actively seeking out opportunities that will bring them closer to achieving career goals, being more assertive and actively competing for leadership positions, and finding admirable leaders to emulate.

Relating To and Impacting the Context

Participants also reported on shifts in the way in which they viewed themselves within their contexts and the macro-institutional environment. Specific themes that emerged relate to how participants "see the same things differently" and have a deeper understanding of the context as enabling or inhibiting their participation and their agency.

Many spoke of a fundamental shift in the way they perceived themselves within their workspaces and a change in how they applied themselves to the challenges therein. There were instances where participants described seeing themselves now as potential "change agents" who could pave the way for others. WiL shifted the way in which participants viewed their power, or lack thereof, with many noting that they felt more empowered within their contexts since participating in the program.

Some participants have strengthened and improved their relationships with their staff and team members because of increased leadership confidences, capacity, and management skills. Leadership outcomes were not only related to how to lead for the completion of tasks but also how to develop junior staff members while being cognizant of the nuances of relationship building.

Many participants reported how these changes had started a ripple effect in their immediate and broader contexts, either as plans they are intending on actioning in the near future or as activities that they have already undertaken. Participants spoke of being inspired by WiL to become champions for other women leaders or future leaders within their spheres of influence. They felt a sense of responsibility for the development of other women to join the ranks in affecting change and impacting patriarchy and recognized the need for solidarity with other women leaders to influence positive systemic change within higher education.

Conclusion

The evaluation done on the 2020 cohort of women participants in the WiL program in South African higher education revealed that the program achieved its objectives to embolden women leaders and build capacity around understanding the complexity of their contexts, as well as their agency to impact their context. The WiL built a sense of community around the similarities of experience, normalizing the women leaders' sense of being and leading in their contexts. The relational aspect, the peer groups, the reflections, and networks that emerged were highly valued and enabled "developing a voice" for the participants. There appears to be a pronounced need to access a community of women in higher education and to find support from and solidarity with other women leaders.

Gender advancement in South African higher education is not only about emboldening women. It is also about reducing their sense of "otherness," of being "on their own," being different to their male counterparts in a patriarchal leadership context. Women leaders need to harness their own strength and exercise their agency in contributing toward a fairer and more equitable higher education management and leadership culture.

References

Diezmann, C., & Grieshaber, S. (2019). The higher the fewer. In *Women professors*. Springer. https://doi.org/10.1007/978-981-13-3685-0_2

Fish, P. (2019). *Hunting down the elephant in the room: Transformation and institutional culture*. Retrieved January 10, 2020, from https://www.newssite.co.za/usaf/culture.html

Franklin, M. (2020). *MESURE SA evaluation report* [Internal report]. USAf HELM.

Freire, P. (1970). *Pedagogy of the oppressed*. Continuum.

Freire, P., & Freire, A. M. A. (1994). *Pedagogy of hope: Reliving pedagogy of the oppressed*. Continuum.

Freire, P., & Freire, A. M. A. (1997). *Pedagogy of the heart.* Continuum.

Garavan, T., & McCarthy, A. (2008). Collective learning processes and human resource development. *Advances in Developing Human Resources, 10*(4), 451–471.

Gmelch, W., & Buller, J. (2015). *Academic leadership capacity – A guide to good practice*. Jossey Bass.

Higher Education and Training (HET). (2019). *Republic of South Africa. Department of Higher Education and Training: Report of the Ministerial Task Team on the recruitment, retention and progression of Black South African academics*. Compress Publishers. https://www.dhet.gov.za/SiteAssets/Report_MTT_RRP%20of%20Black%20Academics_web%20final.pdf.

Higher Education Leadership and Management (HELM). (2020). *HELM conceptual framework – Women in leadership programme*. Universities South Africa.

Jarboe, N. (2016). *Australian universities 2016: Women count*. Retrieved February 21, 2023, from www.women-count.org

Johnson, H. (2017). *Pipelines, pathways, and institutional leadership: An update on the status of women in higher education*. American Council on Education (ACE).

Jones, C., Connolly, M., Gear, A., & Read, M. (2006). Collaborative learning with group interactive technology: A case study with postgraduate students. *Management Learning, 37*, 377–396. https://doi.org/10.1177/1350507606067173

Keet, A., Zinn, D., & Porteus, K. (2009). Mutual vulnerability: A key principle in humanising pedagogy. *Perspectives in Education, 27*(2), 109–119.

McCarthy, A., & Garavan, T. N. (2008). Team learning and metacognition: A neglected area of HRD research and practice. *Advances in Developing Human Resources, 10*(4), 509–524.

Mouton, J., & Wildschut, L. (Eds.). (2015). *Leadership and management: Case studies in training in higher education in Africa*. African Minds.

Salazar, M. (2013). A humanising pedagogy: Reinventing the principles and practice of education as a journey towards liberation. *Review of Research in Education, 37*(1), 121–148.

Seale, O., & Cross, M. (2017). Executivism and deanship in selected South African universities. *Oxford Review of Education, 44*(3), 275–290.

Seale, O., Fish, P., & Schreiber, B. (2021). Enabling and empowering women in leadership in South African universities – Assessing needs and designing a response. *Management in Education, 35*(3), 136–145. https://journals.sagepub.com/doi/10.1177/0892020620981951

Yemiscigil, A., Born, D., Ling, H. (2023). What makes leadership development programs succeed? *Harvard Business Review*, February 28. https://hbr.org/2023/02/what-makes-leadership-development-programs-succeed

Zinn, D., & Rodgers, C. (2012). A humanising pedagogy: Getting beneath the rhetoric. *Perspective in Education, 30*(4), 76–87.

Chapter 7

Building Diverse and Inclusive Faculty Teams: Practices in Inclusive Leadership in Higher Education

Jacqueline N. Gustafson and Charles Lee-Johnson

California Baptist University, USA

Abstract

Diversification of faculty within higher education has been a topic of focus within the academy for decades. Further, there has been a call to create academic departments composed of faculty teams which are more representative of gender, racial, and ethnic diversity, often with the ideal of representing student and community demographics. Though challenges remain in recruiting, hiring, and retaining diverse faculty, higher education institutions (HEIs) rarely represent the racial and ethnic diversity of the communities that they serve, and benchmarks or definitions of success have been vague at best. However, evidence does support the notion that both student and community outcomes are strengthened by the skills, talents, perspectives, and contributions offered by diverse faculty and leadership teams. First, a review of the current obstacles and challenges of creating diverse and inclusive faculty teams is covered. Second, the *Five I's of Inclusive Leadership Practices in Higher Education*, lessons and successes from building diverse and representative faculty teams are shared. This model includes Intentionality, Invitation, Influence, Investment, and Innovation. Finally, recommendations for future practice, as well as application across institutional type, setting, and location, are included. Building diverse and inclusive faculty teams is important, urgent, and rewarding work. Diversification gives birth to lively classroom conversations, thriving campus environments, enhanced growth in the personal and professional lives of

Inclusive Leadership: Equity and Belonging in Our Communities
Building Leadership Bridges, Volume 9, 75–85
ISSN: 2058-8801/doi:10.1108/S2058-880120230000009007

students and faculty, establishment of equitable and affirming cross-racial and gender relationships, population and financial growth of the HEI, and more equitable service to communities.

Keywords: Faculty diversification; inclusion; diversity; higher education; equity; inclusive leadership

Diversification of faculty within higher education has been a topic of focus and inquiry within the academy for decades. Further, there has been a call to create academic departments composed of faculty teams which are more representative of gender, racial, and ethnic diversity, often with the idea of representing student and community demographics. At times, these efforts have been focused on the diversification of faculty across the institutions, and in other cases, the focus has been more specific, such as strategies that have sought to increase the number of women in science, technology, engineering, and math (STEM) fields. Though challenges remain in recruiting, hiring, and retaining diverse faculty, higher education institutions (HEIs) rarely represent the racial and ethnic diversity of the communities that they serve, and benchmarks or definitions of success have been vague at best. However, evidence does support the notion that both student and community outcomes are strengthened by the skills, talents, perspectives, and contributions offered by diverse faculty and leadership teams. Additionally, challenges related to social justice, equity, and access cannot and should not be adequality addressed in environments where those who have historically been, and currently are, the most vulnerable or marginalized are not represented and included as decision-makers. This is of particular importance in HEIs given the role of the academy in contributing to discourse, generating research data and outcomes, and preparing future professionals and leaders across disciplines and fields of practice.

First, a review of the current obstacles and challenges of creating diverse and inclusive faculty teams will be covered. Challenges persist in both policy and practice and are further complicated by factors related to specific fields of study (i.e., an underrepresentation of women or racial and ethnic minority groups in certain academic disciplines), geographic location and setting (e.g., urban vs rural), institutional type (e.g., public, private, non-profit, and for-profit), and other institutional factors to include mission or faith and religious orientation. Second, lessons and successes from building diverse and representative faculty teams will be shared. Some practices that were correlated with successful outcomes included building diverse and inclusive spaces and environments (e.g., cultural celebrations), prioritizing the diversification of leadership roles within the organization, providing opportunity for affinity group organization (both formally and informally), and evaluation of curriculum and programming through diverse and representative lenses. Finally, recommendations for future practice, as well as application across institutional type, setting, and location will be included.

Part I: Current Obstacles and Challenges

> An excellent and diverse faculty is vital to individual colleges and universities and to our communities, states, nation and globe. A diverse faculty brings diverse perspectives, and these diverse perspectives enhance teaching and advising, research and scholarship, clinical practice, and engagement with the community and world. (Perna, 2023)

A review of the scholarly and policy/practice literature the historical and current obstacles and challenges for faculty diversification, inclusion, and retention in higher education. The National Center for Education Statistics (2022), in their survey of 1.5 million faculty at postsecondary institutions found that nearly three-quarters were White, only 4% were Black females, and only 3% were Black males. Additionally, these numbers vary by academic rank, with the highest-ranking positions having the fewest number of women and racial and ethnic groups as compared to other categories (McChesney & Bichsel, 2020; National Center for Education Statistics, 2022). While these challenges have persisted for decades (Moreno et al., 2006), more recently, students, faculty, professional organizations, and other stakeholders have called for change to include increased efforts at systemic and structural levels (Griffin, 2020). One of the major challenges is the real or perceived underrepresentation of Black, Indigenous, and People of Color (BIPOC) and women receiving graduate degrees and training, the requisite experience to enter into faculty appointments within the academy. This obstacle has been conceptualized as a "pipeline" issue and therefore many strategies to address faculty diversification have focused primarily on increasing the diversity in graduate programs (Griffin, 2020, p. 279). While there is merit to this approach, alone it is anemic, failing to address deeper challenges of equity at structural levels. In addition, "great differences [still] exist by race, ethnicity, and gender in where students go to college and what they study, signaling an uneven playing field in the labor market and a threat to the opportunity for intergenerational upward mobility" (Espinosa et al., 2019, p. 17). Additionally, there is evidence that changes to the "pipeline" have not necessarily impacted changes in employment, and disparities persist within specific fields of study, geographic locations and settings, institutional types, and other factors (e.g., religious affiliation). As one example, Casad et al. (2020) signaled to gender stereotypes, social capital, and climate (e.g., unwelcoming environments) as factors impacting the representation of women in STEM fields. Evans and Chun (2007) focusing on both women and BIPOC faculty, specifically in the context of public, doctoral-granting research universities, identified asymmetric institutional power and "isms" as underlying structures and barriers to advancement. Additionally, White-Lewis (2020) highlighted discourse that described institutional "fit" "as code to exclude marginalized candidates in hiring procedures" (p. 851). Even if the "playing field" could be evened, Griffin (2020) argued that

> institutions must acknowledge how administrators, faculty, policies, and structures create and maintain (un)welcoming campus environments. Institutional leaders must understand and address how sexism and racism are embedded in academic structures,

systems, departments, colleges, and programs in a comprehensive way to truly understand why they have failed to or have made minimal progress towards increasing the number of women and men of color on their faculties. (pp. 279–280)

Continued investment and effort in understanding challenges and obstacles to faculty diversification are necessary and important to the work of advancement for women and BIPOC and the building of more equitable and sustainable institutions. Additionally, faculty, student, and community outcomes are positively impacted by gains in faculty diversification, inclusion, and other practices that promote equity and belonging. Over the last decade, significant gains have been made in the diversification of the student body, with aspirational goals of reflecting both local and national community demographics; though faculty diversification has not kept pace (Perna, 2023). Abdul-Raheem (2016) underscored the importance of faculty diversity for students, "Faculty members who are tenured have the ability to advocate for cultural equality in their institutions and serve as mentors for students" (p. 53), and asserted that increased faculty diversity was related to student success in areas such as mentorship, research, and equity advocacy. An introduction to this topic would not be complete without also mentioning the role of HEIs in generating data and knowledge and shaping discourse (macro-level impact), in addition to the individual (micro) and group (mezzo) outcomes. There is much at stake for the individual faculty member, students, and for the well-being of society as a whole. Evans and Chun (2007) underscored this final element, the well-being of society, by recounting the words of W. E. B. DuBois, in *The Souls of Black Folk*: "The function of the university is not simply to teach breadwinning … it is, above all, to be the organ of that fine adjustment between real life and the growing knowledge of life." Evans and Chun (2007) went on to then highlight the "barriers that obstruct [women and BIPOC] their empowerment, participation, and retention" (p. 1) in this process.

Faculty retention, advancement (Perna, 2023; Townsend, 2020), and satisfaction (O'Meara et al., 2019) are also important factors in faculty diversification efforts. These opportunities, experiences, and successes should not be overshadowed by efforts that focus solely on diversification by numbers. Settles et al. (2019), drawing upon data from 118 interviews, identified themes related to the experiences Black, Hispanic/Latinx, Asian, and American Indian faculty members had at a predominantly White, research-intensive university. Faculty in this study reported tokenism, exclusion, visibility and invisibility, working-harder, and disengagement as significant factors impacting their experiences. Similarly, Fortner and Inman (2023) identified five emerging themes gathered from their sample of faculty who were recently employed or seeking a role in an HEI: invisibility, authoritarian, unconscious (implicit) bias, marginalization, and silencing. Frazer and Hunt (2011), stated that "There is a shared anxiety that underlies the literature on change in higher education in the United States, one that goes beyond specific conceptual or empirical permutations; the concern is that despite extensive research – and many calls for reform – there is no consensus as to the capacity of institutions to effect meaningful organizational change" (p. 185). Now, over a decade later, some of this sentiment remains the same, though, while challenges persist, some gains have been made.

Part II: The Five I's of Inclusive Leadership Practices

This model, the *Five I's of Inclusive Leadership Practices in Higher Education*, includes Intentionality, Invitation, Influence, Investment, and Innovation and is designed to provide a framework for HEIs in faculty diversification and inclusion work.

Intentionality (and the Challenge of "Institutional Fit")

Racial and gender oppression are not always obvious, apperceptive, or readily identifiable, as they are often systemic and structural. HEIs are guided by written and unwritten policies and practices that are deeply embedded in the ethos of the organization and consciously or unconsciously create atmospheres that can be oppressive to BIPOC and women. Intentionality in diversification for HEIs challenges power brokers within an institution to be aware of implicit bias, structural and systemic inequity, and toxic cultural practices. In addition, intentionality in hiring engages organizations in a preplanning process of thinking beyond the prospective position and to the possibilities of growth of the organization and its constituents. It considers not only the position and job duties that need to be fulfilled but also the welfare of society and the advancement of opportunities for historically marginalized populations. This macro-orientation is important because it proactively seeks to dismantle the strongholds of historical oppression, bias, and exclusion by intentionally identifying racial and gender inequities within the organization, and it seeks to keep these issues at the forefront.

The term "institutional fit" is often used in the hiring process to convey the desire to hire someone that will not be disruptive to the organizational composition and culture. One HEI that stated it wanted diversity in its executive leadership interviewed several racially different candidates, but the search committee only advanced White candidates. While the committee noted that the other candidates met the qualifications and had excellent interviews, the committee felt they were not a good "institutional fit." After further conversation, the committee discovered that they were looking for a candidate that resembled the people they already had, and they were hiding behind "institutional fit" to avoid the institutions' need to expand and welcome difference.

Diversification often will lead to a disruption in the normal processes and practices of an organization, as it challenges the institution to incorporate the "differentness" in thought, culture, and presence of its new diverse partners. Diversification, however, is a positive disruption as its benefits far outweigh the challenges and can open the organization to greater markets, service provision, and productivity. The following questions can be considered as a starting place to begin this first step:

(1) Does our hiring/search team include BIPOC and women?
(2) Is our idea of diversity tokenism, or are we truly open to the changes diversity brings?
(3) Is our construct of "fit" functional or is it exclusionary and counterproductive to our goals?

Invitation

Hiring candidates involves inviting people outside the current work sphere to enter their respective worlds. Often, the first round of invitation is to people known in the network, generally who look and think like insiders. The challenge in the invitation phase of this model is to re-examine the invitation process and to consider BIPOC and gender. Systemic and structural racism and gender exclusive practices have long disbarred these populations from being invited into positions of influence and power. Frequently, hiring committees will state "diverse candidates didn't apply." This response is reflective of a lack of awareness of how oppression works and the need to proactively, persistently, and purposefully seek diverse candidates. The process of invitation is twofold: (1) job postings should reflect language that promotes diversity and inclusion and (2) target areas in which prospective candidates from underrepresented groups gather. For example, an inclusive posting might read: *Tenure track faculty – seeking a doctoral-level engineer, with two years post-education experience, to work in a diverse workforce that promotes equity and inclusion.* Using the terms "diverse workforce" or "equity and inclusion" in a job posting can serve as key identifiers for diverse applicants that the invitation is for them. This language identifies that the organization is being intentional in its pursuit of diversification and welcomes the diverse prospective candidate to be a part of that change.

With that same position, the HEI can create connections with local chapters of the National Society of Black Engineers (NSBE) or Women in Engineering (WIE) to promote the position within their respective networks. This kind of "grassroots" invitation increases the likelihood of attracting diverse applicants and demonstrates that the organization is a partner in diversification and inclusion for BIPOC and women candidates. While invitation can take many forms, and should not be confined solely to early engagements with faculty (and prospective faculty), the following two questions can guide tangible application of invitation during faculty searches:

(1) Does the posting include diverse and inclusive language?
(2) Was the posting shared with professional groups and networks that reflect BIPOC and women?

Influence

People want to work where they are empowered to make a difference. HEIs seeking to attract, hire, and retain underrepresented populations must consider the level of influence it will extend to new constituents. Historically, BIPOC and women candidates have been hired into positions, only to find themselves without influence, decision-making ability, and power that should accompany the position they are employed to fulfill. This can look like a woman not being invited to represent the department at a conference because of her "home obligations" or a BIPOC employee being required to obtain multiple layers of permission to accomplish tasks in which others are exempt from these requirements. BIPOC and women employees often work under a veil of suspicion and skepticism that doesn't permit them the same benefits, privileges, and opportunities that are often granted to their dominant group colleagues in similar positions. The inability to do the job one was hired for leads to immense frustration and stress, as these employees are constantly fighting to "prove" their worthiness, competency, and capability. Additionally, this often disqualifies underrepresented candidates from advancement opportunities within the organization, not because they were incapable of the job but quite often because they were not given the opportunity to display their preparedness for advancement within the organization.

Institutions that are intentional in diversification, and want to invite underrepresented candidates, must consider influence early in the hiring process. In an interview with a Black woman, she shared "I want to be in a place where my work will matter. A place where I will be empowered to make a difference, and sometimes I wonder if a place like that exists." Search committees must possess an awareness that historically underrepresented groups often enter interviews wondering if the institution will actually give them the influence and power to do their job. Expressing to a candidate that they will be empowered, equipped, and supported to effectively perform in their prospective position is a difference-maker in the candidate choosing to work for, and stay with, the organization. Though not exhaustive, the following questions should be considered in evaluating institutional practices related to influence:

(1) Are BIPOC and women given the same opportunities, privileges, and power as other employees, and how is this assessed?
(2) In what ways are opportunities for advancement offered and communicated to underrepresented candidates and employees in the organization?

Investment

HEIs that are committed to diversification understand that attracting and hiring racially and gender diverse candidates is the beginning, but it will not be sustainable without investment. While BIPOC and women employees arrive with a plethora of talents, competencies, and abilities, they will undoubtedly face some adversities in performing within positions that historically have excluded them. Diversification requires investment in the personal and professional life of the racially or gender diverse candidate, to extend support and allyship as they navigate the cultural norms and practices of the institution. Attention should be extended to ensure racially, and gender different individuals are not excluded from the social activities such as lunch tables, after work gatherings, and work conversations and interactions.

One Latinx professor, who was offered a faculty position at a prestigious university, was asked why she accepted a job at a lesser-known university with a smaller compensatory package stated:

> I knew from the beginning that the position at the [prestigious university] would be the highest position I would ever have there.

> I also felt like I wouldn't be included in the social life of the col-
> leagues in that institution. I accepted the job at the smaller univer-
> sity, because they communicated very early how they would invest
> in me professionally and personally. More than just having a job, I
> wanted to be in a place where I was wanted for who I am not just
> what I can do.

The investment of time should not suggest inaptitude on the part of the employee but should show an interest in their growth and development in the job and support for their advancement within the institution and in life. This can take on many different forms and might include opportunities for informal meetings, check-ins, mentoring, and publicly and regularly affirming their work. For example:

(1) How does the organization champion underrepresented employees once they are a part of the team, both formally and informally?
(2) In what ways do BIPOC and women speak into and inform the practices in this phase?

Innovation

Diversification within HEIs must include elevating the voices, perspectives, and cultural practices of BIPOC and women employees. HEIs in pursuit of being more equitable and inclusive must be committed to innovation, embracing that new racial, cultural, and gender representation is an invitation to new and often different ways of conducting business.

For example, a primarily White institution (PWI), HEI that hired an Asian-American faculty member, was asked by that new hire, if he could help organize a celebration of the Lunar New Year. In response to this question, the organization is presented with an amazing opportunity to learn more about this celebration, and to possibly host a Lunar New Year celebration, creating a welcoming environment for its newest hire and possibly attracting new students, communities, and partners to the institution. Institutional readiness to incorporate cultural holidays, ideas, practices, and perspectives can lead HEIs to being more inclusive spaces that invite freshness in instruction, service, and scholarship.

In the hiring process, HEIs should carefully consider that diversification in key positions can become critical hires that will bring immeasurable impact and value to the institution. Racial and gender inclusivity in key positions signals to others that the institution is ready for innovation and attracts new partners, donors, and constituents. In one HEI, the hiring of a Latinx faculty member as a program director led to an influx of Latinx student applicants, new cultural celebrations that attracted community partners, and a collaborative grant proposal. Diversity gives birth to innovation, and innovation opens the door for new opportunities. The innovation phase represents a deeper level of engagement in the process of diversification and inclusion and can also be one of the most rewarding. Unfortunately, many approaches (e.g., tokenism) stop far short of innovation and never realize these benefits for employees or the institution. The following questions can serve HEIs in beginning to engage in this step:

(1) How is the organization including diverse stakeholders in the innovation process?
(2) What opportunities can be sought by leveraging innovation within the organization?

Part III: Recommendations for Practice and Application Across Institutional Type

Recommendations for practice, to improve faculty diversification and inclusivity within HEIs, should consider institutional type (type can include size, structure, mission, and affiliation), setting, and location as well as the current institutional strengths, opportunities, and challenges related to representation and leadership for underrepresented populations. The following four recommendations provide a starting place for HEIs who seek to begin or improve faculty diversification and inclusion; they are neither exhaustive nor exclusive. First, faculty diversification and inclusion are intentional processes and require both planning and strategy. The nature of the plan will depend upon the HEIs current strengths, opportunities, and challenges and should be tailored to the institutional type. For example, the challenges faced by HEIs in rural settings may differ from those in more urban or suburban settings, with the same being the case for very small institutions as compared to large comprehensive universities. This recommendation relates directly to the component of *Intentionality*.

Second, BIPOC and women must be represented and included in leadership roles where their perspectives and experiences can inform and shape faculty diversification and inclusion processes from planning to implementation and assessment. For HEIs who are early in the process, this may initially be more difficult if pipelines for diverse and representative leadership have not been developed. However, plans and practices that are created and deployed without the influence and voice of stakeholders who are most impacted can, even if unintentionally, further perpetuate systems and structures that are not only ineffective but exclusionary and damaging to underrepresented groups. This recommendation relates to both the *Invitation* and *Influence* components of the model.

Third, strategies and plans are strengthened when there is a clear and well-articulated shared purpose or vision for faculty diversification and inclusion that aligns with the ethos of the institution. For example, HEIs that are religiously affiliated or intentionally mission driven for a particular purpose can leverage the opportunity to develop and implement plans which are thoughtfully tied to collective and cohesive goals shared by institutional stakeholders to include faculty and administration. This strategy can help to protect against the backlash that can occur in the *Investment* component of the model. When resistance occurs, and cohesion and collaboration is threatened, shared purpose and vision can be utilized as a rallying point for the team.

Finally, faculty diversification and inclusion efforts must include regular evaluation and assessment work serving as a continual feedback loop leading to ongoing and iterative adaptation and improvement. Plans and practices must continually be evaluated and adapted to be responsive to both what is working and what is not working as well as how the HEI may change over-time. This recommendation is directly related to the *Innovation* element of the model and recognizes that faculty diversification and inclusion efforts are neither "one-size-fits-all" nor independent of changing contexts and needs over time.

Conclusion

Building diverse and inclusive faculty teams is important, urgent, and reward-ing work. Diversification gives birth to lively classroom conversations, thriving campus environments, enhanced growth in the personal and professional lives of students and faculty, establishment of equitable and affirming cross-racial and gender relationships, population and financial growth of the HEI, and more equitable service to communities. HEIs hold the privileged position of setting the standard for the constitution of the workplace and society at large, and diversi-fication within HEIs can lead to the dismantling of long-standing structural and systemic inequities that have infected society. By being more intentional, invita-tional, influential, investing, and innovative, HEIs respond to the words of Rever-end Doctor Martin Luther King, Jr., who stated "We are caught in an inescapable network of mutuality, tied in a single garment of destiny. Whatever affects one directly affects all indirectly" (King, 1986, p. 290). Building diverse and inclusive faculty teams engages HEIs in the mutual work of making the garment of tomor-row more beautiful for future generations.

References

Abdul-Raheem, J. (2016). Faculty diversity and tenure in higher education. *Journal of Cultural Diversity, 23*(2), 53–56.

Casad, B. J., Franks, J. E., Garasky, C. E., Kittleman, M. M., Roesler, A. C., Hall, D. Y., & Petzel, Z. W. (2020). Gender inequality in academia: Problems and solutions for women faculty in STEM. *Journal of Neuroscience Research, 99*(1), 13–23. https://doi.org/10.1002/jnr.24631

Espinosa, L. L., Turk, J. M., Taylor, M., & Chessman, H. M. (2019). *Race and ethnicity in higher education: A status report.* American Council on Education. https://www.equityinhighered.org/wp-content/uploads/2019/02/Race-and-Ethnicity-in-Higher-Education.pdf

Evans, A., & Chun, E. B. (2007). Special issue: Are the walls really down? Behavioral and organizational barriers to faculty and staff diversity. *ASHE Higher Education Report, 33*(1), 1–139. https://doi.org/10.1002/aehe.3301

Fortner, K., & Inman, L. (2023, January 3). *Equitable education: Experiences voiced by women of color* (conference session). Hawaii International Conference on Education 2023, Honolulu, Hawaii, United States.

Fraser, G. J., & Hunt, D. E. (2011). Faculty diversity and search committee training: Learning from a critical incident. *Journal of Diversity in Higher Education ,4*(3), 185–198. https://doi.org/10.1037/a0022248

Griffin, K. A. (2020). Institutional barriers, strategies, and benefits to increasing the representation of women and men of color in the professoriate. In L. Perna (Ed.), *Higher education: Handbook of theory and research* (Vol. 35, pp. 277–349). Springer. https://doi.org/10.1007/978-3-030-31365-4_4

King, M. L. (1986). *A testament of hope: The essential writings of Martin Luther King, Jr.* (J. M. Washington, Ed.). Harper and Row.

McChesney, J., & Bichsel, J. (2020). *The aging of tenure-track faculty in higher education: Implications for succession and diversity.* CUPA-HR. https://doi.org/10.13140/RG.2.2.18555.95521

Moreno, J. F., Smith, D. G., Clayton-Pedersen, A. R., Parker, S., & Teraguchi, D. H. (2006). *The revolving door for underrepresented minority faculty in higher education – An analysis from the campus diversity initiative.* James Irvine Foundation. https://folio.iupui.edu/handle/10244/50

National Center for Education Statistics. (2022). *Race/ethnicity of college faculty.* https://nces.ed.gov/fastfacts/display.asp?id=61

O'Meara, K., Lennartz, C., Kuvaeva, A., Jaeger, A., & Misra, J. (2019). Department conditions and practices associated with faculty workload satisfaction and perceptions of equity. *The Journal of Higher Education ,90*(5), 744–772. https://doi.org/10.1080/00221546.2019.1584025

Perna, L. W. (2023). *Why we need better data on faculty diversity.* Inside Higher Ed. http://https://www.insidehighered.com/views/2023/01/10/why-we-need-better-data-faculty-diversity-opinion

Settles, I., Buchanan, N., & Dotson, K. (2019). Scrutinized but not recognized: (In)visibility and hypervisibility experiences of faculty of color. *Journal of Vocational Behavior, 113*, 62–74. https://doi.org/10.1016/j.jvb.2018.06.003

Townsend, C. V. (2020). Identity politics: Why African American women are missing in administrative leadership in public higher education. *Educational Management Administration & Leadership, 49*(4), 584–600. https://doi.org/10.1177/1741143220935455

White-Lewis, D. K. (2020) The facade of fit in faculty search processes. *The Journal of Higher Education ,91*(6), 833–857. https://doi.org/10.1080/00221546.2020.1775058

Chapter 8

Inclusive Leadership for Social Justice: DEIB Leadership Programs and Organizations

Antonio Jimenez-Luque and Lea Hubbard

University of San Diego, USA

Abstract

Organizational initiatives to address diversity, equity, inclusion, and belonging (DEIB) have multiplied with many different courses and training programs in the last three decades. Despite these efforts, some recent studies have pointed out that disadvantages among minoritized social groups continue to persist, and thus far, organizations have failed to address them. University graduate leadership programs are, at least theoretically, able to respond in a way that better prepares future formal and informal organizational leaders with the knowledge, skills, and dispositions needed to be inclusive individuals in the 21st century committed to social change and social justice. This study aimed to understand how some graduate programs were currently teaching DEIB issues; more specifically, to understand if universities implementing DEIB programs were using a critical lens in their program design and to assess if these programs were indeed intended to be transformative. The review of 40 graduate programs in the United States indicated that the majority of them view diversity training and the work of DEIB leadership as "managing diversity" to keep the status quo and for economic profit contributing to the commoditization and tokenism of people; there was no mention of power in terms of asymmetries but rather a legitimizing of the accumulation of power with the leader at the top; and, finally, except for five programs, there was little attention given to DEIB as a transformative project committed to social justice.

Keywords: Inclusive leadership; social justice; managing diversity; graduate leadership programs; social change; organizational leadership

Inclusive Leadership: Equity and Belonging in Our Communities
Building Leadership Bridges, Volume 9, 87–96
Copyright © 2023 by Emerald Publishing Limited
All rights of reproduction in any form reserved
ISSN: 2058-8801/doi:10.1108/S2058-880120230000009008

Introduction

In the last few decades, the diversity of the United States' demographic has increased considerably. The workforce belonging to marginalized social groups among American organizations has increased too. Alongside this growth, organizational efforts to address DEIB have multiplied since the 1980s when organizational initiatives such as courses and training programs started to be implemented through workplace education, organizational structures, and managerial policies and practices. Despite these efforts, some recent studies have pointed out that disadvantages among minoritized social groups continue to persist, and thus far, organizations have failed to address them (Adeyumo, 2021; Rahim, 2010; Sorenson & Garman, 2013; Sue, 2010).

As an example, when it comes to positions of leadership in US organizations today, data show that White individuals typically occupy these spaces (Adeyumo, 2021). More specifically, 84% of management positions in structured organizations are occupied by individuals who identify as White, and 88% of those in chief executive positions also identify as White (U.S. Bureau of Labor Statistics, 2020). When it comes to higher education institutions, according to the National Center for Education Statistics, in 2019, for the 259,986 management positions, 195,243 or 75% were occupied by Whites.

Additionally, besides the lack of people from the non-dominant social group in positions of leadership, there is a high disengagement and turnover at work for people belonging to marginalized communities. According to a Gallup survey from 2013, more than half of the American workforce claims to be disengaged at work. Disengaged employees cost the United States around $500 billion in lost productivity per year (Sorenson & Garman, 2013). When employees feel that they are being mistreated or not supported, it affects their sense of belonging and sense of worth in the organization (Sue, 2010).

Given this larger context, attention to creating initiatives that address issues of DEIB have, more than ever before, increased dramatically. Thus, many American universities have taken up the opportunity and challenge to develop effective DEIB training, including developing graduate programs designed around these issues. University graduate leadership programs are, at least theoretically, in a position to respond in a way that better prepares future organizational formal and informal leaders with the knowledge, skills, and dispositions needed to be inclusive individuals in the 21st century committed to social change and social justice.

The aim of this study was to understand how some graduate programs are currently teaching DEIB issues; more specifically, to understand if universities implementing DEIB programs are using a critical lens in the design of their program and to assess if these programs are indeed intended to be transformative. In other words, are these programs developed and marketed for the stated purpose of readying leaders to lead organizations merely for managing diversity or for social justice or for both? Do these programs examine the role of power in shaping organizational and social relations? Finally, do they acknowledge the sociohistorical context that has constructed inequality – a space that goes beyond the individual and the organization and views DEIB as a systemic issue?

We begin by reviewing the existing literature around the origins of DEIB in organizations. Next, we present our findings from a content analysis of our research on leadership development programs across the United States. We conclude with a call for a more critical and holistic rendering of diversity to best support leadership development for DEIB.

DEIB Origins and Evolution: Reproducing Power Differentials and the Status Quo

Discussions of leadership, in general, and educational leadership, in particular, as it relates to diversity and social justice emerged from global social movements in the 1970s with the civil rights movement and second-wave feminism, as well as with the multicultural and postcolonial movements in the 1980s and 1990s. "It is a discourse mobilized largely by the political and educational aspirations of racial, ethnic and linguistic social groups together with the resurgence of new knowledges" (Blackmore, 2006, p. 196). Feminist and postcolonial scholars and practitioners advocated for a more collective and participatory leadership and argued that leadership processes needed to be more "inclusive" of women and marginalized social groups (Fraser, 1997; Mirza, 2005).

The call for transformative equity practice stemming from these global social movements of the past faced a backlash from conservative political and economic sectors of society. In this case, it was the idea of "managing diversity" that emerged with the document published by the conservative Hudson Institute in 1987: *The Workforce 2000: Work and Workers for the Twenty-first Century*. In Bourdieu's terms (1989), any process of heterodoxy or challenge of doxa (dominant assumptions) is always counter challenged by a strong orthodoxy. Thus, the idea of "managing diversity" was the orthodoxy that tried to control diversity within organizations and keep the status quo.

This report pointed out that by the year 2000, most workers in the United States would be African-Americans, Hispanics, Native Americans, women, and other minority groups (Beasley, 1996). According to a great number of quantitative analyses that proliferated after the publication of the report, by the year 2000, White males would no longer comprise the majority of their labor forces (Hammond & Kleiner, 1992). Thus, organizations began to reconsider who their future managers might be, focusing on "managing diversity" in a way that was functional in controlling diversity and maintaining the status quo.

According to Lorbiecki and Jack (2000), "interest in diversity management turned political when its inclusive philosophy was seen as an attractive alternative to 'affirmative action' policies, which were causing widespread unease" (p. 20). The idea of "managing diversity" resonated with the new-right thinking that began with the Reagan administration in the 1980s and continued throughout the 1990s (Gordon, 1992). "Diversity management was seen by the right wing as an acceptable response to the 'political correctness' lobby against liberal or left-wing policies, and to the 'cult of ethnicity' exhibited by the Black (and White) power movements" (Lorbiecki & Jack, 2000, p. 20).

As Lorbiecki and Jack (2000) argue, diversity is a highly political concept that does not relate to all aspects of difference but to those aspects of difference that may be seen as "unacceptable" or problematic by the dominant group. In other words, some group differences matter more than others but always from the point of view of the dominant social group or culture. Thus, diversity is a social and political construct defined by the dominant group and, as such, created to serve their ends (Lumby, 2006).

Moreover, political interest around diversity turned economic with the intro-duction of new arguments stating that only those organizations that decide to manage diversity will be economically successful in the future (Lorbiecki & Jack, 2000), thus tying numbers or representation of diversity to economic gain. A great number of quantitative analyses emphasized the connection between diver-sity and organizational performance, turning the issue of diversity into a "busi-ness" case (Lorbiecki & Jack, 2000). From then on, social identities were framed as potential repositories of economic value for employers for the first time. The notion of managing diversity that focused on managing potential conflict and keeping the status quo added a new element of economic profit when social dif-ferences were turned into resources to be deployed by firms to attract specific skills, foster innovation and creative solutions, and enhance client orientation (Robinson & Dechant, 1997).

The whole idea of "managing diversity" that emerged by the end of the 1980s and is still very present within US organizations and university departments of leadership and management can be seen as a retreat from equal opportunities strategies that could challenge power differentials and discrimination (Wilson & Isles, 1996). In essence, because the mainstream concept of "managing diversity" transforms radical challenges to power and inequity into manageable human resource management processes, it may camouflage the intention to retain the status quo (Sinclair, 2000).

In this study, we used the literature described above as a lens to examine the 40 graduate programs identified from a google search. We specifically questioned: (a) the mainstream DEIB perspective of the program, whether it has been con-cerned with "managing diversity" to avoid potential conflict and keeping the status quo, and/or managing diversity for economic aims rather than transform-ing unjust structures and inequities within organizations and society; and (b) the extent to which it indicated a connection with global systems and structures – an approach that is key to understanding how constructed differences are connected with issues of power. We were also attentive to emerging consistent patterns found within these programs.

Methodology

In this study, we used the literature described in the first part of this chapter as a lens to examine the 40 graduate programs identified from the google search. See Table 8.1 for a distribution list of universities by the US state.

We coded each program description using a combination of a priori codes (i.e., codes initially informed by the research questions) such as "managing

Table 8.1.   List With the Distribution of Universities and States.

State	Number of Universities
Arkansas	1
California	4
Colorado	2
Connecticut	1
Florida	1
Georgia	1
Illinois	4
Iowa	2
Kansas	2
Kentucky	1
Maryland	1
Massachusetts	4
Michigan	1
Missouri	1
Nebraska	1
New Jersey	2
New York	2
North Carolina	1
Ohio	2
Pennsylvania	1
South Carolina	1
Texas	3
Wisconsin	1
Total number of universities	40

diversity," "social justice," "power," and "international or global." We also used inductive codes developed in an ongoing manner during the analysis process. We used axial coding assembling the data in new ways to identify patterns, core categories, and subcategories as proposed by Creswell (2013).

We specifically questioned: (a) the mainstream DEIB perspective of the program; the extent to which it was concerned with "managing diversity" (managing potential conflict and keeping the status quo) and/or for economic aims and profit rather than transforming unjust structures and inequities within organizations and society; and (b) the extent to which it indicated a connection with global systems and structures – an approach that is key to understanding how constructed differences are connected with issues of power. We were also attentive to emerging consistent patterns found within these programs.

DEIB Program Perspectives on Leadership Development

A review of the DEIB programs' description, courses' descriptions, and some syllabi in this study indicated that 90% of the programs view diversity training as "managing diversity," that is, for the purposes of controlling diversity and getting economic profit. In these cases, there was no mention of how power shapes relations in either the program or course descriptions, and there was little attention given to DEIB training that was explicitly intended to be transformative and committed to social justice. There were just a few programs implementing a critical perspective that emphasized social change. In essence, managing diversity for keeping the status quo and economic profit seemed to be the main orientations of the different programs. We will describe these orientations within some of these programs next.

Economics and Diversity

One common theme found in the content analysis of the 40 different programs' websites was their attention to how diversity training can give an organization an economic advantage. The idea is that diversity training is essential because it is inextricably connected to economic success. One Florida program suggests that diversity training has the potential to "increase revenue." A similar economic orientation was seen in the statement from a Colorado university program that promises to help individuals: "Learn to create an inclusive workplace culture that increases innovation, productivity and profits – and stand out as a valuable, inclusive leader who drives the economic benefits and competitive advantage of gender diversity at your company."

A program in California also described diversity training as important for business success in this way: "Research from multiple studies confirms that organizations that succeed in implementing an effective culture of inclusion show measurable improvement of key metrics that drive business success and sustainability of the enterprise." And an executive leadership program from a university in Colorado connected DEIB topics and profit in their program description by stating that individuals need to:

> Learn to create an inclusive workplace culture that increases innovation, productivity and profits – and stand out as a valuable, inclusive leader who drives the economic benefits and competitive advantage of gender diversity at your company.

Another program at a Californian university claimed the importance of DEIB training by also focusing on economic gain. The program description explained how: "inclusion stimulates productivity and growth." Similarly, a program in Iowa emphasized the connection between DEIB training and productivity stating how its program helps organizational leaders "Identify, recognize and remove barriers that impede productivity for the 21st century workforce."

No one would argue against adopting strategies that increase an organization's profit. The concern however is that if DEIB training is merely seen as "managing diversity" for economic advantage and is absent the overall goal of addressing social justice, people belonging to marginalized backgrounds are seen as tokens, that is, DEIB training helps to respond to a diversity quota, and individuals merely occupy subaltern positions within the organization reproducing the same asymmetries of power that are experienced in society. When diversity is merely seen as a commodity, employees from marginalized social groups are seen as objects and not subjects (Blackmore, 2006; Lorbiecki & Jack, 2000) and arguably, the goals of DEIB may be overlooked.

The general assumption that lies within this DEIB strategy is that the only goal of any business organization is profit, but this assumption needs to be challenged. Thinking of business organizations as spaces committed to social justice could transform businesses and create healthier relationships among employees at work. A deeper discussion of these issues could, at a minimum, create some balance when designing DEIB programs.

Power and Diversity

When reviewing graduate programs of DEIB, we found that DEIB course descriptions typically did not capture the relational aspect of power in shaping inequity and exclusion but rather treated DEIB training as empowering or giving power to those charged with leading change. Understanding policies and practices and how they shape a workplace culture demands attention be given to how power is distributed, who has power, and who does not, and how those with power use it (Courpasson, 2000; Gordon, 2011; Jimenez-Luque, 2021). Power and privilege are likely the result of positional authority and socio-historical events (Courpasson, 2000; Gordon, 2011; Jimenez-Luque, 2021), and power shapes present-day interactions and relationships that influence whether employees feel valued or devalued within their organizations. Race, ethnicity, class, gender, and so on construct the relations between leaders and followers within organizations. These relationships need to be acknowledged and, particularly, that hierarchies and inequities in society distribute power in unequal ways that are reproduced within organizations. For example, daily routines within organizations, such as granting equal access to information, communication, or processes of decision-making, although presented in a technical, bureaucratic, or even neutral way, are connected to power. Leadership is a relational process within a context, and power is a relation.

The leader-centered approach with a leader at the top of a hierarchy accumulating power appeared to be legitimized and reproduced in most of these programs. A university from Colorado mentions power this way:

> This course will empower and equip you to develop inclusive cultures where everyone feels valued and respected. You will learn

how highly inclusive leaders from around the world use processes of social influence to interact effectively with individuals from a wide variety of backgrounds.

Another Boston university program discussed power as something that participants in their program would gain by enrolling in their program. They noted how DEIB training empowers individuals with the "leadership practices that builds others up."

None of the programs reviewed explicitly addressed leadership as a relational process or in terms of relationships of power between positional leaders and followers. Accumulating power instead was discussed as something held at the hands of a few individuals at the top of a hierarchy and was legitimized through the idea that the leader would contribute to the work of DEIB "building others up" without asking if the "other" wants to be built up or if the other could co-create or collaborate in the DEIB effort. As some research has pointed out, this leadership approach has resulted over the last several decades in unethical behaviors and practices that Dennis Tourish (2013) defined as the dark side of transformational leadership.

DEIB for Transformative Change

The primary impetus behind the development of DEIB leadership programs suggested by educational leaders in the 1970s and 1980s in the United States was that these programs would teach individuals the knowledge and skills needed for transformative organizational change. Participants would learn how to restructure and re-culture an organization to be more responsive to the needs of a diverse workforce and remedy some of the problems of work inequity and exclusion.

We found, however, that the backlash from the report *Workforce 2000*, published in the 1980s with the aim of keeping the status quo, is still very alive. For example, out of the 40 programs reviewed for this study, only 5 defined transformative change as their goal which implies a conceptualization of "managing diversity" around the idea of avoiding conflicts and keeping the status quo. However, a university program in Missouri was one of these exceptions. Their program claimed that they would teach DEIB leadership from a critical and cultural consciousness lens so that students would understand the "systems change process" and able to do the DEIB work needed in their organization:

> This certificate is designed to provide students with the practical knowledge necessary to understand the challenges surrounding equity, inclusion, and cultural consciousness through the examination of institutional and community cultures. As leaders, locally, nationally, or globally, the DEI Leadership Certificate will prepare students to understand the systems change process through a cultural conscious lens as they work with their organizations on DEI initiatives.

This leadership program addressed DEIB in a systemic way by recognizing the role of local, national, and global forces. It is a program that is community oriented and acknowledges the distribution of power and the need for systems change.

Similarly, an Illinois program also explicitly promised to train individuals to lead transformative change. Students would learn to: "Demonstrate the value of diversity, equity, and inclusion in your organization in order to turn dialogue into action and lead transformative change." Their DEIB certificate with a specialization in social-justice promised to take "a transformative approach in addressing diversity and equity issues within the P-16 learning environment." Finally, one other university program in Pennsylvania also emphasized the importance of training individuals in how to design more inclusive policies that would create the "transformative change" needed in their organization.

Discussion and Conclusion

The review of the DEIB programs of 40 graduate programs in the United States indicated that the majority of them view diversity training and the work of DEIB leadership as "managing diversity" for economic profit contributing to the commoditization and tokenism of people; there was no mention of power in terms of asymmetries but rather a legitimizing of the accumulation of power with the leader at the top; and, finally, except for five programs, there was little attention given to DEIB as a transformative project committed to social justice. This current approach to DEIB training is likely to continue to lead to the reproduction of inequality and the current system that maintains the status quo.

When it comes to limitations, this research reviewed 40 graduate programs from the United States in total. Although 40 programs are a significant number, the study could be more exhaustive since most universities in the country have graduate programs. While this content analysis included a review of the websites of each program, program descriptions, lists and contents of courses, and a few syllabi, it would have been ideal to have access to all the syllabi of the courses offered in each program and have a deeper understanding of each course and how it is taught. Additionally, future research would benefit from disaggregating by the type of the university, differences between academic units where programs are housed, and other relevant demographic information.

This study aimed to start a conversation around reviewing current and future DEIB leadership programs from a critical lens and conceptualizing leadership, in general, and particularly DEIB leadership, as a process committed to issues of transformation and social justice to build fairer societies and organizations. In essence, building a world of social justice for all will be a difficult and long process. However, to think about this possibility, means, in part, creating training opportunities that emphasize individual, organizational, and global connections of DEIB issues; acknowledging socio-historic asymmetric relationships of power; and conceptualizing the role of business organizations as more than making profit for the stakeholders. This work has become more important than ever.

References

Adejumo, V. (2021). Beyond diversity, inclusion, and belonging. *Leadership*, *17*(1), 62–73.

Beasley, M. A. (1996). Keys to managing diversity. *Food Management*, *31*(7), 36.

Blackmore, J. (2006). Deconstructing diversity discourses in the field of educational management and leadership. *Leadership, Educational Management and Administration*, *34*(2), 188–199.

Bourdieu, P. (1989). Social space and symbolic power. *Sociological Theory*, *7*(*1*), 14–25.

Courpasson, D. (2000). Managerial strategies of domination. Power in soft bureaucracies. *Organization Studies*, *21*(1), 141–161.

Creswell, J. (2013). *Qualitative inquiry and research design: Choosing among five traditions.* Thousand Oaks, CA: Sage.

Fraser, N. (1997). *Justice interruptus: Critical reflections on the 'Postsocialist' condition.* Routledge.

Gallup. (2013). *State of the American workplace.* www.gallup.com/services/178514/state-american-workplace.aspx

Gordon, J. (1992). Rethinking diversity. *Training*, *29*(2), 23–30.

Gordon, R. (2011). Leadership and power. In A. Bryman, D. Collinson, K. Grint, B. Jackson, & M. Uhl-Bien (Eds.), *The Sage handbook of leadership* (pp. 195–202). Sage.

Hammond, T., & Kleiner, B. (1992). Managing multicultural work environments. *Equal Opportunities International*, *11*(2), 6–9.

Jimenez-Luque, A. (2021). Decolonial leadership for cultural resistance and social change: Challenging the social order through the struggle of identity. *Leadership*, *17*(2), 154–172.

Lorbiecki, A., & Jack, G. (2000). Critical turns in the evolution of diversity management. *British Journal of Management*, *11*(3), 17–31.

Lumby, J. (2006). Conceptualizing diversity and leadership: Evidence from 10 cases. *Educational Management Administration & Leadership*, *34*(2), 151–165.

Mirza, H. (2005, June). *Race, gender and educational desire* [Inaugural Professorial Lecture]. Middlesex University. https://core.ac.uk/download/pdf/82963.pdf

National Center for Education Statistics. (2019). *Digest of education statistics.* https://nces.ed.gov/programs/digest/2018menu_tables.asp

Rahim, E. (2010). An application of change management for confronting organizational stigmatization. *Journal of Business and Leadership: Research, Practice and Teaching*, *6*, 25–37.

Robinson, G., & Dechant, K. (1997). Building a business case for diversity. *Academy of Management*, *11*(3), 21–31.

Sinclair, A. (2000). Teaching managers about masculinities: Are you kidding? *Management Learning*, *31*(1), 83–101.

Sorenson, S., & Garman, K. (2013). How to tackle U.S. employees' stagnating engagement. *Business Insider*, June 11.

Sue, D. (2010). *Microaggressions and marginality: Manifestation, dynamics, and impact.* Wiley.

Tourish, D. (2013). *The dark side of transformational leadership: A critical perspective.* Routledge.

U.S. Bureau of Labor Statistics. (2020). *Household data annual averages.* https://www.bls.gov/cps/cpsaat11.pdf

Wilson, E., & Iles, P. (1996). Managing diversity: Evaluation of an emerging paradigm. In *British Academy Conference Proceeding* (pp. 6.62–6.76). Aston Business School.

Chapter 9

Addressing the Goal of Inclusive and Equitable Quality Education and Lifelong Learning for All

Carolyn M. Shields

Wayne State University, USA

Abstract

In this chapter, the author argues that in order to meet the United Nations' sustainable development goal 4 which calls for education to "ensure inclusive and equitable quality education and promote lifelong learning opportunities for all by 2030," transformative leadership may be key. Transformative leadership goes well beyond traditional technical and rational approaches to leadership; it includes but extends theories such as social justice leadership and transformational leadership and involves two general principles and eight interconnected tenets. These include knowing oneself, one's community and organization; deconstructing frameworks that perpetuate inequity and reconstructing them in more equitable ways; addressing the inequitable distribution of power; emphasizing individual and collective good; focusing on democracy emancipation, equity, and justice as well as interconnectedness and global awareness; and offering both critique and promise. Transformative leadership theory is a critical, holistic, and normative approach that focuses on values, and on beliefs and mindsets as well as knowledge and action. It is characterized by its activist agenda and its overriding commitment to social justice, equity, and democratic society. Thus, it is an approach to leadership that is anti-racist, anti-homophobic, anti-xenophobic, etc.; it calls for rejection of deficit thinking and for inclusive and equitable practices that require moral courage. It is such a holistic and critical theory that would help to promote the United Nations' education goal by the target of 2030.

Keywords: Transformative leadership; inclusion; equity; justice; excellence; United Nations' sustainable development goals

Inclusive Leadership: Equity and Belonging in Our Communities
Building Leadership Bridges, Volume 9, 97–106
ISSN: 2058-8801/doi:10.1108/S2058-880120230000009009

Today, 57 million primary-aged children will not be in school: in developing countries, three out of four will be girls. Moreover, education in many places is so poor that over 103 million youth lack basic skills and competence in math or reading. As adults, they then fail to obtain positions that either support families or enhance society. These abysmal statistics have long been matters of concern. In 1948, the United Nations (UN) proclaimed article 26: "Everyone has the right to education" (UN, 1948). Since then, the UN has been making proclamations and identifying goals intended to fulfill that statement. For example, in 1989, the UN Convention on the Rights of the Child was adopted, and as of today, it has been ratified by every country in the world except the United States (UN, 1989). Similarly, the UN's Millennium Development Goal 2, Achieve Universal Primary Education, was created but not reached by the deadline 2015 (UN, 2015).

Undaunted, at the UN meeting in Incheon, Korea, in 2015, 160 nations signed on to 17 interconnected sustainable development goals (with 169 targets) (Education 2030 ..., 2015). This set of goals was intended to "end poverty, protect the planet, and ensure that by 2030 all people enjoy peace and prosperity." The fourth goal (sustainable development goal 4 (SDG4)) is the education goal: "to ensure inclusive and equitable quality education and promote lifelong learning opportunities for all." Given such a worldwide emphasis, a book focused on inclusion and equity is particularly timely if we are to meet the SDG4, transform schools, and improve democratic society.

To begin, it is perhaps important to reflect on these terms. Inclusion does not simply imply permission to participate in an event. It requires that everyone is welcomed, valued, and treated with respect; it ensures their voices are heard, and their perspective is carefully considered. I recall the stinging feeling of exclusion, years ago, when an adult said of me, "She's just a child" and, hence, dismissed my voice. Similarly, it is important to differentiate between equality and equity. We cannot and should not treat everyone equally. If one child needs glasses, we do not provide them to all; if one needs a crutch, we do not teach everyone to use one. Instead, equity involves providing each person what is needed to participate in society fully and successfully, whether we are talking about success academically or more broadly.

Unless we ensure that all girls and boys complete free, equitable, and quality primary and secondary education, their future participation in both lifelong learning and civil society will be impeded. Therefore, it is important to consider the kind of leadership that may best assist in attaining this goal.

Moving Beyond Technical Leadership

In this chapter, I briefly make a case for replacing the dominant technical and rational approaches to leadership that have prevailed since the managerial approaches of the early twentieth century with leadership that is critical (in that it foregrounds those whom Burns (1978) called, "in the direst want" (p. 12)). Critical approaches engage in both advocacy and action. It is no longer sufficient to focus simply on whether formal leaders emphasize tasks or relationships (Blake & Mouton, 1982; Hersey et al., 1979) or to consider the effectiveness and efficiency of an organization as a whole because overall success can, and does, mask the marginalization, exclusion, and oppression of subgroups of people.

Even transformational leadership, said by Bass and Riggio (2006) to be "the approach of choice for much of the research and application of leadership theory" (p. xi), falls short. Bass and Riggio (2006) emphasize repeatedly that "the strongest effects of transformational leadership seem to be on followers' attitudes and commitment to the leader and the organization" (p. 32) and assert that "the commitment and loyalty of members of organizations are multifaceted. There is commitment to the larger organization, to the work group or team, and to the leader" (p. 34).

I argue that instead of a commitment to either the leader or the organization, what is needed is a commitment to specific values, in this case to the values of diversity, equity, inclusion, belonging, and accessibility (DEIBA). Without emphasis on the desired values, there is little reason to expect that the SDG4 will be met. Thus, I propose here that we need a theory that clarifies the components of inclusion, equity, justice, and high quality and reflects on how to offer opportunities for ongoing development to all. I assert the necessity for a critical theory that emphasizes the needs of those who are the most marginalized, oppressed, and excluded, one that directs our vision and grounds it in the needs of a specific context and in explicit values and beliefs. Moreover, research has shown that what is good for the least advantaged students will also result in equity and excellence for all (Berryman, 2022; Bieneman, 2011; Salinas & Garr, 2009). Further, empowered students result in more empowered citizens. There are many recent studies and theories focused on elements of intersectionality and DEIBA which tend to be ignored when researchers and scholars engage in reviewing approaches to leadership. In large part, these current theories take seriously the context of the research, take pains to describe it carefully, but do not include measures of effect sizes, power, or other statistical measures. In part for this reason, theories like social justice leadership (Theoharis, 2007), culturally responsive leadership (Khalifa et al., 2016), critical democratic leadership (Møller, 2011), and transformative leadership (Shields, 2018, 2020) are rarely foregrounded. Nevertheless, it is these more critical, more activist, and more normative (values-based) theories that have the potential to move the needle toward more equity and inclusion and increasingly toward socially-just organizations and societies.

Transformative Leadership Theory (TLT)

Despite the fact that other theories also meet the above criteria, I argue here for the comprehensive, holistic, normative, and critical approach of Transformative Leadership Theory (TLT) (see Table 9.1) to attain the goal of equitable and inclusive education that also offers high-quality instruction for everyone.

In 2013, van Oord argued that the term is not new, but that for many years, the concepts of transformational and transformative leadership were used as synonyms. He continued:

> Recognizing this conceptual murkiness, scholars such as Shields (2010, 2012) have in recent years successfully endeavored to define and theorize transformative leadership as distinctively separate

Table 9.1.   Transformative Leadership Theory.

Principle 1: When all are safe, respected, included, and their voices are heard, they are better able to learn, and performance improves.

Principle 2: When schools focus on democratic inclusion and excellence, civil society also strengthens and advances.

Tenets:

1. Accept a mandate for deep and equitable change.
2. Deconstruct knowledge frameworks that perpetuate inequity (and reconstruct them in more equitable ways).
3. Address the inequitable distribution of power.
4. Emphasize both individual and collective (private and public) good.
5. Focus on democracy, emancipation, equity, and justice.
6. Emphasize interconnectedness, interdependence, and global awareness.
7. Balance critique and promise.
8. Exercise moral courage.

(Shields, 2018, 2020)

> from the transformational approach. Transformative leadership is characterized by its activist agenda and its overriding commitment
>
> to social justice, equality and a democratic society. (pp. 421–422)

The distinctions are increasingly recognized. Blackmore (2011), for example, stated that "while seductive, transformational leadership discourse appropriates critical perspectives while depoliticizing their social-justice intent," and further that transformative leadership promotes "emancipatory pedagogies" and raises questions about the "purposes of education and leadership and about issues of social justice" (p. 21).

Table 9.1 demonstrates how TLT truly comprises a holistic, interactive leadership theory. In fact, that is one distinguishing feature. While Khalifa et al. (2016) insist that their approach to culturally responsive leadership focuses on urban schools and "describe[s] CRSL behaviors" (p. 1274), transformative leadership concentrates on beliefs, mindsets, and knowledge frameworks, as well as behaviors and actions. It takes seriously Johnson's (2008) finding that "what separates successful leaders from unsuccessful ones is their mental models or meaning structures, not their knowledge, information, training, or experience per se" (p. 85).

A theory, according to the University of California, Berkeley, is "a broad, natural explanation for a wide range of phenomena" (Bradford, 2017). It is also "coherent, systematic, predictive, and broadly applicable." TLT is consistent with this definition because one can manipulate the principles (or hypotheses) in order to assess their ability to be predictive in terms of the goals of equity, inclusion, and belonging. For example, principle 1 argues the need for ensuring that all are safe, respected, included, and their voices heard. One can learn empirically if a student is trying to avoid being bullied at recess, or worried about where their family will sleep that night, whether that student is fully focused on the learning at hand and whether, ultimately, academic performance is suffering. Similarly, if an adult is concentrating on an upcoming performance appraisal, or on a conflict with a peer, will she be able to focus fully on the work at hand? Principle 1 is balanced by the second principle that asserts that TLT also improves civil society by helping to promote democratic, civic engagement, and global curiosity. This too may be tested empirically.

TLT as outlined in *Transformative Leadership in Action: Allyship, Advocacy & Activism* (Bruce & McKee, 2020) is said to offer "a deeply reflective and reflexive account of the bravery and vulnerability necessary for substantive social change" (front pages). Building on that volume and using examples from research, I briefly elaborate TLT's guiding principles and tenets and demonstrate how it grounds education, and hence society, in equity, inclusion, excellence, and justice and thus promotes the DEIBA space.

The bravery begins with the commitment required of the first tenet. It is not enough to identify an inequity but requires leaders to carefully examine their own commitment, their nonnegotiables, and willingness to follow through, despite the unavoidable pushback that happens when deep transformation occurs. Here, context is important. What inequities are present in the organization? Which are the most salient and should be addressed first? In the current American context, for example, we know that racism and xenophobia are playing inordinately important roles. In January 2023, the Anti-Defamation League reported, for example, that 85% of the American public subscribe to at least one anti-Jewish trope. In addition, tropes regarding the "inferiority" of African-Americans abound, as do those perpetuating the notion that Asian-Americans are inherently alien to the United States. These and other racial narratives suggest that leaders in American schools and organizations ignore race and racism at their peril.

Bravery is immediately joined by vulnerability when the second tenet comes into play. Here addressing knowledge frameworks is hard work as it involves challenging one's own mindsets and beliefs as well as those of others. It involves taking seriously the title of Nguyen's 2022 book, also a common poster that states, "Don't believe everything you think" for we have been taught to believe many incorrect ideas. It is this second tenet that truly makes TLT an anti-racist, anti-homophobic, and anti-xenophobic theory. Tenet 2 requires that one address deficit thinking as well as implicit bias and conduct myriad conversations and activities to foreground the inequity of much current thinking, both individual and systemic. Moreover, there are multiple ways to approach deconstructing knowledge frameworks that perpetuate inequity and to replace them with more appropriate knowledge frameworks.

For example, one African-American school principal had never considered the concept of deficit thinking (Shields et al., 2005; Valencia, 2012) prior to her doctoral program. Recognizing that the concept also often applied to her, she set about to determine ways in which other Black leaders had also adopted the pervasive and systemic negative mindset about many students and to counteract them through many contested and uncomfortable conversations.

Tenet 3 takes seriously the concept expressed more than 30 years ago by Quantz et al. (1991) who asserted that "transformative leadership does not imply the diminishing of *power*, but the diminishing of *undemocratic power relationships*" (p. 102). They argued the necessity of working for more symmetrical power relations in which there is mutual recognition of skill and leadership. Half a century ago, Schwartz and Ogilvy (1975) asserted the need for heterarchic leadership similar to the child's game of "scissors, stone, paper" in which no element is always on top, but each sometimes is. Symmetrical leadership works similarly, with mutual respect for times when each person's skills and abilities propel them into leadership.

In today's climate of fear, racism, and polarization, teaching children from an early age to work positively with others, to reject hate, and to address the discrimination that society perpetuates is one way to ultimately change societal behavior and attitudes. It is not easy; nor is it quick. But it is essential. Hence, the preservation of democratic society may depend on the fourth tenet. My friend's adopted Black child should never have to hear, when rounding an aisle in a grocery store, "Mom, I hate black babies." No teacher should receive a phone call stating, "My son cannot read a biography of Jackie Robinson, because my husband will not permit a book about a Black man in the house." And no principal should have to deal with parents insisting, out of prejudice, that their child be moved from a classroom with a Black teacher. There is no doubt that students must participate in critical democratic discourse from a young age if such widespread societal discrimination is to cease.

Tenets 5 and 6 move beyond general policy and practice to the center of the school or organization itself. Tenet 5 focuses on democracy, emancipation, equity, and justice, while tenet 6 emphasizes interconnectedness, interdependence, and global awareness. I recently attended a presentation of August Wilson's (2015) *Gem of the Ocean*, in which one character states more than once that he cannot be free until everyone is free. This is in some ways the crux of these two tenets. It is imperative to teach children, regardless of their privilege, or perhaps at times, because of it, that there still exist discrimination, marginalization, and oppression, including human trafficking and enslavement.

Transformative leadership does not advocate that teachers ignore the legislated standards and curriculum, simply that they use them as occasions for critical democratic discourse. Whether students are learning about taxation, sources of energy, or local history, it becomes imperative to engage them in critical discourse. As Grumet (1995) argued,

> What is basic is not a certain set of texts, or principles or algorithms, but the conversation that makes sense of these things. Curriculum is that conversation. It is the process of making sense with a group of people of the systems that shape and organize the world that we can think about together. (p. 20)

Making sense cannot ignore discriminatory policies or practices but must, instead, help students to understand their place in an inequitable world and how to change it.

Tied to the concept of critical democratic engagement is the recognition that we are irrevocably tied to those we have never known who may live either close to us or in a foreign country. Arousing global curiosity helps children to understand that even in the same city, others may have quite different lived experiences from them. At the same time, it is important to create awareness of the 771 million people (World Health Organization (WHO) & The United Nations Children's Fund (UNICEF), 2021) who do not have access to a basic clean water service near their houses, or of the "828 million people in 2021, an increase of about 46 million since 2020 and 150 million since the outbreak of the COVID-19 pandemic" who experienced severe hunger (World Health Organization (WHO), 2022).

New understanding may help them to see how the world is moving farther away from meeting the UN's proposed sustainable development goals by 2030. This emphasizes the importance of the seventh tenet of transformative leadership: the need for both critique and promise, in other words, for both awareness and action. Understanding is hollow unless it leads to change that enhances both inclusion and equity at home and abroad.

It goes without saying that the mindsets and strategies associated with transformative leadership are not easy; there is often resistance and pushback. Moral courage itself requires deliberation and careful thought. It requires doing the right thing regardless of the consequences. As Weiner (2003) noted of transformative leader Paulo Freire, one "must have one foot in the dominant structures of power and authority" and, at the same time, learn how to "combat the seduction of official power and knowledge, maintain a critical stance, and disrupt the hegemony of dominant cultural formatives" (p. 91).

Concluding Reflection

The transformative leadership agenda outlined here provides one comprehensive way for leaders to approach achieving the UN's SDG4: to ensure "inclusive and equitable quality education and promote lifelong learning opportunities for all" (United Nations Sustainable Development Goals Report, 2022). This report further states that "Providing quality education for all is fundamental to creating a peaceful and prosperous world. Education gives people the knowledge and skills they need to stay healthy, get jobs and foster tolerance." Yet it also acknowledges that "cascading and interlinked crises are putting the 2030 Agenda for Sustainable Development in grave danger, along with humanity's very own survival" (p. 3). These crises include the COVID-19 pandemic, global conflicts, and other events that have negatively affected education.

We also know that basic school infrastructure is far from universal. According to the UN Report: Global Hunger Numbers Rose to as Many as 828 Million in 2021 (2022) "about one quarter of primary schools worldwide lacked access to electricity, drinking water and basic sanitation facilities. Only half of primary schools had computers and Internet access or facilities that were fully accessible" (p. 35). Yet we also know that, at least in developed countries, school leadership is second only to classroom teaching in its impact on student learning (Leithwood et al., 2008, p. 27). Others, too, have noted the power of educational leaders. Winston Churchill recognized this power in a memoire when he asserted that "Headmasters have powers at their disposal with which Prime Ministers have never yet been invested" (Gibb, 2016). Moreover, good leadership grounded in the values of intersectionality, inclusion, equity, and belonging can overcome myriad challenges including poor facilities, limited fiscal resources, and diverse student bodies.

Transformative leadership is an appropriate leadership theory for the twenty-first century. It moves beyond technical leadership to be a critical and holistic approach to leadership that acknowledges the importance of mindsets and beliefs as well as skills and practices. Grounded in the explicit values of equity, inclusion, justice, and excellence, TLT is a theory that is anti-racist, anti-homophobic, anti-xenophobic, and much more. Moreover, TLT goes well beyond schools, to offer institutions, whether nonprofit or for-profit, governments, nongovernmental organizations (NGOs) and others, a way to ensure the success and well-being of all participants. Thus, transformative leadership has guided the charitable Mastercard foundation's work promoting education in underserved countries in Africa; it has been found to promote learning in Bolivia (Anello et al., 2014) and is the chosen theory in engineering (Jones et al., 2017) and of business writers (Caldwell et al., 2012). TLT is activist and committed to societal transformation. Thus, it is my hope that the advocacy and action inherent in transformative leadership will help leaders to achieve sustainable transformation that is both equitable and inclusive, transformation that will help to address the UN's SDG4 in schools and lead to increased development throughout the world.

References

Anello, E., Hernandez, J., Khadem, M. (2014). *Transformative leadership*. Harmony Equity Press.

Anti-defamation League. (2023). Over 85% of Americans believe in antisemitic tropes, conspiracies – Survey. Retrieved January 2023 from *I24NEWS*. https://www.i24news.tv/en/news/international/americas/1673590010-over-85-of-americans-believe-in-anti-semitic-tropes-conspiracies-survey

Bass, B. M., & Riggio, R. E. (2006). *Transformational leadership* (2nd ed.). Lawrence Erlbaum Associates.

Berryman, M. (2022). Poutama Pounamu equity, excellence, and belonging: Address delivered at the annual BELMAS/CCEAM conference, Liverpool, July. Retrieved November 2022 from https://CCEAM.net/. Understanding historical events: Leaders building stronger connections for 'all' learners (vimeo.com/735601367/0d0e9efe71).

Bieneman, P. D. (2011). Transformative leadership: The exercise of agency in educational leadership. In C. M. Shields (Ed.), *Transformative leadership* (pp. 221–237). Peter Lang Counterpoints.

Blackmore, J. (2011). Leadership in pursuit of purpose: Social, economic and political transformation. In C. M. Shields (Ed.), *Transformative leadership* (pp. 21–36). Peter Lang Counterpoints.

Blake, R. R., & Mouton, J. S. (1982). Theory and research for developing a science of leadership. *The Journal of Applied Behavioral Science, 18*(3), 275–291.

Bradford, A. (2017). What is a scientific theory?*LiveScience*. Retrieved May 2020, from, https://www.livescience.com/21491-what-is-a-scientific-theory-definition-of-theory.html

Bruce, J., & McKee K. (2020). *Transformative leadership in action: Allyship, advocacy & activism*. Emerald.

Burns, J. M. (1978). *Leadership*. Harper & Row.

Caldwell, C., Dixon, R. D., Floyd, L. A., Chaudoin, J., Post, J., & Cheokas, G. (2012). Transformative leadership: Achieving unparalleled excellence. *Journal of Business Ethics, 109*(2), 175–187.

Education 2030 Incheon Declaration and Framework for Action.(2015). Incheon Declaration and SDG4, UNESCO, Incheon, Korea. https://reliefweb.int/report/world/education-2030-incheon-declaration-towards-inclusive-and-equitable-quality-education#:~:text=The%20Education%202030%20Framework%20for%20Action%2C%20which%20provides,and%20global%20level%2C%20the%20commitment%20made%20in%20Incheon

Gibb, N. (2016). *The power of leadership, speech delivered for the Department of Education, London.* https://www.goc.uk/government/speeches/the-importance-of-school-leadership

Grumet, M. (1995). The curriculum: What are the basics and are we teaching them. In J. L. Kincheloe & S. R. Steinberg (Eds.), *Thirteen questions* (pp. 15–21). Peter Lang.

Hersey, P., Blanchard, K. H., & Natemeyer, W. E. (1979). Situational leadership, perception, and the impact of power. *Group & Organization Studies, 4*(4), 418–428.

Johnson, H. H. (2008). Mental models and transformative learning: The key to leadership development. *Human Resource Development Quarterly, 19*(1), 85–89.

Jones, S. A., Michelfelder, D., & Nair, I. (2017). Engineering managers and sustainable systems: The need for and challenges of using an ethical framework for transformative leadership. *Journal of Cleaner Production, 140*, 205–212.

Khalifa, M. A., Gooden, M. A., & Davis, J. E. (2016). Culturally responsive school leadership: A synthesis of the literature. *Review of Educational Research, 86*(4), 1272–1311.

Leithwood, K., Harris, A., & Hopkins, D. (2008). Seven strong claims about successful school leadership, *School Leadership & Management: Formerly School Organisation, 28*(1), 27–42.

Møller, J. (2011). Leadership: Democratic. In E. Baker, P. Peterson, & B. McGaw (Eds.), *International Encyclopedia of Education* (3rd ed.). Elsevier.

Nguyen, J. (2022). Don't believe everything you think: Why your thinking is the beginning & end of suffering. Amazon Kindle.

Quantz, R. A., Rogers, J., & Dantley, M. (1991). Rethinking transformative leadership: Toward democratic reform of schools. *Journal of Education, 173*(3), 96–118.

Salinas, M. F., & Garr, J. (2009). Effect of learner-centered education on the academic outcomes of minority groups. *Journal of Instructional Psychology, 36*(3), 226.

Schwartz, P., & Ogilvy, J. A. (1979). *The emergent paradigm: Changing patterns of thought and belief* (p. 13). SRI International.

Shields, C. M. (2018). *Transformative leadership in education: Equitable change in an uncertain and complex world* (2nd ed.). Routledge.

Shields, C. M. (2020). *Becoming a transformative leader*. Routledge.

Shields, C. M., Bishop, R., & Mazawi, A. E. (2005). *Pathologizing practices: Deficit thinking in education*. Peter Lang, Counterpoints.

Theoharis, G. (2007). Social justice educational leaders and resistance: Toward a theory of social justice leadership. *Educational Administration Quarterly, 43*(2), 221–258.

United Nations. (1948). Article 26. Universal Declaration of Human Rights. https://www.un.org/sites/un2.un.org/files/2021/03/udhr.pdf

United Nations. (1989). Convention on the Rights of the Child. United Nations Human Rights, Office of the High Commissioner. https://www.ohchr.org/en/instruments-mechanisms/instruments/convention-rights-child

United Nations. (2015). Millennium Development Goals and Beyond 2015. https://www.un.org/millenniumgoals/

United Nations Sustainable Development Goals Report. (2022). Retrieved January 2023 from https://un.org/sustainabledevelopment/progress-report/

UN report: Global hunger numbers rose to as many as 828 million in 2021. (2022). In *World Health Organization.* https://www.who.int/news/item/06-07-2022-un-report--global-hunger-numbers-rose-to-as-many-as-828-million-in-2021#:~:text=The%20number%20of%20people%20affected%20by%20hunger%20globally

Valencia, R. R. (2012). *The evolution of deficit thinking: Educational thought and practice.* Routledge.

van Oord, L. (2013). Towards transformative leadership in education. *International Journal of Leadership in Education: Theory and Practice, 16*(4), 419–434.

Weiner, E. J. (2003). Secretary Paulo Freire and the democratization of power: Toward a theory of transformative leadership. *Educational Philosophy and Theory, 35*(1), 89–106.

Wilson, A. (2015). *August Wilson's gem of the ocean.* Concord Theatricals.

World Health Organization (WHO). (2022, July 6). *UN report: Global hunger numbers rose to as many as 828 million in 2021.* https://www.who.int/news/item/06-07-2022-un-report--global-hunger-numbers-rose-to-as-many-as-828-million-in-2021

World Health Organization (WHO), & The United Nations Children's Fund (UNICEF). (2021). *Progress on household drinking water, sanitation, and hygiene 2000–2020: Five years into the SDGs.* https://data.unicef.org/wp-content/uploads/2021/06/JMP-2021-progress-report.pdf

Chapter 10

Research–Practice Partnership to Reform Special Education Service Delivery in Boston Public Schools

Aashna Khurana[a], Martin Scanlan[a], Julia Bott[b] and Ethan d'Ablemont Burnes[b]

[a]Boston College, USA
[b]Boston Public School, USA

Abstract

Historically, learners labeled with disabilities have been denied equal access to and opportunities in mainstream classrooms. Globally, the task of addressing marginalization entails two main approaches. Firstly, there is a need to prevent stigmatization, discrimination, and neglect. Secondly, efforts must be directed toward establishing structures and systems that enable complete and meaningful involvement within educational institutions and various sectors. Educational inequality is associated with various aspects of identity beyond disability status. Factors such as culture, language, race, and gender impact the classroom experiences of children. Consequently, schools must adopt an intersectional approach in their quest to deliver effective, accessible, and inclusive education to all children. Building from the work of UNESCO, we define inclusivity as a transformative process of educators ensuring that all children experience high-quality learning opportunities that respect and value multiple dimensions of diversity. This chapter describes an emerging research–practice partnership focused on organizational learning advancing inclusivity. The partnership is premised on supporting central office administrators and the school-based inclusion planning teams (IPTs) in a public school district implementing a comprehensive reform of their service delivery model for students labeled with disabilities. It involves supporting administrators in Boston Public Schools (BPS) in fine-tuning a theory of action (ToA), designing organizational learning processes to enact this ToA, and evaluating

Inclusive Leadership: Equity and Belonging in Our Communities
Building Leadership Bridges, Volume 9, 107–118
ISSN: 2058-8801/doi:10.1108/S2058-880120230000009010

the efficacy of the initiative in advancing effective, inclusive education for students labeled with disabilities.

Keywords: Inclusive leadership practices; organizational learning; research–practice partnership; community engaged design; system change; diversity, equity, and inclusion

Traditionally, children labeled with disabilities have been marginalized from mainstream classrooms. Around the world, efforts to confront this marginalization involve, on one hand, preventing stigma, discrimination, and neglect and, on the other hand, building infrastructure that fosters full and meaningful participation within schools as well as across sectors (United Nations Children's Fund, Disability Inclusion Policy and Strategy (DIPAS), 2022). Disability status is just one dimension of identity that correlates with educational inequity. Many other dimensions – from culture and language to race to gender – affect children's classroom experiences. Therefore, schools need to take an intersectional lens as they pursue their goal of providing teaching and learning that is effective, accessible, and inclusive for all children (Theoharis & Scanlan, 2020).

This chapter describes an emerging research–practice partnership (Penuel & Gallagher, 2017) focused on organizational learning advancing inclusivity. Building from the work of UNESCO (2019), we define inclusivity as a transformative process of educators ensuring that all children experience high-quality learning opportunities that respect and value multiple dimensions of diversity. Educators nurture inclusivity by identifying and eliminating exclusionary barriers that children experience (Scanlan, 2023). Organizational learning advances inclusivity by shaping the teaching and learning environment in a purposive manner. Our research–practice partnership uses barriers associated with service delivery to students labeled with disabilities as a starting point. We are exploring how a combination of factors – including articulating an imaginative and audacious ToA, implementing innovative policy reforms, leveraging external pressure from community stakeholders, and allocating resources strategically – is combining to overcome historic barriers to inclusivity for students labeled with disabilities, as well as barriers associated with other dimensions of identity.

The research–practice partnership we describe in this chapter is focused on supporting central office administrators and the school-based planning teams in a public school district implementing a comprehensive reform of their service delivery model for students labeled with disabilities. We begin this chapter by describing the historical context of this research–practice partnership. We then describe our theoretical framework. Next, we describe the emerging partnership itself. We conclude with implications for scholar-practitioners to improve practices of inclusive leadership.

Historical Context

For many decades, students labeled with disabilities in BPS have faced barriers to equitable opportunities to learn. In 1972, the Massachusetts General Court enacted a special needs education law, Chapter 766 of the Statutes of 1972, which was widely accepted as the far-reaching and inclusive legislation on educating people with disabilities mandating that educational services ensure the "maximum feasible benefit" to students identified with special needs and that these services be provided in the "least restrictive environment" possible. In 1975, the Massachusetts Advocacy Center released a report called "Special Education in Boston: The Mandate and the Reality," which detailed Boston's failure to comply with Chapter 766 (*Allen* v. *McDonough working files*). Following this, a lawsuit was filed on June 10, 1976, in Suffolk Superior Court by the plaintiffs of *Allen* v. *McDonough*. The suit claimed that the school system had not conducted regular reviews to track progress, failed to evaluate and prepare educational plans for referred special education students, and estimated that over 1,400 children were waiting for educational plans for more than 30 school working days. The suit was the first-class action brought against a Massachusetts school system for non-compliance with Chapter 766, and it was reported that approximately 7,250 students were awaiting a review of their educational progress.

Allen v. *McDonough working files* further mention that the *Allen* v. *McDonough* class action lawsuit (1976–1998) pressured BPS to comply with the state Special Education law Chapter 766. In the late 1980s, BPS focused on school-based management. However, the State Auditor's Report on Special Education in Massachusetts (DeNucci, 1991) published by the Office of the State Auditor, Division of Local Mandates highlighted that between 1980 and 1989 statewide public school enrollment declined by 17.4% (from 1,011,933 to 836,189 students), while special education enrollment grew by 5.6% (from 135,739 to 143,373 students). Further, as of October 1, 1990, special education enrollment (pupils ages 3–21) as compared to the total public school enrollment was 17.1%. This increase in enrollment led to a dramatic rise in the cost of providing special education services and far outpaced inflation. Of even more concern was the trend of placing more and more children in separate educational settings outside the regular classroom. This trend was expensive and, more importantly, contradicted Chapter 766 objectives by stigmatizing students through segregation from their peers and regular school activities. During 1980–1989, there was a 28% increase in the number of special education students placed in substantially or completely separate classrooms. Despite these trends, in the early 1990s, as mentioned in "A Response to the BPS Inclusion Plan" prepared by Massachusetts Advocates for Children (2013), a ray of hope was seen when three outstanding principals established varied inclusive school models at the Henderson Elementary School, the Mary Lyon School, and the Mason Elementary School.

Further, the Allen Case History section of the *Allen* v. *McDonough working files* mentioned the Arthur D. Little Report (1992) focused on mainstreaming, which became a central component of the 1993 Master Plan for Training which the superintendent sought to implement. After this, Rossman, Rallis, and Uhl (1996), who were part of the UMass Amherst School of Education research team carried out an extensive evaluation of special-education systems in eight BPS schools to examine both promising practices and systemic barriers that exist in the school system. As the *Allen* v. *McDonough* case ended in 1998, the department focused on bringing many students in segregated settings to mainstream classrooms.

Decades later, in 2013, the BPS administration reiterated its commitment to educating students labeled with disabilities in a report submitted to the School Committee titled "Increasing Inclusive Practices in the BPS." They highlighted in the report that special education must be linked with BPS Citywide Learning Standards, professional development of general and special-education teachers, linking the special education department with other BPS departments, and planning to institute data-driven instruction with standards and benchmarks. In the 2015 inclusion rollout, inclusion was understood as a "place," that is, "inclusion schools" and "inclusion rooms" in schools, wherein categorical placement of students was considered, and students were placed in rooms based on their diagnostic category. The rollout followed a service delivery model of 15:5 with a teacher and a paraprofessional.

However, despite the vast resources invested, these historical efforts have not succeeded in improving educational opportunities for students labeled with disabilities. As of October 1, 2021, the enrollment data of Massachusetts state (Massachusetts Department of Elementary and Secondary Education, 2021) and the nation (Rename this as National Center for Education Statistics, 2021) shows the rate of students in substantially separate classrooms in BPS is over twice as high as state and national rates. The students labeled with disabilities are underserved in these classrooms and face barriers that affect their learning and participation. The situation is even worse when disability status is considered alongside other dimensions of identity. For instance, in BPS, a student with an identified communication disability and who is also an English learner is over two and a half times more likely to be placed in a substantially separate classroom than native English-speaking students. As another example, BPS is over three times as likely to place Black male students experiencing emotional impairment in substantially separate classrooms than other student groups.

In response to these long-standing challenges, the central office of BPS recently embarked on a new "Inclusion Initiative" – a systematic effort to improve service delivery for students with disabilities. The Inclusion Initiative began in the summer of 2022 with a renegotiated contract between the BPS administration and the teachers' union. This new contract established a historic shared vision for and commitment to reforming special education and ensuring district-wide inclusive practices. At the heart of this reform effort is a school-based IPT, which is responsible for implementing this Inclusion Initiative in their schools. They not only play a critical role at the school level, but there are equally responsible for important systemic visions and structural changes. The ToA also focuses on the IPT learning, planning, and design work within the school should be paired with school-level efforts, supported through district-level coaching, to build educator knowledge, skill, and capacity to be effective inclusive practitioners. Further, it is pertinent for the successful implementation of this work, the central office has to change its systems, policies, and processes. If the central office does not change, it will be a barrier to IPTs making the needed changes in schools. The IPT would comprise racially diverse and include members with a variety of roles, experiences, and perspectives; at least half of the slots on the IPT are reserved for members of the Teachers Union. The size of the IPT can vary based on the principal's discretion. Beyond school employees, the IPT can include parents and caregivers, school council members, and community partners. The research–practice partnership discussed in this chapter aims to assist both the BPS central office administrators and the school-based IPTs in implementing this Inclusion Initiative.

Theoretical Framework

Research–practice partnerships, generally speaking, are collaborations between educators and external partners seeking to leverage research in manners that advance educational improvement (Penuel & Gallagher, 2017). Guiding principles include sustaining the partnerships over time, leveraging diverse expertise, and sharing power in decision-making among the partners (Farrell et al., 2021).

Our research–practice partnership seeks to support organizational learning to advance inclusivity. Literature on the education of students labeled with disabilities points to important educational and social benefits of inclusion (Florian, 2015; Florian et al., 2017). Further, such literature emphasizes that models of service delivery structure the degree of inclusivity in a school community (Capper & Frattura, 2009), and that school administrators play a central role in creating and implementing policies to transform these service delivery models toward inclusion (McLeskey et al., 2016; Villa & Thousand, 2017).

Theoharis et al. (2020) describe a multifaceted process for organizational learning advancing inclusivity. A foundational element is establishing, committing to, and communicating a bold, clear vision of inclusion. The process requires engaging varied stakeholders (e.g., teachers, parents, and administrators) on a collaborative team charged with articulating and pursuing this vision. This collaborative team uses techniques to establish a shared understanding of the current situation. These include auditing current practices to determine trends and patterns and mapping service delivery to illustrate human resource allocation. The team then formulates strategies for reforming the teaching and learning environment to come into alignment with their new vision of inclusion. These strategies transform classroom practices through shifts in staffing structures and improved instructional capacity. The process is iterative and adjusted based on ongoing formative feedback from all stakeholders (educators, students, and families).

One specific assessment tool supporting organizational learning advancing inclusivity is the Schoolwide Integrated Framework for Transformation-Fidelity Integrity Assessment (SWIFT-FIA). SWIFT-FIA focuses on five major domains (see Table 10.1). Schools and school systems use SWIFT-FIA to monitor their progress in these domains and to adjust their action plans based on this progress. Since BPS has adopted the SWIFT-FIA framework, we incorporate this tool in our theoretical framework for the research–practice partnership.

Emerging Research–Practice Partnership

We now turn to describe how an emergent research–practice partnership between Boston College and BPS is striving to support organizational learning advancing inclusivity. This collaborative work seeks to be mutually beneficial, with BPS

Table 10.1.   SWIFT Domains and Core Features.

SWIFT Domain	SWIFT Core Features
Administrative leadership	• Strong and engaged site leadership
	• Strong educator support system
Multi-tiered system of support	• Inclusive academic instruction
	• Inclusive behavior instruction
Integrated education framework	• Fully integrated organizational structure
	• Positive and strong school culture
Family and community engagement	• Fully integrated organizational structure
	• Positive and strong school culture
Inclusive policy structure & practice	• Strong LEA (district)/school relationship
	• LEA (district) policy framework

driving the research focus. The goal of the research–practice partnership is to support BPS in implementing its Inclusion Initiative. The work of the research–practice partnership began in the fall of 2022, with a series of meetings between BPS administrators leading the Inclusion Initiative and members of the Boston College community. These four individuals served as the planning team guiding the emergent partnership. The work has focused on three areas: articulating a coherent ToA shaping it, building human resource capacity to enact it, and crafting formative and summative processes to evaluate the progress and performance.

Articulating the ToA

Initial planning team meetings surfaced the centrality of the ToA guiding the implementation process. The team discussed how an explicit ToA (see Fig. 10.1) provides clear guidance for allocating resources, testing hypotheses, and iterating action.

Early in the process, the BPS administrators captured their ToA in an Inclusion Implementation Process Guide (see Fig. 10.2). This guide identifies a bold, clear vision to educate students labeled with disabilities inclusively as the foundational driver of implementation (top row). It also identifies collaboration among all stakeholders as an essential component of the process (row 2). These two dimensions work in tandem.

Framing this vision statement will require the participation of all the stakeholders (community, parents, students, teachers, staff), considering their voices, their collective agreement, and the circulation of the final statement among all of them. While the vision statement is being framed, it is pertinent to think about how the vision centers the students/communities with the greatest needs, particularly Black, Latinx, Asian, and Multilingual learners, students with disabilities, students, and families. Part of collaborative planning and implementing inclusive

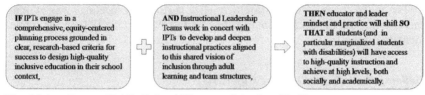

Fig. 10.1.   Boston Public School Theory of Action (ToA)

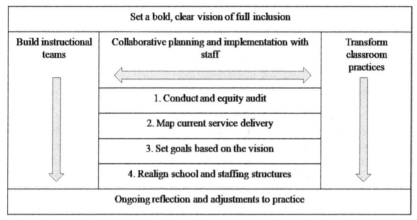

Fig. 10.2.   Inclusion Implementation Process Guide.

reform is creating a climate of belonging. Further, this aligns with the BPS Equity Impact Analysis Tool that lays out a clear process and a set of questions to guide the development, implementation, and evaluation of significant policies, initiatives, professional development, programs, instructional practices, and budget issues to explicitly and intentionally create equity.

The center column of the Process Guide presents four steps to enact the vision, specifically by reforming the service delivery model. The first steps involve assessing the current situation in the school community by gathering data about current trends and patterns (equity audit) and mapping the existing service delivery model. The next step is to set goals aligning with the school's vision. The final step is to develop a plan for realigning the staffing and scheduling in a manner that meets these goals. The IPT is charged with leading these four steps. "Setting the vision" is not just the first step in this process, but it is also iterative. This allows schools to think about their unique context – demographics, programming, the concentration of need and begin to envision what a more inclusive school community would look like for the students they serve.

Finally, the Process Guide articulates two parallel processes that must accompany these steps: building instructional teams (left column) and transforming classroom practices (right column). Thus, this Process Guide strives to create a visual representation of how the IPT can lead the school community in implementing the Inclusion Initiative.

The initial focus of the research–practice partnership meetings was making this working ToA explicit, helping BPS administrators guide IPTs in the implementation process.

Building the Human Resource Capacity

A second focus of this research–practice partnership is building human resource capacity to enact the working ToA illustrated in the Process Guide (Fig. 10.2). Toward this end, the BPS administrators planned and engaged in a series of meetings to coach an initial cohort of IPTs during the fall and spring of 2022. Ongoing research–practice partnership planning team meetings created space for critically reflecting on this process.

Data Analysis Steps

The first two steps of the Process Guide both involve engaging with data. For the equity audit step, the BPS administrators coached team members to examine current data (i.e., student achievement data, student staff/climate data, agendas, classroom observations) to notice pertinent patterns and trends (e.g., disproportionality in student achievement across classroom setting, discipline referrals, classroom assignments). IPTs synthesized components to identify bright spots, areas for growth, and lingering questions.

For mapping the current service delivery model, BPS administrators guided IPT members in creating new data in the form of visual representations of the student patterns and human resource distribution. These indicated the classrooms, special education service provision, general education classrooms, and how students receive their related services. These provided a comprehensive picture of how and where staff at the school work and showed patterns of the student movement, including movement among classrooms. Again, BPS administrators provided coaching to focus attention. For instance, they used reflection prompts to draw attention to trends for students labeled with disabilities, as well as across other dimensions of identity, such as race and ethnicity, gender identity, and cultural and linguistic diversity. These led to discussions of where concentrations of need exist, followed by brainstorming possible ways to reconfigure service delivery.

To promote the analysis of data from both the equity audit and service delivery map, BPS administrators invited IPT members to read the chapter on "proportional representation" from Theoharis and Scanlan's (2020) book, *Leadership for Increasingly Diverse Schools*. This helped establish a baseline understanding for critiquing service delivery models for students labeled with disabilities in particular while attending to the intersection of this with other dimensions of identity. They provided IPTs guiding questions to bring to their data analysis, such as:

- Where do you notice that students are concentrated? Why do you think this is?
- Where do you notice staff are allocated to service students? Why?
- Where and how does this align (or misalign) with our school's vision of inclusive education?

Goal Setting and Realignment

The third and fourth stages of the Process Guide (Fig. 10.2) involve setting goals based on the vision and realigning school and staffing structures to pursue these goals. Again, BPS administrators focused on building the human capacity within the IPTs to pursue both of these goals, which worked in tandem. They guided IPTs to set goals that were specific, measurable, achievable, relevant, and time-bound and how to make specific shifts in areas of staffing, professional learning, and school routines to pursue these. For example, a school setting a broad goal: "We will increase partial- to full-inclusive opportunities for students in the Social and Academic Remediation (SAR) and Applied Behavior Analysis (ABA) setting for further access to grade-level standards." To achieve this goal, they identified objectives in various domains:

- *Staffing:* Increasing staffing to match the level of need across grade levels and specials, working toward multi-licensed staff, and increase in inclusion specialist positions.
- *Professional learning:* Build coaches/admin capacity to support educators to implement high-quality, accessible tier 1 instruction; equitable coaching across the school that includes Applied Behavior Analysis/Substantially separate classroom (ABA/SAR).
- *Structures and systems:* Grade-level alignment with schedules that allows for inclusive specials and related services scheduled by grade span and not caseload.
- *Family engagement:* Supporting families to understand human differences; providing clear, strength-based language to engage in dialogues and shared learning around human differences (cognitive disabilities and autism), and increased opportunities for conversations around supports and inclusive models.

The last stage involved realigning the school structures. This stage involved the rethinking of and reconfiguring structures and the use of staff to create teams of professionals to better serve the heterogeneous student groups, in other words, creating a new service delivery map. This necessitated balanced student needs across all classrooms and kept the natural proportion front and center. Centering the natural proportion meant that there will be an equal distribution of children with disabilities and/or racially diverse learners across all sections. The proportion of students who need support in each classroom should mirror the total proportion of students labeled with disabilities and/or racially diverse learners in the school.

As the teams progressed through these stages, they also focused on building instructional teams. This meant rethinking their staffing models and structures that involved creating teams of general education teachers, specialists, and paraprofessionals to serve the students inclusively. Developing teams involved bringing together professionals to work together to inclusively meet the needs of all children and also involved revising roles if needed. IPTs in the school reconsidered their coaching models, staffing structures, and teaching preferences. They carried out long-term planning with their staff to identify areas such as hiring, licensure, co-planning, professional development, family/community engagement, student

Fig. 10.3.   Inclusion Initiative Evaluation Process.

participation and engagement, collaboration, etc. that they want to focus on to reform inclusive practices in their school. Additionally, there was also a focus on transforming classroom practices, wherein the school leaders observed the teaching practices, gave feedback to their staff, and encouraged collaboration to improve the delivery of instruction. There has been a focus on strengthening the instructional core (tier 1 practices) and building all educators' capacity to provide access to rigorous content in the Least Restrictive Environment (LRE). This has been concurrent development work with schools and will also emerge as a continuous focus from the planning process. During the meetings, BPS Central Office personnel referenced Department of Elementary and Secondary Education's (DESE's) Multi-Tiered System of Supports (MTSS) blueprint a lot to emphasize the importance of tier 1 as the foundation of successful inclusive schools.

Formative and Summative Evaluation Processes

A final focus of this emerging research–practice partnership is evaluation. In the initial planning meetings, BPS administrators raised queries regarding what made for an effective IPT. The discussions led to conceptualizing ways to measure progress across each step of the Inclusion Initiative Process Guide – from setting the vision to engaging in the four stages of implementing this vision (Fig. 10.2). This led to explicating a process for providing IPTs formative feedback on this implementation to help them make course-correcting decisions as they implement the working ToA (Fig. 10.3). The goal is for all BPS to establish an IPT and move through this process, so clear evaluation criteria for each stage are essential.

Some examples of the iterative process of evaluation work are illustrative. For instance, during the fall, it became clear that the preliminary work – namely "setting a bold, clear vision for inclusion" – varied across IPTs. As a result, BPS coaches engaged in providing feedback to each team. The coaches created a working document entitled "What is a vision/What is not a vision" to level-set expectations among the IPTs. As another example, the university partners drafted a preliminary multi-stage evaluation plan for IPTs that aligned with the four stages of implementation. This plan includes formative feedback to measure progress at each of these stages. Currently, they are gathering feedback from IPT members on these tools. The outstanding questions related to this work relate to determining the right scale to measure the progress and identifying ways to capture the supporting evidence.

Implications

The goal of the emerging research–practice partnership between Boston College and BPS described in this chapter is to support organizational learning advancing inclusivity in BPS. In this final section, we step back from this to discuss two implications for how research–practice partnerships can help catalyze and drive systemic service delivery reform for students labeled with disabilities, in particular, and with traditionally marginalized students more generally.

One implication is the important ways that research–practice partnerships scaffold a "research practitioner stance" among all participants: those in the institute of higher education as well as those working in the schools and district. The three initial steps in this partnership, normalizing the use of theory, data, and measurement, illustrate this. The research practitioner's stance nudges all participants to reflect critically on policy implementation. Given the considerable existential pressures they face, Prekindergarten to Grade 12 (PK-12) educators often find themselves approaching policy implementation with a compliance-driven mindset. Given their distance from the practice, university partners often find themselves detached from the complicated realities of policy implementation. Collaboratively working together can create synergies allowing partners to complement one another. A research practitioner stance pushes the educators working at the school and district level to explicate the theory driving their work and pushes the educators in institutes of higher education to identify in a more grounded manner how theory is enacted.

A second implication is that research–practice partnerships scaffold boundary-spanning within complex educational ecosystems. In such ecosystems, formal and informal barriers tend to divide individuals. These occur both intra- and inter-organizationally. In intra-schools, educators are often divided from one another both within roles (e.g., teachers divided from fellow teachers) and across roles (e.g., teachers divided from support staff and administrators). Such divisions are exacerbated at other levels, such as inter-schools and between schools and central offices. Research–practice partnerships present novel opportunities for interrupting these divisions insofar as external partners – in this case, university personnel – can serve to broker roles, enhance communication, and promote collaboration.

These two implications – encouraging participants toward a research-practitioner stance and scaffolding boundary-spanning – point toward how this nascent research–practice partnership is helping promote organizational learning advancing inclusivity in BPS. While it remains to be seen whether this partnership will take root and mature in a sustainable, iterative manner, initial indications are hopeful.

References

Allen v. McDonough working files, 0450.003-II. City of Boston Archives. Retrieved February 24, 2023, from https://archives.cityofboston.gov/repositories/2/resources/201

Capper, C., & Frattura, E. (2009). *Meeting the needs of students of all abilities: How leaders go beyond inclusion* (2nd ed.). Corwin Press, Inc.

DeNucci, A. J. (1991). *The state auditor's report on special education in Massachusetts.* Division of Local Mandates. https://www.mass.gov/doc/special-education-in-massachusetts/download

Farrell, C., Penuel, W., Coburn, C., Daniel, J., & Steup, L. (2021). *Research–practice partnerships in education: The state of the field.* William T. Grant Foundation.

Florian, L. (2015). *Inclusive pedagogy: A transformative approach to understanding and responding to individual differences* (C. of H. and S. Science, Ed.). University of Edinburgh. https://youtu.be/LeeDwzZwTj8

Florian, L., Black-Hawkins, K., & Rouse, M. (2017). *Achievement and inclusion in schools* (2nd ed.). Routledge.

Inclusion plan 2013 response – Boston Public Schools. (n.d.). Retrieved February 28, 2023, from https://www.bostonpublicschools.org/cms/lib07/MA01906464/Centricity/Domain/249/Inclusion%20Plan%202013%20Response.pdf

Massachusetts Department of Elementary and Secondary Education. (2021, October 1). *Enrollment of students with disabilities.* Retrieved January 24, 2023, from https://www.doe.mass.edu/infoservices/reports/enroll/default.html?yr=sped2122

McLeskey, J., Billingsley, B., & Waldron, N. L. (2016). Principal leadership for effective inclusive schools. In J. P. Bakken & F. E. Obiakor (Eds.), *General and special education inclusion in an age of change: Roles of professionals involved* (Vol. 32, pp. 55–74). Emerald Group Publishing Limited. https://doi.org/10.1108/S0270-401320160000032005

National Center for Education Statistics. (2021, October 1). *Students with disabilities.* Retrieved January 24, 2023, from https://nces.ed.gov/programs/coe/indicator/cgg/students-with-disabilities

Penuel, W., & Gallagher, D. (2017). *Creating research–practice partnerships in education.* Harvard Education Press.

Rossman, G. B., Rallis, S. F., & Uhl, S. (1996). *A formative evaluation of the Boston Public Schools' special education initiative on inclusion.* University of Massachusetts at Amherst School of Education. http://works.bepress.com/gretchen_rossman/57/

Scanlan, M. (2023). *Navigating social justice: A schema for educational leadership.* Harvard Education Press.

Theoharis, G., Causton, J., Woodfield, C., & Scriber, S. (2020). Inclusive leadership and disability. In G. Theoharis & M. Scanlan (Eds.), *Leadership for increasingly diverse schools* (2nd ed., pp. 17–55). Routledge.

Theoharis, G., & Scanlan, M. (Eds.). (2020). Leadership for Increasingly Diverse Schools (2nd ed.). Routledge. https://doi.org/10.4324/9780429356261

UNESCO. (2019). *Cali commitment to equity and inclusion in education.* UNESCO. https://unesdoc.unesco.org/ark:/48223/pf0000370910

United Nations Children's Fund, Disability Inclusion Policy and Strategy (DIPAS). (2022). *UNICEF disability policy and strategy: 2022–2030.* UNICEF.

Villa, R. A., & Thousand, J. S. (2017). *Leading an inclusive school: Access and success for ALL students.* ASCD.

Part Three

The Application and Practice of Diversity, Equity, Inclusion, and Belonging/Accessibility

Chapter 11

An Inclusive Language of Diversity

Bjørn Zakarias Ekelund

Human Factors AS, Norway

Abstract

In this chapter, I present a concept named Diversity Icebreaker® where the participants in a seminar are categorized along red, blue, and green dimensions based on a psychological assessment. The participants co-create the meaning of the dimensions in mono-colored groups due to their dominant scores where they describe themselves and others from inside and outside perspectives. Blue is more task and detail oriented. Green is more holistic and future oriented. Red is more social and communicative oriented. The language as a metaphorical structure as well as the seminar builds a culture of inclusivity. The simplicity and easiness of mastery of the categories make it easy for everyone to apply the categories. The social co-creation of the categories makes every participant at an even level. The colors are defined reciprocally strengthening the needs of the others. Everyone has all colors which makes it easier to connect and see commonalities that build cohesion. In the seminar, participants experience uncertainty followed by dialogues with others. Positive emotions and insight reinforce the script of "dialoguing with others when uncertainties arise." The positivity and humor in the seminar reinforce the behavior of being together. The closure is a collective reflexivity process where all participants have even possibility to contribute due to their unique perspectives on their shared experience. I end this chapter with reflections and questions on leadership models in this seminar that has evolved in a Norwegian context and their relevance in a global context.

Keywords: Co-creation; language; inclusion; diversity; leadership; culture

Inclusive Leadership: Equity and Belonging in Our Communities
Building Leadership Bridges, Volume 9, 121–131
Copyright © 2023 by Emerald Publishing Limited
All rights of reproduction in any form reserved
ISSN: 2058-8801/doi:10.1108/S2058-880120230000009011

Introduction

> Unifying and diversifying are two interdependent processes.
> (Ekelund & Matoba, 2015, p. 85).

In the professional context for diversity, equity, inclusion, and belonging, there has been a strong focus on groups that are discriminated against and measures taken to compensate. Dominating distinctions have been made in gender and race or sexual preferences and cultural background. Other types of diversity categories are included when talking about diversity management. Most often categories are made that make distinctions between people, where people are or they are not. Often diversity categories lead to making distinctions and organizing people in groups. In this chapter, I will introduce a concept that introduces a diversity model of cognitive and social style that categorizes people and make distinctions, but the distinctions belong to a larger whole. As such, the diversity model unifies and diversifies at the same time. The diversity model is named Diversity Icebreaker®.

Diversity Icebreaker® History

Diversity Icebreaker® is a seminar where participants are categorized along red, blue, and green dimensions. These diversity categories were defined in 1995 as three distinct communication styles that were chosen for public communication and consultation to reduce energy consumption (Ekelund, 1997). Blue communication style was detailed, facts oriented, and practical. Green communication style was enthusiastic, visionary, and creative. The red communication style focused on relations, feelings, and harmony. Savings were five times the costs in five months in one of the largest counties in Norway. Due to the success, more research was asked for, and a questionnaire was made to map individual differences along the red, blue, and green dimensions. The questionnaire looked like a very simple team-role concept, a reduced version of the Margerison & McCann Team Performance Inventory (Margerison & McCann, 1991). In the consultation company, we started to use this questionnaire as an icebreaker in team development (Ekelund & Jørstad, 2002), and since we at that time had very little empirical research that clarified the meaning of the three colors, we created a seminar where participants were asked to identify the qualities of each color. The Diversity Icebreaker® seminar found its standard form five years later. It has gradually become a starting point of learning and development processes where the scope is much wider than team development. Today, diversity issues, communication, teamwork, leadership development, and change in organizational culture seem to be the dominant areas of use. A high degree of involvement and engagement seems to be an essential quality that makes it easier to move on to other subjects of concern.

From Classical Psychological Assessment of an Individual's Qualities to a Multidisciplinary Approach

The structure of the Diversity Icebreaker® seminar is like this:
Stage 1: Participants fill out the questionnaire and receive their scores.

Table 11.1.   Core Concepts in Each Color.

Red	Blue	Green
Feelings	Concrete	Big picture
People-oriented	Practical	Possibilities
Interaction	Facts	Future
Easygoing	Details	Ambitions
Patient	Logical	New ideas

Stage 2: Participants are divided into three, color-specific groups (red, blue, or green) depending upon the color in which each individual scores highest. Most often, we recommend creating even numbered groups, an element that creates a kind of equal balance in the room. If there are too few people with, for example, red-dominant preference, we ask participants who are close to red as a dominant preference to join the red group. Each group gets 2 questions: What are the positive qualities of your color? How do you describe the other two colors? The last question opens the possibility of writing both positive and negative qualities. But since the group starts with a positive self-description, they enter question 2 with a primary positive approach. The duality in question 2 most often is a topic that is discussed internally in each group during the writing.

The meaning of the categories is co-created in the seminar when participants anchor and objectify the categories in a relevant way for themselves. They create a local meaning around the core concepts of each color (see Table 11.1).

Stage 3: Each of the color-specific groups presents their work to the whole group – one color per round. For example, the blue group starts with their color, followed by the red and green groups presenting what they wrote about blue. This series is then repeated for the other two colors.

Stage 4: The facilitator asks: "What can we learn from this? What can we apply to the practice of interacting with others on a day-to-day basis?" Participants share their reflections as a whole group and arrive at various learning points (e.g., "We need all the colors" or "We all share some qualities of each of the colors, but to different extents," "It is ok to be different if I know that the others appreciate this and I have a role to play," etc.).

Multidisciplinary Ground Structure

The seminar is a multidisciplinary experience inspired by modern disciplines such as psychology, sociology, linguistics, and pedagogics (Ekelund et al., 2009). Its paradigmatic ground structure is constituted by three main differences in scientific traditions. Stage 1 where participants assess themselves using a psychological assessment is a natural science-inspired test psychology. In stages 2 and 3, there are elements of social psychological traditions with group dynamics (Tajfel & Turner, 1979) and attribution theories (Jones & Nisbett, 1972). Participants are anchoring and objectifying (Moscovici, 1984) the red, blue, and green categories.

In the fourth stage, participants are invited to reflect upon the process where a natural scientific-oriented product becomes meaningful by groups exemplifying the different color categories. In the reflexivity process in the fourth stage, there are possibilities of facilitating the process in many directions, including asking the essential humanistic questions "Who am I/we? Who do I/we want to be?" It is also possible to make participants aware of the different scientific paradigms in the seminar and use the pedagogical structure as an entrance to theories of science and a model of multidisciplinarity (Ekelund, 2019).

Validity and Reliability of the Assessment

When introducing a new concept with three dimensions that have not been described before, the question of reliability and validity in the assessment tool is a critical element for legitimacy and applicability in research. The first assessment in 1997 had an ipsative format with reliabilities between 0.62 and 0.75. The semi-ipsative format in 2005 had 0.75–0.81 which is satisfactory (Langvik, 2009). The version in 2015 where we use the Likert format when participants score themselves have reliabilities at the same level. The assessment has since 2013 been certified due to European test-psychology standards, so internal consistency is good.

Concerning validity, it is not easy to use criterion validity since what we assess are new categories. The categories of red, blue, and green were formed by focus groups searching for answers to the question "What types of communicative behavior are relevant to consider to make the receiver/consumer change consumer behavior." The assessment was meant to map preferences for information content and form for senders and receivers. Factor analysis was not applied when categories first time was tested in a questionnaire but cluster analysis (Hegge, 1997).

Construct validity is a validity form (Campbell & Fiske, 1959; Cronbach & Meehl, 1955) that is most relevant since this gives us some indication of how the red, blue, and green dimensions are related to already established concepts and knowledge. And with this ambition, studies have been done in relation to Big 5, Myers-Briggs type indiciator (MBTI), emotional intelleigence (EQ), etc. (Ekelund & Pluta, 2015). This type of knowledge seems to also create legitimacy among people who have a preference for natural and social science model in mind when evaluating the quality of psychological tests. This is also important to create an attractive research interaction with empirically oriented academics leading to both important practices and research. Our history of the two edited research volumes illustrates this aim (Ekelund & Langvik, 2008; Ekelund & Pluta, 2015).

I strongly believe this type of knowledge has contributed to the success of the Diversity Icebreaker®. But I look upon this knowledge as a necessity for legitimacy among professionals. I think there are other qualities in the seminar that is important to understand the extended growth of the concept in the market. I think the effect of the Diversity Icebreaker® seminar in the short and long terms is important to consider to explain its success. This is described as functional validity in the context of validity studies (Messick, 1995). I also think that these effects lead us to a better understanding of what I call the inclusivity effect of the Diversity Icebreaker® seminar and the language of red, blue, and green.

How to describe this? I will in the next section highlight seven different perspectives that I think are explanatory factors. I will refer to research and use phrases heard during seminars and feedback from long-term customers in an organization where the language has become a part of their organizational culture and sentences gathered in qualitative research (Ekelund & Langvik, 2008).

The Inclusive and Functional Qualities of the Diversity Icebreaker® Seminar

What are the seven perspectives I think can explain the inclusivity effect?

1. Simplicity and mastery of the model:

It has been argued by one of our largest customers when they decided to use the model in their global merger with 2,000 leaders: "The model is easy to understand and it easy to master."

It is only three dimensions, red, blue, and green. And the categories look like other three-dimensional models like heart, head, and hand; thinking, feeling, and behavior; task, people, and change; ethos, logos, and pathos. The simplicity makes it easy for everyone involved independent of positions and knowledge to grasp the main elements. It makes everyone feel like to be at the same mastery level.

The participants develop a language that can be used approaching strangers. Participants whom you do not know can be identified and named in the language of red, blue, and green. "Reframing Others in Colours of Mastery" is one of our conference titles that is inspired by these qualities (Ekelund & Pluta, 2017).

2. The social co-creation of the categories seen from inside and outside:

In stage 2, the mono-colored in-groups define their positive qualities. This is the actor's self-perspective. When they describe others, it is from the other's perspective. The short time for in-group self-description, normally about 5–10 minutes, does not allow for a deeper search for inner personal unconscious dynamics. Most normally, the descriptions describe communication, behavior, and motivation. Then, the focus in stage 3 is on sharing and learning from others, the social interaction, and reciprocal perception between people in the mono-colored groups. It is about perceptions of self and others with a positive approach and a minor focus on the negative sides. There is no expert knowledge or experts that know better. The answer is not in an advanced book or research that the more competent people know of.

3. Reciprocal definition of social identity that does not exclude:

The psychological research tells us that participants' answers on the Diversity Icebreaker® questionnaire are formed by personality, cognitive style, and values (Ekelund & Pluta, 2015). In the seminars, their social identity is formed by what words they create about themselves inside the mono-colored group and through the lenses of others defined by participants with other color qualities. As an individual participant, you are not alone. You belong to a group with similar color preferences. And in the learning process in stage 4, the focus will often be: "Each group has qualities that are important for the others. All colors are needed to solve a complex problem. All people are needed to complete the full picture of diversity."

While categorizing participants in groups based on their dominant color, the Diversity Icebreaker® process simultaneously unifies all individuals in a kind of Yan–Yin relationship. Blue is detailed oriented, and green is not detail-oriented but sees the large picture. Red is concerned with the harmony of blue and green when working together. Colors are partly defined by the qualities of the others. At the end of stage 4, the participants expressed that people from all colors are needed to solve a complex problem. At the collective level, each person in the whole group is unified, while diversified at the individual level and yet still belonging to the whole group. They are a part of the Gestalt (Ekelund & Matoba, 2015).

Unlike many other categorization processes, the Diversity Icebreaker® categories of red, blue, and green do not exclude. For this reason, "re-inclusion" is not an issue when these categories are applied. This fundamentally inclusive quality makes the categories of Diversity Icebreaker® systematically different from categories founded on visible and less visible physiological and socially constructed differences, like "race, ethnic/cultural background, gender, sexual orientation, religion, and genetic, physical and mental differences."

4. *No one is either or*:

In the seminar, people are at the beginning positioned in groups based on their dominant color. But the results given to each individual reflect the results on all three dimensions. For example, blue: 75, red: 30, and green: 45. It seems that this reduces single-minded stigmatization of having only one preference. And it makes it easier and more relevant to perceive oneself and others as flexible persons. A button is given to participants as a funny reminder and an identity marker. The blue button has the text "… but also Red and Green."

Since each individual has all three colors as personal qualities at different levels, it makes a platform of common ground even though each person has a dominant score in one color. It makes it easier to see the other's primary preference through the lenses of one's nondominant preferences.

Red, blue, and green are categories that diversify and unify at the same time. They are categories of diversity where everyone has three colors in common. In working together in teams, people with different primary preferences need each other to solve problems.

5. *An inclusive learning culture*:

We often see that participants leave the room after the seminar, dialogically interested in talking with each other. This can be explained by the classical and operant conditioning of talking with each other when there is something you do not know.

Three times participants are in anxious situations of not-knowing, and the solutions evolve as a consequence of talking with others. It happens the first time when they do not know what the colors mean, but inside the mono-colored group, some positive answers are created. Second, when the awareness evolves of behaving politically not correctly by self-bragging and both negative and positive descriptions of the other groups. This is reconciled when communication between the groups shows that they all have been doing the same and that it is not dangerous to voice negativity if it can be phrased in a way and context where it is meant to be a part of developing a shared understanding. Third time when participants are uncomfortable with the disparities of perspectives from the mono-colored groups and would like to see a collective meaningful integration. This integration evolves when participants share answers to the question, "What have we learned from this experience?" From a behavioral learning perspective, participants are reinforced three times with new knowledge and relief from uncomfortable feelings. The consequence is that when the stimulus is "I/we do not know," the reinforced behavior is "communicate with others."

Experimental research shows that following the Diversity Icebreaker® seminar, the participants seem to be in a climate with positivity and awareness of others leading to a creative psychological safe situation where it is easier to voice (Arieli et al., 2018). This safe learning space may be one of the reasons why it is easy for participants to discuss more sticky diversity issues that have history, identity, and unconscious elements embedded in them (Ekelund & Maznevski, 2008).

6. *The positivity and humor*:

There are many elements of positivity and humor in the Diversity Icebreaker® seminar. Being together with positive affect reinforces the behavior of being together. The memory of having fun together with people voicing different perspectives promotes the attractiveness of meeting others in a similar multiple perspectives dialogue. The diverse perspective is an integrated part of wishes for how to be together. It forms expectations of future behavioral qualities of being together (Arieli et al., 2018; Brannen et al., 2016; Pluta, 2015; Straume & Ekelund, 2005).

7. *Collective reflexivity as a unifying process*:

When participants reflect upon their shared seminar experiences in stage 4, they execute a process where everyone is involved at the same level. They are invited to share ideas, from a bird's perspective, and what they all experienced. Insightful comments from individuals contribute to creating shared learning points. Most often, the participants mention qualities of equality, complementarity, inclusion, and belonging. The Diversity Icebreaker® diversity concepts of red, blue, and green are unified through the need for each other to solve complex problems. It unifies and diversifies at the same time managing the important complexity paradox in diversity management. As such, the categories contribute to building an organizational culture with an inclusive language representing shared mental models that have high levels of functional validity in interpersonal interactions and problem-solving.

Alternative Models of Leadership

Although leadership is often related to the individual behavior of the leader, inclusiveness is an interpersonal phenomenon where employee feelings of belonging and interdependency are important success criteria. The Diversity Icebreaker® is an experiential learning that does *not* have the individual leader behavior in focus. A leader can decide to invest time to arrange these seminars and promote a design of work and communication aligned with these ideas, meaning creating space. A leader can role model and communicate in a supportive way the appreciation of diverse perspectives from employees with diverse backgrounds. But the essential elements of learning are co-created among the participants without any contribution from an organizational leader due to his/her role as a leader. As such, it illustrates a leadership model that focuses on how to facilitate employees in their goal-setting, problem-solving, and self-understanding through these processes.

Cross-cultural Issues

The Diversity Icebreaker® concept was developed in Norway in the period from 1995 to 2005. Since 2007, the assessment and seminar have been applied by more than 400,000 participants in more than 75 countries. It has been described as a valuable tool in cross-cultural teaching processes in international journals (Orgeret, 2012; Romani, 2013), in diversity processes for innovation (Urstad, 2012), and it has been presented at multiple international professional and academic conferences (Ekelund, 2019). Even though it has been used in multiple countries, it is still a hidden treasure for most trainers and leaders worldwide. Of course, one explanation is the historical importance of local path dependency, and a company that is inside a national market pushes the concept. And then, the liability of foreigners is always a hindrance in another country.

But besides these normal economic considerations, are there any unique cultural components?

What Cultural Qualities Have Stimulated This Growth in Norway?

Norway is an anti-authoritarian, people-oriented society with a high degree of involvement, and the team focuses on work contexts (Ekelund, 2009; Hofstede, 2001; Smith et al., 2003). There is a high degree of trust, and economic disparities are low. An internal cultural self-description for all Scandinavian countries is the Jante-law (Sandemose, 1936), which states that no one is better than others. If you try to stand out by acting differently, sanctions are easily triggered (Gelfand et al., 2011). The Diversity Icebreaker® highlights the unique positive qualities of each color but at the same time does not indicate that one color is more important than the other. The seminar format where people are distributed with even numbers in each color group reinforces this implicit understanding of the balance between the colors. As such, the Diversity

Icebreaker® promotes positive self-representation, but at the same time, no one is more important or better than others. In one way, it becomes an element of the anti-Jante-law discourse in Scandinavian societies but with elements of equality (Levison, 2012).

What Cultural Qualities Are Important to Consider in a Global Application of the Concept?

The field of cross-cultural management brings forward the awareness of cultural differences in managerial practices (Hofstede, 2001; Lane et al., 2000). Considering Diversity Icebreaker® in different cultures, we see similarities with what should be expected due to similarities in individual and collective value systems, meaning that the prevalence of red correlates with collectivism (Ekelund et al., 2009). Concerning the seminar experiences, in African contexts, no significant cross-cultural challenges have been reported after 35 seminars in 14 different African countries (Canney-Davison et al., 2016). In the Scandinavian context, the Diversity Icebreaker® contributes to individuals standing out positively, expecting to be included based on their unique contribution and being respected for voicing their perspectives in discussions. In more authoritarian societies, we may expect that participants will be more restrained by the leader's explicit and implicit norms. In more individualistic societies, we may expect the qualities of awareness of others (Arieli et al., 2018) and the need for others to solve complex problems to be potential benefits. These are questions for further research.

References

Arieli, S., Rubel-Lifshitz, T., Elster, A., Sagiv, L., & Ekelund, B. Z. (2018, January 3). *Psychological safety, group diversity, and creativity* [Conference session]. Israel organizational behavior conference, Tel-Aviv, Israel.

Brannen, M. Y., Brannen, N. C., Ekelund, S. M., & Ekelund, B. Z. (2016, May 18). *A trajectory theory of language development in organizations following Diversity Icebreaker seminars* [Conference session]. EAWOP congress, Oslo.

Campbell, D. T., & Fiske, D. W. (1959). Convergent and discriminant validation by the multitrait–multimethod matrix. *Psychological Bulletin* ,*56*, 81–105.

Canney-Davison, S., Ekelund, B. Z. Gjerde, S. Boodhun, V., Guttormsgard, I., Malde, Y. S., Handeland, A. Dahlmann, O. P., Gyan, K. A., Dybwad, A. Johnston, K., Fjell, K., & Lane, H. (2016, January 8). *Trainer experiences applying Diversity Icebreaker in 15 African countries* [Paper presentation]. African Academy of Management, Nairobi, Kenya.

Cronbach, A. B., & Meehl, P. E. (1955). Construct validity in psychological tests. *Psychological Bulletin, 52*, 281–302.

Ekelund, B. Z. (1997). *The application of a model which integrates market segmentation and psychological theories to change energy consumption in households* [MBA Dissertation]. Henley Management College/Brunel University.

Ekelund, B. Z. (2009). Cultural perspectives on team consultation in Scandinavia: Experiences and reflections. *Scandinavian Journal of Organizational Psychology, 2*, 31–40.

Ekelund B. Z. (2019). *Unleashing the power of diversity: How to open minds for good.* Routledge.

Ekelund, B. Z., Davcheva, L., & Iversen, J. V. (2009, December). Diversity Icebreaker: Developing a shared understanding of cooperation. *Bulgarian Journal of Psychology, 46*(3), 370–381.

Ekelund, B. Z., & Jørstad, K. (2002). *Team Climate Inventory intervention manual* (Danish). Danish Psychological Publisher.

Ekelund, B. Z., & Langvik, E. (Eds.). (2008). *Diversity Icebreaker: How to manage diversity processes.* Human Factors Publishing.

Ekelund, B. Z., & Maznevski, M. L. (2008, August 6). *Diversity training. Are we on the right track* [Paper presentation]. Academy of Management annual meeting, Anaheim. Published in Ekelund, B. Z., & Langvik, E. (2008). *Diversity Icebreaker. How to manage diversity processes* (2nd ed., pp. 135–154). Human Factors Publishing.

Ekelund, B. Z., & Matoba, K. (2015). The Diversity Icebreaker for third culture building: A social constructionist approach for managing diversity. In B. Z. Ekelund & P. Pluta (Eds.), *Diversity Icebreaker II. Further perspectives* (pp. 62–103). Human Factors Publishing.

Ekelund, B. Z., & Pluta, P. (2015). Diversity Icebreaker II. *Further perspectives* (pp. 62–103). Human Factors Publishing.

Ekelund, B. Z., & Pluta, P. (2017). Reframing Others in Colors of Mastery. Nordic Intercultural Communication, Conference 23. Nov. 2017. Jyväskylä, Finland.

Gelfand, M. J., Raver, J. L., Nishii, L., Leslie, L. M., Lun, J., Lim, B. C., & Yamaguchi, S. (2011). Differences between tight and loose cultures: A 33-nation study. *Science, 332*(6033), 1100–1104.

Hegge, T. I. (1997). *Rapport om arbeidet med segmenter, utprøving av kommunikasjonsbiter rød, blå og grønn og utprøving av kWh-kur.* Rapport til Akershus Eneriverk.

Hofstede, F. (2001). *Culture's consequences* (2nd ed.). Sage.

Jones, E. E., & Nisbett, R. E. (1972). The actors and observer: Divergent perspectives of the causes of behavior. *Journal of Personality and Social Psychology, 27*(2), 79–94.

Lane, H. W., & DiStefano, J. J., & Maznevski, M. (2000). *International management behavior* (4th ed.). Blackwell.

Langvik, E. (2009 July 10). *The ipsative format of Diversity Icebreaker* [Paper presentation]. 11th European Psychological Conference, Oslo.

Levison, C. (2012). *Cultural semantics and social cognition: A case study on the Danish universe of meaning.* De Gruyter, Inc.

Margerison, C., & McCann, D. (1991). *Team management. Practical approaches.* Mercury Books.

Messick, S. (1995). Validity of psychological assessment: Validation of inferences from persons' responses and performances as scientific inquiry into score meaning. *American Psychologist, 50*(9), 741–749.

Moscovici, S. (1984). The phenomenon of social representations. In R. M. Farr & S. Moscovici (Eds.), *Social representations* (pp. 3–69). Cambridge University Press.

Orgeret, K. S. (2012). Intercultural educational practices: Opening paths for dialogue. *Intercultural Communication Studies, 21*(1), 189–204.

Pluta, P. (2015, August 12–14). *Systematic use of humor in HR training concepts – An example of the Diversity Icebreaker* [Paper presentation]. 23rd Nordic Academy of Management conference NFF 2015 – Business in Society, Copenhagen Business School.

Romani, L. (2013). Diversity Icebreaker for cross-cultural management teaching: Much more than breaking the ice!*Academy of Management Learning and Education, 12*(3), 534–536.

Sandemose, A. (1936). *A fugitive crosses his tracks.* AA Knopf.

Smith, P. B., Andersen, J. A., Ekelund, B. Z., Graversen, G., & Ropo, A. (2003). In search of Nordic management styles. *Scandinavian Journal of Management, 19,* 491–507.

Straume, L. V., & Ekelund, B. Z. (2005, September). *FLOW following the introduction of a diversity tool* [Conference session]. Positive psychology conference, NPF, Oslo, Norway.

Tajfel, H., & Turner, J. C. (1979). An integrative theory of intergroup conflict. In W. G. Austin & S. Worchel (Eds.), *The social psychology of intergroup relations* (pp. 33–47). Brooks/Cole.

Urstad, B. (2012, December). Keeping a diverse work-force: More than glossy rhetorics?. *Scandinavian Journal of Organizational Psychology, 4*(2), 23–31.

Chapter 12

Inclusive Leadership: Guide and Tools

Yael Hellman

Los Angeles County Sheriff's Department, USA

Abstract

Groups once marginalized by culture, ethnicity, class, sexuality, age, and physical ability have entered and impacted business, service, and educational institutions. To unify their widening communities, leaders must pursue inclusivity, which demands more than equitable demographics. Inclusivity integrates each individual's perspective, regardless of group – the tougher goal of equitable belonging. Most diversity, equity, inclusion, and belonging programs agree that inclusivity starts with leaders' acknowledging their own biases and committing to organizational reform. Yet few apply leadership principles to gain crucial team collaboration in the project. This chapter explicitly shows public- and private-sector executives and instructors how to guide staffers and students to understand and welcome unfamiliar cultural, social, and personal variances so they themselves create an inclusive cohort. Experiential activities, games, performance arts, and focused, reflective debriefings help make inclusivity the norm by playfully but persistently uncovering even unconscious exclusionist assumptions and replacing them with informed, diversity-positive interactions. These emotionally engaging exercises reveal that exclusionism emerges most bluntly in casual conversation, which both displays and perpetuates preconceptions. Fortunately, self-corrected speech can become the avatar and instrument of inclusivity. So the gentle unearthing and disproving of biases about cultural, social, and personal differences allow participants to construct a diversity-enhanced unity deeper than uniformity. Albeit temporary and simulated, such visceral learning experiences dramatically immerse players in the hurtful disregard caused by microaggressions of privilege and prejudice about cultures, ethnicities, classes, sexualities, ages, and abilities. These exercises and leaders' modeling grow collegiality despite – indeed, through – human variety, letting all celebrate their individuality while greeting new views and voices.

Inclusive Leadership: Equity and Belonging in Our Communities
Building Leadership Bridges, Volume 9, 133–143
Copyright © 2023 by Emerald Publishing Limited
All rights of reproduction in any form reserved
ISSN: 2058-8801/doi:10.1108/S2058-880120230000009012

Keywords: Community-based leadership guide; experiential diversity
training; diversity-positive leadership; inclusive leadership practices;
inclusive everyday speech; inclusive team behaviors

Global and domestic demographics, economics, and movements have reshaped
every US enterprise. Groups once marginalized by culture, ethnicity, class, gender
and sexuality, age, and physical ability have entered business, service, government,
and educational mainstreams. Unifying this diversity of diversities is crucial since
differences can derail workspace and community collaboration or – when effectively addressed – strengthen it. To do so, leaders and those they lead must not
merely accept diversity as a legal and economic necessity, but pursue inclusivity as
an enriching aim (University of California Los Angeles Office of Equity, Diversity
and Inclusion, 2019). Inclusivity goes beyond attaining an equitable demographic
make-up through hiring and promoting persons of varied characteristics. It values and integrates all individuals' perspectives, regardless of group – a broader,
tougher goal that requires ensuring the equal belonging of all.

Most diversity, equity, and inclusion (DEI) programs agree inclusivity starts
with leaders' honest acknowledgment of their own biases, self-correction, and
commitment to reforming organizational culture, and that their modeling power-
fully inspires the same in personnel (Bourke & Titus, 2021; Harvard University
Office for Equity, Diversity, Inclusion, and Belonging, 2023). Yet few DEI plans
draw on leadership principles and on-the-ground techniques to gain consensus as
well as compliance (Chang et al., 2019).

In contrast, this chapter shows public- and private-sector instructors and executives step by step how to guide classes and workers to understand and welcome – not
just tolerate – human differences, so they themselves create an inclusive cohort. This
hands-on roadmap provides teaching and tools that let students and staffers comprehend, then actually practice supporting, unfamiliar cultural, social, and individual
variances. This chapter, then, meets and surpasses diversity aims by making venue-
wide inclusivity the customary norm rather than a parroted motto. And that requires
making conversation upholding everyone's equal worth habitual – as noted, harder
than attaining statistical equity among groups (Copdei, 2019).

How? By uncovering even unconscious exclusionism and replacing it, through
guided practice, with informed, diversity-positive interactions, students or workers get comfortable with human variation and realize how it can fuel productivity. This chapter offers materials and directions for experiential tools: games,
performance art, crisp tutorials on groups represented but imperfectly received,
followed by inclusivity-focused debriefings (with sample responses you may hear)
to help you process them. Albeit temporary and staged, emotionally engaging
experiential learning playfully but persistently exposes and amends exclusionist
assumptions (Hellman, 2014; Stoltz, 2021). These beliefs emerge most bluntly
in casual talk because everyday chat both displays and perpetuates prejudices
(University of Massachusetts Lowell Office of Multicultural Affairs, n.d.). Fortunately, this also means that self-examination and self-correction can make daily
speech the avatar and instrument of inclusivity. So the respectful but relentless

unearthing and disproving of biased comments about different cultures, sexualities, age groups, and abilities advance cultural sensitivity, everyone's sense of fitting in, collaboration, and innovation. Most important, team members or classmates practicing diversity-supportive conversation build a unity far greater than uniformity – one that connects all in a difference-enhanced *esprit de corps*.

Specifically, a progression of vetted tools (at Hellman, 2023), talking points, and inclusivity-oriented debriefings explores exclusionary paradigms and boosts everyone's feeling of belonging. Initial activities teach the universal basis of communication – first, listen – then train in avoiding verbal and nonverbal cross-cultural gaffes, observing cultural modesty, and practicing respectful (thus effective) interactions. These early exercises prepare participants to investigate subtler, sometimes more controversial verbal markers of privilege and prejudice about ethnicity, class, sexuality, age, and physical ability (including COVID-19 views). After raising awareness of microaggressions visited on many American minorities (appropriation, idealization, discounting), they consider those confronting specific groups, and learn about cisgender perks; the multiplicity of sexual identities and orientations; and hurtful versus helpful reactions to coming out. Next, a foray into different generations' "slanguage" shares the mindset, and wisdom, of each. Later, experiential performances briefly but dramatically acquaint participants with challenges to sight, hearing, speech, and mobility – along with the pity, disregard, and denial of access accompanying them. You will tackle divisiveness over COVID-19 as well. Finally, you will give guidance in diplomatically but firmly correcting exclusionist speech. And you will always model how a safe, inclusive team talks by sharing in exercises yourself but assuring others they'll never be pressured to disclose.

In brief, this chapter supports your and your team's actively incorporating rather than just managing a wider community. Activities advancing real listening and truthful reflection grow collegiality despite – in fact, through – cultural, social, and individual variety. "Inclusive Leadership: Guide and Tools" shows how your example and recognition of honesty and self-correction let all maintain their individuality while greeting new views and voices.

First, Listen

Since inclusivity honors all persons' perspectives, the starting point is making respectful conversation your organization's norm by practicing its essence: good listening. This 10-minute, one-line "script" demonstrates that different vocal tones convey vastly different meanings (adapted from Garber, 2016; see more at Hellman, 2023). The debriefing highlights how a single sentence, or even sound, can reveal the speaker's attitude toward the listener.

Debriefing

- Ask:
  - "Why did I have you do this?" (Expect: "To show attitude is more important than words;" "So we hear the messaging in our tone of voice").
  - "Do you use different tones of voice to specific people? Why?"
  - "How might this experience change how you speak at work? At home?"

The following 10-minute exercise analyzes the Chinese pictograph for "listening" (adapted from Bates, 2022; see more at Hellman, 2023) and the debriefing underscores its universal wisdom.

Ting: "Listen"

Debriefing

- Ask:
  - "Why does the pictograph include an ear?" (This "silly" question might elicit deep comments, e.g., "You use your own body to hear someone else's mind").
  - "Why do we need the mind? ... Presence? ... Focus? ... Holding? ... Heart?" ("We need to think about the speaker's message," "To really be there," "Not zone out," "Retain what they said," "Use our feelings to understand the message sent, with or without words").
  - "Don't we do this anyway?" ("No, we get wrapped up in on our own thoughts and feelings and need to remember to use all our abilities to hear someone else's").
  - Ask how remembering *Ting* might change work conversations.

Cultural Inclusivity

While everyone wants respectful communication, what is thought of as respectful conversational *content* (what you can say) and *style* (how you can say it) varies hugely among cultures. Nonverbal communication presents even trickier unspoken rules, which may further vary with different genders, ages, and statuses of the people conversing. Being conscious of these cultural characteristics does not make you or your team prejudiced, since you're not assuming all persons buy into their ancestral culture and you're not judging which is best. In fact, such awareness expands cultural modesty and thus your ability to achieve shared understanding. This 30-minute game and debriefing alert your students or workforce to potential verbal and nonverbal intercultural gaffes and help them practice respectful communication (adapted from CultureWise, n.d.; see more at Hellman, 2023).

Including Other Cultures

Debriefing

- Ask:
  - "Was the questionnaire hard? Why or why not?"

Invite all to share any uncomfortable cross-cultural interactions. (Offer one yourself first.)

- Ask:
  - "Did content (business; personal life; criticism) make it uncomfortable?"
  - "Did style (voice tone and volume; interrupting) make it uncomfortable?"
  - "Did nonverbal aspects (personal space; touch; laughing; gestures; dress; being of different genders/ages/status) make it uncomfortable?"
- If participants answered "yes" to any item, ask how it might differ in another culture.
- If participants answered "do not know" to any item, ask for ways to find out.
- If participants answered "no" to any item, ask others if they agree or disagree, and why.
- Ask:
  - "How can we speak more inclusively with persons from other cultures?"

Are American Minorities and Classes "Cultures?"

Learning about cultural differences in earlier exercises already sensitized participants to cross-cultural communication offenses, so now they are ready to weigh how members of American ethnic and economic minorities – whether identifying with their roots or assimilated – may be marginalized by generalizations, even those meant as compliments. As a leader, you can present these conversation-starters in a staff meeting or class session – always with your own "confession" of errors before soliciting missteps made or received by others.

Talking Points About Talking: American Minorities and Classes

- Few Black people will appreciate the praise for "their" athletic prowess.
- Most Jews will dislike being informed they are "all" smart with money.
- Asians will not universally welcome characterization as studious.
- Native Americans will probably resent hearing how "sensitive to nature" they are.
- Most people who rose above their family's economic and educational status (which many scholars call "the culture of poverty") may not relish being hailed as icons of "the American Dream."
- Another source of "exclusion by admiration," *cultural misappropriation*, is copying a minority's words or arts (inventing "American Indian" mascots for sports teams; using group-specific words, music, or fashions).
  - Minority individuals – many of whom have assimilated into mainstream culture – may feel mocked rather than flattered by others' repeated insertion of group-specific lingo, even if intended as a bridge or done unconsciously.
- Minimizing the many privileges non-minority, financially stable, fluent English speakers with full citizenship enjoy excludes those who lack them.

Since inclusivity means valuing everyone as an individual, you will model conversation that's free of these sometimes-inadvertent exclusionist microaggressions. Interacting with all as individuals requires consciously dropping even unconscious but perpetuating spoken symbols of cultural and social prejudice and privilege.

Social Inclusivity: Sexualities

Even within a culture, social factors like gender, gender identity, and sexual orientation impact people's roles and behaviors along with how they convey and receive communications. Of course, being male or female, cisgender or nonconforming, gay or straight should not pigeon-hole a person, but it happens. Knowledge about sexualities lets personnel and learners establish an inclusive community. Why? As seen, understanding the concerns of individuals in specific groups builds unity far better than either exaggerating or ignoring them. And whatever lets everyone converse safely lets them work constructively.

Gender Identity and Sexual Orientation

Here you and your team or class come to appreciate the variety of gender *identities* (the sex one identifies as, including transgender, questioning, intersex or asexual) and sexual *orientations* (one's sexual feelings). Using the initials LGBTQ+ (lesbian, gay, bisexual, transgender, queer/questioning, others) reminds listeners that not everyone is heterosexual or displays binary masculinity or femininity. You will also alert them to the way sexuality-based labels or "jokes" (including plain old sexism) can damage *esprit de corps*, since – be they closeted or proudly out, gender-normative or gender-bending – human beings want to be treated as individuals, not reduced to types. As with any element of diversity, appreciating others' uniqueness makes us less likely to isolate them. The LGBTQ+ awareness activities below (taking 30 and 10 minutes, respectively; adapted from GLSEN, 2022; see more at Hellman, 2023) help you teach how to get beyond prejudice and ignorance – which gender minorities can display, too! – to create cohort-building speech.

An LGBTQ+ Glossary

Debriefing

- Ask:
  - "What terms were new?"
  - "Were any terms disturbing? Why?"
  - "Which words exclude which people?"
  - "What terms should we use here, and what terms should we avoid?"

When Someone Comes Out: What Not To Say, What To Say, and Why

Debriefing

- Ask, "Did this increase your comfort level about LGBTQ+ persons? Why or why not?"
- Suggest a thought experiment: "Imagine we live in a *gay-majority* community, with mostly same-sex parents, clubs, and congregations. How would you want to be responded to when you 'come out' as heterosexual?"
- Direct discussion toward respectful conversation tips:
  - Do not assume everyone is heterosexual or fits traditional gender roles, identities, attractions, and behaviors.
  - Use inclusive language even (especially!) in casual conversation: "partner," "spouse," or "husband" for a male spouse and "wife" for a female spouse in same-sex marriages.
  - Ask yourself if gendered pronouns in your speech ("he" and "she") might unconsciously perpetuate sexism, homophobia, or transphobia.
  - Remember that a person who has come out hasn't changed – just how well you know them. Then consider whether the disclosure hurt, or improved, your relationship.

Social Inclusivity: Generations

If you are a Baby Boomer, you probably grew up hearing, "Don't trust anyone over 30." But contemporary business, educational, and service venues merge later-retiring, GenZ, Millennial, and GenX populations and depend on their mutual trust. And as with any element of inclusivity, trust grows best when we neither exaggerate nor deny individuals' differences, but learn and speak about them through honest, personal talk.

Interestingly, the greatest gap between generations seems to center precisely on conversation – both terms used and topics broached – which are more explicit and confessional among the younger and more euphemistic and classics-based among the older. It's both fun and enlightening to learn other generations' "slanguage" in this 40-minute game (adapted from Montanarogers, 2022; Zoghlami, 2022; Publications International Ltd., 2022; see more at Hellman, 2023). Most importantly, your multigenerational assembly will discover a conversation that is respectful without feeling stifled or uncomfortable.

"Slanguage" Throughout the Ages

Debriefing

- Ask:
  - "Which terms were new?"
  - "Which do you like or dislike? Why?"

- "Where do they mostly come from?" (e.g., Bible; literature; science; Internet; music).
- "What wisdom do these terms offer?"
  - "What does that say about that generation's mindset?" (traditional education; euphemisms; calling out phoniness; practicality; media focus).
- "How can younger persons respect older persons' discomfort with topics like sex, but still have a good conversation?" ("Find other topics;" "Avoid crude slang;" "Observe and ask about comfort level.")
- "How does cross-generational tact resemble cross-cultural diplomacy? How does it differ?" ("You have to see if someone is getting uncomfortable;" "Older folks know more young people's expressions than young people know theirs.")

Personal Inclusivity: Physical Ability

Now you will (if only for 30 minutes) experience challenges facing differently abled individuals to appreciate their contributions and difficulties – not just physical ones but also ableist pity and exclusivist disregard. As you are learning, the way to integrate persons is to explore differences so you can move beyond them to function as a partnership. This performance exercise has participants express themselves as, and with, a differently abled individual (adapted from Rodgers, 2023; see more at Hellman, 2023). Always inclusive of individuals, you will randomly assign a physical challenge to any differently abled person, just as for other participants. Everyone pairs up, so be ready to take part.

Walk in my Shoes – Then We Can Talk

Debriefing

- Ask:
  - "What did it feel like to imagine yourself with your physical challenge?" ("Interesting;" "Infuriating;" Embarrassing).
  - "What did it feel like to have to hear questions about it?" ("Rude;" "Relieving").
  - "What did it feel like to ask questions about your partner's challenge?"
  - "What did you learn from walking in (or with) your partner's shoes?"
  - "Will this exercise change how you feel when interacting with differently abled people?"
    - Direct conversation to the point that understanding, rather than ignoring, a physical challenge lets you get beyond it and have more comfortable interactions.

Personal Inclusivity: COVID-19: Inclusivity's Perfect Storm

Perhaps more than any individual difference, pandemic waves intertwine physical, psychological, and ideological divisions. Some staffers or students (and leaders) fear infected or unvaccinated associates, and essential workers may resent forced exposure. Others disdain the COVID-19-cautious as worrywarts succumbing to "fake news," government shills, or closet racists promoting harmful vaccines. Fear and denial (often two sides of the same coin), as well as resistance to government mandates, threaten camaraderie. They also complicate leaders' and institutions' taking legally required or reasonable precautions. The depersonalizing effects of masking and distance work or study further fray inclusive collegiality.

Yet, as with other diversities, listening and respectful discussion prevents or heals rifts. Gentle humor helps, too, and there's plenty in stories of Zoomers – including teachers and bosses – trying to get away with business shirts on top and p.j.'s below! Figure on 30 minutes for this performance activity, though large units will take more time (see more at Hellman, 2023).

The Petrified, the Pooh-Poohers, and the Put-Upon

Debriefing

- Ask each person in each group (if you took part, have a volunteer ask you):
  - ○ "Which view fits you best?"
  - ○ "Which fits you worst?"
  - ○ "What did you learn from the view that fits you worst?"
  - ○ "How might you relate better to people holding that view?"
  - ○ "Did stating different views change your view at all?"

How an Inclusive Cohort Converses

Your modeling listening, self-reflection, and non-exclusivist speech that weaves in culturally, socially, and individually diverse persons as individuals made your crew or class better collaborators. Now you can safeguard each member's sense of belonging. "That's nice," you may say. "But how does their private sense of belonging help me here?" Most organizational psychologists suggest it stimulates innovation: Secure people work on new ideas while insecure people reject them pessimistically. Your take-away? Tough problems do not hurt problem-solving, but exclusionist speech does. So fostering genuine *esprit de corps* is job one.

You will now guide personnel or learners in tactfully correcting any discounting of individuals' contributions which they may hear. Remind them this means rejecting unacceptable *speech*, not the *speaker*: As always, inclusive talk starts with listening and self-reflection, and solves problems as a cohort of unique persons connected by shared goals and respect. This 10-minute exercise and debriefing compare speech that dismisses versus speech that supports ideas from everyone (adapted from Garber, 2016; see more at Hellman, 2023).

Words That Exclude or Include

Debriefing

- Ask:
  - ○ "How do you think people using these phrases felt? Why?"
  - ○ "How do you think people hearing these phrases felt? Why?"

○ "How can each of these 'innovation crushers' be changed to encourage innovation?" ("Instead of 'Don't be ridiculous', say, 'I've never heard that idea. How would it work?'").

○ "What do you think of my mantra? 'Seeing Without Stereotyping Brings Unity Without Uniformity; Knowing Yourself and Others Teaches You the Most!'"

Quick tips remind everyone how to reap the rewards of inclusive talk.

Rules of Thumb

- Practice the honesty and connectivity you want from others.
- Converse respectfully to learn from everyone.
- View inclusivity as an advantage since individual belonging fuels collective achievement.

Summary

This chapter's goal is to help teach organizational leaders and teams how to approach cultural, social, and personal diversities as enriching, and at the same time to treat everyone not as a group's representative but as an individual. Utilizing the tools provided can help those you lead practice inclusive speech and behavior with persons of unfamiliar cultures, ethnicities, classes, sexualities, ages, and abilities. That practice goes beyond meeting diversity targets to incorporate individuals irrespective of sector, ensure their sense of belonging, and value their contributions equally. Habituating all to inclusive speech (starting with modeling honest self-correction) made it safe for employees, trainees, or colleagues to express themselves while respecting others. Besides being the right thing to do, you saw it benefit the organization when a unit could interdependently untangle conflicts, defuse divisiveness, collaborate with confidence, and function fairly and successfully. Making respectful listening, honest reflecting, and supportive conversing the cohort's everyday norm is the ultimate accomplishment of your inclusive leadership and their inclusive community.

References

Bates, C. (2019, January 1). *5 listening insights from the Chinese character for listening.* SkillPacks. https://www.skillpacks.com/chinese-character-listening-5day-plan/

Bourke, J., & Titus, A. (2021, August 30). The key to inclusive leadership. *Harvard Business Review.* https://hbr.org/2020/03/the-key-to-inclusive-leadership

Chang, E., Milkman, K., Zarrow, L., Brabaw, K., Gromet, D., Rebele, R., Massey, C., Duckworth, A., & Grant, A. (2019, July 9). Does diversity training work the way it's supposed to? *Harvard Business Review.* https://hbr.org/2019/07/does-diversity-training-work-the-way-its-supposed-to

Copdei. (2019, October 9). *The language of diversity.* Diversity Equity and Inclusion. https://copdei.extension.org/the-language-of-diversity/

CultureWise (n.d.). *Intercultural Training Exercise Pack, 5-7, 24-27, 33-34*. https://www.culturewise.net/wp-content/uploads/2019/04/Cultural-awareness-training-exercise-pack.pdf

Garber, P. (2016). *50 communications activities, icebreakers, and exercises*, 155-159, 147-149. HRD Press. https://downloads.hrdpressonline.com/files/6820080609105844.pdf

GLSEN. (2022, May 6). *Safe space kit: A guide to being an ally to LGBT students*. https://www.nctsn.org/resources/glsen-safe-space-kit

Harvard University Office for Equity, Diversity, Inclusion, and Belonging. (2023, February 17). https://edib.harvard.edu/

Hellman, Y. (2014). *Learning for leadership: A facilitative approach for training leaders*. ASTD Press. http://www.astd.org/Publications/Books/Learning-for-Leadership

Hellman, Y. (2023). *ILA inclusive leadership guide and tools: Materials*. http://www.dryaelhellman.com

Montanarogers. (2022, February 9). *Make your lesson lit: 5 activities for teaching slang in ESL class*. FluentU English Educator Blog. https://www.fluentu.com/blog/educator-english/teaching-slang-esl/

Publications International, Ltd. (2022, July 5). *67 slang terms by decade*. HowStuffWorks. https://people.howstuffworks.com/53-slang-terms-by-decade.htm

Rodgers, L. A. (2023, January 19). *Team building activity for trust: Walk in my shoes*. https://better-teams.com/walk-in-my-shoes-team-building-activity

Stoltz, R. (2021, December 28). *Your complete guide to adult learning theory*. New England Institute of Technology. https://www.neit.edu/blog/what-is-adult-learning-theory

University of California Los Angeles Office of Equity, Diversity and Inclusion. (2019). *Communication best practices*. Communication-Best-Practices.pdf (ucla.edu). https://equity.ucla.edu/wp-content/uploads/2017/07/Communication-Best-Practices.pdf

University of Massachusetts Lowell Office of Multicultural Affairs. (n.d.). *Diversity and social justice glossary*. https://www.uml.edu/student-services/Multicultural/Programs/dpe-glossary.aspx

Zoghlami, F. (2022, October 25). *A list of generational slang words and phrases – X, Y and Z*. Pangea Translation Experts. https://www.pangea.global/blog/2022/10/25/a-list-of-generational-slang-words-and-phrases-x-y-and-z/

Chapter 13

How Inclusive Leaders Can Influence Employee Engagement

Rosalind F. Cohen

Socius Strategies LLC, USA

Abstract

Treating team members fairly, valuing different voices, and celebrating unique-ness are the behaviors that successful inclusive leaders exhibit and role models within the workplace. Actions such as these can impact how engaged (the active and intentional use of physical, cognitive, and emotional energies put into job responsibilities) employees are in their relationships with colleagues and how they feel about their work. Research revealed that when leaders act in ways that demonstrate inclusivity (such as treating others fairly, being open to differences, valuing unique perspectives, and authenticity), women, people of color, and those individuals at small or midsized companies feel stronger connections with their colleagues. This is valuable as engaged employees positively affect the organization's success. We know that perceived or actual commonalities can cause individuals to feel a sense of connection to others based solely on that perception, so it should only follow that the level of engagement should be impacted when team members and managers feel a sense of connection based upon actual or perceived identity similarities. This provides a unique opportunity for leaders to create spaces of bravery and safety through inclusive leadership actions that allow all individuals to share the aspects of their identity that allow these connections to occur. This chapter identifies behaviors and actions of inclusive leaders, explores original research on the connection between perceptions of identity and employee engagement, and provides practical advice on how leaders can support and encourage employee engagement regardless of the perception of identity.

Keywords: Inclusive leadership; employee engagement; human resources; shared social engagement; belonging; connection

Inclusive Leadership: Equity and Belonging in Our Communities
Building Leadership Bridges, Volume 9, 145–153
Copyright © 2023 by Emerald Publishing Limited
All rights of reproduction in any form reserved
ISSN: 2058-8801/doi:10.1108/S2058-880120230000009013

Introduction

My professional "people" experience began in higher education whereby providing differing or counter perspectives, students could challenge their values and beliefs that had previously been accepted as truth. This exploration allowed students to make active decisions about what they believed and what they held to be true. When I changed industries to work in financial services in the capacity of HR, I realized that the environment did not provide a supportive culture where individuals could challenge their beliefs and evolve. I began questioning how I could create an environment where personal and organizational growth could co-exist. I asked myself, "What are the pieces that would need to be in place to allow individuals to continue to grow professionally and personally while delivering value for the company?"

This is important because research has shown how engaged a team member is within an organization positively affects its success. Specifically, employee engagement behaviors are positively related to motivation, job satisfaction, organizational commitment, and organizational citizenship (Bedarkar & Pandita, 2014); financial performance, work climate, and employee participation (Cameron et al., 2011); productivity, turnover, and managerial effectiveness (Choi et al., 2015); corporate profits and business outcomes (Harter et al., 2002); and higher quality relationship with organizational members, which lead to more positive attitudes, intentions, and behaviors (Saks, 2006). It is these behaviors that impact an organization's success as measured by customer satisfaction, productivity, profit, employee retention, employee safety, employee empowerment, levels of organizational citizenship, job satisfaction, and organizational commitment (Al Mehrzi & Singh, 2016; Harter, 2002; Saks, 2006).

This desire to understand employee and organizational growth led me to research how inclusive leadership, employee engagement, and identity interact and can impact individual and organizational success. This chapter is drawn from my Ph.D. research (Cohen, 2022) and will identify behaviors and actions of inclusive leaders, exploring the connection between perceptions of identity and employee engagement, and providing practical advice on how organizations can support and encourage inclusive leadership impacting employee engagement.

Part 1: The Relationship Between Inclusive Leadership and Employee Engagement

Feelings of belonging and inclusivity are primal; individuals want to have positive (or not negative) interactions with others to develop long-term connections and concern with and for others (Jansen et al., 2014). When these connections happen in a work environment, research shows that employee engagement can be positively affected, benefiting both the individual and the organization (Bedarkar & Pandita, 2014). This possible symbiotic relationship became the basis of my research. The purpose of the research was to ask the question of what affects employee engagement, defined as the active and intentional use of physical, cognitive, and emotional energies that an employee dedicates to their job responsibilities, their relationships with others, and their relationship with the organization (Kahn, 1990; Rich et al., 2010; Rothbard & Patil, 2012). To do so, I refined the measuring Intellectual, Social, Affective Engagement Scale developed by Soane et al. (2012) into three groups: 11 engagement (how intellectually engaged a person is within their work), shared social engagement (SSE; how connected employees are to their colleagues based on shared values, goals, and attitudes), and positive affective engagement (PAE; how employees feel about their work).

I then adapted and organized an inclusive leader behaviors tool (Ratcliff et al., 2018) in addition to those associated with belonging and authenticity from Jansen et al. (2014) into seven categories identifying behaviors of inclusive leaders:

- *Fair treatment of people and processes*: challenging systematic processes and structures for fairness and equity while treating all members fairly and with respect.
- *Openness to differences*: creating teams/organizations where individuals can include all aspects of their identity, both visual and unseen.
- *Connection*: constructing environments for uniqueness, belonging, and collective engagement.
- *Unique perspectives and expertise*: actively seeking out diverse voices and perspectives.
- *Shared communication*: facilitating honest and open dialogues to achieve goals, actively inviting diverse perspectives.
- *Belonging*: the motivation to form and maintain strong and stable relationships with other people (Jansen, 2014).
- *Authenticity*: the extent to which group members perceive that they are allowed and encouraged by the group to remain true to themselves (Jansen, 2014).

The research showed that SSE and PAE) are most effectively increased ($p < 0.01$) through inclusive leadership behaviors such as role-model fair treatment, being open to differences, facilitating connection, encouraging unique perspectives, promoting shared understanding and authenticity, and nurturing a sense of belonging.

Part 2: Inclusive Leadership and Shared Identity

My research then explored the relationship between inclusive leadership and shared identity and found that when an employee perceived that their manager is "very similar" or "somewhat similar," there is a positive effect on both SSE and PAE. When employees perceive that their manager is very or somewhat similar to them and act in ways that reinforce inclusivity, they are more connected to their colleagues and feel better about their work. Inclusive leadership behaviors, such as creating a culture of brave spaces (Arao & Clemens, 2013), facilitate trust and honest communication; the manager creates the opportunity to share aspects of a person's identity that are immediately apparent and form a relationship based on commonalities.

This concept is known as affinity bias, where people gravitate toward individuals with whom they share a value or belief. This bias can provide comfort and safety because of a perceived or actual commonality with another person. such as race, gender, age (Lambert & Bell, 2013), or deep identity, such as attitudes, beliefs, intellectual abilities, recreational habits, or parental status.

This additional work includes creating brave spaces that encourage participants to engage in "deep learning" (Wergen, 2019, p. 84), where individuals not only react to experiences but reflect on the information in the context of their previously held beliefs or values. This "critical reflection" (Wergen, 2019, p. 84) can cause disquietude and an opportunity to challenge closely held values and ideals in light of new information. During this time, individuals must choose whether to continue to hold on to previous knowledge or adapt and change their thinking to accommodate this new information.

Consider this process in the context of inclusion and belonging. We may enter the workplace with certain beliefs about individuals based upon societal, religious, or other systems-shaped thinking. However, when we encounter an individual that does not fit into the paradigm of our previous understanding, we need to consider our next steps. Do we incorporate these new experiences and information into our previously held beliefs or continue our initial understanding despite the new knowledge? Learning about the diversity of others in an environment that allows open communication and reflection provides an opportunity to assimilate new information and create a new belief or idea. This, in turn, may allow for a stronger connection between individuals based upon this new information, on the surface, may not have much in common.

Part 3: Recommendations and Next Steps for HR Professionals

As discussed previously, when identity is perceived to be shared in a relationship, the connection between individuals can be more easily fostered. However, the same cannot be said when there is no perceived identity in common. Because we tend to prefer those with whom we have perceived similarities instead of an intentional desire to exclude others (Dwertmann & Dijk, 2020), organizations must provide opportunities for individuals to share their identities and learn about one another beyond any perceptions of surface identity. Then, individuals can see commonalities and similarities that may not be initially visible, allowing for deeper connections and a greater sense of belonging. The opportunity to share similar identities raises the question of how inclusive leaders can create cultures that foster and support inclusivity when aspects of shared identity are not readily apparent. My research suggests three ways leaders can create an inclusive culture and positively impact employee engagement.

Model Inclusive Leadership Behaviors

The results of the regression analysis in my study indicated a significant positive relation between leader behaviors that demonstrate inclusivity and SSE of members of marginalized groups. Specifically, women, people of color, and individuals at small (fewer than 500 employees) or mid-sized companies (501–5,000 employees) reported higher degrees of SSE within their organizations ($p < 0.01$) when leaders act in inclusive ways. Earlier, it was noted that seven categories of behaviors are shown by inclusive leaders – fair treatment of people and processes, openness to differences, connection, unique perspectives and expertise, shared communication, belonging, and authenticity. Critical knowledge areas, skills, and attributes contribute to competence within these categories. While some of these skills are unique to a specific category, some are shared among more than one category; specifically, challenging biases, challenging the status quo, active listening, creating space for discussion, facilitation, self-awareness/humility, and vulnerability are vital skills needed by leaders within the several categories. Table 13.1 provides additional information on the skills found in several categories.

In addition, there are skills that are unique to a specific Inclusive Leadership behavior category that can be found in Table 13.2.

There is a pragmatic people development reason for understanding and evaluating an individual's level of mastery of these skills. During the recruiting process, interviewers can ask questions such as, "Tell me about a time when you questioned a process or procedure for fairness of equity. What was the catalyst

Table 13.1.   Shared Skills and Attributes Found in Successful Inclusive Leaders.

Inclusive Leadership Behavioral Categories	Skill and Attribute
Belonging Fair treatment Valuing unique perspectives	Active listening
Authenticity Belonging Openness to difference Valuing unique perspectives	Challenging biases
Belonging Fair treatment	Challenging the status quo
Belonging Connection Shared understanding	Creating space for discussion
Valuing unique perspectives, Connection	Facilitation
Openness to difference	Self-awareness/humility
Authenticity Belonging	Vulnerability

Table 13.2.   Unique Skills and Attributes Found in Successful Inclusive Leaders.

Inclusive Leadership Behavioral Categories	Skill and Attribute
Authenticity	Actions = words
	Empathy
Belonging	Shares decision-making
Connection	Collaboration
	Establishes a process for engagement and discussion
Fair treatment	High emotional intelligence
	Self-awareness
Openness to difference	Acts with respect and dignity
Shared understanding	Invites input and feedback
Valuing unique perspective	Cultural awareness and intelligence
	Open communication

that caused you to question? What did you do? What was the end result, or what happened?" By doing so, the manager can determine the candidate's "challenging the status quo" skill level within the Belonging, Connection, and Shared Understanding categories and if the organization can provide them any support needed to be an inclusive leader.

During the performance management process, team members can be asked to evaluate the Belonging category by asking questions about shared leadership. Questions such as, "How has your manager given you an opportunity to be a leader within your team?" can give insight to senior leaders about the culture of inclusivity being created by the manager. Where there is a deficiency or lack of experience, individual goals can be set to provide exposure or increase proficiency in the area needed.

Collaborate in Creating Team Cultural Norms and Team Behaviors

The "forming" stage of team development (Tuckman, 1965) presents a critical opportunity for team members to establish the behaviors and ways in which they will work together. The behaviors of inclusive leaders, such as collaboration, allow individuals to provide their input, understanding, and perspectives on tasks and how to achieve team goals. Creating space for discussion where all members have the opportunity to contribute, for example, allows for the creation of shared mental models (Gentner & Stevens, 2014) of how teams can achieve goals or solve problems.

Suppose inclusive leaders facilitate conversations early on to establish cultural norms and behaviors that will guide the team members throughout their relationship. In that case, team members have opportunities to work together during a pivotal time in developing belongingness and connection and receive direction on holding each other accountable during difficult times or in resolving conflict. Leaders can pose questions to team members such as

- How can we ensure that decisions are communicated to all team members?
- How will we create meetings where all voices have the opportunity to contribute?
- How will we determine the following steps to move forward when we disagree as a team?

Just as crucial in answering these questions, it is imperative that during this type of exercise, leaders create an environment wherein those with diverse perspectives have an opportunity to give input and opinions about how the group will operate. Creating a space where individuals can show up as their authentic selves is crucial for leaders in creating a successful team.

Commitment to Ongoing Development

To create a culture that promotes employee engagement, senior leaders in organizations must demonstrate a commitment to the practice of inclusive leadership throughout the organization. Because inclusive leadership behaviors "extend our thinking beyond assimilation strategies or organizational demography to empowerment and participation of all, by removing obstacles that cause exclusion and marginalization" (Booysen, 2014, p. 298), the environment or culture that needs to be created is one of safety, empowerment, and group identification (Shore & Chung, 2021).

Diverse individuals indicate that they are more engaged, feel more connected to their colleagues, and feel that they are doing a good job in work cultures that support a diversity of thought and provide opportunities for unique contributions (Ashikali et al., 2021).

A commitment to inclusive leadership includes opportunities for managers and leaders to

- assess and evaluate their inclusive leadership skills, behaviors, and actions,
- have access to training and education that enhances inclusive leadership skills and behaviors,
- be vulnerable with respect to sharing mistakes and lessons learned without concern about backlash or retaliation, and
- create space and opportunity for sharing identities within teams to enhance connections, belonging, and inclusivity.

Conclusion

The difference between success and mediocrity may be focusing on creating inclusive leaders and communities. As community leaders and CEOs look at differentiating their message or brand to their constituents, they need to look beyond the traditional ways of defining success; there may always be another business or program that can reproduce their deliverable. However, creating unique organizations of belonging and connection where employees feel engaged and empowered to do their best work is not easily duplicated.

References

Al Mehrzi, N., & Singh, S. K. (2016). Competing through employee engagement: A proposed framework. *International Journal of Productivity and Performance Management, 65*(6), 831–843. https://doi.org/10.1108/IJPPM-02-2016-0037

Arao, B., & Clemens, K. (2013). From safe spaces to brave spaces. In L. M. Landreman (Ed.), *The art of effective facilitation: Reflections from social justice educators* (pp. 135–150). Stylus Publishing, LLC.

Ashikali, T., Groeneveld, S., & Kuipers, B. (2021). The role of inclusive leadership in supporting an inclusive climate in diverse public sector teams. *Review of Public Personnel Administration, 41*(3), 497–519. https://doi.org/10.1177/0734371X19899722

Bedarkar, M., & Pandita, D. (2014). A study on the drivers of employee engagement impacting employee performance. *Procedia – Social and Behavioral Sciences, 133*, 106–115. https://doi.org/10.1016/j.sbspro.2014.04.174

Booysen, L. A. E. (2014). The development of inclusive leadership practice and processes. In B. Ferdman & B. Deane (Eds.), *Diversity at work: The practice of inclusion* (pp. 296–329). Jossey-Bass.

Cameron, K., Mora, C., Leutscher, T., & Calarco, M. (2011). Effects of positive practices on organizational effectiveness. *Journal of Applied Behavioral Science, 47*(3), 266–308. https://doi.org/10.1177/0021886310395514

Choi, S. B., Tran, T. B. H., & Park, B., Il. (2015). Inclusive leadership and work engagement: Mediating roles of affective organizational commitment and creativity. *Social Behavior and Personality, 43*(6), 931–944. https://doi.org/10.2224/sbp.2015.43.6.931

Cohen, R. F. (2022). The *relationships between dimensions of inclusive leadership and aspects of employee engagement: Crucial connections for organizational success* [Doctoral dissertation]. Antioch University, AURA. https://aura.antioch.edu/etds/871

Dwertmann, D. J. G., & van Dijk, H. (2020). A leader's guide to fostering inclusion by creating a positive diversity climate. In B. M. Ferdman, J. Prime, & R. E. Riggio (Eds.), *Inclusive leadership: Transforming diverse lives, workplaces, and societies* (1st ed., pp. 1–16). Routledge. https://doi.org/10.4324/9780429449673

Gentner, D., & Stevens, A. L. (2014). *Mental models.* Taylor and Francis.

Harter, J. K., Schmidt, F. L., & Hayes, T. L. (2002). Business-unit-level relationship between employee satisfaction, employee engagement, and business outcomes: A meta-analysis. *Journal of Applied Psychology, 87*(2), 268–279. https://doi.org/10.1037/0021-9010.87.2.268

Jansen, W. S., Otten, S., van der Zee, K. I., & Jans, L. (2014). Inclusion: Conceptualization and measurement. *European Journal of Social Psychology, 44*(4), 370–385. https://doi.org/10.1002/ejsp.2011

Kahn, W. A. (1990). Psychological conditions of personal engagement and disengagement at work. *Academy of Management Journal, 33*, 692–724. https://doi.org/10.5465/256287

Lambert, J. R., & Bell, M. P. (2013). Diverse forms of difference. In *The Oxford handbook of diversity and work* (Vol. 1, Issue June 2019, pp. 1–33). Cambridge University Press https://doi.org/10.1093/oxfordhb/9780199736355.013.0002

Ratcliff, N. J., Key-Roberts, M., Simmons, M. J., Ratcliff, N., & Jimenez-Rodriguez, M. (2018). *Inclusive leadership survey item development* [Research Note 2018-03].

Consortium of Universities of the Washington & U.S. Army Research Institute. https://www.researchgate.net/publication/330552640_Inclusive_Leadership_Survey_Item_Development

Rich, B., Lepine, J., & Crawford, E. (2010). Job engagement: Antecedents and effects on job performance. *Academy of Management Journal, 53*(3), 617–635. https://doi.org/10.5465/AMJ.2010.51468988.

Rothbard, N., & Patil, S. (2012). Being there: Work engagement and positive organizational scholarship. In K. S. Cameron & G. M. Spreitzer (Eds.), *The Oxford handbook of positive organizational scholarship* (pp. 56–69). Oxford University Press.

Saks, A. M. (2006). Antecedents and consequences of employee engagement. *Journal of Managerial Psychology, 21*(7), 600–619. https://doi.org/10.1108/02683940610690169

Shore, L. M., & Chung, B. G. (2021). Inclusive leadership: How leaders sustain or discourage work group inclusion. *Group & Organization Management, 47*(4), 723–754. https://doi.org/10.1177/1059601121999580

Soane, E., Truss, C., Alfes, K., Shantz, A., Rees, C., Gatenbytt, M., Soane, E., & Shantz, A. (2012). Development and application of a new measure of employee engagement: The ISA engagement scale. *Human Resources Development International, 15*(5), 529–547. https://doi.org/10.1080/13678868.2012.726542

Tuckman, B. (1965). Developmental sequence in small groups. *Psychological Bulletin, 63*(6), 384–399.

Wergin, J. F. (2019). *Deep learning in a disorienting world* (1st ed.). Cambridge University Press.

Chapter 14

Fostering an Inclusive Organization Through the Power of Storytelling

Cary Snow[a], Valencia Gabay[b], Tamarah Danielle Brownlee[c] and Trenae Thomas[d]

[a]North Carolina Central University, USA
[b]The American College of Financial Services, USA
[c]IU Health, USA
[d]The Markle Foundation, USA

Abstract

Leaders need diverse talent to leverage organizational success; however, leaders must also develop inclusive working environments that meet the diverse needs of their employees. This chapter seeks to support organizational leaders in using storytelling to foster a culture of inclusivity and drive inclusive leadership practices throughout their organizations. Dimensions of the inclusive leadership compass (ILC) model (embrace, empower, enable, and embed) are used to highlight organizational areas that are rich with opportunities to facilitate mindset shifts at the individual, team, and system levels. This chapter explores strategies and highlights methods leaders can use to effectively implement the powerful learning and communication technique of storytelling in each of the critical areas of the inclusive leadership model. Starting with self-knowledge, leaders can devise ways to embrace difference and expand their understanding of inclusivity to inspire others to do the same. The authors propose a phenomenological approach to advancing efforts toward an inclusive organization in a way that honors the lived experience of others. This chapter includes methods for developing psychologically safe environments and other storytelling criteria that amplify the power of storytelling in a healthy approach that will be received and reverberate throughout the organization and enhance the benefits of inclusive leadership practices.

Inclusive Leadership: Equity and Belonging in Our Communities
Building Leadership Bridges, Volume 9, 155–165
Copyright © 2023 by Emerald Publishing Limited
All rights of reproduction in any form reserved
ISSN: 2058-8801/doi:10.1108/S2058-880120230000009014

Keywords: Storytelling; inclusion; leadership development; organizational change; phenomenology; diversity

During a new-hire orientation event, Taylor, a mid-level manager, encouraged everyone to share their story about joining the organization. Through their stories, Taylor discovered the group is ethnically and experientially diverse. These stories inspired Taylor to invite the new hires to join the organization's culture committee which was charged with cultivating a more inclusive organization. Without the opportunity to listen to other's lived experiences, Taylor would have missed the opportunity to reflect, share knowledge, and promote learning across the organization. Taylor's actions demonstrated the importance of creating a space for storytelling to influence inclusion within the organization.

Communication drives inclusion (Vohra et al., 2015) and storytelling represents one of the oldest forms of communication. Through storytelling, individuals articulate their cultural heritage, histories, and influential situations of the past (Silva & Silva, 2022). Storytelling, whether through dance, pictures, or verbal expression, has been used throughout history to comfort, teach life lessons, and create a sense of community. da Silva and Larentis (2022) noted that within the cycle of organizational learning, which includes experience, reflection, sense, meaning, and learning (ERSML), stories encourage people to connect around a common purpose. Storytelling is an amorphous mechanism that can create, sustain, and grow an environment conducive to inclusivity.

According to Dillon and Sable (2021) "Creating a diverse and inclusive environment is a moral and business imperative" (p. 2). For the last two decades, organizational leaders have worked to dissolve barriers to inclusion that permit employees to show up as their authentic selves (Roberson & Perry, 2022). Fostering an inclusive work environment requires leaders to consider their workers' characteristics, needs, and perceptions (Davidson & Ferdman, 2002). Well-intended efforts to foster inclusive environments are often met by unforeseen challenges, therefore, leaders must design organizational structures and policies that make individuals feel valued and treated fairly (Davidson & Ferdman, 2002). According to Vohra et al. (2015), in addition to specific values (i.e., humility) and knowledge types (i.e., self-awareness), skills such as open communication are essential to creating inclusion.

If effectively executed, communication can provoke feelings that motivate action. Storytelling is a powerful communication and phenomenological tool that can bridge the gap between striving and current inclusive organizations wanting to connect perception to reality. This chapter explores storytelling to facilitate inclusive leadership and promotes diversity and inclusion throughout an organization's structure. Through the lens of the ILC, we will explore how storytelling can be used to embrace, embed, empower, and enable leadership and other organizational stakeholders to establish and facilitate an inclusive environment.

Inclusive Leadership

Inclusive leadership relies on the antecedents of inclusion where belongingness and uniqueness must be balanced (Ashikali et al., 2021). Shore et al. (2011) referred to uniqueness and belongingness as conflicting but necessary constructs commonly identified within the inclusion literature. Leveraging the notion of uniqueness and belonging, Ashikali et al. (2021) defined inclusion as the "degree to which an employee perceives that he or she is an esteemed member of the work group through experiencing treatment that satisfies his or her needs for both elements, belonging-ness, and uniqueness" (p. 1265). In the leadership ethos, inclusive leadership resides in the leader-follower dynamic in which both leader and follower are contributing to a shared goal through shared decision-making (Roberson & Perry, 2022).

Dillon and Sable (2021) defined inclusive leadership as a leader's capacity to "adapt to and empower diverse talent and to harness team diversity to create value" (p. 4). A leader's motivation to embrace difference and equality drives inclusive leadership practices. Inclusive leadership is nuanced in the leadership literature and therefore, is challenging to contextualize (Dillon & Sable, 2021). Leaders struggle to identify the behaviors that influence their follower's inclusion experiences and leaders struggle to measure their own level of inclusivity (Dillon & Sable, 2021). Knowing these challenges, the ILC provides a practical application framework.

The ILC

The ILC is a framework intended to help leaders demonstrate inclusive leadership outlined in four critical areas threaded through self, other, team, and organization: (a) embrace difference (self), (b) empower diverse talent (others), (c) enable diverse think-ing (teams), and (d) embed diversity and inclusion across the organization (Dillon & Sable, 2021). To facilitate meaningful change, leaders must start by focusing on stories that unearth personal values, beliefs, and attributes that produce authentic behaviors (Dillon & Sable, 2021). Leaders must connect on an interpersonal level, sharing a genuine concern for others' well-being while facilitating a psychologically safe envi-ronment. Finally, leaders must thread diversity and inclusion into every aspect of the organization to nurture an inclusive workplace (Dillon & Sable, 2021).

Storytelling and Leadership

The relationship between storytelling and leadership is rooted in the griot method – a Sub-Saharan African tradition of storytelling (Dodd, 2021). This storytelling tradition benefits both listener and storyteller by using the power-ful tool of language to illustrate thoughts and experiences. This method of storytelling design can be used at the individual, team, and organizational levels.

At the individual level, storytelling can create opportunities to assess the implicit bias of leaders derived from their personal experiences (Bolkan et al., 2020). Much like fables, and parables, storytelling allows teams to learn and consider new perspectives (da Silva & Larentis, 2022). This process permits individu-als to collectively identify commonalities, assess norms, and actively engage in a learning process. Storytelling at the organizational level is effective in studying processes and culture, creating a new vision, and playing a role in sustaining organizational identity (Rossile et al., 2013).

This powerful multilevel impact of storytelling can evolve into a roadmap for inclusive leadership development. Based on Senge's (2006) five disciplines of a learning organization (systems thinking, personal mastery, mental models, building a shared vision, and team learning), Denning (2011) postulated that storytelling could be the sixth discipline. Storytelling can facilitate change and is an effective method of knowledge transference. The knowledge of self and others and the lessons learned through the lived experience are transferred through storytelling. The knowledge transfer allows organizations to move beyond exposure to differences to actively exploring those differences, which is a critical component of establishing inclusive organizations (Prime et al., 2018).

A Storytelling Criteria

A common principle of effective communication is "it's not what you say, but how you say it." This idiom summarizes the Mehrabian communication model (Mehrabian, 1966) which emphasizes that presentation is often more important than the content. When used as a pathway to create inclusive organizations, storytelling can be more harmful than helpful if not executed properly. The authors developed a storytelling criterion adopted from da Silva and Larentis (2020) and Muriithi (2022) to serve as a framework for practitioners to maximize the effectiveness of storytelling.

The first criterion, as noted in Fig. 14.1, is the importance of creating psychological safety. Unfortunately, all too often stories can re-traumatize the teller and create division between the storyteller and listener. Ensuring adequate support, consent, and guidelines for engagement can help to create the psychological safety required to avoid trauma mining. The second criterion is the promotion of learning and knowledge sharing (see Fig. 14.1). This criterion ensures that selected stories are told with intentionality and integrity. The final criteria are that the stories amplified should promote reflection through shared experience. These criteria will guide the practitioner to help listeners connect to the story and the embedded lessons to enact change. When these criteria are met organizations will benefit from the full presence of storytelling (da Silva & Larentis, 2020; Muriithi, 2022).

Integrating Storytelling with ILC

The ILC hosts four progressive domains where the principal character, the leader, focuses on developing through embracing self, curating interpersonal connections by empowering others, cultivating team essence through enablement, and embedding diversity, equity, and inclusion throughout the organization (Dillon & Sable, 2021). The next section examines how storytelling can amplify the execution of the four inclusive leadership practices outlined in the ILC framework. Each area of the framework is explored through the lens of storytelling methods that support leader, employee, and organizational growth.

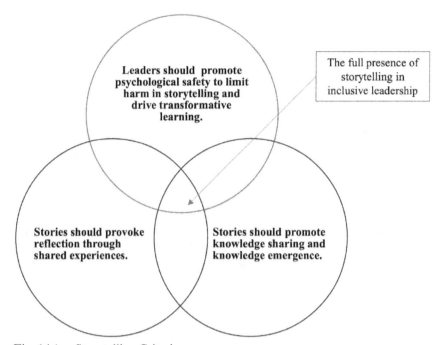

Fig. 14.1.   Storytelling Criteria.
Note. Based on research from da Silva and Larentis (2020) and Muriithi (2022), leaders can reference this criterion to awaken the full presence of storytelling on an individual and organizational level. Criteria are not exhaustive but rather a working guide to support storytelling practices in inclusive leadership.

Embrace

A leader's behavior seeds an organization's culture; therefore, the development of inclusive leadership begins with a leader's motivation to embrace differences (Dillon & Sable, 2021). According to Robertson and Perry (2022) a leader's values and actions impact followers' experiences in working groups and create an inclusive environment. Nishii and Leroy (2022) noted that leaders, regardless of their level within an organization, are instrumental to their follower's inclusion experiences which include fostering states of competence, autonomy, and belonging. Leaders must be aware of their personal values, belief systems, and attributes that trigger their desire to sustain inclusivity authentically and design inclusive workplaces (Dillon & Sable, 2021).

According to Armstrong (2021), through stories, leaders develop their identity and unearth the norms that support or impede the belief in difference and the development of inclusive leadership behaviors. Intentional leader identity work involves an examination of cultural norms and lays the groundwork for gaining valuable self-knowledge (Armstrong, 2021). Ganz et al. (2022) defined identity as "an unfolding story that we weave from a lifetime of narrative moments we have experienced as participants, recounted to others as tellers, or identified with as listeners, learning what we value in ourselves, in others, and in the world" (p. 8).

Mahoney (2017) referenced the "story of self," as a component of Ganz's (2011) three-part Model of Public Narrative: story of self, story of us, story of now (p. 282). The model serves as a framework for using storytelling as a method for public leadership development and social agency (Ganz, 2011). The story of self is the story that articulates the values and convictions that drive a leader's motivation to lead others (Mahoney, 2017). A story of self coalesces around what Ganz (2011) described as "choice points" (p. 283). Choice points include moments when leaders made a choice, faced a challenge, experienced an outcome, or learned a moral lesson. Sharing stories of self helps bypass feelings of anxiety and impossibility and fosters agency to enact change in oneself, others, or the community (Mahoney, 2017).

The belief in the value of difference and the ability to stay open to different people, their ideas, and opinions is paramount to inclusive leadership (Dillon & Sable, 2021). A leader's personal attitudes such as a willingness to be vulnerable and stay humble also promotes a culture of inclusion (Dillon & Sable, 2021). Through stories of self, leaders can reflect on past experiences where they demonstrated behaviors that shaped the inclusion experiences of others.

Empower

Dillon and Sable (2021) identified in their ILC the need for empowerment, which assists in constructing an inclusive organization. The empowerment domain included the concepts of respect, equality, personalization, and participation as ways to empower the diverse talent within the organization. Establishing an environment where individuals willingly communicate, share, learn, and garner meaning from their and others' lived experiences disseminates a level of empowerment from leadership to followers. According to Nishii and Leroy (2022), empowerment creates a space for inclusion and engagement that allows individuals to add their knowledge and experience, knowing their peers will recognize and respect their competence. Furthermore, as empowerment expands, so does organizational learning, the engenderment of trust, and inspiration and motivation will rise. What encapsulates all these ideologies and concepts of empowerment is storytelling.

Hoffer (2020) stated, "A story invites us to see the world through different points of view" (p. 75). Storytelling allows individuals to use their lived experiences to break down barriers and connect with others. Influential professional speakers often begin with a personal story that connects them to the audience. The stories will tell of inspiring experiences or challenging hardships the speaker encountered on the way to this point in their life. The story will crescendo, bringing the audience closer and giving more clarity to the speaker's worldview. Denning (2005) wrote that stories are a way to show others who you are and to remove the veil that makes you feel like a stranger to others. As leadership encourages followers to share their stories in tandem with demonstrating respect and equality, a space will form where other employees will begin to share, enriching the knowledge of those around them and giving voice to and empowering those who may feel alienated or hesitant.

There is a fundamental need for learning and reflecting in the criteria for storytelling. Researchers have noted the correlation and impact between the level of empowerment of those within an organization and organizational learning (Dahou et al., 2016; Marquardt, 2002; Watkins & Marsick, 1993). One of the more effective ways to use storytelling as an empowering tool toward organizational learning is using Kolb's experiential learning theory (ELT). The concept of learning defined by ELT is the process of creating knowledge through the grasping and transforming of experience (Kolb et al., 2001). Applying the lived experiences of others through storytelling and guided by the principles of ELT creates a framework for leadership to establish a foundational building block toward creating an inclusive organization.

Enable

The enable domain illustrates how the leader actively engages other facets of the ILC to draw out diverse thinking and behavior (Dillon & Sable, 2021). This exchange occurs by fostering team unity, artfully facilitating, including diverse perspectives and personalities, curating psychologically safe spaces, and coaching to success (Dillon & Sable, 2021). Barker and Gower (2010) argued that storytelling as a leadership communication tool holds many opportunities to provoke a sense of community and cohesion, unifying a heterogeneous workforce. According to da Silva and Larentis (2022), organizational storytelling evokes a type of informal learning that promotes positive social interactions as a part of the culture.

Stories convey complex ideas and perspectives that support the dynamism of problem-solving among teams (da Silva & Larentis, 2022). One common aspect of storytelling is reflection and its contributions to learning leveraging experiences (da Silva & Larentis, 2022). This concept is demonstrated through experience, reflection, sense, meaning and learning as captured in the cycle of organizational learning which is germane to the facilitation of storytelling (da Silva & Larentis, 2022). The ERSML conceptually integrates with the concept of team unity which begins with a leader sharing a story, and levering the experience and knowledge, enabling the team to do the same. This exchange results in sense-making through reflection, which can birth new ways of thinking and behaving that enhance work performance and organizational success (da Silva & Larentis, 2022).

The leadership compass highlights team unity as a mechanism to enable diverse thinking in navigating inclusion as a leader (Dillon & Sable, 2021). Regardless of the role as storyteller or listener, the reasons for storytelling are compelling. da Silva and Larentis (2022) found that the act of telling and listening to stories fostered "team unity" by engaging both teller and listener emotionally. Telling stories connected them through the sentiments shared while harnessing empathy for the storyteller personally and participating in the story as a listener (da Silva & Larentis, 2022).

Embed

The ILC leans into the concept that change happens on multiple levels to create inclusive leadership. We explored the change in the self, others, and team, but it is also essential to explore change at the organizational level. In the ILC, Dillon and Sable (2021) emphasized the need for organizations to embed diversity and inclusion across the organization highlighting four core areas of focus: work flexibility, systems and processes, accountability and vision, and strategy (p. 4). The formal operating structures of an organization are essential to bring close monitoring, heightened coordination, and visibility to key initiatives (Osman, 2020, p. 278).

There are multiple ways storytelling can be effective in embedding inclusive practices at the organizational level, one of which is by helping to diagnose the existing culture. According to Cameron and Quinn (2011), the most effective way to create organizational change is through culture. Culture is best illustrated through stories. Within a culture of psychological safety, storytelling is key to unlocking the truths about an organization and how it functions (Parrish, 2023).

When an organization gains access to the lived experiences of its members, organizational leaders can effectively determine a course of action toward change. For example, there is often a disconnect between policies and their impact on those that belong to marginalized groups. Intentionally listening – a key component of effective storytelling (da Silva & Larentis, 2020, p. 695), to diverse experiences can assist in developing inclusive and equitable workplace policies. Policies that lack inclusivity can be observed in those related to access (e.g., training and development, mentorship, and remote work) or identity (e.g., hairstyle restrictions, neurodiversity, and parenting status). Creating opportunities to reflect on experiences can empower individuals to speak out against policies that impede their ability to show up as their true selves without the worry of threatening group cohesiveness – specifically related to topics deemed as "undiscussable issues" (Cameron & Quinn, 2011, p. 129).

Storytelling is also an effective method to co-create a future vision for the organization that expresses dreams, ultimate concerns, and communicates the unique experiences to develop an inclusive vision (Cooperrider & Whitney, 2005; Teller, 2021). Equally amplifying diverse stories in this process is a powerful method for casting a new organizational vision and embedding inclusion and diversity into the systems, processes, and culture of an organization.

Conclusion

As this chapter concludes, we anticipate readers have strengthened their belief in the importance of an inclusive organization and the power of storytelling. Organizational leaders should recognize the power and responsibility they have in facilitating inclusive leadership in a way that embraces, empowers, enables, and embeds inclusive policies and practices. Leaders must consider the value of storytelling as a method for leader identity development and a method for examining choice points to enact change.

The exploration of storytelling applied in key areas of organizational influence (self, others, team, and organization) identified through the ILC (Dillon & Sable, 2021) demonstrated the variety of ways storytelling can foster inclusive organizations. Storytelling can empower others to use their voice to represent the lived experiences of those that feel alienated and can promote community and cohesion among teams. At the organizational level, stories can reveal organizational culture and create and cast a vision for the future of the organization (Dillon & Sable, 2021).

Equally as important are the methods for capturing and sharing stories. This chapter provided readers with a set of criteria to effectively maximize the storytelling technique. The criteria promoting psychological safety, promoting knowledge sharing and emergence, and reflection through shared experience provide a filter for practitioners to apply their efforts to use storytelling and increase the potential for success. Storytelling is a familiar form of communication that can effectively be used to meet current organizational needs on multiple levels. We encourage practitioners to explore how storytelling can effectively achieve organizational goals aimed at creating inclusive organizations.

References

Armstrong, J. P. (2021). Guest editor's introduction: Storytelling and leadership. *Journal of Leadership Studies, 14*(4), 45–49. https://doi.org/10.1002/jls.21727

Ashikali, T., Groeneveld, S., & Kuipers, B. (2020). The role of inclusive leadership in supporting an inclusive climate in diverse public sector teams. *Review of Public Personnel Administration, 41*(3), 497–519. https://doi.org/10.1177/0734371X19899722

Barker, R., & Gower, K. (2010). Strategic application of storytelling in organizations: Toward effective communication in a diverse world. *Journal of Business Communication, 47*(3), 295–312. https://doi.org/10.1177/0021943610369782

Bolkan, S., Goodboy, A. K., & Kromka, S. M. (2020). Student assessment of narrative: Telling stories in the classroom. *Communication Education, 69*(1), 48–69. https://doi.org/10.1080/03634523.2019.1

Cameron, K. S., & Quinn, R. E. (2011). *Diagnosing and changing organizational culture* (3rd ed.). Jossey-Bass.

Cooperrider, D. L., & Whitney, D. (2005). *Appreciative inquiry: A positive revolution in change.* Berrett-Koehler Publishers.

da Silva, E. R., & Larentis, F. (2022). Storytelling from experience to reflection: ERSML cycle of organizational learning. *The International Journal of Human Resource Management, 33*(4), 686–709. https://doi.org/10.1080/09585192.2020.1737831

Dahou, K., Hacini, I., & Bendiabdellah, A. (2016). Empowering employees to promote organizational learning. *Revue Algérienne des Ressources Humaines* (1), 148–158. https://www.researchgate.net/publication/315664975_Empowering_Employees_to_Promote_Organizational_Learning

Davidson, M. N., & Ferdman, B. M. (2002). Inclusion: What can I and my organization do about it? *The Industrial Organizational Psychologist, 34*(4), 80–85. https://doi.org/10.1037/E576932011-010

Denning, S. (2011). *The leader's guide to storytelling: Mastering the art and discipline of business narrative.* Jossey-Boss.

Dillon, B., & Sable, S. C. (2021). Navigating inclusion as a leader. Lessons from the field. In B. M. Ferdman, J. Prime, & R. E. Riggio (Eds.), *Inclusive leadership: Transforming diverse lives, workplaces, and societies* (pp. 379–393). Routledge.

Dodd, J. G. (2021). Reclaiming inheritance: Enacting leadership in African storytelling contexts. *Journal of Leadership Studies, 14*(4), 71–80. https://doi.org/10.1002/jls.21726

Ganz, M. (2011). Public narrative, collective action, and power. In S. Odugbemi & T. Lee (Eds.), *Accountability through public opinion: From inertia to action* (pp. 273–289). The World Bank.

Ganz, M., Lee Cunningham, J., Ben Ezer, I., & Segura, A. (2022). Crafting public narrative to enable collective action: A pedagogy for leadership development. *Academy of Management Learning & Education, 22*(2). https://doi.org/10.5465/amle.2020.0224

Hoffer, E. R. (2020). Case-based teaching: Using stories for engagement and inclusion. *International Journal on Social and Education Sciences, 2*(2), 75–80. https://www.ijonses.net/index.php/ijonses

Kolb, D. A., Boyatzis, R. E., & Mainemelis, C. (2001). Experiential learning theory: Previous research and new directions. In R. Sternberg, & L. Zhang (Eds.), *Perspectives on thinking, learning, and cognitive styles* (pp. 227–248). Routledge.

Mahoney, A. D. (2017). Being at the heart of the matter: Culturally relevant leadership learning, emotions, and storytelling. *Journal of Leadership Studies, 11*(3), 55–60. https://doi.org/10.1002/jls.21546

Marquardt, M. J. (2002). *Building the learning organization: Mastering the 5 elements of corporate learning* (2nd ed.). Davies-Black Publishing.

Mehrabian, A. (1966). Attitudes in relation to the forms of communicator object relationship in spoken communications. *Journal of Personality, 34*(1), 80–93. https://doi.org/10.1111/j.1467-6494.1966.tb01700.x

Muriithi, C. W. (2022). Healing stories: How storytelling and metaphor build capacity for healing and transforming organisational and racial trauma. *Organization Development Review, 54*(3), 10–17.

Nishii, L. H., & Leroy, H. (2022). A Multi-level framework of inclusive leadership in organizations. *Group & Organization Management, 47*(4), 683–722.

Osman, L. H. (2020). Cliques role in organizational reputational influence: A social network analysis. *Iranian Journal of Management Studies, 13*(2), 263–288.

Parrish, D. (2023). Ready the canons: The role of canonical stories in organizational sensemaking. *International Journal of Business Communication, 60*(1), 202–233. https://doi.org/10.1177/2329488420918389

Prime, J., Ferdman, B. M., & Riggio, R. E. (2021). Inclusive leadership insights and implication. In B. M. Ferdman, J. Prime, & R. E. Riggio (Eds.), *Inclusive leadership: Transforming diverse lives, workplaces, and societies* (pp. 421–429). Routledge.

Roberson, Q., & Perry, J. L. (2022). Inclusive leadership in thought and action: A thematic analysis. *Group & Organization Management, 47*(4), 755–778. https://doi.org/10.1177/10596011211013161

Rossile, G. A., Boje, D. M., Carlon, D. M., Downs, A., & Saylors, R. (2013). Storytelling diamond. *Organizational Research Methods, 16*(4), 557–580. https://doi.org/10.1177/1094428113482490

Senge, P. M. (2006). *The fifth discipline: The art & practice of the learning organization.* Doubleday.

Silva, T., & Silva, P. (2022). *Making sense of work through collaborative storytelling: Building narratives in organisational change.* Palgrave Macmillan. https://doi.org/10.1007/978-3-030-89446-7

Shore, L. M., Randel, A. E., Chung, B. G., Dean, M. A., Holcombe Ehrhart, K., & Singh, G. (2010). Inclusion and diversity in work groups: A review and model for future research. *Journal of Management, 37*(4), 1262–1289. https://doi.org/10.1177/0149206310385943

Teller, T. C. (2021). Inspiring inclusion with the appreciative leadership lotus model. In B. M. Ferdman, J. Prime, & R. E. Riggio (Eds.), *Inclusive leadership: Transforming diverse lives, workplaces, and societies* (pp. 396–406). Routledge.

Vohra, N., Chari, V., Mathur, P., Sudarshan, P., Verma, N., Mathur, N., Thakur, P., Chopra, T., Srivastava, Y., Gupta, S., Dasmahapatra, V., Fonia, S., & Gandhi, H. K. (2015). Inclusive workplaces: Lessons from theory and practice. *Vikalpa: The Journal for Decision Makers, 40*(3), 324–362. https://doi.org/10.1177/0256090915601515

Watkins, K., & Marsick, V. (1993). *Sculpting the learning organization: Lessons in the art of science of systemic change.* Jossey-Bass.

Chapter 15

Achieving Societal Equality by Building Inclusive Corporate Boards

Karen Perham-Lippman[a], Yolanda Caldwell[b] and Tissa Richards[c]

[a]*Jensen Hughes, USA*
[b]*Titus Enterprises, LLC, USA*
[c]*Tissa Richards, USA*

Abstract

Leadership diversity promotes inclusive decision-making, innovation, and sustainable performance. This chapter examines the relationship between corporate board diversity and social criteria under the environmental, social, and governance (ESG) framework, emphasizing gender parity on boards. ESG data are linked to one-fourth of the world's professionally managed assets, worth $20 trillion (Eccles et al., 2019). Despite progress, less than 20% of corporate boards worldwide include women (Deloitte, 2021). Social psychology's conformity theory describes how group dynamics affect individual behavior. Minority views are not easily expressed or heard in groups as social constraints favor conformity with the majority's viewpoint (Asch, 1955; Glass & Cook, 2017; Yarram & Adapa, 2021). When a group encounters persistent minority viewpoints from multiple individuals, it is more likely to consider and learn from the minority voice (Asch, 1955). Decision-making and problem-solving increase when a board has diverse perspectives and critical mass can contribute to normalizing diversity on boards removing communication impediments. In the context of corporate board diversity, this theory can be applied to address diversity challenges, improving decision-making and problem-solving. To promote board diversity and inclusion, we developed BOARDS, a six-step process to assist current boards on increasing their capacity for inclusion. Our four-step process SKIM can be used to prepare potential board members for future opportunities. This chapter underlines the necessity to eliminate diversity gaps on corporate boards to develop a sustainable model of social equality

Inclusive Leadership: Equity and Belonging in Our Communities
Building Leadership Bridges, Volume 9, 167–176
ISSN: 2058-8801/doi:10.1108/S2058-880120230000009015

to build inclusive corporate boards. Future research should consider other diversity variables including age, sexual orientation, and cultural and language diversity.

Keywords: Gender diversity; board diversity; environmental, social, and governance inclusive leadership, social equality

Historically, homogenous boards produced acceptable results and decision-making based on a limited scorecard profitability, but a single group making recommendations for a heterogeneous society is shortsighted. The expanded scorecard, which includes ESG measurements advances our collective focus on what is acceptable. For example, ineffective corporate governance, including a lack of boardroom diversity, contributed to the previous global financial crisis caused by the collapse of the US housing market (Nguyen et al., 2020). Crises such as this have led to obligatory and voluntary quotas to address board diversity, particularly for female board presence. Moreover, to address the chronic gender imbalance on corporate boards, some governments, starting with Norway in 2003, have introduced gender quota laws (Marisetty & Prasad, 2022). Although research points to a degree of progress in narrowing the gender gap, women on corporate boards continue to experience a wage discrepancy (Marisetty & Prasad, 2022; Nguyen et al., 2020). Despite gains in gender representation, Deloitte's (2021) global study of nearly 10,500 companies in more than 50 countries found that less than 20% of boards include women, a mere 2.8% rise from their 2019 report. At the current pace of progress, achieving gender parity on boards will not be possible until 2045, as per a recent report by Deloitte (2021).

Research shows that gender-diverse boards improve monitoring for firms with poor governance (Adams & Ferreira, 2009), increase profitability (Noland & Moran, 2016), and improve social and community outcomes (Deloitte, 2021). Nonetheless, significant gender disparities in corporate board representation remain. Furthermore, a primary factor contributing to women's underrepresentation on corporate boards is the gender gap in executive leadership positions (Deloitte, 2021; Nguyen et al., 2020). Considering these trends, what will be the strategy for building the leadership bridge that results in corporate board governance harnessing the power of diversity of thought, experience, culture, and gender to address global social and environmental challenges and profitability?

This chapter begins by analyzing the gender diversity gap present in corporate boardrooms and its influence on organizational performance, while also considering the broader scope of diversity. The authors examine additional underrepresented groups that contribute to diversity gaps on corporate boards. Leadership diversity, characterized by gender balance and overall diversity on corporate boards, has been shown to improve decision-making, financial performance, and inclusive leadership. Boards with diverse representation demonstrate higher returns on equity, reduced volatility, and superior stock performance. Such diversity in leadership enables alternative problem-solving approaches, leading to innovative and efficacious solutions (Adams & Ferreira, 2009; Noland & Moran, 2016). This chapter accordingly reviews the correlation between board diversity and social criteria within the ESG framework. The authors propose that critical mass can contribute to normalizing diversity on boards, for which Asch's Conformity Theory can be applied to address diversity challenges. Finally, the chapter recommends strategies we have developed to improve diversity and inclusiveness on boards, followed by suggestions for future research. This chapter is relevant for corporate board leadership, organizational leaders, HR, and diversity and inclusion professionals.

The Influence of ESG

ESG refers to a set of non-financial criteria used to evaluate the sustainability and societal impact of companies, organizations, and investments. The environmental criteria within ESG assess a company's impact on the natural world, including issues such as climate change, pollution, and resource depletion. The impact of a business on society, including labor practices, human rights, and community relations, is evaluated using social criteria, while governance criteria evaluate a company's leadership, ethics, and overall management structure. The term ESG was introduced by the United Nations in the 2004 Global Compact, during which 20 different financial institutions agreed to endorse the development of guidelines and recommendations that integrate ESG concerns into investment decisions (United Nations, The Global Compact, 2004). Since that time, the early demand for ESG data has grown into an industry of vendors with more than 100 organizations collecting data, 500 ESG rankings, 170 ESG indices, and numerous awards and standards related to ESG (Eccles et al., 2019). According to Eccles et al. (2019), approximately one-fourth of the world's professionally managed assets, valued at an estimated $20 trillion, are connected to ESG data.

The increasing body of research demonstrating the link between a company's environmental and social impact and its financial performance highlights the potential risks of lacking a comprehensive ESG strategy (Adams & Abhayawansa, 2021). This is becoming more evident as companies face pushback from consumers and employees seeking more than "token programs and philanthropic side projects" (O'Leary & Valdmanis, 2021, para. 10). For this reason, ESG has become an important area of focus for investors and companies, providing insight into a company's long-term financial performance, risks, and opportunities. According to O'Leary and Valdmanis (2021), competitive differentiation increasingly hinges on the ability to demonstrate a forward-looking vision that incorporates resiliency, agility, and adaptability; ESG plays a crucial role in this. ESG can be integrated into a company's financial analysis and decision-making process to identify opportunities for operational efficiency and cost savings, as well as to identify risks such as reputational damage, legal and regulatory changes, and community opposition. Furthermore, many investors use ESG criteria to screen potential investments. Companies are increasingly being held accountable for their ESG performance through various reporting frameworks. Organizations like Global Reporting Initiative (GRI), Sustainability Accounting Standards Board (SASB), and the Task Force on Climate-Related Financial Disclosures (TCFD) provide guidelines and frameworks for companies to report their ESG performance, as well as research and guidance on ESG practices (Adams & Abhayawansa, 2021). While ESG analysis has become more mainstream, there is still much work to be done in the development of uniform standards for reporting disclosures and metrics (Adams & Abhayawansa, 2021). Despite the existing challenges and the demands for more consistent and comparable measurements, the growth in ESG investing and the pressure to integrate risk factors have not diminished. Furthermore, a focus on ESG has become a critical component of corporate board strategy, 79% of directors report their boards are focused on ESG and how it materially contributes to value creation (National Association of Corporate Directors, 2019). The global pandemic propelled ESG to the forefront, highlighting the vulnerability of supply chains, labor markets, and financial systems (Adams & Abhayawansa, 2021). Ultimately, these factors reveal the need to advance the social component of ESG.

Gender Diversity and ESG's Social Pillar

Diversity in leadership and the workforce, particularly gender diversity, is a crucial element of ESG investing's social pillar. Despite modest progress toward gender equality in the workplace, most organizations fall short when it comes to boardrooms and management. A 2020 progress report on gender diversity on the corporate boards and C-suites of corporations in the MSCI All Country World Index (ACWI) revealed fewer than one-fifth of over 3,000 companies had achieved a level of sustained board diversity (Milhomem, 2020). Moreover, more than 30% of companies still had all-male boards, a decrease of nearly 35% from 2019 levels (Milhomem, 2020). In 2015, the Australian Institute of Company Directors (AICD) implemented the 30% Club to achieve 30% or more representation of female directors on the boards of ASX 200 companies by December 2018 (Yarram & Adapa, 2021). By that time, the average percentage of female directors had increased to 29.7%, up from 19.4% in May 2015, such that the number of companies with 30% or more female directors more than doubled to 96, yet over half of the ASX 200 companies still have not met the 30% target (Yarram & Adapa, 2021). According to Milhomem (2020), most European companies that are obligated to comply with representation mandates have made notable strides in promoting gender diversity. Specifically, over 80% of these firms have established boards of directors with three or more female members, representing approximately 60% of overall board representation. These accomplishments are noteworthy given the economic challenges presented by the COVID-19 pandemic, which have disproportionately impacted women in the workforce. Nevertheless, these advancements are not happening fast enough nor receiving the appropriate attention, particularly given the substantial benefits from enhancing gender diversity on boards.

Research demonstrates that companies with more women on their boards tend to have higher environmental and social performance. Paoloni et al. (2023) sampled 660 European companies listed between 2017 and 2020 and found that European companies with greater female representation on corporate boards were more effective in communicating human rights issues. For example, women directors who shared corporate social responsibility (CSR) information externally contributed to an enhanced corporate reputation and the adoption of CSR practices. Bernardi et al.'s (2009) research analyzing the presence of Fortune 500 companies on the list of "100 Best Companies to Work For" during a span of 24 years revealed that increased representation of women on corporate boards corresponded with a considerable presence on the list. Gender diversity on corporate boards has been found to have a positive impact on decision-making and governance. Specifically, the inclusion of diverse perspectives reduces groupthink, allowing for more comprehensive consideration of ideas, enhancing risk management and decision-making (Catalyst, 2020). This is particularly important considering the growing focus on stakeholder capitalism, which emphasizes considering the needs and interests of all stakeholders, including employees, customers, and the broader community.

Board gender diversity has been found to positively predict management gender diversity within organizations (Adusei et al., 2017), which also has favorable effects on profitability and performance. For example, companies that are in the top-quartile for gender diversity on executive management teams increase the representation of diverse talent, are 21% more likely to outperform on profitability, and 27% more likely to experience greater value generation (Hunt et al., 2018). The highest-performing firms in profitability and diversity report having a greater number of women in revenue-generating positions on executive teams than staff positions (Hunt et al., 2018). However, Glass and Cook (2017) emphasize that evaluations should also extend beyond financial outcomes. They demonstrate that companies with interlinked (multiple directorships) women directors and CEOs have significantly stronger governance, product strength, diversity, and community engagement. Gender-diverse boards reflect the company's commitment to both diversity and an inclusive work culture, which is a crucial part of ESG. Advancing gender diversity on corporate boards can improve decision-making, performance, and sustainability, ensuring businesses maintain their commitment to a diverse and inclusive corporate culture.

The Diversity Gap

The diversity gap refers to the lack of women and other underrepresented groups as well as background and functional expertise on corporate boards. Gender diversity remains one of the most well-known diversity gaps found on corporate boards in many countries, especially given that women account for only 6% of board seats globally (Deloitte, 2021). However, there are other significant gaps related to a dearth of racial and ethnic diversity on corporate boards. In the United States, for example, the Alliance for Board Diversity found that people of color hold just 12.5% of board seats at Fortune 500 companies (Deloitte & Alliance for Board Diversity, 2021). In response to the Confederation of British Industry's (CBI) 2020 announcement that firms must include at least one Black, Asian, or minority ethnic (BAME) board member by 2021, the United Kingdom has taken the initiative to increase ethnic diversity on boards in contrast to other European nations (Diligent Institute, 2022). However, while a 2022 report published by the Parker Review Committee showed that almost all companies in the FTSE 100 now have at least one racial minority member, only 16% of board positions are held by members that represent racial and ethnic diversity (Diligent Institute, 2022; Parker, 2022). Diversity gaps on corporate boards are also found for the underrepresentation of individuals with disabilities. As reported in the *DEI Disability Equality Index 2022* (American Association of People with Disabilities & Disability:IN, 2022), a mere 6% of S&P 500 companies have someone on their corporate board who openly identifies as having a disability, indicating the need to address both diversity and inclusion gaps.

While more work needs to be done to address various demographic factors associated with diverse representation on boards, reports have also found gaps in business strategy and international experience. According to Spierings (2022), only 67.5% of board members report having business strategy experience and less than 15% have international experience, a 5% decrease from 2018. In contrast, functional skills (operations, finance, and technology) saw overall increases. With ESG topics now integrated into board strategy rather than siloed across organizations, boards should not forgo business strategy experience for functional knowledge in technology, cybersecurity, and human resources. Instead, directors will provide substantial value when they draw the connection between these functional areas and company strategy (Spierings, 2022).

Improving Board Diversity Through Asch's Conformity Theory

Asch's (1955) conformity theory suggests that individuals are influenced by the opinions and behavior of the group they belong to. Given that research shows diverse representation is often limited to one or very few minority members, the group may tokenize them, disregarding their opinions or contributions. Research indicates that minority views are not easily expressed or heard in groups because social constraints favor conformity with the majority's viewpoint (Asch, 1955; Glass & Cook, 2017; Yarram & Adapa, 2021). However, when a group encounters persistent minority viewpoints from multiple individuals, it is more likely to consider and learn from the minority voice (Asch, 1955). This concept has important implications for the representation of underrepresented groups on corporate boards as the presence of a critical mass of three or more individuals on a board could create "normalization" thereby reducing barriers to communication. Bear et al. (2010) found that as gender diversity on boards increases, communication obstacles diminish and minority voices become more assertive, lending these contributions more credence. Furthermore, corporate social responsibility increases as gender diversity increases, as seen in the board group dynamics shifting from tokenism to normalcy (Bear et al., 2010). For example, token representation of a lone female director on boards may prohibit "the ability to curb the 'agentic' behavior of male board members" (Yarram & Adapa, 2021, p. 9). With two or three female directors, significant associations emerge between gender diversity and positive ESG factors, while decreasing negative CSR, which includes global media controversies (Yarram & Adapa, 2021). Therefore, we provide several strategies for addressing diversity gaps on boards to improve critical mass.

Recommendations

We have designed the subsequent actionable approach for boards and prospective board members to increase diversity and foster inclusive leadership using acronyms to increase understanding and retention of concepts by creating a link between terms through a memorable abbreviation. These foundational strategies are essential for establishing a sustainable model of social equality within corporate boards.

Boards

We recommend implementing *BOARDS*: board assessment, onboarding, awareness, recruitment, development, and succession planning as a six-step process to effectively improve social equality for existing boards.

Board assessments can annually evaluate board diversity based on gender, race, ethnicity, culture, ability, and experience using a board skills matrix. Assessments can also identify potential members for board peer mentorship. The evaluation of assessments is vital to developing actionable steps to address gaps or reinforce strengths.

Onboarding procedures and training for new board members should integrate inclusion and cultural competency training. The participation of the board in inclusion training is a key step in effective board development and operations. Board members can meet with the company's diversity officer or collaborate with a consultant to provide training annually.

Awareness and opportunity campaigns related to corporate governance within management development programs can increase knowledge on finance, governance, compliance, and regulation, while also providing presentation opportunities for middle and senior leadership.

Recruitment can be improved by expanding the circle of influence through mentoring and informational interviews. Board member engagement in these activities can widen the network of potential board members and increase the candidate pool for open board seats.

Development plans for board members to enhance board behavioral competencies will also help first-time members gain a better understanding of building a board career. This plan could include inclusion training and how to effectively serve on and recruit for a diverse board.

Succession plans can be reviewed annually during board assessment periods to ensure the plan is inclusive for effective transitions of board leadership, off boarding, and on boarding of directors.

Aspiring Board Members

Aspiring board members can prepare themselves for future opportunities by implementing a four-step process, *SKIM:* skill up, keep a record, inform yourself and others, and manage the process. Fewer than 25% of surveyed board directors actively planned to pursue their first board opportunity (Little, 2014). Therefore, executives who plan and prepare earlier are more likely to secure a directorship where they can add value.

Skill up: Aspiring board members should develop skills in three key areas of board selection matrices: board-specific, industry-specific, and behavioral competencies. According to Landers (2018), financial literacy is the top skill sought by 97% of selection committees, followed by compensation and HR at 86%, governance at 81%, and regulatory and compliance at 80%. Additional board-specific skills include risk management, strategic planning, capital allocation, stakeholder management and mergers and acquisitions. Selection committees prioritize industry-specific knowledge as the second most important skill, with a prevalence rate of 95% (Landers, 2018). Governance positions require a thorough understanding of the relevant industry, such as manufacturing and supply chain experience, oil and gas, eCommerce, retail channels, health and safety, or pension or hedge fund management. Skill development for behavioral competencies includes traits such as being collaborative, insightful, a good listener, diplomatic, and accountable.

Keep a record: Aspiring board members can keep a record of their experiences in the key areas of board selection matrices and develop a board resume based on their career experiences. Attending public board meetings of relevant organizations as an observer can provide valuable insights into governance practices and enhance their understanding of board operations. As an observer, an aspiring board member can take note of key takeaways, questions, and insights that may help build knowledge and familiarity with governance.

Inform yourself and others: Aspiring board members should network purposefully to increase their chances of securing future board seats, as one-third of first-time board directors report that early relationship building could have better prepared them for their board journeys (Landers, 2018). To do so, aspiring board members can attend educational sessions, research current board members for insights, request informational interviews, seek mentorship, and communicate their value proposition based on board competencies, industry knowledge, and behavioral competency. During informational interviews, they can inquire about securing a board seat, responsibilities, time commitment, challenges, and available resources. It is also important to inform others of their interest in pursuing board opportunities.

Manage the process: Aspiring board directors should proactively prepare for the board journey process. Although some board members did not formally prepare for board service, their career progressions equipped them with the necessary skills when the opportunity arose. Aspiring board members can curate their experience and manage the process by managing their careers, developing their skills, building their business reputation, and expanding their network. Upskilling can be achieved by learning about what boards seek, becoming familiar with board skills matrices, increasing financial literacy, articulating value propositions, and developing interviewing skills. Some large public tech companies invite high-potential board candidates to observe their meetings, providing a greater level of familiarity and fluency in navigating the dynamics of "the room" and "the table."

Conclusion

Within the context of the social pillar of ESG, there is a clear connection between diversity in corporate boardrooms and its impact on organizational outcomes. Despite progress in some areas, such as increased gender diversity on boards, there are still significant diversity gaps that need to be addressed, including the underrepresentation of individuals from different racial and ethnic backgrounds as well as those with disabilities. Asch's conformity theory provides a useful framework for understanding the potential impact of increasing diversity on boards, with critical mass being key in creating normalization and reducing communication barriers. To improve diversity and inclusion, we recommend that boards implement *BOARDS*, a six-step process focused on board assessment, onboarding, awareness, recruitment, development, and succession planning. We also recommend that aspiring board members prepare themselves for future opportunities by implementing the four-step process *SKIM*. Lastly, further research is needed to explore the potential impact of other diversity factors, such as age, sexual orientation, and cultural and linguistic diversity, to develop effective strategies for addressing these gaps. Overall, it is crucial for corporate boards, organizational leaders, HR, and diversity and inclusion professionals to prioritize building a sustainable model of social equality by addressing diversity gaps on corporate boards.

References

Adams, C. A., & Abhayawansa, S. (2021). Connecting the COVID-19 pandemic, environmental, social and governance (ESG) investing and calls for "harmonisation" of sustainability reporting. *Critical Perspectives on Accounting, 82*(1), 102309. https://doi.org/10.1016/j.cpa.2021.102309

Adams, R. B., & Ferreira, D. (2009). Women in the boardroom and their impact on governance and performance. *Journal of Financial Economics, 94*(2), 291–301. https://doi.org/doi:10.1016/j.jfineco.2008.10.007

Adusei, M., Akomea, S. Y., & Poku, K. (2017). Board and management gender diversity and financial performance of microfinance institutions. *Cogent Business & Management, 4*(1360030), 1–14. https://doi.org/10.1080/23311975.2017.1360030

American Association of People with Disabilities (AAPD) & Disability:IN. (2022). *DEI disability equality index 2022*. American Association of People with Disabilities (AAPD) and Disability:IN. https://disabilityin-bulk.s3.amazonaws.com/2022/DEI+2022+Report+Final+508.pdf

Asch, S. E. (1955). Opinions and social pressure. *Scientific American, 193*(5), 31–35. https://www.jstor.org/stable/24943779

Bear, S., Rahman, N., & Post, C. (2010). The impact of board diversity and gender composition on corporate social responsibility and firm reputation. *Journal of Business Ethics, 97*(2), 207–221. https://doi.org/10.1007/s10551-010-0505-2

Catalyst. (2020, June 24). *Quick take: Why diversity and inclusion matter*. Catalyst. https://www.catalyst.org/research/why-diversity-and-inclusion-matter/

Diligent Institute. (2022). *Board diversity gaps the global modern leadership report | 2022*. https://www.diligentinstitute.com/wp-content/uploads/2022/09/Board_Diversity-Gaps_2022_Modern_Leadership_Report_FINAL.pdf

Deloitte. (2021). *Progress at a snail's pace women in the boardroom: A global perspective* (7th ed.). Deloitte.

Deloitte & Alliance for Board Diversity. (2021). *Missing pieces report: The board diversity census of women and minorities on fortune 500 boards* (6th ed.). Deloitte & Alliance for Board Diversity. https://www2.deloitte.com/content/dam/Deloitte/us/Documents/center-for-board-effectiveness/missing-pieces-fortune-500-board-diversity-study-sixth-edition.pdf

Eccles, R. G., Lee, L.-E., & Stroehle, J. C. (2019). The social origins of ESG: An analysis of innovest and KLD. *Organization & Environment, 33*(4), 575–596. https://doi.org/10.1177/1086026619888994

Glass, C., & Cook, A. (2017). Do women leaders promote positive change? Analyzing the effect of gender on business practices and diversity initiatives. *Human Resource Management, 57*(4), 823–837. https://doi.org/10.1002/hrm.21838

Hunt, V., Prince, S., Dixon-Fyle, S., & Yee, L. (2018). *Delivering through diversity* (pp. 1–40). McKinsey & Company.

Landers, P. (2018, October 22). *An essential tool for improving board composition*. Global Governance Advisors. https://ggainc.com/an-essential-tool-for-improving-board-composition/

Little, K. (2014). *Beyond "if not, why not": The pathway to directorship for women in leadership* (pp. 1–38). Korn Ferry Institute.

Marisetty, V. B., & Prasad, S. (2022). On the side effects of mandatory gender diversity laws in corporate boards. *Pacific-Basin Finance Journal, 73*, 1–22. https://doi.org/10.1016/j.pacfin.2022.101741

Milhomem, C. (2020). *Women on boards 2020 progress report*. MSCI ESG Research LLC.

National Association of Corporate Directors. (2019). *2019–2020 NACD public company governance survey*. National Association of Corporate Directors. https://www.nacdonline.org/insights/publications.cfm?ItemNumber=66566

Nguyen, T. H. H., Ntim, C. G., & Malagila, J. K. (2020). Women on corporate boards and corporate financial and non-financial performance: A systematic literature review and future research agenda. *International Review of Financial Analysis, 71*(101554), 1–24. https://doi.org/10.1016/j.irfa.2020.101554

Noland, M., & Moran, T. (2016, February 8). Study: Firms with more women in the C-Suite are more profitable. *Harvard Business Review*. https://hbr.org/2016/02/study-firms-with-more-women-in-the-c-suite-are-more-profitable

O'Leary, M., & Valdmanis, W. (2021, March 4). An ESG reckoning is coming. *Harvard Business Review*. https://hbr.org/2021/03/an-esg-reckoning-is-coming

Paoloni, P., Lombardi, R., & Principale, S. (2023). The impact of gender diversity on corporate social responsibility knowledge: empirical analysis in European context. *Journal of Knowledge Management, ahead-of-print*. https://doi.org/10.1108/jkm-07-2022-0512

Parker, J. (2022). *Improving the ethnic diversity of UK boards*. The Parker Review Committee. https://assets.ey.com/content/dam/ey-sites/ey-com/en_uk/topics/diversity/ey-what-the-parker-review-tells-us-about-boardroom-diversity.pdf

Spierings, M. (2022). *Board composition: Diversity, experience, and effectiveness*. The Conference Board. https://www.conference-board.org/pdfdownload.cfm?masterProductID=39366

Yarram, S. R., & Adapa, S. (2021). Board gender diversity and corporate social responsibility: Is there a case for critical mass? *Journal of Cleaner Production, 278*, 123319. https://doi.org/10.1016/j.jclepro.2020.123319

United Nations, The Global Compact. (2004). *Who cares wins: Connecting financial markets to a changing world*. United Nations, The Global Compact. https://www.unglobalcompact.org/docs/issues_doc/Financial_markets/who_cares_who_wins.pdf

Part Four

Diversity, Equity, Inclusion, Belonging/Accessibility: A Community and Global Perspective

Chapter 16

Creating Inclusive Leadership in Rural Communities: Lessons Learned in Rural Minnesota

Jennifer Aranda, Scott Chazdon, Jocelyn I. Hernandez-Swanson, Tobias Spanier and Ellen Wolter

University of Minnesota – Extension, USA

Abstract

Minnesota's rural communities are becoming increasingly more racially, ethnically, and culturally diverse. The state shares territory with 11 Sovereign Nations and one in five Minnesotans identifies as Black, Indigenous, People of Color (BIPOC) today, compared with just 1% in 1960. In collaboration with communities, University of Minnesota's Extension Department of Community Development works to develop leadership capacity for residents to address inclusiveness, belonging, community climate and culture. The Welcoming and Inclusive Communities Program (WICP) focuses on measurement of community readiness within seven sectors combined with an educational stakeholder cohort experience leading to identification of challenges and best practices happening across a community. Curriculum includes exploring concepts of race and intersectionality and emphasizes the growth of leadership as participants work to promote equity and inclusion. Growing Local, another program in our community toolkit, is an intentional cohort series for BIPOC growth into leadership, more specifically, into decision-making arenas and positions of leadership, like their town/city/county committees, boards, and commissions. From learning the language of the oppressor (e.g., Robert's Rules of Order) to understanding the dynamics and nuances of power-mapping and social capital, participants address the barriers facing BIPOC. This chapter highlights program design elements, assessments and evaluation, and lessons learned from program implementation to date. Scholars, researchers, practitioners, and leaders will find globally relevant and replicable tools to

Inclusive Leadership: Equity and Belonging in Our Communities
Building Leadership Bridges, Volume 9, 179–189
Copyright © 2023 by Emerald Publishing Limited
All rights of reproduction in any form reserved
ISSN: 2058-8801/doi:10.1108/S2058-880120230000009016

support the development of leaders who can shape their communities through the lens of inclusive leadership, increase and strengthen capacity to lead, build networks, and facilitate community-owned change.

Keywords: Rural; community readiness; community leadership; leadership capacity; assessment; representation

Introduction

Rural communities in Minnesota are becoming more racially, ethnically, and culturally diverse, despite population loss in many regions (Johnson & Lichter, 2022). One in five Minnesotans (20%) identify as BIPOC today compared with just 1% in 1960. Minnesota also shares territory with 11 Native Nations. Unfortunately, rural Minnesota communities have historically struggled to create welcoming and inclusive spaces that provide the same opportunities to all community members. Within the United States, Minnesota is among the states with the starkest disparities by race/ethnicity ranking 45th among all 50 states with one of the largest employment gaps between White and BIPOC populations, and it ranks 49th with the employment gap between White and Indigenous populations (Minnesota Compass, 2022).

In collaboration with Minnesota communities, University of Minnesota's Extension Department of Community Development works to develop leadership capacity to address inclusiveness, belonging, community climate, and culture. The WICP is a cohort learning experience open to anyone in the community. The curriculum ranges from Diversity, Equity, and Inclusion (DEI) 101 to exploring concepts of race and intersectionality, and it emphasizes the growth of leadership for participants to feel more confident as they work to change the face of their home. Growing Local is another program in our community toolkit. In contrast to WICP, this is an intentional cohort series for BIPOC growth into decision-making arenas and positions of leadership such as town/city/county committees, boards, and commissions. From learning the language of the oppressor (e.g., *Robert's Rules of Order*) to understanding the dynamics and nuances of power-mapping and social capital, participants address the barriers that keep BIPOC from being invited and welcomed to the table.

This chapter highlights design elements from these two Extension programs as well as lessons learned from program implementation and evaluation to date. Scholars, researchers, practitioners, and leaders will find globally relevant and replicable tools to support the development of leaders who can shape their communities through the lens of inclusive leadership, increase and strengthen capacity to lead, build networks, and facilitate community-owned change.

Literature Review

Our conceptual approach to understanding leadership capacity to promote inclusion is informed by the broader rural sociology literature, the interpretive/relational turn in leadership theory, and themes from several research articles specifically addressing leadership for inclusion.

In rural sociology, community field theory (Wilkinson, 1972) offers the perspective that a community is made up of overlapping social "fields" or sectors that each have their own interests. For example, education, law enforcement, or business might be considered social fields in a rural community. True community development, according to this theory, is a cross-cutting effort that pushes through the parochial interests of specific sectors of the community in favor of a "generalized" or collective interest that benefits all. A key insight for inclusion work from community field theory is that any effort to promote a broader vision of inclusion in a community must be integrated across the specialized motivations of the particular sectors that want to be inclusive. If the business community wants to promote inclusion because of workforce needs, that is a private interest of that sector. If inclusion is to be a collective interest, all sectors must find common wisdom in the idea that inclusion benefits all. A mindset, in the words of US Senator Paul Wellstone, that "we all do better when we all do better" (Cunningham, 2010).

The most vital concept to note about leadership theory is its evolution from a positivistic, linear, and hierarchical approach, mostly derived from research on male, positional leaders in formal roles and organizations, to a more interpretive and systems-oriented approach focusing on leadership as a process, incorporating perspectives long held by women and people of color who historically value collaboration, interdependent relationships, community responsibility, and systemic views (Komives & Dugan, 2010, p. 112). Some contemporary leadership models explored the types of leadership traits and characteristics that fit best with a more relational approach to leadership. Kouzes and Posner (2007) noted that "leadership is not a solo act; it is a team effort" (p. 224). Kendrick and Sullivan (2009) identified several leadership opportunities and challenges to promote inclusion in an organization or community. Among these challenges are the need to create clear thinking so that inclusion is not "a convenient and fuzzy political slogan" (p. 70), the need to recruit and develop emerging leaders, and the need to work with existing leaders who are independent enough to challenge social exclusion. Echoing the message of Wilkinson's rural sociology, Meehan et al. from the Leadership Learning Community (2019) noted "solving community problems requires an integrated cross-sector leadership approach focused on systems-wide change rather than individual leadership that tackles problems as isolated special interests" (p. 5).

Specific to education administrators and professionals, Ngounou and Gutierrez (2017) identified principles for confronting racial inequity, repeating the emphasis on a system-thinking approach, but also highlighting that the process of learning about race and equity requires a willingness to experience discomfort as well as share stories. Reflecting on community change efforts as a Black female sociologist working in a rural Texas community, Grant-Panting (2021) also emphasized the importance of storytelling and the importance of engaging youth voices in racial equity efforts because, "not only do they have valid and valuable experiences worth sharing, but they are also the ones who will carry the movement forward" (p. 101).

In the remainder of this chapter, we describe two rural community leadership programs, the WICP and Growing Local, in which we have employed distinct approaches to promoting leadership for racial equity. We conclude with a set of lessons learned based on our review of the insights from the literature integrated with our own on-the-ground experience.

The WICP

In 2017, a regional development organization, a diversity council, and University of Minnesota Extension collaborated on an innovative idea to help community members yearning for a more inclusive, equitable, and welcoming environment. Working together to solicit funds and resources, develop curriculum, recruit community team members across six rural towns, and facilitate learning sessions for the educational cohort beginning in 2018, they named the initial program the Rural Equity Learning Community (RELC). RELC delivered a learning experience leading to broader self-awareness about diversity, racial equity, and inclusion. The focus of the initial curriculum was helping community teams see racial equity work for their towns as a community development process rather than a specific training or one-time event/action. For this community development approach to take hold, leadership development was identified as a critical component.

Following the RELC cohort, the initiative was renamed Welcoming Communities Program to make clearer the purpose and characteristics of the program. The project incorporated a newly created Welcoming Communities Assessment (Chazdon et al., 2020), a mixed-methods survey, and a group interview tool to measure dimensions of inclusion across community sectors. This provided a way for future cohorts to determine how prepared their communities were to engage in inclusion efforts. The Welcoming Communities Program partnered with each new community to advance leadership, address racial inequities, and respond to community needs in a relational and effective manner. As the program evolved, adjustments were made to keep pace with the ever-changing understanding of how best to approach equity and inclusion education through a community leadership lens. As the program expanded into rural communities across the state, the Extension team adapted program components as needed to be responsive.

Shifting Our Colonized Lens

With the expansion of the program into areas also home to Native Nations, the question arose as to the use of the term "welcoming" as many community residents were already Indigenous to this land. We began to confront our own colonized lens by changing the program name to WICP. With the continued increase in Minnesota's populations of color, there was also a desire to integrate Extension educators who reflected marginalized community cohort members. We felt having one White and one BIPOC educator would lead to increased learning by challenging our own implicit bias. BIPOC participants claiming "leadership," exercising their power, and redefining *who* leaders are has been foundational for our work (Komives & Dugan, 2010). Continued shifts in curriculum included holistic and intentional offerings including race-based affinity group breakouts during cohort sessions (Everyday Democracy, 2023). Race-based groups allow Whites to own their power and privilege, start to deconstruct systems, and significantly lessen the emotional labor and tax (Travis et al., 2016) paid for by BIPOC working within predominantly White spaces.

Ensuring Safety

As the Extension team included BIPOC colleagues, we felt the need to address all aspects of safety for educators, including threats to physical safety when working with communities that house a segment of people who are reactionary toward anti-racist initiatives. During one community's WICP planning sessions, the design committee identified community members who were adamantly against (what they termed) critical race theory or any type of diversity being discussed. At the town's WICP kickoff, Extension educators were warned of potential for violence by this faction of residents. Afterwards, reviewing logistical concerns, the need for heightened security and possible interventions, our colleague with knowledge of the community cautioned the team to take safety precautions and vigilance seriously because "people in that town carry," meaning they carry guns on their person.

Defining Inclusion Broadly

WICP began to support rural communities wanting to create a more inclusive, equitable, and welcoming environment primarily for communities of color and/or immigrants. However, as WICP expanded, the definition of inclusion differed and expanded to include other identities and marginalized communities. Some community members expressed concern that the initial WICP definition of inclusion was not "inclusive" of all as it overlooked individuals with disabilities, individuals with low-income, LGBTQ+ communities, and underrepresented religious communities. The WICP definition of inclusion broadened to focus on social inclusion to better meet the needs and context of communities (Table 16.1). Perspectives varied on the broadened social inclusion definition. In critics' eyes, this "watered-down" approach to inclusion reduced or eliminated the focus on race, in particular BIPOC communities, and the vital need for Whites to confront racism in their communities.

Growing Local

One challenge facing inclusion efforts in rural communities is the need to attract, recruit, and develop emerging leaders, especially from underrepresented groups. By focusing efforts to involve non-traditional leaders in local boards and committees, Growing Local, the second rural community leadership program this chapter discusses, builds inclusive leadership.

Table 16.1.   WICP Definitions of Inclusion, 2019–2022.

Inclusion Focus	2019	2021	2022
Race/ethnicity	X	X	X
Immigrant status	X	X	X
Socioeconomic status		X	X
Location of residence		X	X
Gender identity		X	X
Sexual orientation		X	X
Religion		X	X
Disability status		X	X
Political affiliation			X
Marital status			X
Use of public assistance			X
Family status/structures			X
Age			X

Inclusive Purpose

Prior to Growing Local, rural community leadership programs in Minnesota had not been very successful in developing leaders from underrepresented communities. It takes intention and sustained effort to create opportunities for marginalized community members to lead, or even participate, in formal opportunities of positional power. Though communities have residents with innate leadership abilities, there was no education on accessing that talent and learning the tools needed to navigate formal spaces of leadership.

Begun in Northfield, Minnesota, Growing Local strengthens the knowledge/ skills, networks, and confidence of underrepresented residents to aspire to and serve on local boards and commissions. The initial cohort in 2020 attracted a mix of gender, age, race, and ethnicity groups that had little or no representation on town committees and boards. Cohort sessions guided emerging leaders in exploration of the "what now," while also identifying the "what could" leadership in vital communities be and do. The curriculum and approach of the program were continuously developed. COVID-19 forced the first cohort to move online after only two sessions and pushed the program to think of new ways to mitigate inequities. And participant experiences, including encounters with barriers, forced Extension educators to acknowledge equity gaps in the program.

With the changes from the pandemic and rise in racial consciousness after the murder of George Floyd in Minneapolis, Minnesota, the second cohort brought even more perspective and modifications. Educators taught how to serve in formal leadership roles, but participants shared there was more to just stepping into these spaces; they were used to being silenced and made invisible in their rural community.

Leadership was thought of as a distant achievement, reserved for those who fit in most with Whiteness. As people who were BIPOC, queer, of a non-traditional age, or who spoke English as a second language, participants needed to know how they could be involved while also dealing with racism and an unwelcoming environment. Extension educators needed to address the role of race, gender, age, immigration status, and power. An asset-based approach spoke to the collective leadership style of historically marginalized cohort participants, but there was a deeper need for agility in the traditional leadership curriculum to acknowledge the realities of leading as marginalized people. This included teaching to multiple generations, translating concepts into Spanish, and leaving space for participants to discuss their lived experiences.

Fostering an Environment of Inclusivity

Adapted from a community program within the Minneapolis/St. Paul metropolitan area, Growing Local brought a rural lens to the gap in representation and knowledge needed to create robust, inclusive local boards and commissions. To build a learning opportunity designed for success, the program's framework encompassed a multifaceted approach: recruit/build a cohort of participants for the once-a-month educational workshop; facilitate/activate community networks by engaging existing community leaders as mentors; and provide parallel training for existing boards and commissions to members to ensure they were prepared to be open to new voices and set the stage for success of "graduating" cohort.

The Extension team needed to navigate and address White saviorism (Marcantonio, 2017) and generations of systemic practices that allowed exclusion of community members who did not reflect the majority or who were non-positional leaders – active change agents within their communities such as the single mom who led afterschool activities or the deacon serving through church outreach. We were tasked with creating a leadership program for participants to (re)claim their space at the table and realize that they were already leaders, and we were supporting the enlargement of the table to accept their contributions. A statement made by one participant, "I thought I was coming in to learn leadership and left realizing I was already a leader," highlights this challenge of building diverse leadership in rural communities. In tandem with equipping participants to navigate politics and procedures of local boards and commissions, was the knowledge that these same entities lacked the skills and foundations to become spaces that valued diversity of people and thought. The Extension team developed parallel work including seminars for readiness education for positional power holders in cultural agility basics, challenging the group normative, inspiring the interrupter (Belfer, 2015), empowering the boundary spanner (Miller, 2008), and curating behaviors that promote inclusion of every member.

Lessons Learned For Moving Forward

Based on the existing literature and our experiences in these two programs, we offer the following lessons for developing inclusive leadership programs in rural communities.

Think Broadly About Inclusion to Meet Communities Where They Are At

Rural communities in the United States are experiencing demographic changes at different rates. Kendrick and Sullivan (2009) noted the challenge, and necessity, to create clear thinking about social inclusion to ensure clear leadership, strategy, and accountability. In our experience, defining social inclusion in collaboration with the local community will meet the varying contexts and needs of rural communities. Consider ways intersectionality is key to helping individuals understand their own identities and the myriad identities in their communities. Within a rural context, where many communities are predominantly White and beginning their journey to understand how/why to be more inclusive, broadening the definition may be a pathway to increase empathy and understanding through an intersectionality lens.

Attract, Recruit, and Develop Emerging Leaders

Leadership through the Western tradition is often viewed as dependent on positional power, which is not where marginalized communities may actually perceive real power. Religious and spiritual leaders or community elders exemplify other types of leadership held through social capital in the collective. When working with communities, it is important to reframe how leadership is defined and to recognize leadership wherever it is taking place. Community development through linking and relationships was one key to identifying and growing leaders. A ripple effects mapping (REM) evaluation (Chazdon et al., 2017) found that emerging leaders lacked connections to influential people in the community and how to create them. An invitation to leadership is powerful (Hoelting et al., 2012). A personal invitation, through a boundary spanner (Miller, 2008) or other opinion leader recognizes the leadership capacity of the potential participant by honoring their present impact within the smaller community. Community members who are non-positional leaders can become positional leaders with the simple act of extending an invitation, which has proven to be an effective recruitment tool when communities struggle to include those who are not representative of the norm.

Nurture Dominant Culture Leaders to Be Independent and Courageous, and to Challenge Social Exclusion

A key issue for dominant culture leaders working to improve social inclusion is to understand how one goes about including individuals and groups in a set of structured social relationships and structures responsible for excluding them in the first place (Labonte, 2004). To improve social inclusion through a systems lens, dominant culture leaders must first grapple with "making the invisible visible." Dominant culture leaders must do the work of understanding the systems in which they live and how those systems are set up to primarily support their inclusion. This will require courage and may force difficult confrontations with sentiments, agendas, and vested interests that actively uphold regimes of social exclusion (Kendrick & Sullivan, 2009).

Activate the Community Field Through Cross-sector Collaboration and Innovation

Developing leadership capacity to focus on systems requires developing methods, processes, and networks to identify and leverage intersections for additional impact (Auspos & Cabaj, 2014). Activating cross-sector collaboration is built into the process of WICP which develops leadership capacity across community sectors instrumental in defining how a community includes members of marginalized groups. The WICP process builds leadership networks across a wide spectrum of interests, which are often more intertwined in small, rural communities, and effectively aligns support for inclusion (Kendrick & Sullivan, 2009).

Create Safe Spaces for Positive Contact and Discomfort. In That Space, Share Stories

Diversity is a very personal identifier and journey. When convening educational cohorts, we guide community decision-makers to embrace diversity of thought during the selection process. As one committee member shared, we don't want only participants who think as we do. What is important is that everyone possesses the "spirit to learn." When educating on subjects that challenge the core of a person's sense of justice, self, and place in the world, we found storytelling to be a fundamental strategy for creating safe spaces. Stories are the bridge that elicit empathy and connect people to relate to another's lived experiences. Spoken from the personal "I," stories are owned by the storyteller, yet can offer others a perspective from which they can relate their own stories.

Engage Youth Voices

Young people have played key roles in social movements such as the civil rights and environmental movements, yet in many rural communities, youth voices are often excluded in conversations about racial justice (Grant-Panting, 2021, p. 101). We have found that intentional efforts to engage youth add needed perspective and energy. Madelia, a WICP community, started an Equity Club in their high school. This effort has resulted in club members advocating for gender inclusive restrooms and improved Spanish language signage in the school.

Attend to Participant Safety

In predominantly White spaces, the onus for DEI education may unfairly be placed on any marginalized person present, particularly BIPOC. Not only is the person representative of an entire race, but there is also an unspoken belief they should be responsible for solutions to "fix the problem." Agile educators, versed in understanding racial justice and White supremacist structures, must be alert to psychological safety of participants and ensure there is time and space for breaks and debriefs. They must also serve as interrupters to the expectations from others in the cohort for BIPOC to take on the heavy lifting with this work (Cooper, 2017). Even BIPOC educators, we acknowledge, are not immune to the redirected anger that can arise from White silence and fragility. Being aware of the depth of intolerance in a community is one step in addressing what safety measures may need to be put in place.

Conclusion

Building leadership capacity in rural communities around diversity, inclusion, belonging, and justice, is not a one-time accomplishment. As Extension educators, we have found agility is a must to meet the continued evolution of shifting demographics and changes in the DEI arena. To foster leadership capacity that leads to inclusive rural communities, practitioners will need to stay attuned to the opportunities and challenges inherent in the lessons learned while simultaneously supporting local community leadership needs and context.

References

Auspos, P., & Cabaj, M. (2014). *Complexity and community change: Managing adaptively to improve effectiveness*. The Aspen Institute. https://www.aspeninstitute.org/wp-content/uploads/files/content/docs/pubs/Complexity_and_Community_Change.pdf

Belfer, A., (2015). *How to be an interrupter: A white person's guide to activism*. Living Water Association. https://livingwaterone.org/wp-content/uploads/2021/11/How-to-be-an-interrupter.pdf

Chazdon, S., Emery, M. E., Hansen, D., Higgins, L., & Sero, R. (Eds.). (2017). *A field guide to ripple effects mapping*. University of Minnesota Libraries Publishing. https://publishing.lib.umn.edu/publication/a-field-guide-to-ripple-effects-mapping/

Chazdon, S., Hawker, J., Hayes, B., Linscheid, N., O'Brien, N., & Spanier, T. (2020). Assessing community readiness to engage in diversity and inclusion efforts. *The Journal of Extension, 58*(6), Article 24. https://tigerprints.clemson.edu/joe/vol58/iss6/24

Cooper, C. L. (2017). Can bias interrupters succeed where diversity efforts have stalled. *Perspectives, 25,* 4. https://www.americanbar.org/groups/diversity/women/publications/perspectives/2017/summer/cbiinterrupters-succeed-where-diversity-efforts-have-stalled/

Cunningham, G. (2010, September 22). We all do better when we all do better. *Star Tribune*. https://www.startribune.com/we-all-do-better-when-we-all-do-better/103588254/

Everyday Democracy. (2023) *Dialogue to change*. https://everyday-democracy.org/dialogue/

Grant-Panting, A. (2021). "We're not done yet": Public intellectuals, rural communities, and racial equity organizing. *Journal of Research in Rural Education, 37*(7), 94–104. https://doi.org/10.26209/jrre3707-10

Hoelting, J., Caldwell, P., & Hennen, M.A. (2012). The power of invitation: The west central leadership academy. *Rural Minnesota Journal, 7*. https://www.ruralmn.org/rmj/2012-vol-7/the-power-of-invitation-the-west-central-leadership-academy/

Johnson, K. M., & Lichter, D. (2022). *Growing racial diversity in rural America: Results from the 2020 census* [Carsey Research National Issue Brief #163 Spring 2022]. University of New Hampshire, Carsey School of Public Policy. https://scholars.unh.edu/cgi/viewcontent.cgi?article=1450&context=carsey

Kendrick, M., & Sullivan, L. (2009). Appraising the leadership challenges of social inclusion. *The International Journal of Leadership in Public Services*, *5*, 67–75. http://www.iimhl.com/files/docs/20170518b.pdf

Komives, S. R., & Dugan, J. P. (2010). Contemporary leadership theories. In R. A. Couto (Ed.), *Political and civic leadership: A reference handbook* (pp. 111–120). Sage Publications.

Kouzes, J. M., & Posner, B. Z. (2007). *The leadership challenge* (4th ed.). Jossey-Bass.

Labonte, R. (2004). Social inclusion/exclusion: Dancing the dialectic. *Health Promotion International*, *19*(1), 115–121. https://doi.org/10.1093/heapro/dah112

Marcantonio, N. (2017). "Reason to hope?": The White savior myth and progress in "post-racial" America. *Journalism & Mass Communication Quarterly*, *94*(4), 1130–1145. https://doi.org/10.1177/1077699017691248

Meehan, D., Reinelt, C., & Perry, E. (2009). *Developing a racial justice and leadership framework to promote racial equity, address structural racism, and heal racial and ethnic divisions in communities*. Leadership Learning Community. https://silo.tips/download/prepared-for-and-supported-by-the-wk-kellogg-foundation-center-for-ethical-leade

Miller, P. M. (2008). Examining the work of boundary spanning leaders in community contexts. *International Journal of Leadership in Education*, *11*, 353–377. https://doi.org/10.1080/13603120802317875

Minnesota Compass. (2022). *Quality of life workforce*. Minnesota Compass. https://www.mncompass.org/topics/quality-of-life/workforce

Ngounou, G., & Gutierrez, N. (2017). Learning to lead for racial equity. *Phi Delta Kappan*, *99*(3), 37–41. https://kappanonline.org/ngounou-learning-lead-racial-equity/

Travis, D. J., Thorpe-Moscon, J., & McCluney, C. (2020). *Emotional tax: How black women and men pay more at work and how leaders can take action*. Born Digital Publications. https://digital.hagley.org/Ebook_20200003

Wilkinson, K. P. (1972). A field-theory perspective for community development research. *Rural Sociology*, *37*(1), 43.

Chapter 17

Inclusive Leadership From a Force Commander's Perspective

Cornelis Johannes (Kees) Matthijssen[a] and Anne-Marij Strikwerda-Verbeek[b]

[a]*Lieutenant General Royal Netherlands Army*
[b]*Lieutenant Colonel Royal Netherlands Army*

Abstract

This chapter is based on the experiences of lieutenant general Cornelis Johannes (Kees) Matthijssen in his period as the Force Commander of the UN Mission in Mali. His military Force consisted of men and women from 60 nationalities. The authors clearly explain what has been done to turn this diversity into a strength that benefits effectiveness. In the first part, they address the challenges like differences in cultural and doctrinal backgrounds that every nationality brings, as well as the language and the interoperability challenges. Part of the latter is the human aspect, which is mainly about understanding and respecting other cultures and how to bridge differences for the benefit of effective cooperation. The authors conclude with the importance of having a good understanding of the challenges. The second and main part of this chapter brings a wealth of practical experiences when the authors discuss how they turned diversity into a strength. Overarching they stress the importance of the tone at the top since it sets the example. Thereafter, they discuss five elements in their ways of working: continuously showing respect and understanding, exploiting all perspectives, encouraging unit cohesion, utilizing collaborative planning to enhance a common focus and teamwork, and finally continuously appreciating everyone's efforts equally. Intersecting with the diverse nationalities is the critical issue of gender equality. A final paragraph in this chapter explains how this was an essential theme within the responsibility of the Force Commander. As a conclusion, the authors again stress the importance of leadership.

Keywords: Diversity; United Nations; military; gender; cohesion; leadership

Inclusive Leadership: Equity and Belonging in Our Communities
Building Leadership Bridges, Volume 9, 191–198
Copyright © 2023 by Emerald Publishing Limited
All rights of reproduction in any form reserved
ISSN: 2058-8801/doi:10.1108/S2058-880120230000009017

From January 10, 2022, until January 10, 2023, I had the privilege to be the Force Commander of the United Nations (UN) Multidimensional Integrated Stabilization Mission in Mali (MINUSMA). My co-author was my personal assistant, and she had an important advisory role including diversity and gender-related aspects. It was not only a particularly challenging period, commanding a peacekeeping mission while there is hardly any peace to keep, but also a fascinating period, dealing with a multitude of challenges. One of those challenges was the cooperation within and interoperability of this Force consisting of about 13,000 men and women from 60 different nations. Notwithstanding the complexity of the different challenges, from the start as a Force Commander, I considered the diversity of the Force as a potential strength.

This chapter will elaborate on how the diversity of the Force was turned into a strength. To this end, first the broader context of the mission will be given. Thereafter, a view on the challenges related to diversity will be provided, followed by the ways and means of coping with this to turn diversity into a strength. More specifically, gender will be discussed as an intersecting theme, as this was an important element in the approach as well. Finally, some conclusions will be drawn.

Minusma

MINUSMA is a UN mission that was established in 2013. It is an extraordinarily complex mission – within a complex environment – that includes a military Force with about 13,000 soldiers from around 60 nations. The purpose of this mission is twofold:

(1) To support the implementation of the Mali Peace Agreement: the agreement between the three entities involved in the initial conflicts, which was the 2012–2013 uprising in northern Mali.
(2) To help restore state authority and protect civilians in the central part of Mali.

Since the signing of a peace agreement, the already-difficult situation in Mali has become much more complex because of the increased influence and violence of jihadi-motivated armed groups. The military Force has the task to enable and facilitate the efforts of MINUSMA's civilian pillar by providing security in support of the host nation's armed forces.

Challenges

Prior to discussing how diversity can be leveraged as a strength, it is imperative to comprehend the obstacles that arise from multinationalism. This comprehension is particularly important within a military and mission context. Firstly, every nationality brings its own culture and its own ways of working based on one's own doctrine and training. Since there is no universal military doctrine, nations have their own doctrine. Sometimes, some nations do have a (more) common doctrine, for example, when they are part of a multilateral organization. For example, many North Atlantic Treaty Organization (NATO) member states use NATO doctrine, although this is not a guarantee for a similar application of this doctrine. Doctrine and military ways of working are influenced by a nation's own military history, its experience, and its military culture. Fighting power has three components: a physical component, which is the means to fight, such as equipment and the physical skills of military personnel; a mental component, which is more about mindset and leadership; and a conceptual component, which refers to doctrine or ways of operational thinking. To some extent, all aspects are influenced by national and cultural backgrounds.

Second, we all speak different languages. This is a considerably basic aspect, and one could argue that it is part of the national background that we touched upon previously. Nevertheless, it deserves to be mentioned separately because there is more to say. Of course, every nation has its own language, and in a mission with 60 nationalities, we need an agreement on the language to use. That is easier said than done. The working language in the Force is English, so all documents are written in English, and people are expected to speak English. However, not every nation is equally able to speak English. That is why French is the second language within the mission. For example, many African nations (being 67% of the Force) are more accustomed to speaking French than English. However, some individuals are proficient in English, and at the very least, officers possess this language skill. Nonetheless, there are instances where some nations have no familiarity with the English language. For instance, colleagues from Chad receive their education in French and Arabic within their school system. An example of the language challenges: in one of our smaller camps, we have a unit from Chad, not speaking English, and two smaller units from Bangladesh and Nepal, both not speaking French. Despite this, the cooperation between the three is excellent.

Third, the aspect of interoperability. How to make sure that all units can operate in a coherent and effective way. Interoperability has three elements: cultural, procedural, and technical. Let us shortly explain these. Cultural interoperability is basically about mutual understanding and mutual respect as important preconditions for cooperation. Or to frame it differently, are we able and willing as human beings to get to know one another a little bit better to facilitate our cooperation. It is more about the human dimension. Procedural interoperability is about developing common procedures that everyone adheres to. This is about aligning ways of working. It prevents surprising one another, and it ensures predictability of procedures. Technical interoperability means having the technical equipment that allows us to communicate with each other and to operate together. This is related to command and control, and it is mainly about using networks and other communication systems collectively. Looking at the elements of interoperability, my experience is that in international military cooperation, we tend to look more at the technical and the procedural parts. I would say that the cultural interoperability is the most underestimated part. This is often neglected too much.

Comprehending all these challenges is a critical prerequisite for identifying strategies and tactics to effectively manage them and, subsequently, transform diversity into an asset. This does not happen automatically. It needs attention and more than that. Actual action is needed. This will benefit the military Force by optimizing its effectiveness and being able to operate in a cohesive way. So, what have we done within the Force? And what is the role of leadership?

Turning Diversity into a Strength

Before discussing relevant elements in the approach, we first want to say something about the importance of the tone at the top. The tone at the top in this regard is the standard or the bar for organizational character, performance, and culture. This tone needs to be set by the organization's leadership, so in our case by the Force Commander primarily. Setting the tone is not just a matter of sending a message. It is more. The tone is comprehensively set by providing clarity on the intent and by behavior that is fully in accordance with the intent. Basically, it is about setting the example. As a leader, one cannot afford to do something different or something outside of the intent. If you want your organization to act within your thoughts and intent, you must provide the right example.

In this regard, I wanted to provide clarity on my intent early on to be sure that I could be consistent with my message throughout my tenure. Supported by my Command Advisory Group (CAG), we developed a mission statement:

> MINUSMA Force Mission Statement:
>
> As a part of the integrated MINUSMA mission, the Force supports cohesive partner efforts who together enhance vital security and stability necessary to protect civilians (being a relevant contribution to the political transition). We do so while ensuring a population-centric focus and applying a civil-military integrated approach. Hence, the Force contributes to Unity of Effort.
>
> The Force enables decisive unified action by being a reliable and transparent team player, operating robust, pro-active and flexible. Meanwhile, we will adhere to the highest human rights standards. Moreover, our Force's diversity strengthens our perspectives and professionalism.
>
> The Force ensures to create awareness of both the environment and the mission in order to carry out its mandate and facilitate the integrated action of MINUSMA as a whole. We will maintain an adoptive attitude to continuously improve the way we operate, in the service of peace.

The MINUSMA Force Mission Statement was meant to provide clarity on how I see the Force's role, not only tactically but also comprehensively. Included in this mission statement was a sentence recognizing the value of diversity: "our Force's diversity strengthens our perspectives and professionalism." While articulating this idea is valuable, it is more imperative to lead by example and embody it daily. In the following section, I will illustrate how I accomplished this.

First, as a Commander for 60 nationalities, I considered it essential that everyone felt equally part of the team. Continuously showing respect and understanding is an important starting point for that. The challenge for a commander at this level and particularly in a mission in such a huge country is to visit all units on a regular basis. I have put a lot of effort into that for several reasons. Visiting all units and listening to all personnel throughout the Force is an essential instrument that helps to have everyone "on board" in the team. Demonstrating understanding and respect during a visit necessitates attention to detail. It begins with recognizing the impact of one's own position. There is a lot of respect for a three-star general, so the challenge is to expose yourself in such a way that you break the ice. For me, it is always important to be yourself, to listen carefully and pay attention, and to have a conversation – not based on status but as human beings, as colleagues in the same mission. It is also a matter of taking time because it allows the other to get to know you a little bit more. This is particularly important, especially at the level of a commander. They must understand and grasp your intent, but they also must feel comfortable to speak freely. Showing attention and respect for traditions and important national moments is another element that is appreciated and that lowers the threshold for participation and open communication.

Second, I wanted to make sure that we utilized all perspectives. Like in any other military operation, it is important to have the best possible understanding about the conflict and the dynamics in the country. Never think you may have a rather good feel for the situation but continuously try to improve and try to use all sources available to build that understanding. With so many nationalities as part of the Force, it feels rich to have many perspectives on the situation within the organization. African colleagues, for example, may have an excellent understanding about the situation in Mali. Some officers and even units come from neighboring countries like Burkina Faso, Niger, and Senegal. Having many of those colleagues in the Force enables everyone to have a much better understanding. Part of that is encouraging those colleagues to share their views. Out of respect and/or culture, they may not be used to giving their opinion if not explicitly asked for. So, encouraging them not only helps but is also appreciated.

A third relevant element is unit cohesion. Cohesion can be seen as the cement that binds the members of a unit. This cement consists of social attraction, group prestige, and task commitment (Burroughs & Ruth, 2022). I have personally witnessed the commitment and spirit within units to be willing and able to meet any challenge in a military operation. The better the bonding and the commitment to each other, the stronger the confidence and willingness within a unit.

In the Force, I encouraged commanders to pay attention to unit cohesion. One of my subordinate commanders once said, "it does not cost anything, just the energy that one puts into it." This is so true. It costs nothing and the benefit is huge, simply because a common activity binds and creates a collective memory. Especially at a unit level, investing in unit cohesion is important and relatively easy. But above the unit level, at the sector level, and above that at the Force level, we also paid attention to it. At those levels, it is more about facilitating events that help to build bridges among units and doing so benefits cooperation. One possible approach to promoting inclusion in camps is to introduce competitive activities, such as cricket or volleyball matches between contingents. However, organizing cultural events can also be an effective means of achieving this goal. In my experience, I have witnessed many inspiring examples of the latter approach. For example, cultural evenings in which the members of the contingents presented their countries through song, dance, and other performances. What is particularly fascinating to observe is that participants take great pride in presenting their respective cultures and traditions. Equally intriguing is the mutual fascination and interest that each person exhibits toward the other's culture. So, this appeared to be another way to build bridges and to build relationships which in the end benefit mutual understanding and cooperation.

Fourth, having a unified purpose brings another binding element in a Force with 60 nationalities. It starts with having a clear and unifying intent. Previously, we mentioned the MINUSMA Force Mission Statement. Additionally, the binding aspects also come from collaborative ways of working. Collaborative planning brings a common focus and strengthens team spirit. A Force-wide plan or a quarterly order, setting priorities and tasks for a quarter of the year, provided those opportunities. Instead of using the more traditional sequential approach, in which planning is done at the higher level and once ready it is distributed to the units, we used parallel and collaborative planning. This means that the subordinate unit headquarters participated in the planning from the start. It is more challenging than the traditional way of planning because it requires more organization, coordination, and communication throughout the process. Despite the initial investment required, the benefits of undertaking this endeavor far outweigh the costs. There are three main advantages that we have experienced:

(1) The plan itself has more support because subordinate levels have been involved.
(2) As a result, the plan becomes more viable, as feasibility checks have been conducted at subordinate levels throughout the entirety of the process.
(3) Intense coordination and communication provide a much better understanding on both sides. It becomes a shared product that people take responsibility for.

For those reasons, I strongly believe in the value of collaborative ways of working.

A fifth and final element is to appreciate everyone's efforts equally. Having worked with so many nationalities from all over the world, and having seen all of them in their work, one of my most important conclusions is that "soldier's commitment" is universal. Whatever nationality, soldiers want to do their job as good as they can, and they are all proud of the fact that they are deployed on a mission. The differences come from different leadership, different equipment, and different training, but their commitment is the same. Therefore, always value and appreciate everyone's contribution instead of looking at differences and judging people based on potential individual biases. Appreciating men's and women's efforts was something that I continuously paid attention to. This by the way is not just a matter of words. Of course, that is important too, but I have also seen the value that people see in the simple fact that you visit them everywhere, including some of the small outposts that are the most difficult to travel to. It is also important to give attention to units that have been facing incidents resulting in loss of life. Paying respect and expressing sympathy is not just a simple part of a commander's responsibility, it was a priority for me. As an example, when our battalion from Chad stationed in Tessalit was confronted with four deadly casualties in October 2022, I traveled to the unit. Tessalit is our most Northern UN camp, which is a three-hour flight from Bamako, meaning six hours back and forth in one day. That makes it quite an effort, but showing empathy to the unit and sharing their mourning far outweighs the effort to get there.

Gender

Intersecting with the diverse nationalities is the critical issue of gender equality. It is not an aspect that is specifically related to multinationalism, although it is heavily influenced by nation's culture, tradition, and religion. The United Nations Security Council Resolution (UNSCR) 1325 on Women, Peace, and Security constitutes a crucial and fundamental starting point (UN Security Council, 2000). Furthermore, the UN has developed a gender equality strategy to increase women's participation in peace and security and to empower their role. This strategy also clearly identifies leadership as one of the important building blocks by stating "leaders foster listening and open spaces for self-reflection, pushing beyond comfort zones to change behaviors while modelling power-sharing in practice" (United Nations Development Programme (UNDP), 2022, p. 11).

I fully concur with the importance of the role of women. Their role should not be underestimated. That is why for me, gender equality was an essential theme in my role as Force Commander. And that was not just because of the UN strategy, but also because I personally believe in the added value of women in peace processes. The world population consists of both men and women, so both should have an equal role in conflict resolution.

Regarding the issue of gender equality, I have directed my attention toward several key areas. This commitment was evident from the onset of the selection process for my personal staff, as I sought to establish a balanced representation of genders, thereby setting a positive and influential precedent. Examples include engaging female peacekeepers in the Force, discussing the theme with my subordinate commanders, posting messages about gender inclusivity UNSCR 1325 on social media, and paying specific attention to gender-related aspects during my visits to units. On top of this, I provided direction and guidance on how to promote and implement UNSCR 1325 to sensitize the Force and to improve awareness. I did this through organizing, hosting, and attending events linked to International Women's Day and the anniversary of UNSCR 1325. For the latter, we organized a gender retreat which turned out to be a particularly good and lively event with fruitful and open discussions. The significance of women in peacekeeping and the benefits of gender-balanced teams were two of the most prominent messages that emerged. The results were encouraging and inspiring, as well as proving that prioritizing diversity is an effective strategy that merits sustained leadership focus and investment. For leaders, this is also not just a matter of saying it but adhering to it daily with everything you say and do. You must live it, so to say. Like with the other things we discussed in this chapter, leadership sets the tone. Achieving progress cannot just be left to the gender advisor or be viewed as a predicament for female colleagues to resolve independently. Gender equality is everyone's responsibility. This approach is imperative to cultivate the right environment and climate that not only prioritizes gender issues but also facilitates tangible and substantive progress. The important role of leadership in this regard is to empower, encourage, and inspire.

Conclusion

To conclude, while multinational diversity presents certain challenges, proactive measures can be implemented to effectively address them. This chapter provided many practical actions that can be taken, but it cannot be done without leadership that is fully committed to implementation by setting the tone and leading by example. It is imperative that a leader incorporates this approach into their lifestyle and provides ongoing attention and focus to this issue. It was an extremely rewarding and enriching experience to work with so many nationalities. My conclusion is that there is more that binds us than there are differences.

References

Burroughs, J. T., & Ruth, S. G. (2022, February). *Cohesion in the army: A primary group analysis.* Army University Press. Retrieved March 29, 2023, from https://www.armyupress.army.mil/Journals/Military-Review/Online-Exclusive/2022-OLE/Burroughs/

United Nations Development Programme (UNDP). (2022). *Gender equality strategy 2022–2025.* UNDP. Retrieved March 27, 2023, from https://genderequalitystrategy.undp.org/

United Nations (UN) Security Council. (2000, October 31). Resolution 1325(2000) *adopted by the Security Council at its 4213th meeting.* http://unscr.com/en/resolutions/doc/1325

Chapter 18

Diversity From an Organizational Perspective: Building a Culture

Donald Williams, Jr

Independent Researcher and Strategist, USA

Abstract

This chapter explores the many dynamics of diversity initiatives and presents a central argument that diversity initiatives are most effective when organizational leaders create and strategically implement them to form an inclusive organizational culture. This chapter addresses diversity from a global perspective in three ways. First, it defines diversity and emphasizes one goal: diversity of perspectives. Second, it advocates for creating an organizational culture to overcome conflicting aspects of traditional, demographic-centered, or individual-centered diversity initiatives. Third, it introduces the DURCI Diversity Model, which stands for Define, Understand, Review, Communicate, and Implement, as a five-step method to foster a diverse, inclusive organizational culture. This chapter begins with a definition of diversity as efforts to synchronize unique demographic groups. It emphasizes the importance of defining diversity as it applies to an organization and ultimately creating an organizational culture that transcends individual demographics and defines diversity by what it means explicitly to the organization, including what diversity the organization already possesses. This chapter proceeds to use nonprofit, private, and public organizations, such as the US Department of Health and Human Services, Google, the American Red Cross, Cisco Systems, Americans for the Arts, the National Diversity Council, and the Gates Foundation, to illustrate the wide applicability of the DURCI Diversity Model to frame successful organizational diversity initiatives.

Keywords: Diversity; culture; inclusion; implementation; organization; strategy

Inclusive Leadership: Equity and Belonging in Our Communities
Building Leadership Bridges, Volume 9, 199–207
Copyright © 2023 by Emerald Publishing Limited
All rights of reproduction in any form reserved
ISSN: 2058-8801/doi:10.1108/S2058-880120230000009018

This chapter explores the many dynamics of diversity initiatives. It presents a central argument that diversity initiatives are most effective when organizational leaders create and strategically implement them to form an inclusive organizational culture. This chapter addresses diversity from a global perspective in three ways. First, it defines diversity and emphasizes one goal: diversity of perspectives. Second, it advocates for creating an organizational culture to overcome conflicting aspects of traditional, demographic-centered, or individual-centered diversity initiatives. Third, it introduces the DURCI Diversity Model, which stands for Define, Understand, Review, Communicate, and Implement, as a five-step method to foster a diverse, inclusive organizational culture.

Diversity is a broad term that requires thoughtful definition to avoid misinterpretation. Diversity is commonly accepted as beneficial to most organizations, yet many leaders struggle to implement and sustain successful diversity initiatives (Holvino et al., 2004; Kirton & Greene, 2021; Roberson, 2006). Individual-centered diversity initiatives risk an untimely ending if the individual departs the organization or ends their involvement in a program. Diversity initiatives centered on a demographic, such as a gender, race, or ethnicity, risk excluding members, especially in global organizations. Diversity initiatives require a unique approach based on the organization's needs and desired outcomes. The first step in that approach is defining diversity.

Define

Diversity must have a clear meaning as it applies to an organization, and its definition provides a framework by which an organization's members view diversity programs. Every organization has members from different backgrounds, each with its social norms. Hofstede's cultural dimensions provide valuable examples of some dynamics between demographics. Hofstede categorizes cultures as individualist/collectivist, high/low power distance, masculine/feminine, uncertainty tolerant/avoiding, long-term/short-term oriented, and restrained/indulgent (Hofstede, 2001, n.d.). This broad framework demonstrates some considerations associated with diversity, but many others exist. Diversity synchronizes unique demographic groups (Khelifa & Mahdjoub, 2022; Swartz et al., 2019). Any diversity effort aims to increase a group's perspectives: education, age, gender, political affiliation, experience, beliefs, nationality, etc. It likely generates a breadth of perspectives, but it also potentially creates unintended outcomes, such as tension within a group as differences among group members become challenging to balance (Kirton & Greene, 2021; Neblett, 2019). For instance, diversity in education may correlate to conflicts in socio-economic status. Diversity in gender may correlate to differences in experiences and worldviews. In short, diverse organizations must solve the problem of group divergence (Zabelina et al., 2019).

This chapter argues that the solution to the problem of group divergence is creating an organizational culture that transcends individual demographics and defines diversity by what it means explicitly to the organization, including what diversity the organization already possesses. However, defining diversity is the first step in building an organizational culture. Leaders should also understand the constraints and what diversity means to the organization.

Understand

In a sense, authoritative bodies have created a diversity framework for organizations. Leaders must understand and follow laws, regulatory policies, and organizational standards, as well as why diversity matters to the organization. In the United States, for example, dating back to the Civil Rights Act of 1964, federal and state laws prohibit discrimination by race, gender, ethnicity, and religion (Civil Rights Division, 2000), which provides an essential starting point for diversity programs and an organizational culture. An organization may build upon this legal framework by focusing on anti-discriminatory practices, programs, and standards. Some organizations, such as the US Department of Health and Human Services (HSS), have excelled in implementing an organizational diversity program.

The Department of HHS is an Executive Branch office with approximately 65,000 employees, a budget of nearly $700 billion, 11 operating divisions, including 8 agencies in the US Public Health Service, 2 human services agencies, and the Centers for Medicare and Medicaid Services (US Department of Health and Human Services, n.d.). It exemplifies a large, public organization with unique needs for its diversity efforts. It is reasonable to assume that programs that depend on one person would struggle with continuity and scope in the department. Any individual-level diversity effort risks extinction when an administration changes or as its champions leave the department because its leaders are appointed for finite periods. Its dispersed operations nationwide are comparable to large, for-profit, or nonprofit organizations, which face the same logistical challenges when implementing diversity programs. To solve these challenges, the department created and sustains the Office of Equal Employment Opportunity, Diversity and Inclusion (EEODI), which "administers and ensures compliance with the laws, regulations, policies, and guidance that prohibit discrimination in the federal workplace for employees and applicants" (United States Department of Health and Human Services, n.d.). The Department of HHS approached its diversity efforts with a focus on organizational structure and compliance with authoritative guidance. This office enables the department to prioritize its adherence to governing policies and reach the entire organization, assuring that diversity is important to the department and part of its culture.

The EEODI manages, administers, and communicates diversity initiatives to the department. The office is a staple of the department's structure and part of its organization's culture. The Department of HHS represents a unique approach to diversity, a permanent presence guided by an authoritative framework, such as laws or policies. The fact that it is a US federal office provides a helpful lesson for leaders. The department's mission is to inform and uphold federal laws, policies, and programs.

Similarly, every organization has a mission and responsibility. An organization's effort to create a diverse, inclusive culture could succeed if the organization adopts a similar framework to the Department of HHS, creating a permanent office with resources and a guiding framework to provide a sustainable, equitable, legal implementation of diversity efforts as they apply to the needs of that specific organization. Google is an example of a company with a similar model.

Google's unique approach is organizational and leader centric. In 2008, the company created and led a research study named Project Oxygen, which highlighted eight behaviors leaders needed to succeed at Google (Harrell & Barbato, 2018). One of the behaviors involved creating an inclusive environment in which leaders considered the experiences of their team members. This behavior demonstrates how leaders may foster inclusive organizational cultures; by understanding the specific organizational, contextual, and social factors, their teams face. This approach accounts for organizations of all types, sizes, and demographics because diversity initiatives directly relate to the needs of local teams. Legal requirements underpin their approach but work with their organization's unique needs. Leaders hear the concerns of those they supervise, make assessments of their teams' needs, and advocate for solutions that are most applicable to their teams. Successful diversity initiatives lead to an organizational culture when a leader understands the organization beyond the legal framework to include the organization's reach and members' responsibilities.

The American Red Cross shows how an organization builds an inclusive culture when it understands how diversity applies to its mission. It exemplifies how leaders may understand the role of diversity in an organization's internal and external operations. Leaders realized diversity efforts could impact an organization's constituents as much as it impacts its staff. A diverse organizational culture spans beyond how an organization operates; it is what people may associate with the organization itself. The American Red Cross published an Equal Employment Opportunity and Commitment to Diversity, which includes a Diversity, Equity, and Inclusion (DEI) mission and vision (The American Red Cross, n.d.). The American Red Cross' initiative took the innovative approach of focusing on messaging to youth. The organization maintains the DEI Toolkit and a Youth Diversity Pledge for interested volunteers. The organization defines its diversity in thought, background, experiences, and culture categories. It believes its organizational culture depends on its ability to reflect its communities. Leaders' understanding of diversity led them to create a national initiative to reach organizational members and a public audience. This example shows how opportunities emerge when leaders understand how diversity contributes to an organization. An in-depth understanding of diversity initiatives and their impact on an organization may assist leaders in building an inclusive organizational culture that provides tangible and intangible benefits to an organization, many of which improve upon previous solutions or successful initiatives. Therefore, after defining and understanding diversity, leaders must review a diversity initiative to identify these circumstances.

Review

Successful diversity programs depend on organizational structures, market circumstances, and realistic goals, which indicate a necessity to review an organization's preparedness for an inclusive culture. A review of a diversity effort is also an assessment of the organization. Leaders may ask if the organizational structure is adequately positioned to meet its objectives, what comprises an inclusive culture, or if organizational goals align with a diversity effort. This approach emphasizes structural changes in an organization which increases the likelihood of a diversity effort to positively impact the organization (Arsel et al., 2022). The focus is on the organization and its mission rather than the desired outcomes of a specific program. Further, leaders should review precedents to find any similar instances of organizational diversity initiatives. Past events and their outcomes provide valuable insight into the future.

When leaders review these precedents, they may find commonalities between a diversity initiative's objectives, goals, and probable outcomes. Texts from the Americans for the Arts and the National Diversity Council support the need to review a diversity initiative, which resembles how some private companies have approached inclusion programs in their organizations. In 2016, The Americans for the Arts published a Statement on Cultural Equity, which defined cultural equity and detailed organizational support for inclusion initiatives. One of the statement's recommendations called for a review of how leaders used organizational resources to further cultural equity and inclusion programs (The Americans for the Arts, 2016). This technique avoids repetitive mistakes and ensures new ideas build on the successes of previous ideas. On another note, the National Diversity Council measures organizations' commitment to diversity and inclusion annually and publishes a list of best practices. Of the five assessment areas, two areas, *CEO Engagement* and *Policies, Benefits, and Initiatives*, indicate leaders need to review the organization's diversity efforts (National Diversity Council, 2023). Leaders needed a firm grasp of the organization, a diversity initiative's desired outcomes, and its similarity to previous internal or external diversity programs. Leaders have an opportunity to foster inclusive cultures by reviewing organizational structures, goals, and precedents to tailor a diversity program to an organization's needs. History may provide lessons that enable acceptance of the diversity program and the work required to sustain it across the organization. Further, when leaders create a diversity program and complete such a review, it is essential to communicate to internal and external audiences.

Communicate

Communication enables a diversity initiative's success because it helps establish an organizational culture of feedback and transparency (Gomez & Bernet, 2019). Leaders must publicize why and how diversity matters to the organization, such as how diverse perspectives improve organizational tools, knowledge, inclusive policies, or other unique outcomes. People tend to support programs they understand to be transparent and inclusive (Linkov et al., 2022), but leaders may need to explain a program's intent.

Communication supports a diversity initiative and fosters the realization of the organization's commitment to inclusion. In the DURCI Diversity Model, communication is analogous to the lubricant of a diversity effort's engine. Diversity programs rely on effective communication. Two organizations, the Gates Foundation and Cisco Systems, provide exceptional examples of how leaders may communicate a diversity initiative and create an inclusive organizational culture in private and nonprofit sectors.

The Gates Foundation communicates its commitment to diversity by emphasizing transparency and accountability. In 2021, it drafted a DEI strategic framework for internal distribution to its employees. It also released it publicly to enable comprehensive accountability for the framework's implementation (The Gates Foundation, n.d.). The Foundation operates on three continents in over 24 fields, so its constituency is inherently diverse. It identified four pillars for its diversity framework and acknowledged its desire to build a culture of diversity and inclusion (The Gates Foundation, n.d.). This approach requires leaders to recognize diversity of all types and remain vulnerable to feedback and changes that reflect an organizational culture. Cisco Systems provides a similar communication style.

Cisco Systems, the number 1 ranked company in Fortune's 100 Best Companies to Work For (*Fortune Magazine*, n.d.), communicates its diversity as *inclusion* and *collaboration in action*. Its approach highlights organizational and individual actions contributing to its commitment to an inclusive environment. For example, its spotlight on pay parity mentions that it was one of the 28 founding signers of the White House Equal Pay Pledge, an effort to combat discriminatory compensation practices (Cisco Systems, 2020). The company emphasizes its goal of an environment in which people trust one another. This inclusive culture is sustainable because it does not depend on one person, event, or demographic. Communication fosters an inclusive organizational culture because it reflects leaders' commitment to diversity and a culture where everyone participates and has value (Passantino, 2021). However, communication is only one facet of an inclusive organizational culture. Implementation supports the promises of an organization with actionable steps to execute diversity initiatives.

Implement

A diverse, inclusive organizational culture integrates diversity and inclusion into the organization's processes, policies, and priorities. Its outcomes and feedback support leaders' intent, and there are sustainable measures that transcend an individual or specific demographic. Implementation involves establishing a feedback mechanism, and attributable, measurable outcomes, such as recruitment or retention surveys that specifically address an organization's culture or a person's perceived contribution to a team. Implementation often requires metrics varying across public, private, and nonprofit sectors. For example, employee satisfaction may reflect an organization's culture. In 2022, Cisco, Hilton, and Wegman obtained Fortune Top 10 rankings as a "great place to work" (*Fortune Magazine*, n.d.). While the ranking is not the sole indicator of organizational culture, it demonstrates an attributable outcome of diversity programs. Similar indicators include market or employee surveys or how an organization's leaders respond to a contentious event.

Implementing a diversity initiative is often the most challenging aspect leaders face in creating an organizational culture because it likely involves organizational change (Noon & Ogbonna, 2021). However, a leader may address challenges to a diversity initiative by using a proactive, phased-based approach to a diversity program, focused on one specific change at a time. For example, suppose members of the organization have experienced discrimination. In that case, one phase in the diversity initiative could be mandatory training in the organization's laws, policies, and standards. Suppose members perceive favoritism or special privilege for specific demographics. In that case, a program phase may involve a marketing campaign, internally and externally, highlighting a mentorship or leadership development program in the organization, open to all organizational members. Moreover, if a demographic-centered diversity event occurs, leaders should resist the temptation to host a demographic-centered, and by its nature, exclusive event and instead hold informational, interactive events based solely on the context of laws, policies, the organization, its mission, and its commitment to an inclusive culture. Leaders should pay special attention to the risk of excluding individuals in an organization, a possible outcome of demographic-based efforts.

Should organizational leaders still elect to participate in such events, leaders must be sure to emphasize laws, policies, and context for the event, as well as other diverse perspectives that apply to all demographics. For instance, regardless of race, a group's members bring diverse experiences, education, socio-economic status, hobbies, personalities, and interests. These should be celebrated alongside the traits that make the group different. Finally, in such events, leaders should emphasize the organization's values, mission, and goals as the unifying theme for the group. In short, a group may have differences, but it also has commonalities, which form an organizational culture.

All diversity events should reflect the organization's culture and contribute to its goals. The National Diversity Council considers successful diversity initiatives as business imperatives in the private, public, and nonprofit sectors (National Diversity Council, n.d.). A diversity program's implementation may drive quantifiable outcomes for an organization, such as increased productivity, retention, recruitment, or profit (Gomez & Bernet, 2019; Page, 2019), and intangible outcomes, such as engagement and connectedness (Stuart & Ward, 2019). These programs are permanent facets of an employee's experience, and many organizations have realized tangible benefits from their implementation.

In conclusion, diversity is a broad term describing an attempt to increase the perspectives of a group. This chapter argued that organizational culture is uniquely suited for addressing the many aspects of diversity if it capitalizes on the many perspectives within groups and contains efforts aimed at synchronizing those perspectives. Organizations have a global pool of candidates from which to choose and, in many cases, a global customer base to serve. Global reach suggests the introduction of varying worldviews and challenges to harmonizing diversity initiatives. The price of diversity is not exclusion; it requires a thorough understanding of an organization and its specific needs and desired outcomes. Organizational culture provides diversity without sacrificing the unity that organizations value. Creating an organizational culture is challenging, and this chapter presented an innovative model informed by private, nonprofit, and public sectors. The DURCI Diversity Model offers a five-step approach to creating a sustainable, diverse organizational culture: Define, Understand, Review, Communicate, and Implement. The model potentially equips leaders with an inclusive, legal, transparent framework by which to lead potentially contentious changes or programs, and leaders should consider the model's applicability to the unique needs of their organization.

References

Arsel, Z., Crockett, D., & Scott, M. L. (2022). Diversity, equity, and inclusion (DEI) in the *Journal of Consumer Research*: A curation and research agenda. *Journal of Consumer Research, 48*(5), 920–933. https://doi.org/10.1093/jcr/ucab057

Cisco Systems. (2020). *Pay parity at Cisco*. Cisco Systems. https://www.cisco.com/c/dam/en_us/about/inclusion-collaboration/pay-parity.pdf

Civil Rights Division. (2000, October). *Federal protections against national origin discrimination*. The United States Department of Justice. https://www.justice.gov/crt/federal-protections-against-national-origin-discrimination-1

Fortune Magazine. (n.d.). Fortune 100 best companies to work for. *FortuneMagazine*. https://fortune.com/ranking/best-companies/

Gomez, L. E., & Bernet, P. (2019). Diversity improves performance and outcomes. *Journal of the National Medical Association, 111*(4), 383–392. https://doi.org/10.1016/j.jnma.2019.01.006

Harrell, M., & Barbato, L. (2018, February 27). Great managers still matter: The evolution of Google's Project Oxygen. *ReWork*. https://rework.withgoogle.com/blog/the-evolution-of-project-oxygen/

Hofstede, G. (2001). *Culture's consequences: Comparing values, behaviors, institutions, and organizations across nations* (2nd ed.). Sage.

Hofstede, G. (n.d.). *The 6-D model of national culture*. https://geerthofstede.com/culture-geert-hofstede-gert-jan-hofstede/6d-model-of-national-culture/

Holvino, E., Ferdman, B. M., & Merrill-Sands, D. (2004). Creating and sustaining diversity and inclusion in organizations: Strategies and approaches. In M. S. Stockdale & F. J. Crosby (Eds.), *The psychology and management of workplace diversity* (pp. 245–276). Blackwell Publishing.

Khelifa, R., & Mahdjoub, H. (2022). An intersectionality lens is needed to establish a global view of equity, diversity and inclusion. *Ecology Letters, 25*(5), 1049–1054. https://doi.org/10.1111/ele.13976

Kirton, G., & Greene, A. M. (2021). *The dynamics of managing diversity and inclusion: A critical approach*. Routledge.

Linkov, I., Trump, B., & Kiker, G. (2022). Diversity and inclusiveness are necessary components of resilient international teams. *Humanities and Social Sciences Communications, 9*(1), 1–5.

National Diversity Council. (2023). *National Diversity Council NDC index*. National Diversity Council. https://ndc-index.org/ & https://ndc-index.org/our-participants/2022-participating-companies/

National Diversity Council. (n.d.). *Vision and mission*. https://nationaldiversitycouncil.org/about/who-we-are/vision-and-mission/

Neblett, E. W., Jr. (2019). Diversity (psychological) science training: Challenges, tensions, and a call to action. *Journal of Social Issues, 75*(4), 1216–1239. https://doi.org/10.1111/josi.12357

Noon, M., & Ogbonna, E. (2021). Controlling management to deliver diversity and inclusion: Prospects and limits. *Human Resource Management Journal, 31*(3), 619–638. https://doi.org/10.1111/1748-8583.12332

Page, S. E. (2019). *The diversity bonus: How great teams pay off in the knowledge economy*. Princeton University Press.

Passantino, F. (2021). Reflections: Diversity, inclusion and belonging in education post-Covid. *Intercultural Education, 32*(5), 583–589. https://doi.org/10.1080/14675986.2021.1857575

Roberson, Q. M. (2006). Disentangling the meanings of diversity and inclusion in organizations. *Group & Organization Management, 31*(2), 212–236. https://doi.org/10.1177/1059601104273064

Stuart, J., & Ward, C. (2019). Exploring everyday experiences of cultural diversity: The construction, validation, and application of the normative multiculturalism scale. *European Journal of Social Psychology*, *49*(2), 313–332. https://doi.org/10.1002/ejsp.2542

Swartz, T. H., Palermo, A. G. S., Masur, S. K., & Aberg, J. A. (2019). The science and value of diversity: Closing the gaps in our understanding of inclusion and diversity. *The Journal of Infectious Diseases*, *220*(Suppl. 2), S33–S41. https://doi.org/10.1093/infdis/jiz174

The American Red Cross. (n.d.). *Diversity equity inclusion toolkit*. The American Red Cross. https://www.redcross.org/red-cross-youth/resources/diversity-equity-inclusion-toolkit.html

The Americans for the Arts. (2016, October). *Americans for the Arts statement on cultural equity*. The Americans for the Arts. https://www.americansforthearts.org/sites/default/files/pdf/2016/about/cultural_equity/ARTS_CulturalEquity_updated.pdf

The Gates Foundation. (n.d.). *Diversity, equity, and inclusion*. The Gates Foundation. https://www.gatesfoundation.org/about/diversity-equity-inclusion

United States Department of Health and Human Services. (n.d.). *About EEO*. United States Department of Health and Human Services. Department of Health and Human Services: Equal Employment Opportunity. https://www.hhs.gov/about/agencies/asa/eeo/about-eeo/index.html

Zabelina, D. L., Friedman, N. P., & Andrews-Hanna, J. (2019). Unity and diversity of executive functions in creativity. *Consciousness and Cognition*, *68*, 47–56. https://doi.org/10.1016/j.concog.2019.01.004

Chapter 19

Decolonization and Inclusion: Widening the Circle

Niels Agger-Gupta, Shauneen Pete and Nikki Bade

Royal Roads University, Canada

Abstract

This chapter is a conversation between the three authors, an Indigenous person, a multigenerational White settler, and a White immigrant, about how equity, diversity, and inclusion (EDI) connects with the history and pervasive practices of colonialism, White supremacy, and embedded racism, and what might be done to create a new future that is individually and collectively just. EDI has become increasingly embraced by organizations and governments to overcome bias, to increase representation of under-represented groups, and to revise discriminatory policies across almost all areas of intersectionality. But EDI has no answers for the issues of Indigenous reconciliation and decolonization that seem to exist in a parallel world. A deeper understanding is needed about the individual rights roots of "equity," as well as knowledge of Indigenous history, since Indigenous communities are not simply additional cultural groups in Canada. The British *Royal Proclamation* of 1763 initially codified a "nation to nation" relationship, but subsequent broken treaties, and the 1876 *Indian Act*, imposed a White supremist relationship on Indigenous populations, stole lands, and attempted to eliminate traditional cultures. Since 1970, Indigenous organizations have sought a "citizenship plus" relationship with Canadian federal and provincial governments, a direction supported by more recent court decisions. This chapter includes examples of how these ideas have been applied by some organizations and concludes with a model for developing personal stamina and resilience for learning, reconsidering, and interacting with others about identity issues given the complexities of personal learning and system change.

Inclusive Leadership: Equity and Belonging in Our Communities
Building Leadership Bridges, Volume 9, 209–219
Copyright © 2023 by Emerald Publishing Limited
All rights of reproduction in any form reserved
ISSN: 2058-8801/doi:10.1108/S2058-880120230000009019

Keywords: Leadership; collective rights; colonialism; cultural benevolence; cultural tax; Indigenous; transformative learning

This chapter is a learning dialogue among the three authors – an immigrant settler, a settler descendent, and an Indigenous person. "Settler" refers to all non-Indigenous peoples in North America and is about relationships to land/place, structures, and processes, not an accusation or an epithet (Battell-Lowman & Barker, 2015). However, not all non-Indigenous peoples occupy North American spaces with the same complicities in Indigenous oppressions (Dei, 2017; Joyce, 2022).

The concepts of EDI or DEI are increasingly embraced by organizations across North America (Sanford, 2022; Williamson & Kizilcec, 2022), involving work to overcome bias, increase staffing from underrepresented groups, and revise discriminatory systems (CBC News, 2018; Sanford, 2022). The objective of workplace "inclusion" has been creating a sense of belonging and a feeling of acceptance for individual uniqueness (see Agger-Gupta & Harris, 2017; Baumeister & Leary,1995; Sugiyama et al., 2016; Thorpe-Moscon, 2015). However, the "belonging/uniqueness" formulation of "inclusion" hides an uncomfortable truth that for many the concept of inclusion is about fitting into a Euro-centric understanding of the dominant order and is disconnected from the issues of decolonization and ongoing oppression and discrimination, especially for Indigenous people in Canada (see, e.g., Dei, 2017; Lawrence & Dua, 2005).

Indigenous Realities and the Origins of EDI

The context of oppression and discrimination for Indigenous peoples in Canada is underpinned by the systematic oppression of the federal Indian Act (Government of Canada – Legislative Services Branch, 1876), which determined who was an "Indian" (an officially recognized Indigenous person, in the language of the time) and replaced traditional kinship relationships with policies separating "Indian" from "Metis" and "non-status" relatives. The Act was in direct opposition to the first British treaty between North American Indigenous nations and King George III, the Royal Proclamation of 1763, establishing "nation to nation" relationships with the crown (George, 1763). The Act separated Indigenous populations from their lands, their cultural background, language, self-governance, autonomy, resources, and ultimately health and dignity, by enforcing assimilation and calling this "enfranchisement." Residential schools were implemented from the late 1800s onward through various Christian churches, seeking to "remove the Indian from the child," by removing Indigenous children from their families, punishing them for speaking their languages, starving them, and physically and sexually abusing them, before burying over 6,000 in unmarked graves in residential school graveyards when they became sick and died (Milloy, 2017; Srikanth, 2012; Truth and Reconciliation Commission of Canada (TRC), 2015; Wilson-Raybould, 2022). The last residential school finally closed in 1996 (TRC, 2015), but the Indian Act continues to discriminate against Indigenous women and their children (Lafond, 2019).

The roots of EDI in Canada predate the Charter of Rights and Freedoms (Government of Canada, 1982), but the equality provisions under the law are enshrined there. The concept of "equality" – meaning treating everyone identically under the law – within a framework of cultural diversity, found its home in the Canadian Multiculturalism Act (Government of Canada – Legislative Services Branch, 1988). However, multiculturalism was rejected by Indigenous communities as an instrument of assimilation, erasing broken treaties and stolen lands and saying nothing about restitution for the centuries-long history of genocide through systematic racist oppression and colonial White supremacy (Battell Lowman & Barker, 2015; Joseph, 1970; Regan, 2010; Srikanth, 2012; St. Denis, 2011; Tuck & Yang, 2012; Wilson-Raybould, 2022). Multiculturalism also says nothing about relationships to land and place, or about collective rights and responsibilities to one's community, to ancestors, and to seven future generations, as articulated by Indigenous peoples (Battell-Lowman & Barker, 2015; Chief et al., 2016; Eichler, 2019; McDonald, 2022).

Shauneen Pete: Concepts of equity and inclusion place dominant groups at the center, and they assume Indigenous peoples should desire to become members of the dominant group – we should want to assimilate, in much the same way that racialized peoples assimilate to a national identity. The cost of becoming "Canadian" is giving up your cultural identities, but as First Nations, Metis, and Inuit people are not a culture within a nation, we are nations alongside a nation. We are striving to retain, in my case, nationhood through specificity: *niya nehiyawewin*. When I say, "niya nehiyawewin," I am describing not only a cultural positioning but also a political assertion of nationhood.

In my experience working in dominant educational environments, the multicultural assumptions of dominant society shape how they view the inclusion of the other, in my case, as a First Nations person. They believe (and want) a (light) cultural interaction with me, and what I offer is a critical examination of ongoing settler colonialism. I recognize that their views of inclusion center on their comfort. From that positioning, members of the dominant group want to be recognized for the benevolence they extend to Indigenous peoples, and they expect gratitude for our inclusion. "White benevolence" (Gebhard et al., 2022) is "a form of paternalistic racism that reinforces, instead of challenges, racial hierarchies, and its presence is found across Canadian institutions" (p. 1). White benevolence is rooted in "ideals of democracy, multiculturalism, peacekeeping, and tolerance" (p. 1). These ideals support the illusion of Canada and its institutions as being innocent in relation to ongoing colonialism. So deep is this idea entrenched that members of the dominant group expect Indigenous peoples to perform to the required codes of behavior that they have established and coded as "professional." They expect racialized and Indigenous professionals to generously share their cultures so that they (dominant group members) can gain an experience that affirms their tolerance. Performing our culture, and offering lessons, is the cultural tax racialized, and Indigenous peoples pay for inclusion (Pete, 2022, pp. 50–53). The cultural tax is the assumed responsibilities of Indigenous students, staff, and faculty who are expected to share our cultural experiences, offer land acknowledgments, serve as a diversity voice on committees, and provide evidence that the institution is doing its part to promote diversity. We also risk exclusions when we defy the codes of behavior by daring to identify discriminatory practices, and institutionalized racism/colonialism.

Niels Agger-Gupta: "Cultural benevolence" is the invisible and normative colonial project of White supremacy, where a White "settler" finds it almost impossible to understand that everyone does not share his/her perspective or experience, or that anyone would not want an individualistic, neo-liberal lifestyle (DiAngelo, 2022; Joyce, 2022). Without an understanding of the history of Indigenous peoples in Canada, those in the mainstream, and many in immigrant communities, find it hard to understand or accept Indigenous "citizenship plus" (Joseph, 1970; Newman et al., 2016), a reference to the special status and history Indigenous communities within North America have, both legally and ethically. As a White immigrant from Germany, growing up in Saskatoon, Saskatchewan, in the 1960s and early 1970s, with a stepfather from India, there was nothing in my education about residential schools.

Going Beyond the Performative

A second issue is that much of the work labeled as reconciliation has been criticized as being merely performative rather than transformative (see, e.g., Wilson-Raybould, 2022; Jimmy et al., 2019, and the Baroness von Sketch video about land acknowledgement, , 2021). "Reconciliation" is complicated and means different things to different people, say Wilson et al. (2019, p. xi). They identify five different constructs: "improving social relations between Indigenous and non-Indigenous peoples; specific calls to action and processes outlined by national governments; ... healing within ... families and communities ... and within ourselves"; ... and "associated with exploitation and ongoing colonialism" (p. xi). Organizations require deep commitments to foster understanding of the historic and systemic harms that have been perpetuated, to understand and respect cultural differences, and to commit to sustained action for the long term (Jimmy et.al., 2019, Wilson-Raybould, 2022).

One example is the September 30th Canadian national holiday, intended to commemorate and honor the tragic history and ongoing impacts of the Residential School system in Canada. Organizations have embraced this as an opportunity to wear orange shirts (https://www.orangeshirtday.org/). Wearing an orange shirt may involve personal learning for some, but for others could well be a "move to innocence" (Tuck & Yang, 2012), a performative interpretation of reconciliation, requiring no substantive personal or systems change in discarding the racist remnants of a normative White supremacy (Wilson-Reybould, 2022). As suggested by the Governor-General of Canada, Mary Simon, "the time for, 'I didn't know,' is over" (Simon, 2022).

Shauneen: To go further, Gebhard et al. (2022) assert,

> colonial institutions often engage in tokenistic gestures, evading the deeper work of antiracism theory and practice. Educational training models such as diversity and inclusion or implicit bias training that are currently popular in Canadian organizations often lack a foundational analysis of white settler colonialism and the unequal power dynamics that continue to negatively impact Indigenous peoples. (p. 252)

As suggested by the TRC (2015), in order for there to be a mutually respectful relationships between Indigenous and non-Indigenous peoples, "there has to be awareness of the past, acknowledgement of the harm that has been inflicted, atonement for the causes, and action to change behavior" (p. 7). As such, the concepts of equity and inclusion will only have meaning for Indigenous populations, when the almost invisible individualistic White settler colonial assumptions currently embedded in these concepts (see Battell Lowman & Barker, 2015; Joyce, 2022) are recognized, removed, and replaced with action.

Improving Inclusion with Indigenous Employees in the Energy Sector

In research currently being conducted by Nikki, there are multiple examples of how this is emerging in various energy organizations in Calgary, Alberta, Canada.

Nikki Bade: My doctoral dissertation study (forthcoming) considered both the individual and organizational perspectives in answering the question, "How might non-Indigenous organizations foster a culture of inclusion and engagement with Indigenous employees?" The findings suggested that relationship building is central to decolonizing and transforming the predominantly performative work being done in many organizations, to implementing action-based, transformative strategies for engaging Indigenous employees. For example, one participant shared a story of how their leader changed their annual performance review process, so that it was conducted using a circle process, and the evaluation criteria became based on the seven sacred teachings from their community. The participant described this change as a gift that felt more in alignment with the work they were doing and was also in alignment with whom they were as a person. In making this small, but obviously significant, change for the employee, the leader deepened their personal relationship with the employee and learned about the importance of culturally relevant processes in the work of the team. In supporting this change, the organization challenged previously established approaches and found ways to build a deeper understanding of both the employee's needs and Indigenous culture.

Another example from Nikki's organizational interviews was with an Indigenous Relations Manager from a long-standing energy organization that only recently began their journey of reconciliation. They recognized their relationships with the communities in which they operate are a key factor in their ongoing success, both financially and as an employer. To that end, they conducted a mapping exercise of their assets, locating both the Treaty land and the traditional territories that may be impacted by their operations. "Traditional territory" is the geographical area that is identified by a particular First Nation, Métis, or Inuit group as the land that they historically occupied (Wilson, 2018). The intention in identifying the traditional territory is specifically to,

> […] identify where else, along the path of our business, do we impact the traditional rights … of … Indigenous people, by impacting their traditional territories … [It] will tell us where those lands that are reserved for Indigenous peoples are, [and] the traditional

> territory where their hunting and gathering areas are, where they may have culturally sensitive areas …. (Organizational participant)

This approach suggests a deep commitment to the existing communities and is an acknowledgment that the traditional territory supersedes any ownership claims of the organization and opens the way for a new relationship where both the organization and the community may co-exist in a new way.

In both Nikki's research and from the personal experiences of the co-authors, respect and autonomy at both the individual and collective levels are seen to be critical for making inclusive leadership successful. Inclusion seems to work best when organizational stakeholders prioritize building personal and community relationships that connect the broader issues of equitable inclusion with the critical elements of decolonization and reconciliation.

Developing the Stamina and Patience to Learn New Identity Skills

Niels: To accomplish this task requires internal stamina, patience, and accept-ance that there will be discomfort in learning about history, race, and privilege (see, e.g., Battell Lowman & Barker, 2015; Regan, 2010). A recently popular idea is that topics creating discomfort, such racism or intersectionality, should not be taught, thus avoiding feelings of guilt, shame, distress, or victimization – reactions DiAngelo (2018) calls, "White fragility" (see Allen, 2022; Bregman, 2019; Capehart, 2022; Gross, 2022). These topics requires courage and vulnerability, two core elements of leadership (Brown, 2012). But inclusive leadership also requires curiosity, expertise in listening, asking questions, self-disclosure (Pearce, 2007), and an orientation to possibility (Agger-Gupta & Harris, 2017, p. 316), and critical hope that positive steps forward together can be found (Barker, 2021). Mezirow described "disorienting dilemmas," as critical to transformative learning (2000), particularly when expanding socially-constructed understandings through dialogue (Gergen & Hersted, 2016). It is also clear that we need greater tolerance, appreciation, and forgiveness for ourselves and for others (see, e.g., McArthur-Blair et al., 2018).

Shauneen: I have found it essential to explore White settler decolonization in my teaching work within the field of teacher preparation. This work explores the students' settler identity formation, their historical settler family narratives, and the gaps in their learning regarding Indigenous-settler relations. I've learned that we have all been structurally denied the opportunity to learn about Indigenous peoples, and that settler decolonization is necessary if we are to ever achieve any measure of reconciliation.

A reflexive thinking and communications skill set to create the emotional capacity to have emancipatory conversations exploring the damaging impacts of White (male) supremacy and other intersectional oppressions is an essential part of living in a cosmopolitan world and building healthy relationships. These skills include tolerance, patience, respect for others, and the ability to be reflective and curious, even while one's own biases, privilege, and unexamined microaggressions are being challenged. Tolerance for personal discomfort is part of this and includes personal acceptance of ambiguity and the candor to admit the deep socialization of White supremacy – and that there are no easy answers. DiAngelo (2022) says, "We don't need to be rescued from shame; we need to build our tolerance so we don't fall apart whenever our self-image is challenged" (p. 125). The practice of learning from our discomfort, that Shauneen calls, "building stamina for the ambiguity of the work," becomes equivalent to exercising an emotional muscle, if we are to be successful in creating reconciliation and building a new story of inclusion in organizations.

Based on the conversation among the three of us, Shauneen framed out a four-level developmental model (see Fig. 19.1) for building the stamina for challenging learning. It is evident that defensiveness is a "move to innocence" that shuts down learning, while patience, curiosity, reflexivity, and the willingness to stay in the moment supports transformational learning. The model has four different levels:

Here is how we see this process model working:

1. The first level involves the practice of self-location to promote a more honest positioning of oneself in relation with Indigenous peoples. A part of that self-location is claiming one's identity as settler. Reflective questions include:

    - What is the story of your ancestry?
    - What policies/procedures facilitated their relocation?
    - What were the costs to your family for their move?
    - What deeply held values/beliefs did you inherit?
    - What are the legacies of settlement for you today?
    - How did you learn about Indigenous peoples in your home, school, and community? And
    - What are your current relationships with land and Indigenous peoples?

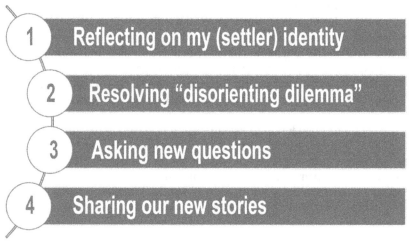

Fig. 19.1.   Process Model for Internal Stamina Development.

2. The second level involves resolving an ongoing, "disorienting dilemma," that one's own worldview or self-location may be blocking understanding or involve biases about others – including Indigenous people. This layer builds on empathy and social justice to develop a larger picture of inclusion/exclusion that respects ways of being and thinking that may be outside of one's current awareness. This level is therefore also about allowing for patience and emergence to increase one's own boundaries of acceptance. Questions for debriefing a disorienting dilemma might include:

    - What am I experiencing that is upsetting me?
    - Can I describe the challenging interaction I am having about something I said, did, or might believe?
    - How did I first learn about this topic?
    - What did I hear from my parents or siblings?
    - How can I be curious about and accept the work I must do to overcome my socialization into a society that ranks people by race and gender and carries elements of White supremacy?

3. The third level is about expanding the ability to develop and ask questions. The questions – and their partial answers – expand one's vocabulary to describe the personal difficulty in the second layer (perhaps through self-location?) and reflect on personal experiences and examples from cultural norms learned in their family and community about "us" and "them" (or others). DiAngelo (2022) suggests: "How is my socialization into systemic racism expressing itself in my daily life, and what can I do to interrupt it in myself, in those around me, and in our institutions? (p. 126).

4. With practice, a necessary fourth level opens, involving sharing one's personal learning journey with others, and co-creating a community of practice to build internal stamina through challenging conversations requiring courage, personal curiosity, profound respect for the other(s), openness to personal learning about the impacts of White supremacy, and an expectation that one will go through a "groan zone" (Kaner, 2014). One's own and collective transformative learning also requires humility and patience for the learning of others. Our purpose is nothing less than creating mutual understanding and an improved set of perspectives in the work of creating a new "inclusion" that incorporates the needs and aspirations of both reconciliation and social equity.

In conclusion, building internal stamina is challenging, but this learning is essential for achieving social justice and true inclusion, for others and for oneself. This is the necessary start of a much longer journey of discovery toward inclusive leadership involving "writing the new story about our (respectful) future together." Paulette Regan (2010) recognized the complex internal dynamics involved in moving out of colonial relationships:

> As a settler ally, I must continuously confront the colonizer-perpetrator in myself, interrogating my own position as a beneficiary of

colonial injustice. Exploring the epistemological tensions of working between these two identities means embracing persistent uncertainty and vulnerability. If we have not explored the myths upon which our identify is based, or fully plumbed the depths of our repressed history, we lack a foundation for living in truth .... But what if we were to offer the gift of humility as we come to the work of truth-telling and reconciliation? Bearing this gift would entail working through our own discomfort and vulnerability, opening ourselves to the kind of experiential learning that engages our whole being – our heads, our hearts, our spirits ... This involves nothing less than a paradigm shift that moves us from a culture of denial toward an ethics of recognition. (pp. 236–237)

References

Agger-Gupta, N., & Harris, B. (2017). Chapter 17: Dialogic change and the practice of inclusive leadership. In A. Boitano & H. E. Schockman (Eds.), *Breaking the zero-sum game: Transforming societies through inclusive leadership – A volume in the International Leadership Association Building Leadership Bridges series* (pp. 303–320). Emerald.

Allen, G. (2022, February 8). *Florida bill bans businesses and schools from making anyone feel guilt about race.* NPR|Race. https://www.npr.org/2022/02/08/1079112803/fla-bill-bans-businesses-and-schools-from-making-anyone-feel-guilt-about-race

Barker, A. J. (2022). *Making and breaking settler space: Five centuries of colonization in North America.* UBC Press.

Baroness von Sketch: Land Acknowledgement. (2021, February 16). *CBC comedy* [YouTube video]. https://youtu.be/LQyFfC7_U-E

Battell Lowman, E. B., & Barker, A. J. (2015). *Settler: Identity and colonialism in 21st century Canada.* Fernwood Publishing.

Barker, A. J. (2022). Making and breaking settler space: Five centuries of colonization in North America. UBC Press.

Baumeister, R. F., & Leary, M. R. (1995). The need to belong: Desire for interpersonal attachments as a fundamental human motivation. *Psychological Bulletin, 117*(3), 497–529. https://doi.org/10.1037/0033-2909.117.3.497

Bregman, P. (2019, August 21). Learning is supposed to feel uncomfortable. *Harvard Business Review.* https://hbr.org/2019/08/learning-is-supposed-to-feel-uncomfortable

Brown, B. (2012). *Daring greatly: How the courage to be vulnerable transforms the way we live, love, parent, and lead.* Gotham.

Capehart, J. (2022, February 9). Opinion|what about black students' 'discomfort'? *Washington Post.* https://www.washingtonpost.com/opinions/2022/02/08/teaching-history-discomfort-black-students/

CBC News. (2018, February 12). Dalhousie only seeking racially visible, Indigenous candidates for senior job. *CBC.* https://www.cbc.ca/news/canada/nova-scotia/dalhousie-university-recruitment-management-racially-visible-indigenous-1.4531723

Chief, C., Sabo, S., Clark, H., Henderson, P. N., Yazzie, A., Nahee, J., & Leischow, S. J. (2016). Breathing clean air is sa'áh naagháí bik'eh hózhóó (SNBH): A culturally centred approach to understanding commercial smoke-free policy among the Diné

(Navajo people). *Tobacco Control, 25*, i19–i25. https://doi.org/10.1136/tobaccocontrol-2016-053081

Dei, G. J. S. (2017). [Re]framing blackness and black solidarities through anti-colonial and decolonial prisms: An introduction. In G. J. S. Dei (Ed.), R*eframing blackness and black solidarities through anti-colonial and decolonial prisms* (pp. 1–30). Springer International Publishing. https://doi.org/10.1007/978-3-319-53079-6_1

DiAngelo, D. R. (2022). *Nice racism: How progressive White people perpetuate racial harm.* Beacon Press.

DiAngelo, R. (2018). *White fragility: Why its so hard for White people to talk about racism.* Beacon Press.

Eichler, J. (2019). *Reconciling Indigenous peoples' individual and collective rights: Participation, prior consultation, and self-determination in Latin America.* https://doi.org/10.4324/9780367220860

Gebhard, A., McLean, S., & St. Denis, V. (2022). *White benevolence: Racism and colonial violence in the helping professions.* Fernwood Publishing.

George, III. (1763, October 7). *Reprinted in RSC 1985, App II, No. 1 and reprinted in Government of Canada – Crown-Indigenous Relations and Northern Affairs Canada (2013, September 19). Royal Proclamation of 1763: Relationships, Rights and Treaties* [Poster – Educational material; promotional material]. https://www.rcaanc-cirnac.gc.ca/eng/1379594359150/1607905375821

Gergen, K. J., & Hersted, L. (2016). Chapter 9: Developing leadership as dialogic practice. In J. A. Raelin (Ed.), *Leadership-as-practice: Theory and application* (pp. 178–197). Routledge.

Government of Canada – Legislative Services Branch. (1876 and updated multiple times into the 2020s). *The Indian Act – Consolidated federal laws of Canada.* https://laws-lois.justice.gc.ca/eng/acts/i-5/

Government of Canada. (1982). *The Canadian Charter of Rights and Freedoms.* https://www.justice.gc.ca/eng/csj-sjc/rfc-dlc/ccrf-ccdl/

Government of Canada – Legislative Services Branch. (1988, July 21). *Canadian multiculturalism act – Consolidated federal laws of Canada.* https://laws-lois.justice.gc.ca/eng/acts/c-18.7/page-1.html

Gross, T. (2022, February 3). *From slavery to socialism, new legislation restricts what teachers can discuss.* NPR|Education. https://www.npr.org/2022/02/03/1077878538/legislation-restricts-what-teachers-can-discuss

Jimmy, E., Andreotti, V., & Stein, S. (2019). Towards braiding. Musagetes Foundation. https://decolonialfuturesnet.files.wordpress.com/2019/05/braiding_reader.pdf

Joseph, B. (1970). *The red paper: A counter-punch to the white paper.* Retrieved March 8, 2023, from https://www.ictinc.ca/blog/the-red-paper-a-counter-punch-to-the-white-paper

Joyce, S. J. A. (2022). Chapter 11: Am I a settler: Considering dominance through racial constructs and land relationships. In A. Gebhard, S. McLean, & V. S. Denis (Eds.), *White benevolence: Racism and colonial violence in the helping professions* (pp. 163–176). Fernwood Publishing.

Kaner, S. (2014). *Facilitator's guide to participatory decision-making* (3rd ed.). Jossey-Bass.

Lafond, D. (2019, February 8). *UN Human Rights Committee rules that Indian act discriminates on the basis of sex.* MLT Aikins Insights. https://www.mltaikins.com/indigenous/un-human-rights-committee-rules-that-indian-act-discriminates-on-the-basis-of-sex/

Lawrence, B., & Dua, E. (2005). Decolonizing antiracism. *Social Justice, 32*(4), 120–143. https://www.jstor.org/stable/29768340

McArthur-Blair, J., Cockell, J., & Cooperrider, D. (2018). *Building resilience with Appreciative Inquiry: A leadership journey through hope, despair, and forgiveness.* Berrett-Koehler Publishers.

McDonald, L. (2022). Can collective and individual rights coexist? In P. Jones (Ed.), *Group rights* (pp. 349–375). https://doi.org/10.4324/9781315253770-22

Milloy, J. (2017). *A national crime: The Canadian government and the residential school system*. University of Manitoba Press.

Mezirow, J. (2000). *Learning as transformation: Critical perspectives on a theory in progress*. Jossey-Bass.

Newman, K., Environics Institute for Survey Research, Canadians for a New Partnership, Circle on Philanthropy and Aboriginal Peoples in Canada, Inspirit Foundation, Institute on Governance, National Centre for Truth and Reconciliation, Reconciliation Canada, & Tides Canada. (2016). *Canadian public opinion on Aboriginal peoples: Final report*. https://nctr.ca/assets/reports/Modern%20Reports/canadian_public_opinion.pdf

Pearce, W. B. (2007). *Making social worlds: A communication perspective*. Wiley-Blackwell.

Pete, S. (2022). Decolonizing equity praxis. In V. C. R. Hackett & B. Allan (Eds.), *Decolonizing equity* (pp. 40–59). Fernwood Publishing.

Regan, P. (2010). *Unsettling the settler within: Indian residential schools, truth telling, and reconciliation in Canada*. UBC Press.

Sanford, S. (2022). *Inclusion, Inc.: How to design intersectional equity into the workplace*. Wiley.

Simon, M. (2022, October 6). *2022 LaFontaine-Baldwin lecture (Calgary)* [Text]. The Governor General of Canada; Government of Canada. https://www.gg.ca/en/media/news/2022/lafontaine-baldwin-speech

Srikanth, H. (2012). Multiculturalism and the Aboriginal peoples in Canada. *Economic and Political Weekly*, *47*(23), 17–21. JSTOR. https://www.jstor.org/stable/23214913

St. Denis, V. (2011). Silencing Aboriginal curricular content and perspectives through multiculturalism: "There are other children here." *Review of Education, Pedagogy, and Cultural Studies*, *33*(4), 306–317. https://doi.org/10.1080/10714413.2011.597638

Sugiyama, K., Cavanagh, K. V., Esch, C. v., Bilimoria, D., & Brown, C. (2016). Inclusive leadership development drawing from pedagogies of women's and general leadership development programs. *Journal of Management Education*, *40*(3), 253–292 .https://doi.org/10.1177/1052562916632553

Thorpe-Moscon, J. (2015). *Inclusion is key to keeping Canadian high potentials* [Research Report]. Catalyst Research Centers. http://www.catalyst.org/system/files/inclusion_is_key_to_keeping_canadian_high_potentials.pdf

Truth and Reconciliation Commission of Canada (TRC). (2015). *Volume 5: Canada's residential schools: The legacy: The final report of the Truth and Reconciliation Commission of Canada*. McGill-Queen's University Press. http://www.myrobust.com/websites/trcinstitution/File/Reports/Volume_5_Legacy_English_Web.pdf

Tuck, E., & Yang, K. W. (2012). Decolonization is not a metaphor. *Decolonization: Indigeneity, Education & Society*, *1*(1), 1–40. https://jps.library.utoronto.ca/index.php/des/article/view/18630

Williamson, K., & Kizilcec, R. (2022). A review of learning analytics dashboard research in higher education: Implications for justice, equity, diversity, and inclusion.*LAK22: 12th international learning analytics and knowledge conference* (pp. 260–270). https://doi.org/10.1145/3506860.3506900

Wilson, K. (2018). *Pulling together: Foundations guide*. Victoria, BC: BCcampus. https://opentextbc.ca/indigenizationfoundations/

Wilson, S., Breen, A. V., & DuPré, L. (2019). *Research and reconciliation: Unsettling ways of knowing through Indigenous relationships*. Canadian Scholars' Press.

Wilson-Raybould, J. (2022, November). *True reconciliation: How to be a force for change*. Penguin Random House Canada.

Chapter 20

Muslimophobia: Overcoming Religious Discrimination and Exclusion in the Workplace

Nurcan Ensari[a] and Ronald E. Riggio[b]

[a]*Alliant International University, USA*
[b]*Claremont McKenna College, USA*

Abstract

Muslimophobia, or prejudice toward Muslims, results in employment dis-crimination, social exclusion of Muslims, anti-Muslim hate crimes, and physical and verbal assaults, in the United States and globally. Moreover, anti-Muslim incidents are on the rise in many countries. In this chapter, we provide a review of Muslimophobia and its dynamics and consequences in the workplace. We also make suggestions for reducing prejudice toward Muslim employees, using social psychological perspectives, particularly intergroup contact theory, and research on prejudice reduction. It is also argued that leaders play an important role in the combating of Muslimo-phobia, including creating opportunities for personalized interactions with Muslim employees and disseminating more information about Muslims and Islam. This chapter concludes with practical implications and sug-gestions for future research directions. Although there is much work to be done in reducing Muslimophobia and discrimination against Muslims, social psychological research emanating from intergroup contact theory suggests that it is a viable path for researchers and practitioners to pursue.

Keywords: Muslimophobia; Islamophobia; discrimination; prejudice; hate crimes; social psychological research

Inclusive Leadership: Equity and Belonging in Our Communities
Building Leadership Bridges, Volume 9, 221–232
Copyright © 2023 by Emerald Publishing Limited
All rights of reproduction in any form reserved
ISSN: 2058-8801/doi:10.1108/S2058-880120230000009020

Muslims all around the world face great scrutiny and discrimination. Events such as the 9/11 attacks in New York City and the
7/7 subway bombings in London triggered further anti-Muslim
rhetoric globally. (Hussain & Bagguley, 2012; Pandith, 2021)

The US Equal Employment Opportunity Commission (EEOC) reported that discrimination against Muslims increased 250%, and 1,040 discrimination charges
were filed by Muslims between 9/11/2001 and 3/11/2012 (https://www.eeoc.gov/
wysk). The Pew Research Center (Mohamed, 2021) reports that 20 years after
9/11, Muslims continue to be discriminated against with nearly half of US Muslims reporting that they have experienced religious discrimination. Both Muslimophobia (i.e., prejudice toward Muslims) and Islamophobia (i.e., prejudice toward
the religion of Islam) result in employment discrimination, social exclusion of
Muslims, anti-Muslim hate crimes, and physical and verbal assaults (Disha et al.,
2011; FBI National Uniform Crime Reporting Program, 2002, as reported in
Rippy & Newman, 2006). The assumption that Muslims pose a high threat to the
public leads to openly stated prejudice toward Muslims (Croucher et al., 2016).

Muslimophobia is not only a problem in the United States but a global concern. For example, many European countries banned hijabs (women's head cover)
in certain professions and restricted Muslims' freedom of religious expression
(Ahmed, 2017). In the past decade, the annual number of anti-Muslim incidents has increased significantly in the Netherlands (Vellenga, 2018) and Ire-
land (Ahmed, 2017). In a study conducted in Canada, 51% of 1,143 participants
viewed Islam as a religion that promotes dominance over other religions and
held negative beliefs toward Islam (Wilkins, 2018). In Australia, Muslimophobia
negatively impacted the bond between Muslim and Australian society and polarized the relationship between Australian Muslims and Australian non-Muslims
(Akbarzadeh, 2016; Mansouri & Vergani, 2018). In 2016, French municipalities
banned the wearing of burkinis (full body-covering swimsuit) which were seen as
a threat to French secularism (Quinn, 2016).

Although such bans and discriminatory practices and rules spark controversy
at the national and international levels, struggles of Muslims continue.

Clearly, Muslimophobia is a growing social issue that has ramifications
for societies and organizations. In this chapter, we provide a review of Muslimophobia and its dynamics and consequences in the workplace. We also make
suggestions for reducing prejudice toward Muslim employees, based on social
psychological perspectives on prejudice reduction. Leaders play an important
role in combating Muslimophobia, and we end this chapter with practical implications and future directions.

Theoretical Approaches to Muslimophobia and its Consequences in the Workplace

Muslims make up less than 2% of the total US population and 6% of the total
European population. A high ratio of non-Muslims to Muslims in the United
States limits interactions and experiences with Muslims which in turn leads to

the expectation that interactions with Muslims would not be pleasant (Plant & Devine, 2003; Stephan & Stephan, 1985). Negative prior experiences with individual Muslims, anxiety about terrorism, and asylum seeker crises further reinforce expectations of negative consequences for working with Muslims and can enhance intergroup anxiety (Stephan & Stephan, 1985). There is strong empirical evidence that shows that intergroup anxiety results in heightened hostility toward and a desire to avoid interacting with out-group members (LausanneRenfro & Stephan, 2010). As a result, avoiding contact with Muslims can serve to reinforce negative stereotypes, enhance tendencies to judge Muslims as a homogeneous group, and increase hostility and continued anxiety (Baumeister & Vohs, 2007).

As the population of Muslim immigrants in the United States and Europe increases, they may be portrayed as threats to economic well-being, job security, physical safety, political power, and traditional American values such as the Protestant work ethic. Intergroup threat theory (Stephan et al., 2016) distinguishes between realistic threats (e.g., threats to physical safety or social status) and symbolic threats (e.g., threats to moral beliefs and values). Perception of out-group members as posing a threat to the ingroup's well-being, resources, values, and power can lead to intergroup anxiety, stereotyping, and consequently prejudice (Stephan & Stephan, 2000). Abrams et al. (2017) examined how psychological threats explain prejudice toward Muslims in Britain before and after the 7/7 London bombings. They distinguished between the economic and safety aspects of realistic threat. Attacks by Islamic terrorists are more likely to increase the safety threat than the economic threat, "because there is little direct economic interdependence between the perpetrators and potential victims" (Abrams et al., 2017, p. 262). In fact, Islam is perceived as a higher threat to public safety compared to other religions (Croucher et al., 2016). Beliefs that Muslims constitute realistic threats (e.g., terrorism and crime) and symbolic threats (e.g., values inconsistent with those of the majority group) are associated with negative stereotypes about Muslims' lack of integration into mainstream culture (Velasco González et al., 2008), which results in greater resentment toward Muslims (Stephan et al., 2016).

There is strong empirical evidence that supports these theoretical approaches to Muslimophobia. For example, Ghumman and Ryan (2013) found that Muslim women who wore hijabs were offered fewer job call backs and were less likely to be allowed to complete the job application process. Muslim job applicants reported more perceived negativity, lowered expectations of receiving job offers, and perceptions that employers were less interested in them (Malos, 2009). Muslim employees' anticipation of rejection can lead to social isolation which reduces their effective job performance (Sayyid, 2014). In a survey of 136 Christians, participants reported that they believed that Muslims have the weakest values of any religion (Moss et al., 2019). These empirical studies are supported by the Pew Research Center's survey that indicated that 41% of non-Muslim participants (total of 1,001) believe that Islam encourages more violence than other religions, and that Muslims are actually more violent (Khan, 2022; Kishi, 2017). There is also supportive evidence from Western European studies that showed that Muslimophobia is displayed in the form of opposition to building mosques, the wearing of headscarves, and opening Islamic schools, as well as increased intolerance of Muslim practices (Adelman & Verkuyten, 2019).

In sum, Muslimophobia poses a serious threat to organizations and workers and presents a challenge to leaders to try to reduce this pervasive form of religious discrimination. Muslimophobia not only affects individuals who are the targets of discrimination, but it can lead to both intra- and intergroup conflict, disrupt organizational harmony, and has ethical and legal implications. Certainly, there is a dire need for further research and intervention.

How Can Muslimophobia Be Reduced?

Based on intergroup contact theory, the personalization model (Allport, 1954; Ensari & Miller, 2002; Pettigrew, 1997), and the Common Ingroup Identity Model (Gaertner et al., 1996), we propose ways to reduce Muslimophobia.

Having positive experiences with an out-group member, whether in the form of a meeting, talking, exchanging personal information, or being friends, can reduce psychological distance between the group members and help to build empathy and trust (Allport, 1954). This, in turn, can reduce intergroup anxiety and tension (Allport, 1954; Reimer et al., 2021). Contact with out-group members results in meta-humanization which refers to perceptions of out-group members as human or as having dignified qualities. Pavetich and Stathi (2021) examined Muslim–non-Muslim relations in Canada and the United Kingdom and found an indirect effect of meta-humanization through out-group humanization, induced by contact, that reduced prejudice. According to the Personalization Model (Ensari & Miller, 2002; Ensari et al., 2012), a personalized interaction between members of different groups has distinct conceptual ingredients. Imagine a Catholic employee who did not have any prior experience with Muslims is assigned to work with a Muslim employee on an important task. During the intergroup contact, naturally, they might talk about their personal, social, and family lives, the sports they play, the boss that they don't like, the project that they succeeded or failed, their feelings and opinions, etc. Engaging in such personalized interaction can serve to individuate that Muslim employee (i.e., individuation) and differentiate him/her from other Muslims (i.e., decategorization). Further, personalized interactions allow for exploration of similarities and differences (i.e., self-other comparison); can replace negative stereotypes with corrective factual information, increase perspective-taking (i.e., empathy); and promote the exchange of intimate, personal, and unique information (i.e., self-disclosure) (Ensari et al., 2012). These processes elicit feelings of trust and would lead the non-Muslim employee to be more accepting toward his/her Muslim coworker. More importantly, if the Muslim employee is seen as a representation of a typical Muslim, the positive attitudes created might generalize to the out-group category as a whole – reducing prejudice (Ensari & Miller, 2002). The creation of peer mentoring programs that includes pairing mentors from diverse backgrounds is one strategy to help reduce prejudicial attitudes.

As previously mentioned, limited knowledge about Muslims and Islam contributes to Muslimophobia. Personalization can help to gain knowledge about

out-group. Sharing corrective information about Muslims and Islam enhances more positive views of Islam, disconfirms negative stereotypes and myths, and fosters reductions in prejudice (Allport, 1954; Pettigrew & Tropp, 2008). Examples of factual information about Muslims include terrorist attacks or suicide bombing are banned in Islam, majority of Muslim Americans (two-thirds) are democrats, not all Muslim women choose to wear covers, and there are many female CEOs and presidents in predominantly Muslim countries. It is incumbent upon leaders to play a role in sharing corrective information that combats stereotypes and misinformation about Muslims and other underrepresented groups.

For intergroup contact to be successful, certain conditions must be met. Group members must (1) be of equal status, (2) share common goals, (3) work in cooperation, and (4) be supported by a power of authority (Allport, 1954). There is substantial evidence from cross-sectional, longitudinal, experimental, and non-experimental studies that show that both small-scale and large-scale contact-based interventions improve intergroup relations (Al Ramiah & Hewstone, 2012; Pettigrew & Tropp, 2006). However, there are lessons learned from these studies. Intergroup contact is more effective if it (a) involves direct contact experiences (Beelmann & Heinemann, 2014), (b) is positive (Paluck et al., 2019), (c) involves high-quality exchanges (such as exchange of personal information, self-disclosure, and cross-group friendship) (Ensari & Miller, 2002; Khan, 2022; Pettigrew & Tropp, 2006), (d) emphasizes individuating information that allows exploration of similarities and differences (Brewer & Miller, 1984), and (e) is frequent (Pettigrew et al., 2011). Furthermore, for beneficial effects of intergroup contact to generalize to the out-group as a whole, the out-group members in the contact situation must be perceived as typical, and the group memberships need to stay salient (Ensari & Miller, 1998).

When considering intergroup contact, both quantity (frequency and duration) and quality (value and depth) of the contact should be considered. More frequent and long-term intergroup interactions are more likely to encompass cooperation and shared goals (Cernat, 2019). High-quality contact involves higher levels of personalization, self-disclosure, meaningful interactions, and intimacy which are associated with a stronger bond and greater trust between the group members (Ensari & Miller, 2002; Khan, 2022). Cross-group friendship is a powerful form of high-quality contact. A meta-analytic review of cross-group friendships revealed that friendships that involve behavioral engagement, such as spending time together or engaging in self-disclosure with out-group friends, are associated with more positive intergroup attitudes than other friendship assessments such as perceived closeness to out-group friend or perceived inclusion of out-group friend (Davies et al., 2011). Cross-group friendships allow individuals to get an "inside look" at the opinions and beliefs of out-group members; this allows individuals to view others in-depth and see them in a way that contradicts prejudices (Cameron et al., 2011).

When employees from different religious groups come together on a collaborative task, leaders need to set shared common goals (Allport, 1954). The Common Ingroup Identity Model (Gaertner et al., 1993) offers ways in which employees with different religious identities can be successfully merged into a superordinate identity. As this new superordinate social identity for team members starts to develop, loyalties to previous identities are transferred to the new common category for collective welfare. In the organizational context, superordinate group identity can be created by making salient an existing inclusive categorization such as a new workforce, team, or the organization as a whole (Gaertner et al., 1993). A group identity can be created by refocusing attention onto common interests (such as the success of the organization as a whole), forming heterogeneous work teams and holding them accountable to the larger organization, or enhancing subgroup members' awareness of their interdependence within a superordinate organization (Brewer & Schneider, 1990).

Practical Implications

To improve intergroup attitudes in the long run, intervention programs should go beyond short-term intergroup encounters (Reimer et al., 2021). Rather, leaders in organizations should consider creating opportunities for personalized interactions with Muslim employees on a regular basis, disseminate more knowledge about Muslims and Islam, and allow more positive contact to develop over time. These opportunities should not only focus on commonalities and similarities but also differences, such as different traditions, holidays, values, etc. Company newsletters, blogs, website, social media outlets are great vehicles for dissemination of such information and for spreading a celebratory and inclusive tone of voice.

One of the necessary conditions of successful intergroup contact is support from a power of authority (Allport, 1954). Leadership support is critical for the intergroup encounters among Muslim and non-Muslim employees, routine or planned, to be ameliorative. Likewise, organizational norms and policies should support inclusive practices, and the organization's mission statement should reflect inclusion as a shared vision. Initiatives and programs that aim to bring employees from different religious groups together toward a shared mission can be planned, developed, and executed under the leadership of the executive team. One such example is the "task-teams projects" (Maoz, 2000) developed for Palestinians and Jewish teachers in Israel. These projects brought Muslim and Jewish teachers together on joint assignments where there was a common goal and interdependence. More specifically, Muslim–Jewish task teams of 5–8 teachers were formed, and they met once or twice a month for one school year. The shared goal was to create a study unit of Jewish and Arab affairs for the schools collaboratively. They were asked not to engage in irrelevant, destructive discussions such as political conflicts. Each team had one Palestinian or Jewish facilitator who made sure that the teachers stayed focused on task. Leaders need to implement such projects when the status of the employees is perceived to be equal; otherwise, Muslim employees might feel threatened or forced to assimilate. That is, as demonstrated in past studies, without continuous and reinforced positive contact, it is not feasible to sustain ameliorative outcomes of intergroup contact.

Bringing employees from different religions together alone does not guarantee positive contact and positive changes. Interventions and programs should aim to alter out-group stereotypes and attitudes. One such model leaders can adopt is the Narrative Model (Bar-On, 2000) in which personal stories are shared by both group members. In a workspace, the mutual telling of personal life stories would enhance empathy and trust and change perceptions of each other. Such interventions require openness and honesty by the participants, and a safe space without being silenced by the dominant side (Bar-On, 2000). For example, sharing reflections during a 9/11 anniversary revealed that Muslim Americans, just like their non-Muslim peers, hold complex emotions: they have sadness for the humanitarian losses, fear of discrimination, avoidance of public places, and anger due to unfair and undeserved treatment (Mosquera et al., 2013). Another approach is interfaith dialogues that can unlock the power of religions and inspire the participants toward intimacy, perspective-taking, trust, and collaboration. The participants who are engaged in interfaith dialogue openly bring with them a deeply lived experience of their own tradition and share its fruits with others. There is no desire to change the other, instead all those involved in the dialogue will be changed in some way as a result of the process.

With the rise of virtual work since the COVID-19 pandemic, developing and encouraging intergroup interactions among employees might be perceived as a challenge. Past research shows, however, that when used appropriately, internet-based interactions with out-group members can reduce prejudice, just like in-person interactions (White & Abu-Rayya, 2012; White et al., 2015). In fact, researchers argued that the Internet can allow for direct contact via synchronous meetings and removes the physical and psychological barriers that separate groups (Amichai-Hamburger & McKenna, 2006). All requirements of successful intergroup contact as described above can easily be met during virtual meetings (i.e., virtual collaboration, common goal, moderators/supervisor, and equal contribution/status). When considering that Facebook users have an average of 338 friends on Facebook (https://truelist.co/blog/facebook-statistics/), similar social connection platforms can be utilized to remove barriers to personalize and make friends with others (Schwab et al., 2018).

There are also legal considerations. Leaders should know the legal principles governing religious accommodations. If an employee has a bona fide religious belief, and the employer is aware of the need for an accommodation, then management is legally responsible to accommodate the employee's request unless it creates an undue hardship (Findley et al., 2014; *TWA* v. *Hardison*, 1977). According to the EEOC (2013), "an accommodation may cause undue hardship if it is costly, compromises workplace safety, decreases workplace efficiency, infringes on the rights of other employees, or requires other employees to do more than their share of potentially hazardous or burdensome work." To prevent discrimination and legal conflicts, it is critical for leaders to understand the basics of Islam, the major customs, rituals, and obligations held by Muslims, such as certain dietary restrictions, clothing obligations, and holidays (Findley et al., 2014). As much as it is critical for the leadership and human resources departments to reasonably accommodate Muslim employees, it is also important to understand that there is diversity among Muslims with respect to the degree of religiosity and practice of the obligations. While Muslims who need accommodations will appreciate the support, those who don't should not be seen as divergent or outliers. Frequent diversity, equity, inclusion, and belonging (DEIB) training and recognition and celebration of different religions will help to create a culture of understanding, acceptance, and inclusion.

Future Directions

Although there are hundreds of studies on prejudice reduction, there is limited research on how to utilize intergroup contact and personalization in the workplace, and very little is known about the association between intergroup contact during work and generalized attitudes to the out-group as a whole and between contact at work and outside work. Although the premise of intergroup contact and the personalization model is to promote tolerance and acceptance, interventions that promote intergroup encounters may be seen as serving the ideological interests of the dominant group, thus unwittingly perpetuating the power imbalance and interpreting the intervention as misuse of goals (Maoz, 2000). Despite this, recent research suggests that an important key to reducing religious prejudice and discrimination is intergroup contact and greater understanding and familiarization with persons from different religions and cultures.

Recently, in a meta-analysis of 98 studies, Reimer and Sengupta (2023) found a positive association between intergroup contact with perceived injustice, collective action, and support for reparative policies, albeit the estimated effect sizes were small. Thus, potential consequences of power struggles, conflict over agenda, coalitions among the subgroups, and perceived asymmetry in status and power should be further understood, and ways in which such consequences can be avoided should be examined in future intergroup research.

When examining Muslimophobia, it is important for leaders to recognize the heterogeneity within the Muslim group, and the existence of disperse subgroups with different geographical regions, traditions, values, government structures, socio-economic levels, etc. For instance, in the United States, Muslims are from 80 different nations, and constitute the second-most racially and culturally diverse group (Pew Research). The persistent stereotype of Islam as being inherently against women's equality creates unique challenges for Muslim women who are seen as submissive and weak and are more likely to face backlash than Muslim men. Furthermore, there is greater heterogeneity among Muslim women than men. For instance, whereas less than 30% of Muslim women in Turkey and Lebanon wear a hijab, this increases to 65% in Tunisia, 97% in Iraq, and 100% in Saudi Arabia. Although Muslim women in some countries such as Saudi Arabia must ask permission to drive a car or open a bank account, they can become presidents in other Muslim countries such as Turkey. As such, intersectionality of religion and gender, age, race, education level, political ideology, country of origin, etc., as well as the role of out-group homogeneity (i.e., the perception that all Muslims are the same) on Muslimophobia, are interesting topics to explore in future research.

Although there is much work to be done in reducing Muslimophobia and discrimination against Muslims, social psychological research emanating from intergroup contact theory suggests that it is a viable path for researchers and practitioners to pursue. A number of programs (e.g., familypicturesusa.com; see FitzGerald et al., 2019) seek to bring together persons from different races and cultures together, under equal status circumstances, to better understand one another and reduce discrimination. Evaluations of the effectiveness of these programs are needed to extract best practices. Similar programs to reduce Muslimophobia are definitely needed.

References

Abrams, D., Van de Vyver, J., Houston, D. M., & Vasiljevic, M. (2017). Does terror defeat contact? Intergroup contact and prejudice toward Muslims before and after the London bombings. *Peace and Conflict: Journal of Peace Psychology*, *23*(3), 260–268. https://doi.org/10.1037/pac0000167

Adelman, L., & Verkuyten, M. (2019). Prejudice and the acceptance of Muslim minority practices: A person-centered approach. *Social Psychology* ,*51*(1), 1–16. https://doi.org/10.1027/1864-9335/a000380

Ahmed, A. (2017). Islamophobia thriving in Europe, new report says. *Huffpost*, March 31.

Akbarzadeh, S. (2016). The Muslim question in Australia: Islamophobia and Muslim alienation. *Journal of Muslim Minority Affairs*, *36*(3), 323–333. https://doi.org/10.1080/13602004.2016.1212493

Allport, G. W. (1954). *The nature of prejudice*. Addison-Wesley.

Al Ramiah, A., & Hewstone, M. (2012). "Rallying around the flag": Can intergroup contact intervention promote national unity? *British Journal of Social Psychology*, *51*(2), 239–256. https://doi.org/10.1111/j.2044-8309.2011.02041.x

Amichai-Hamburger, Y., & McKenna, K. Y. (2006). The contact hypothesis reconsidered: Interacting via the Internet. *Journal of Computer-mediated communication*, *11*(3), 825–843.

Bar-On, D. (2000). *Bridging the gap*. Koerber.

Baumeister, R., & Vohs, K. (Eds.). (2007). Intergroup anxiety. In *Encyclopedia of social psychology* (pp. 492–493). SAGE Publications.

Beelmann, A., & Heinemann, K. S. (2014). Preventing prejudice and improving intergroup attitudes: A meta-analysis of child and adolescent training programs. *Journal of Applied Developmental Psychology*, *35*(1), 10–24. https://doi.org/10.1016/j.appdev.2013.11.002

Brewer, M. B., & Miller, N. (1984). Beyond the contact hypothesis: Theoretical perspectives on desegregation. In N. Miller & M. B. Brewer (Eds.), *Groups in contact: The psychology of desegregation* (pp. 281–302). Academic Press.

Brewer, M. B., & Schneider, S. (1990). Social identity and social dilemmas: A double-edged sword. In D. Abrams & M. A. Hogg (Eds.), *Social identity theory: Constructive and critical advances* (pp. 169–184). Harvester-Wheatsheaf.

Cameron, L., Rutland, A., Hossain, R., & Petley, R. (2011). When and why does extended contact work? The role of high quality direct contact and group norms in the development of positive ethnic intergroup attitudes amongst children. *Group Processes & Intergroup Relations*, *14*(2), 193–206.

Cernat, V. (2019). When cross-ethnic friendships can be bad for out-group attitudes: The importance of friendship quality. *Journal of Community & Applied Social Psychology*, *29*(2), 81–89. https://doi.org/10.1002/casp.2385

Croucher, S., Homsey, D., Brusch, E., Buyce, C., DeSilva, S., & Thompson, A. (2016). Prejudice toward American Muslims: An integrated threat analysis. *Journal of Intercultural Communication*, *32*, 1–18.

Davies, K., Tropp, L. R., Aron, A., Pettigrew, T. F., & Wright, S. C. (2011). Cross-group friendships and intergroup attitudes: A meta-analytic review. *Personality and Social Psychology Review*, *15*(4), 332–351. https://doi.org/10.1177/1088868311411103

Disha, I., Cavendish, J., & King, R. (2011). Historical events and spaces of hate: Hate crimes against Arabs and Muslims in Post-9/11 America. *Social Problems*, *58*(1), 21–46.

Ensari, N., Christian, J., Kuriyama, D. M., & Miller, N. (2012). The personalization model revisited: An experimental investigation of the role of five personalization-based strategies on prejudice reduction. *Group Processes & Intergroup Relations*, *15*(4), 503–522. https://doi.org/10.1177/1368430211434576

Ensari, N., & Miller, N. (1998). Effect of affective reactions by an out-group on preferences for crossed categorization discussion partners. *Journal of Personality and Social Psychology*, *75*(6), 1503–1527. https://doi.org/10.1037/0022-3514.75.6.1503

Ensari, N., & Miller, N. (2002). The out-group must not be so bad after all: The effects of disclosure, typicality and salience on intergroup bias. *Journal of Personality and Social Psychology*, *83*(2), 313–329.

FBI National Uniform Crime Reporting Program. (2002). United States Department of Justice, Federal Bureau of Investigation. (September 2002). Crime in the United States, 2002.

Findley, H., Hinote, H., Hunter, R., & Ingram, E. (2014). Accommodating Islam in the workplace. *ASBBS Proceedings*, *21*(1), 243–253.

FitzGerald, C., Martin, A., Berner, D., & Hurst, S. (2019). Interventions designed to reduce implicit prejudices and implicit stereotypes in real world contexts: A systematic review. *BMC Psychology*, *7*(29). https://doi.org/10.1186/s40359-019-0299-7

Gaertner, S. L., Dovidio, J. F., Anastasio, P. A., Bachman, B. A., & Rust, M. C. (1993). The common ingroup identity model: Recategorization and the reduction of intergroup bias. *European Review of Social Psychology*, *4*(1), 1–26.

Gaertner, S. L., Dovidio, J. F., & Bachman, B. A. (1996). Revisiting the contact hypothesis: The induction of a common ingroup identity. *International Journal of Intercultural Relations*, *20*, 271–290.

Ghumman, S., & Ryan, A. (2013). Not welcome here: Discrimination towards women who wear the Muslim headscarf. *Human Relations*, *66*(5), 671–698.

Hussain, Y., & Bagguley, P. (2012). Securitised citizens: Islamophobia, racism and the 7/7 London bombings. *The Sociological Review*, *60*(4), 715–734. https://doi.org/10.1111/j.1467-954X.2012.02130.x

Khan, T. (2022). *How to reduce prejudice towards Muslim employees: The mediational role of out-group trust on the relationship between intergroup contact and Muslimophobia* [Doctoral dissertation, Publication No. 29207001]. Alliant International University. ProQuest Dissertation Publishing.

Kishi, K. (2017, November 15). *Assaults against Muslims in U.S. surpass 2001 level.* Pew Research Center. https://www.pewresearch.org/fact-tank/2017/11/15/assaults-against-muslims-in-u-s-surpass-2001-level/

LausanneRenfro, C., & Stephan, W. G. (2010). Intergroup anxiety. In J. Levine & M. Hogg (Eds.). *Encyclopedia of group processes and intergroup relations*. (pp. 465–468). SAGE.

Malos, S. (2009). Post-9/11 backlash in the workplace: Employer liability for discrimination against Arab- and Muslim-Americans based on religion or national origin. *Employee Responsibilities and Rights Journal*, *22*(4), 297–310.

Mansouri, F., & Vergani, M. (2018). Intercultural contact, knowledge of Islam, and prejudice against Muslims in Australia. *International Journal of Intercultural Relations*, *66*, 85–94. https://doi.org/10.1016/j.ijintrel.2018.07.001

Maoz, I. (2000). Multiple conflicts and competing agendas: A framework for conceptualizing structured encounters between groups in conflict – The case of a coexistence project of Jews and Palestinians in Israel. *Peace and Conflict: Journal of Peace Psychology*, *6*(2), 135–156. https://doi.org/10.1207/S15327949PAC0602_3

Mohamed, B. (2021). *Muslims are a growing presence in U.S., but still face negative views from the public.* Pew Research Center. https://www.pewresearch.org/fact-tank/2021/09/01/muslims-are-a-growing-presence-in-u-s-but-still-face-negative-views-from-the-public/

Mosquera, P. M. R., Khan, T., & Selya, A. (2013). Coping with the 10th anniversary of 9/11: Muslim Americans' sadness, fear, and anger. *Cognition and Emotion*, *27*(5), 932–941. https://doi.org/10.1080/02699931.2012.751358

Moss, A., Blodorn, A., Van Camp, A., & O'Brien, L. (2019). Gender equality, value violations and prejudice toward Muslims. *Group Processes & Intergroup Relations*, *22*(2), 288–301.

Paluck, E. L., Green, S. A., & Green, D. P. (2019). The contact hypothesis re-evaluated. *Behavioural Public Policy*, *3*(2), 129–158. https://doi.org/10.1017/bpp.2018.25

Pandith, F. (2021, September 1). *The U.S., Muslims, and a turbulent post-9/11 world.* Council on Foreign Relations. https://www.cfr.org/article/us-muslims-and-turbulent-post-911-world

Pavetich, M., & Stathi, S. (2021). Meta-humanization reduces prejudice, even under high intergroup threat. *Journal of Personality and Social Psychology*, *120*(3), 651–671. https://doi.org/10.1037/pspi0000259

Pettigrew, T. (1997). Generalized intergroup contact effects on prejudice. *Social and Personality Psychology*, *23*(2), 173–185. http://dx.doi.org/10.1037/pspi0000259

Pettigrew, T. F., & Tropp, L. R. (2006). A meta-analytic test of intergroup contact theory. *Journal of Personality and Social Psychology*, *90*(5), 751–783. https://doi.org/10.1037/0022-3514.90.5.751.

Pettigrew, T. F., & Tropp, L. R. (2008). How does intergroup contact reduce prejudice? Meta-analytic tests of three mediators. *European Journal of Social Psychology*, *38*(6), 922–934.

Pettigrew, T. F., Tropp, L. R., Wagner, U., & Christ, O. (2011). Recent advances in intergroup contact theory. *International Journal of Intercultural Relations*, *35*(3), 271–280.

Plant, E. A., & Devine, P. G. (2003). The antecedents and implications of interracial anxiety. *Personality and Social Psychology Bulletin*, *29*(6), 790–780. https://doi.org/10.1177/0146167203029006011

Quinn, B. (2016, August 23). French police make woman remove clothing on Nice beach following burkini ban. *The Guardian*. https://www.theguardian.com/world/2016/aug/24/french-police-make-woman-remove-burkini-on-nice-beach

Reimer, N. K., Love, A., Wölfer, R., & Hewstone, M. (2021). Building social cohesion through intergroup contact: Evaluation of a large-scale intervention to improve intergroup relations among adolescents. *Journal of Youth and Adolescence*, *50*, 1049–1067.

Reimer, N. K., & Sengupta, N. K. (2023). Meta-analysis of the "ironic" effects of intergroup contact. *Journal of Personality and Social Psychology*, *124*(2), 362–380. https://doi.org/10.1037/pspi0000404.supp (Supplemental)

Rippy, A. E., & Newman, E. (2006). Perceived religious discrimination and its relationship to anxiety and paranoia among Muslim Americans. *Journal of Muslim Mental Health*, *1*, 5–20.

Sayyid, S. (2014). A measure of Islamophobia. *Islamophobia Studies Journal*, *2*(1), 10–25. http://doi:10.13169/islastudj.2.1.0010

Schwab, A. K., Sagioglou, C., & Greitemeyer, T. (2018). Getting connected: Intergroup contact on Facebook. *The Journal of Social Psychology*, *159*(3), 344–348. https://doi:10.1080/00224545.2018.1489367

Stephan, C. W., & Stephan, W. G. (2000). The measurement of racial and ethnic identity. *International Journal of Intercultural Relations*, *24*(5), 541–552.

Stephan, W. G., & Stephan, C. W. (1985). Intergroup anxiety. *Journal of Social Issues, 41*(3), 157–175.

Stephan, W. G., Ybarra, O., & Rios, K.(2016). Intergroup threat theory. In T. D. Nelson(Ed.), *Handbook of prejudice, stereotyping, and discrimination* (pp. 43–60). Psychology Press.

TWA v.*Hardison*, 432 U.S. 63, 97 S. *Ct.* 2264 (1977).

Velasco González, K., Verkuyten, M., Weesie, J., & Poppe, E. (2008). Prejudice towards Muslims in the Netherlands: Testing integrated threat theory. *British Journal of Social Psychology, 47*(4), 667–685.

Vellenga, S. (2018). Anti-semitism and Islamophobia in the Netherlands: Concepts, developments and backdrops. *Journal of Contemporary Religion, 33*(2), 175–192.

White, F. A., & Abu-Rayya, H. M. (2012). A dual identity-electronic contact (DIEC) experiment promoting short-and long-term intergroup harmony. *Journal of Experimental Social Psychology, 48*(3), 597–608.

White, F. A., Harvey, L. J., & Abu-Rayya, H. M. (2015). Improving intergroup relations in the Internet age: A critical review. *Review of General Psychology, 19*(2), 129–139.

Wilkins, L. S. (2018). Islamophobia in Canada: Measuring the realities of negative attitudes toward Muslims and religious discrimination. *Canadian Review of Sociology, 55*(1), 86–110.

U.S. Equal Employment Opportunity Commission. (2013). *Religious discrimination.* U.S. Equal Employment Opportunity Commission. http://www.eeoc.gov/laws/types/religion.cfm

Chapter 21

The Reciprocity of Dignity: Transforming Us/Them Narratives Through Inclusive Dialogue

Linda Kligman[a], Justin Mui[b], Henry L. McClendon, Jr[a] and Flor García Mencos[c]

[a]*International Institute for Restorative Practices, USA*
[b]*Lutheran Community Care Services, Singapore*
[c]*Circula, Centro de Liderazgo Restaurativo, Guatemala*

Abstract

People who are "othered" confront an epistemic injustice that silences and discards their knowledge. Rather than being actors in their own future, people in positions of authority dictate prescriptive procedures, removing marginalized individuals – and often the communities that care about them – from participating in what could be real and sustainable solutions to harmful social conditions. These injustices create us/them narratives, which can become social landmines that may explode under pressure. Restorative practices prize shared learning and decision-making to harness collective energies around a common purpose to repair relationships. Dialogue facilitated in a circle format ritualizes acts of inclusion and utilizes the power of followership – those without formal authority – to create a shared understanding. Revealing complexities beyond a myopic us/them perspective expands cognitive empathy and refocuses participants on unmet needs to help defuse social landmines. This chapter illustrates three inclusive circle processes that can be employed to uphold human dignity by affirming belonging within a diverse community and honoring all people's voice and agency. Dialogue circles respond to the injustice of being othered by granting people the right to interpret their own lives. In Detroit, Guatemala, and Singapore, facilitated circles create space for reciprocal storytelling and foster social connections among neighbors, police, and migrants. Most significantly, people become stewards of their future, not problems to be managed, kindling life-affirming resolve collectively supported within their communities.

Inclusive Leadership: Equity and Belonging in Our Communities
Building Leadership Bridges, Volume 9, 233–241
Copyright © 2023 by Emerald Publishing Limited
All rights of reproduction in any form reserved
ISSN: 2058-8801/doi:10.1108/S2058-880120230000009021

Keywords: Restorative practices; circles; dignity; followership; empathy; community

For our survival, biology favors our own families and those in our closest relationships (Bloom, 2018; Lieberman, 2013). Simple words like "us" and "them" initially allow us to identify our people and distinguish our stories. Bloom (2018) warns this evolutionary bias creates limitations on who we naturally care for and associate with and, conversely, who we punish and fear. When us/them narratives are paired with power, there is a schism of participation, sometimes outright exclusions, that diminishes people's voice, agency, and belonging – their very dignity. People who are "othered" confront an epistemic injustice that silences and discards their knowledge. It removes them – and often the communities that care about them – from participating in what could be real and sustainable solutions to harmful social conditions. Restorative practices prize shared learning and decision-making to harness collective energies around a common purpose. Often, dialogue facilitated in a circle format ritualizes acts of inclusion. Circles create space where people can come together and sit side by side; they can see and be seen, hear and be heard, and together their narratives create a shared understanding. Bailie (2019) contends such processes uphold dignity by affirming belonging within a diverse community and honoring voice and agency. Most promising for a divided world, this chapter suggests how leaders can kindle life-affirming resolve and meaningful social connections facilitating inclusive discourse.

Across communities, a reductionist approach thwarts collaboration and limits possibilities (Block, 2008; Bloom, 2018; Palmer, 2011). Even if us/them discernment benefited our immediate families' survival, it creates social landmines that can detonate under pressure. These human-shaped bifurcations erupt and cause harm, violence, and global tragedy. They might lie below the surface, perhaps hidden by history or manners, but a field of landmines harbors violence and trauma for generations. Knowing these polarizing bombs exist, people might dash ahead, willing to accept casualties, or perhaps react with avoidance and refuse to risk engaging with others. Fortunately, when discovered, us/them landmines can be defused. Transformation is possible when we recognize that "us" and "them" need not be oppositional. Intentional discipline, consistent practices, and open minds help people to recognize the creative possibilities in diversity (Palmer, 2011).

Followership is a study within leadership that harnesses the full potential of community by recognizing the reciprocal influence of followers in any leader's hierarchy (Chaleff, 2009; Kellerman, 2012). Fixating on leadership alone negates the power that comes from people's decisions to support, ignore, or resist authority. Restorative practices is an emerging field dedicated to building relationships and strengthening a sense of community (Bailie, 2019; Wachtel, 2013). Processes routinely employ dialogue circles with both leaders and followers, bringing people together to sit side by side and take turns speaking without interruption to share their experiences. Inclusive dialogue invites multiple perspectives and utilizes what Bloom (2018) terms "cognitive empathy," an expanded and more considered lens that helps us care about others beyond those with whom we most easily identify. When leaders become facilitators, empowering followership with an inclusive structure for participation, there is a collective shift. Peacemaking circles favor healing and reintegration, not punishment; engagement is bounded by guidelines, not rules; and decision-making emerges through consensus, not adversarial judgment (Pranis et al., 2003). Dialogue circles can be intentionally inclusive to restore what Fricker (2007) terms "hermeneutical injustice," the act of people being denied the right to interpret their own lives. As illustrated below, storytelling can rebalance this injustice by intentionally structuring discourse to create relational connections. Revealing complexities beyond a myopic us/them perspective refocuses participants on unmet needs and helps deconstruct social landmines and restore people's dignity.

Sharing Agency: Inviting Participation

In Singapore, a densely populated country, 80% of the population lives in high-rise public housing that might consist of 120 families with Chinese, Malay, Indian, or Eurasian ethnicities practicing more than 10 different religions (Tan, 2020). Living in close proximity, neighbors can experience persistent distress, triggering us/them landmines by conflicts over noise, smells, and the encroachment of space along the common corridors. When conflicts erupt, residents in public housing have the option to file a complaint in court. Outcomes are determined by a judge deciding the veracity of the claim, the gravity of the offense, and what remedies worked for others in the past. But harms that feel like grievous disrespect cannot be solved by a judge ordering someone to feel respected. Alternatively, a community organization utilizes restorative practices to divert cases from the justice system and empower neighbors to co-create sustainable solutions.

Facilitators at Project Restore were asked to work with an elderly woman who was continually awakened by the sounds of her neighbors' dripping air conditioner above her apartment and bothered by their dragging furniture overhead during her prayer time. In a peacemaking circle, dialogue does not revolve around establishing facts or deciding who is right or wrong. Instead, it is premised on the individual's subjective experience to express the harm felt and assert their individual needs. In this case, facilitators needed to create conditions for neighbors to willingly participate to find a meaningful resolution. They first identified people who had been affected. They engaged each member of both households to provide an unfettered opportunity for their stories to be heard while validating instances of emotional expression. In such situations, there are often others who have been impacted by the residential conflict: family members and neighbors who listen to the complaints, police who are called to the building, and even community leaders concerned with discord in the building. Creating the space to be inclusive of all parties' participation provides transparency to how resolution occurs and builds trust in the process and outcomes.

A hypothesis of restorative practices is that "human beings are happier, more cooperative and productive, and more likely to make positive changes in their behavior when those in positions of authority do things *with* them, rather than *to* them or *for* them" (Wachtel, 2013, p. 3). Before any explosive can be cleared, it must be located. To discover the us/them landmines, the facilitator establishes a participatory approach, based on the conviction that discourse is the conduit of change. Maroosis (2008) describes a facilitator's role structuring followership as,

> a partnership of reciprocal flowing. It is like a conversation where the leader and follower both are learning about the law of the situation. And like any conversation, leadership and followership can move from person to person as the dialogue twists and turns. (p. 23)

To learn together, the facilitator prompts neighbors to share what happened and listen to others' experiences without interruption. Multiple perspectives unearth a diversity of impacts and feelings. Once heard, the facilitator prompts conversation, so the dialogue shifts away from "getting even" and orbits around "getting well" (Pranis et al., 2003, p. 10). To clear a path forward and collectively remedy harms, agreements are recorded, and there is recognition of their collective efforts.

Peacemaking circles do not rely on precedent set by others, as each circle is unique to the participants and their situation. Facilitators employ the principles of followership, directing their authority away from themselves to empower neighbors to activate their own agency and determine what will work best for them. Storytelling inspires empathy regardless of participants' ethnic background, religious practices, and other constructs. When residents have the authority to resolve conflicts, their solutions aspire to create a harmonious home for their families. Sometimes, the outcomes are symbolic – parties exchange paper cranes at the closing of a circle to symbolize peace, or they might cook and share an ethnic dish to partake in the communal activity of eating together. The outcomes of Project Restore have been promising; claims that were initiated before the courts were withdrawn, and post-peacemaking circle feedback revealed a reduction in the frequency of noise almost immediately after the circle (Lutheran Community Care Services, 2019).

In this case, the upstairs neighbors agreed to minimize their noise because they could sympathize with having felt disrupted and disrespected, though that was not their intent. And continued compliance is much easier when your actions are by your own choice rather than someone else's mandate. The woman's son shared how the circle created a sense of psychological safety (Goh, 2021): "It was a very neutral setting where everyone was relaxed and sat down to voice their matters and differences." In contrast to a disputed argument in court, this relational approach focused on the families' needs, recognizing the importance of their relationship as people who would return home and continue to each other in the halls.

Honoring Voice: Asking Questions That Matter

Miles away, Detroit is an American city scarred by a legacy of abusive policing. Entrapped by structural systems that limit their agency, poor urban communities occupy a "second-order agency" (Simpson, 2017). Police hold authority – as well as tasers and guns. Cries of "Black Lives Matter" are countered by "Blue Lives Matter," a rhetoric implying the safety of police officers, often wearing blue uniforms, is somehow in opposition to focusing on the harms committed against Black and Brown peoples.

Detroit's Police Community Summits invite citizens and police officers to come together to participate in dialogue circles to restore relational trust in the community. Police intentionally invite people who have previously filed complaints and officers who had been the subject of complaints for a facilitated day of teambuilding and storytelling.[1] Facilitators try to mitigate us/them landmines by instructing officers not to wear their blue uniforms and attend in casual clothing like that of the other citizens. To get started, everyone stands in a large circle facing one another and is asked to step forward to indicate experiences, such as *Who here sings in the shower? Who has dated someone your parents didn't like?* Commonalities are humanizing, and it is impossible to discern who among the crowd is a police officer. After the officers identify themselves, participants are placed in groups comprising two officers and two civilians. To prompt dialogue, officers ask the citizens to share: *What memory/encounter has shaped your attitude toward police officers? Who was impacted by the encounter and in what way? How did the experience impact the way you viewed police officers? If the experience was negative, what was the hardest thing for you?* They listen without interruption. Then, the citizens ask the officers: *What was your most challenging encounter with citizens during your career? How did that experience impact the way you do your job? What's been the hardest thing for you?* The small group discussions allow participants to reveal problematic behaviors and learn about these impacts from diverse perspectives.

Similar to the followership framework, Vaandering (2013) defines restorative encounters through a lens of reciprocity, seeing one another not as objects to be managed but as subjects worthy of hearing and respecting. The physical act of all participants showing up in civilian clothes helps all participants to be seen as equal subjects in the dialogue, not as objects to be patrolled or controlled. Participants are in a safe space and have equal agency to choose their level of disclosure and share stories.

The questions we ask matter. Wiesel (1998) observes, "We have learned from history that people are united by questions. It is the answers that divide them" (p. 140). The facilitator asks universally meaningful questions about people's encounters in their neighborhoods so that people could imagine walking in one another's shoes. The social landmines are intentionally triggered by the prompts within the circle to contain the emotional shards.

During one summit, an officer shared he was verbally accosted "just trying to do his job," and a civilian declared: "I think you [police] are all out to kill us!" (H. McClendon, personal communication, April 1, 2017). The questions activated both thinking and feeling, engendering cognitive empathy, observed as a biological resonance when emotions are experienced together (Abramson, 2014; Bloom, 2018). Regardless of skin color, or the uniform worn, they voiced a shared sense of concern for themselves and their families. They all wanted to get home safely.

---

[1]Before attending, all complaints had been resolved by Detroit's Police Commission.

People have different perspectives of what is considered appropriate emotional displays (Cheshin, 2020). One participant shared they had instructed their sons not to make eye contact or move when their cars were pulled over for fear of upsetting the police. An officer expressed the opposite, sharing that people averting their gaze made them feel more nervous. Listening to one another created a new understanding. As one man attested, "because of the discussions we had … I have developed a newfound respect and empathy for the work that officers do" (Detroit Police Department's 11th District, 2022). At the same summit, an officer recognized the reciprocity of dialogue: "It lets law enforcement be involved with the community and the community to be involved with law enforcement so we can both understand each other's perspective of policing." Storytelling humanizes, creates, and restores social connections.

Nurturing Belonging: Strengthening Human Resolve

In Guatemala, many adults and unaccompanied children leave their homes in a desperate act to escape poverty, crime, political violence, human rights abuses, and collapsing natural resources. The presence of loved ones is replaced by remittance offices with lines of women waiting to collect money sent home by those who left. For many, leaving is a matter of survival, yet they end up dislocated, alienated, and unable to send much money home. Entering the United States, many discover Western constructs often impose political structures and solutions that diminish their Indigenous experience and justify their impositions (Tsosie, 2017). In new lands, they discover that only some of "us" belong and others are unwelcomed and deported to countries that did not expect to see them return. As a result of the massive migratory movement, there is a proliferation of agencies authorized to reduce migration, but when the us/them chasm marginalizes those navigating the social mine fields, the issues are not cleared. Relocated individuals often risk their lives to cross borders again.

Hoping to root dislocated migrants back in their original – or sometimes new – communities, one international agency has contracted with a Guatemalan organization to provide entrepreneurial training. Employing circle processes long practiced by their Indigenous communities, facilitators use restorative processes to develop leadership and communication skills. Their program, "Learning from One's Own History: Participation, Restoration and Strengthening the Sense of Community," works with deported individuals to co-create narratives that nurture social cohesion in their new communities. Facilitators convene circles with prompts to honor their inherent leadership capabilities such as courage, perseverance, and decisiveness. At the age of 10, one girl was put on a bus and cleaned homes across the border to send money back to her mother and younger siblings. She shared feeling more estranged from her town and family upon each return from her three trips across the border (F. García Mencos, personal communication, August 25, 2021). In words and pictures, participants create images illustrating where they came from and the paths they traveled to respond to prompts of: "I am made of … I come from …." Facilitators guide the conversation about the impact of dislocation but leave flexibility to allow for the unplanned to emerge.

Stories of courage, decision-making, and adaptability are illustrated with villages, trains, rivers, and tall buildings.

Authorities might control the political and economic agendas, but those who walked through the social mine fields gained important knowledge along their journey. As relayed in a conversation between adult educators Paulo Freire and Myles Horton, creating circles of learners is compelling (Bell et al., 1990):

> It was so enriching, you see, to have a person learn that they knew something. Secondly, to learn that their peers knew something, and learn that they didn't have to come to me, the expert, to tell them what the answers were. (p. 168)

Sharing knowledge is critical for survival and dignity. For people who have been "othered" – marginalized by systems that control their citizenship – having a sense of belonging can evoke positive feelings and correlate to improved thinking and decision-making (Walton & Cohen, 2011).

Sometimes, circles are convened in a local pizzeria, a successful business owned by an entrepreneur who had also once been a migrant. He shares his own stories and his success to show what is possible. Creating a sense of belonging and social connections helps people thrive (Block, 2008; Lieberman, 2013). The facilitators recognized that many youth already possessed some of the planning skills and risk-taking required of entrepreneurs. But to restart a life in a country that had almost nothing to offer them, there was a need to nurture communication skills and interpersonal competencies for social cohesion. Training included nonviolent communication skills (Rosenberg, 2015) to help participants bridge their embodied experiences and connect to the impact they have had on others. Storytelling strengthened their relationships and resolve. Providing programmatic feedback, participants wrote: "I can't believe we did this project with our own ideas; I can see myself in it and I can lead!" and "I have always wanted to help my community and now I feel more confident to do so" (International Learning Institute for Social Reconciliation, 2021). The process also strengthened a sense of belonging among participants.

Conclusion

Dialogue is not a panacea for personal healing and institutionalized disparities. It is predicated on the ability to find one's voice and honor voices that are different. To defuse us/them landmines, preparation is key to success. It takes a skilled facilitator to be intentionally inclusive and create clear expectations: you may not get the last word, there may not be a "happily ever after" resolution, and you are not able to change anyone's thinking but your own. Tokenistic engagement by people in positions of authority will erode trust, making it more difficult to bring people together. For those with less power, it requires courage to engage.

Approaching complex problems using mutual influence to rebalance authority requires a population willing to strive for justice over expediency (Hawkins, 2002).

To transform injustice "to change, the system needs to learn more about itself from itself. The system needs processes to bring it together" (Wheatley, 2006, p. 145). In these three very different countries, circles structured a space for all participants to speak and be heard. Restorative practices rely heavily on willing participation and access to one another to craft discourse in a dignified manner: sharing agency, honoring voice, and nurturing belonging. Leadership must become adept at followership to shift the assumptions of those in positions of authority, balance voice, and create a respect for sharing wisdom (Kellerman, 2012).

These stories show discourse can be applied in various stages of conflict to validate people's dignity. When one lacks the authority to resolve disputes on their own, the need for relational repair remains. Detroit's summits bring polarized parties together to hear perspectives of the other. Because no one speaks for the other, circles balance a flow of narratives that validates the perspectives of those that are different and diffuses the us/them landmines. In Guatemala, participants do not have even symbolic access to the authorities who have crafted the immigration restrictions; but even without an encounter with "them," dignity can be restored by the act of authoring one's own story. In contrast, Singapore's peacemaking circles restore a mutual sense of belonging to a shared residence by providing the agency and support to resolve conflicts and repair relationships on their own. Regardless of the typology of divide or juncture of conflict, when "people suffer an injury to their sense of worth, the antidote is time with people who know how to treat them in a dignified way" (Hicks, 2011, p. 197). The reciprocity shown witnessing one another's stories humanizes both "us" and "them."

References

Abramson, L. (2014). Being emotional, being human: Creating healthy communities and institutions by honoring our biology. In V. C. Kelly Jr & M. Thorsborne (Eds.), *The psychology of emotion in restorative practices: How affect script psychology explains how and why restorative practice works* (pp. 84–104). Jessica Kingsley Publishers.

Bailie, J. (2019). A science of human dignity: Belonging, voice and agency as universal human needs. *International Institute for Restorative Practices, 1*, 1–16.

Bell, B., Gaventa, J., & Peters, J. (Eds.). (1990). *We make the road by walking: Conversations on education and social change*. Temple University Press.

Block, P. (2008). *Community: The structure of belonging*. Berrett-Koehler Publishers.

Bloom, P. (2018). *Against empathy: The case for rational compassion*. HarperCollins.

Chaleff, I. (2009). *The courageous follower: Standing up to & for our leaders* (3rd ed.). Berrett-Koehler Publishers.

Cheshin, A. (2020). The impact of non-normative displays of emotion in the workplace: How inappropriateness shapes the interpersonal outcomes of emotional displays. *Frontiers in Psychology, 11*. https://doi.org/10.3389/fpsyg.2020.00006

Detroit Police Department's 11th District [@DPD11Pct]. (2022, September 8). *The Detroit Police Department's Office of Workplace & Community Resiliency conducts precinct-specific meetings periodically to allow citizens to discuss concerns* [video attached Tweet]. Twitter. https://twitter.com/DPD11Pct/status/1567955048625307649

Fricker, M. (2007). *Epistemic injustice: Power and the ethics of knowing*. Oxford University Press.

Goh, Y. H. (2021, July 23). New scheme in Bukit Merah to help feuding neighbours and avoid escalation to courts. *The Straits Times*. https://www.straitstimes.com/singapore/new-scheme-in-bukit-merah-to-help-feuding-neighbours-and-avoid-escalation-to-courts

Hawkins, D. (2002) *Power vs. force: The hidden determinants of human behavior*. Hay House Inc.

Hicks, D. (2011). *Dignity: Its essential role in resolving conflict*. The Maple Press.

International Learning Institute for Social Reconciliation. (2021). Unpublished learning report.

Kellerman, B. (2012). *The end of leadership*. HarperCollins.

Lieberman, M. D. (2013). *Social: Why our brains are wired to connect*. Broadway Books.

Lutheran Community Care Services. (2019). Unpublished raw data on Restorative interventions case closure feedback form.

Maroosis, J. (2008). Leadership: A partnership in reciprocal following. In R. E. Riggio, I. Chaleff, & J. Lipman-Blumen (Eds.), *The art of followership: How great followers create great leaders and organizations* (pp. 17–24). Jossey-Bass Inc.

Palmer, P. (2011). *Healing the heart of democracy: The courage to create a politics worthy of the human spirit*. Jossey-Bass Publishing.

Pranis, K., Stuart, B., & Wedge, M. (2003). *Peacemaking circles: From conflict to community*. Living Justice Press.

Rosenberg, M. (2015). *Nonviolent communication: A language of life* (3rd ed.). PuddleDancer Press.

Simpson, L. C. (2017). Epistemic and political agency. In J. I. Kidd, J. Medina, & G. Pohlhaus Jr. (Eds.), *The Routledge handbook of epistemic injustice* (pp. 254–260). Routledge.

Tan, X. W. A. (2020). *Urban system studies. Religious harmony in Singapore: Spaces, practices and communities*. Centre for Liveable Cities.

Tsosie, R. (2017). Indigenous peoples, anthropology, and the legacy of epistemic injustice. In J. I. Kidd, J. Medina, & G. Pohlhaus Jr. (Eds.), *The Routledge handbook of epistemic injustice* (pp. 356–369). Routledge.

Vaandering, D. (2013). A window on relationships: Reflecting critically on a current restorative justice theory. *Restorative Justice, 1*(3), 311.

Wachtel, T. (2013). *Defining restorative* (p. 12). International Institute for Restorative Practices. https://www.iirp.edu/restorative-practices/defining-restorative/

Walton, G. M., & Cohen, G. L. (2011). A brief social-belonging intervention improves academic and health outcomes of minority students. *Science, 331*(6023), 1447–1451.

Wheatley, M. J. (2006). *Leadership and the new science: Discovering order in a chaotic world* (3rd ed.). Berrett-Koehler Publishers.

Wiesel, E. (1998). The loneliness of Moses. In L. S. Rouner (Ed.), *Loneliness* (pp. 127–142). University of Notre Dame Press.

Chapter 22

Social Justice Leader Case Studies Assessed Through the Lens of Connective Leadership™

Sarah Smith Orr

University Professor, Consultancy Owner, Smith Orr & Associates, USA

Abstract

This chapter draws upon the leadership and work of two social entrepreneurs who believe that inclusion of community members in project/venture planning and design is key to accelerate equitable system change. The social justice leaders featured, through their actions in diverse, marginalized communities, will provide a model of leadership behaviors that utilize a repertoire of styles framed in the Connective Leadership Model™. They are system-changing champions driven by their social justice passion which requires that they provide leadership through planning and design processes to achieve equity in communities and influence policy. Short case studies will define the venture's mission, processes, and social change outcomes with examples of the type of leadership necessary for building inclusive and equitable community-based initiatives. Their words and actions will illustrate how leaders can innovate to create system impacts not by a single intervention but through multilayered processes with a broad range of benefits – for infrastructure, education, social, economic, and environmental justice programs. The results described will emphasize the critical elements of process, the insight and power of community input and involvement, and the influential cross-sector shaping of programs and policy to achieve sustainable change. This chapter concludes with a more detailed description of the Connective Leadership Model™ and how the model enables a leader to "consciously and systematically utilize a variety of behaviors," effectively reacting to the leadership needs of a par-

Inclusive Leadership: Equity and Belonging in Our Communities
Building Leadership Bridges, Volume 9, 243–254
Copyright © 2023 by Emerald Publishing Limited
All rights of reproduction in any form reserved
ISSN: 2058-8801/doi:10.1108/S2058-880120230000009022

ticular situation as well as using the achieving style behaviors most valued for a community-based system change venture (Lipman-Blumen, 2000, pp. 113–114).

Keywords: Connective leadership; inclusive leadership; social entrepreneurship; inclusive community initiatives; social justice change leaders; multi-sector community-based innovation

"Actions speak louder than words" is a frequently used adage. As illustrated in this chapter, for the two social entrepreneurs featured, actions are indeed louder than words. Their collective and community-based actions are designed to disrupt established systems that hinder equitable change. Their words have depth and values-based meaning, words that are integral to a social justice leader's vocabulary. Their words reveal behavioral and leadership models of how to build equitable, sustainable, and system-changing community initiatives rooted in the concept of belonging.

Foundational to social entrepreneurs is understanding community and how its social fabric is shaped: "The social fabric of community is formed from an expanding shared sense of belonging" (Block, 2008, 2009, p. 9). Block describes a society as "healthy" when it involves connection and caring, achieving that "shared sense of belonging" with a wide range of multi-level stakeholders. Ehrlichman (2021) emphasizes the importance of "impact networks, which build on the life force of community" (p. 8); Praszkier & Nowak (2012) define building community as "strengthening the feeling of a shared identity of belonging, co-ownership, willingness to connect and cooperate, resilience in response, and eagerness to contribute" (p. 199) – basically "co-creating with the community" (Chaline, 2016, p. 41); Budak (2022) maintains that to achieve social justice, societies must embody a level of "changemaker leadership and action" (p. 22). Changemakers are generally defined as people who lead systemic change, collaborators, who free up unrealized community abilities or qualities to advance needed change (Bornstein & Davis, 2010; Carlson, 2023; Dees, 2001; Kickul & Lyons, 2012; Osburg & Schmidpeter, 2013; Sharpiro, 2013; Schwartz, 2012; Wei-Skillern, Austin, Leonard & Stevenson, 2007).

"Forging community is not easy," asserts Lipman-Blumen (2000). Community building requires leaders who employ a repertoire of leadership behaviors as they connect with community members and stakeholders. From Lipman-Blumen's perspective, using a paraphrased reference to Abraham Lincoln, "connective leaders represent our 'last great hope' for building community" (p. 20).

Lipman-Blumen (2000) describes our current period as the "Connective Era," where "traditional approaches to leadership cannot address the complexities created by increasing diversity and interdependence" (p. xvi). She offers a model to help the leader assess and address those complexities through a repertoire of behaviors or "*achieving styles*" (p. 113).

Connective Leadership Model™

Through the lens of Connective Leadership™, I challenge the reader to view the words and actions (*achieving styles*) of two exceptional entrepreneurs. More detailed definitions of the Connective Leadership Model™ follow the brief case studies. However, to help the reader assess the work of the social entrepreneurs, an illustrative version is presented below. In short, the model enables a leader to "consciously and systematically utilize a variety of behaviors," effectively reacting to the leadership needs of a particular situation as well as using the behaviors most valued for a community-based system change venture (Lipman-Blumen, 2000, pp. 113–114).

As you, the reader, assess the leadership behaviors articulated by the two social entrepreneurs profiled, consider which of the styles included in the model below are utilized most frequently. Are their behaviors more relational, instrumental, or direct? Or are they using a combination of those styles? Look for words and actions, keeping a tally of behaviors as you learn about each leader (Fig. 22.1).

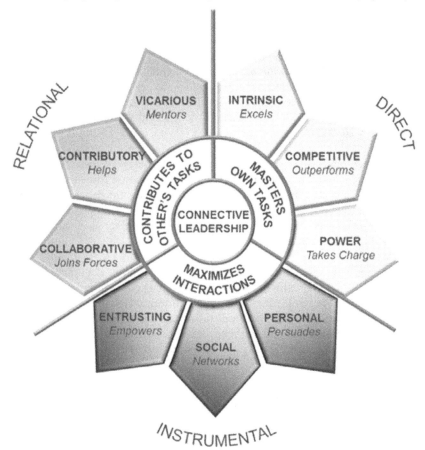

Fig. 22.1.   The L-BL Achieving Styles Model. Copyright ® 1976 Jean Lipman-Blumen. *Source:* Connective Leadership Institute (n.d.).

Case Studies

In early 2023, I conducted personal interviews with social entrepreneurs that I have studied and collaborated with for a decade. This chapter introduces two brief case studies that consist of excerpts from interviews of two internationally recognized leaders; the *passages/quotations* focus on how community social fabric is formed through their actions and ventures, as well as the leadership behaviors they use to achieve their initiative's inclusive, equitable, and belonging goals.

Vicky Colbert, Founder and Executive Director, Fundación Escuela Nueva (FEN), Colombia, South America

Founded in 1987, FEN (n.d.) is

> a nonprofit committed to improve the quality, relevance, and efficiency of education by rethinking the way we learn and promoting active, participatory, cooperative, and personalized learning centered on the learner ... We lead a global movement focused on improving the life chances and opportunities of the underserved through quality education ..., through a coalition of global partners from various sectors ..., extending the reach of the proven Escuela Nueva Activa model and adapting it to meet the needs of the underserved. (https://escuelanueva.org/en/mision-vision/, February 20, 2023)

FEN was established by Vicky Colbert to ensure that the Escuela Nueva (EN) model, that she had initiated through Colombia's National Ministry of Education, was implemented appropriately; with FEN, she continues to innovate and apply the concepts of the educational model to other contexts and population groups, preserving its key features. When asked to describe her vision and inspiration for EN, Colbert replied:

> When you have empathy as your essence and a bit of compassion, you start really thinking about inequity. In Colombia, we started during difficult circumstances [internal civil unrest], trying to reach the marginalized, totally convinced that without quality education and with no development, nothing can be achieved; it is just the only way to reduce inequity and promote democracy.
>
> I was inspired by the concept of democracy and an educational model I learned about in college – how there is an intimate relationship between the way you learn and your social behaviors. It was important to me and my team to incorporate democratic behaviors, problem-solving, and leadership skills in children – basically empowering them to reduce inequities.

> The invisible schools that nobody was reaching were where I started. For me, it's a social, philosophical, personal commitment to work with the most marginalized communities in the rural, isolated areas with bottom-up strategies – to work with rural teachers because they are the ones who know what's going on.
>
> I was young; I started going to isolated areas, even where the revolutionary guerillas were active. Basically, I felt that if the teachers are living and working in those areas, I must go work with them. As a result, I brought the remote schools to the attention of bureaucrats in the Ministry of Education.

As a designer of educational systems, describe your team's foundational philosophy to co-create community initiatives:

> To begin there was no sense early on nor in our program design to not work with the most marginalized and diverse. Community-led planning is crucial to equitable and sustainable change. EN is one of the longest-operating bottom-up educational innovations in the developing world due to that model of planning.
>
> Further, the whole concept of social participation is embedded in what we do and where we see the importance of the participation and involvement of the actors of change. The teachers are the actors of change. Children are the actors of change. Communities are the actors of change. Community members feel it's theirs as they are active participants in this process.
>
> Many of these rural teachers, who, in most cases, did not have formal teaching credentials, have a tremendous sense of belonging and responsibility for their results. In order to support them, we had to find simple ways to equip them with teaching and student learning instruments. But behind each simple instrument, there's a whole concept of social participation. Additionally, anything we did had to be viable, technically speaking, politically speaking, and financially speaking.

Colbert followed with a description of how she has successfully scaled the EN model beyond Colombian rural schools to national and international levels of implementation.

> The most impactful systems involve innovations, not through a single intervention but by thinking systemically from the beginning. It's a multi-layered process. Many of the teachers we work with have been trained in a traditional, conventional way, which means we have to change the way we work with the teachers; we

have to make changes in our work with parents and communities. We had to make changes with school supervisors and local administrators.

We needed to think systemically and transform all this complexity into simple, manageable actions, and, most importantly, we had to make things viable. With the team at FEN, we've continued to innovate new dimensions, adapting our educational model to urban areas and to displaced populations.

To conclude, Colbert discussed her leadership model that she has maintained over the years:

I try to put into practice transformative leadership. My leadership was/is not authoritarian; it is basically promoting the leadership of others. Standing a little bit behind and promoting their leadership and participation.

It is listening to people, dialoguing with them, and helping them reach their own conclusions. Schools should teach children, as in our educational model, how to dialogue. As we have learned, this is the essence of peace processes. (V. Colbert, personal communication, February 9, 2023)

Chelina Odbert, CEO and Founding Principal, Kounkuey Design Initiative (KDI), United States, Nairobi, Kenya, and Sweden

Founded in 2006,

KDI is a community development and design nonprofit. We partner with under-resourced communities to advance equity and activate the unrealized potential in their neighborhoods and cities. KDI works with local residents to transform unsafe and underused sites into "Productive Public Spaces." We believe community-led planning is key to sustainable and equitable change. We work with residents to create plans that advance their long-term visions for equitable communities. We help residents design and implement programming that generates income, energizes culture, builds community capacity, and brings our "Productive Public Spaces" to life for years to come. We believe in co-producing knowledge to catalyze social change. We believe community voices are crucial to advancing equity. (n.d.; https://kounkuey.org/mission, February 21, 2023)

To begin, I asked Odbert to describe her early intuitions and ambitions that led to the co-founding of KDI:

I always expected that I would be a leader contributing to solving global problems. During a post-college year, while teaching in Honduras, I saw the community I was living in rebuilt with the help of outside organizations after a devasting hurricane. It was then that I began to realize the power of design in healing communities and in fixing inequities in communities.

Later, at graduate school, the driving intention was to get back on that path to leadership and to find out how I could use design as a tool for addressing some of our world's most pressing challenges. What I knew intuitively from growing up as a Mexican American and from people in my own communities was that where and what you had, as well as where you lived, made a really big difference in what you had access to and how you thrived in life.

Understanding the importance of a theoretical framework that guides development, I asked Odbert, an urban planner by training, to describe the theory that KDI follows:

At its core, it is sharing the decision-making process with the end user, with the people for whom and with whom you are designing. Whether it's a policy change project or we're actually building something in a neighborhood, it's always through this community-engaged or participatory design process that we are bringing people who know the problem best, better than us, into the process. They have real power to influence and decide the outcome alongside others.

We spend a lot of time just asking people about the place they live. Their answers become the clues for what to build upon and how to effectively create change that is lasting.

That is impressive. Give me some examples of how you, and your team, work within your planning model:

When we started to work in the Eastern Coachella Valley [Southern California], a place we had no previous connection to, we spent the first year just getting to know people, like meeting people that lived there, but also getting to know the institutions and the organizations, whether they be local self-help groups or larger kinds of organizations working for change in the area, foundations, or government officials. We also let them get to know us, such as, here are the things we do, what we've done in other places, and here are the ways we work with community. We would ask what they are already building on: "Are there any places where our particular skills could layer on top of what you are doing or help you move things forward that you did not have a particular skillset for because you are not architects or urban planners?"

Now we've started to work in places where we don't have long histories. We'll only say yes to those projects if there's a really strong community partner that already knows the things that it would take us a year to learn. For example, if there's already a service provider that works with, let's say, unhoused youth, and we're coming in to help with a project with the unhoused, then if that organization invites us as a partner and will share what they know to help us learn, that's another way that we can do it on a faster basis.

Belonging and caring are critical elements of a social justice initiative. Odbert discussed how community members experience those critically important values through KDI ventures.

Our first project was in Nairobi, Kenya, in Kibera, an unincorporated area. From the beginning, we said, if we're going to really do something here, we're going to build the local capacity. If you look at our Kenya team, it's led by Kenyans. We have a similar approach to our work in the U.S. in our Coachella office. It is led by people from Coachella and its rural farm worker communities.

Multi-layering is another KDI feature foundational to system-changing initiatives, involving an evolutionary process that occurs when a venture is truly committed to a community-based change initiative. KDI does that well – please explain:

It is just a necessity for us at the outset to think about projects as layered: physical interventions layered with economic possibility, layered with social change programming or opportunity. Needs are never in just a single sector. It's never just "we need job training," or "we just need you to build a park," or "we just need sidewalks or transportation." They are always intersectional.

The multi-sectoral approach to a particular project became priority number one. You begin to see you're really making headway on one issue. In the process, you uncover another issue that really has to be worked on in order to improve the success of the first intervention. That is why we tend to commit to places for the long term.

As an intersectional example, KDI's Coachella Valley project leaders handled a transportation-related issue that arose during their work with the community; tell me how that came into being:

It was basically a bureaucratic issue. Eastern Coachella Valley is made up of farm communities. Western Coachella is Palm Springs, La Quinta, and a lot of wealthier resort cities. After working with Eastern Coachella Valley residents and assessing their needs, we found a near complete lack of transportation infrastructure: no bus stops, no sidewalks, and no bike lanes. To understand why, we started our inquiry with the county transportation department, the same department serving both sides of the valley. We found there was state money to build transportation infrastructure, but to access that money, a community mobility plan was needed – a transportation planning document that says where the transportation roads and sidewalks go.

The same county transportation planners that make the plans for the West Valley just hadn't prioritized plans for the East Valley. We realized we could fill this gap and offered to make these plans on behalf of the County which could then adopt them as its own. The result? We made the plans; the County adopted them. We applied for the state funds and got eight million dollars to build the first 14 miles of sidewalks!

As we concluded our interview, I sought Odbert's advice for evolving social change leaders:

> The best change agents in any given place are the people that know that place best. The real thing you can offer someone as an outsider is a pathway to grow their leadership in their own community. One of the best practices for a budding social entrepreneur seeking to create change is to look for those people that are native to the experience, to the place, and to the community. And most importantly, to use your capacity as a leader to build their capacity as leaders and as social entrepreneurs. (C. Odbert, personal communication, February 13, 2023)

Profile of Leadership Behaviors

In each of the brief case studies, common themes emerged. For example, each leader has disrupted the "norm" by guiding the design of inclusive systems rooted in community "based upon an understanding, or map, of the community's assets, capacities, and abilities" (Kretzmann & McKnight, 1993, p. 5). Both agree that building community involves a system-wide, long-term perspective that ensures that most individual's needs are reasonably met, which requires that the social entrepreneur and their team work with a wide spectrum of community resources and stakeholders.

At the beginning of this chapter, I noted that the optimal leadership behaviors manifested by the many social entrepreneurs in my study, including the two profiled here, can be framed within the Connective Leadership™/Achieving Styles™ Model (Lipman-Blumen, 2000). As displayed earlier, and illustrated below, the model has three behavioral sets – Direct, Relational, and Instrumental. Within each of the three sets are three behaviors or achieving styles "behaviors used by individuals for achieving their objectives" (Lipman-Blumen, 2000, p. 118). Detailed descriptions of the nine styles can be found in *Connective Leadership: Managing in a Changing World* (Lipman-Blumen, 2000, pp. 119–126). The brief descriptions below of each set have been retrieved from the Connective Leadership Institute website, https://connectiveleadership.com/achieving-styles/ (February 20, 2023). At the site, the reader can learn more about the model and each of the behavioral sets.

Earlier you were asked to tally the leadership behaviors you identified as you read through the interviews. In your review of the descriptions below, and in your assessment of the two leaders' words and actions, have they performed effectively drawing on a repertoire of leadership behaviors?

Direct Set

> People who prefer the direct set of behavioral styles tend to confront their own tasks individually and directly (hence the "direct" label). The three styles within the direct set emphasize deriving intrinsic satisfaction from mastering the task, outdoing others through competitive action and using power to take charge and coordinate everyone and everything. These are the styles most closely linked to diversity and its various expressions of individualism.

Relational Set

> People who prefer to work on group tasks or to help others attain their goals draw on behaviors described in the relational set. The three relational styles emphasize taking vicarious satisfaction from facilitating and observing the accomplishments of others, as mentors do; taking a secondary or contributory role to help others accomplish their tasks; and working in a collaborative or team mode on a group task.

Instrumental Set

> The instrumental set reflects those behaviors described as "denatured Machiavellianism." The political savvy embedded in the instrumental styles helps to diminish the sparks created by the friction among people and groups with different agendas. The three instrumental styles emphasize using one's personal strengths to attract supporters creating and working through social networks and alliances and entrusting various aspects of one's vision to others. Individuals who use themselves and others as instruments for accomplishing organizational goals prefer the instrumental styles (https://connectiveleadership.com/achieving-styles/, February 20, 2023).

From my experience with both, and through their completion of Connective Leadership Institute's Individual Achieving Styles Inventory (ASI), Colbert and Odbert exercise strong relational and instrumental behaviors while using appropriate levels of the direct set to achieve their goals. Through another lens, both "fortify their denatured Machiavellianism with a strong dose of authenticity and accountability" (Lipman-Blumen, 2000, p. 18) and referenced in the instrumental set described above. They recognize the value of being adaptive and inclusive by

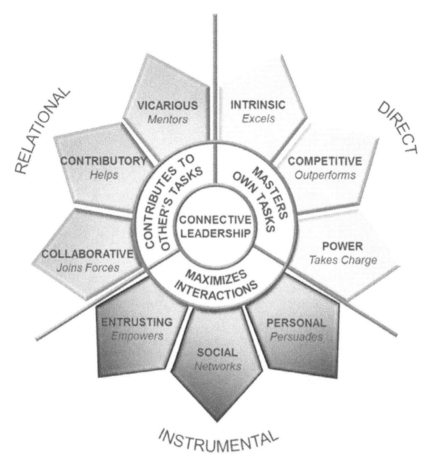

Fig. 22.1. The L-BL Achieving Styles Model. Copyright ® 1976 Jean Lipman-Blumen. *Source*: Connective Leadership Institute.

understanding each stakeholder environment connected to a venture and using the most applicable behavioral set to achieve a successful outcome.

Conclusion

Colbert and Odbert are social mission leaders who have created initiatives demonstrating that including community voices is central to accelerating equitable change. They have led the creative disruption of systems that formerly excluded those relegated to the margins of society; they are visionary and uphold an unrelenting quest to achieve systemic change. They lead innovations designed to eliminate inequities and create opportunities for community members to achieve growth and greater opportunity creation for all (Dees, 2001, p. 4). They are connective leaders through their words and actions. The leadership behaviors both have used to co-produce knowledge, influence actions and achievements within and for designated communities, demonstrate inclusive leadership (Ferdman et al., 2021, p. xxvii; Gundling & Williams, 2019, pp. 79-106), and are rightfully recognized as social justice change leaders.

References

Block, P. (2008, 2009). *Community: The structure of belonging*. Berrett-Koehler Publishers, Inc.

Bornstein, D., & Davis, S. (2010). *Social entrepreneurship: What everyone needs to know*. Oxford University Press.

Budak, A. (2022). *Becoming a changemaker: An actionable, inclusive guide to leading positive change at any level*. Hachette Book Group.

Carlson, C. (2023). *Social entrepreneurship and innovation*. Sage.

Chahine, T. (2016). *Introduction to social entrepreneurship*. CRC Press, Taylor & Francis Group.

Connective Leadership Institute. (n.d.). *Achieving styles*. Retrieved February 20, 2023, from https://connectiveleadership.com/achieving-styles/

Dees, J. G. (2001). *The meaning of social entrepreneurship* (Paper). Kauffman Center for Entrepreneurial Leadership.

Ehrlichman, D. (2021). *Impact networks: Create connection, spark collaboration, and catalyze systemic change*. Berrett-Koehler Publishers, Inc.

Ferdman, B., Prime, J., & Riggio, R. (2021). *Inclusive leadership: Transforming diverse lives, workplaces, and societies*. Routledge.

Fundación Escuela Nueva. (n.d.). *Mission and vision*. Retrieved February 20, 2023, from https://escuelanueva.org/en/mision-vision/

Gundling, E., & Williams, C. (2019). *Inclusive leadership: From awareness to action*. Aperian Global.

Kickul, J., & Lyons, T. S. (2012). *Understanding social entrepreneurship: The relentless pursuit of mission in an ever changing world*. Routledge.

Kounkuey Design Initiative. (n.d.).*Mission*. Retrieved February 21, 2023, from https://kounkuey.org/mission

Kretzmann, J., & McKnight, J. (1993). *Building communities from the inside out: A path toward finding and mobilizing a community's assets*. ACTA Publications.

Lipman-Blumen, J. (2000). *Connective leadership: Managing in a changing world*. Oxford University Press (First publisher, Jossey-Bass, 1996).

Martin, R. L., & Osberg, S. R. (2015). *Getting beyond better: How social entrepreneurship works*. Harvard Business Review Press.

McKnight, J., & Block, P. (2010, 2012). *The abundant community: Awakening the power of families and neighborhoods*. Berrett-Koehler Publishers, Inc.

Osburg, T., & Schmidpeter, R. (Eds.). (2013). *Social innovation: Solutions for a sustainable future*. Springer.

Praszkier, R., & Nowak, A. (2012). *Social entrepreneurship: Theory and practice*. Cambridge University Press.

Schwartz, B. (2012). *Rippling: How social entrepreneurs spread innovation throughout the world*. Jossey-Bass.

Shapiro, R. L. (Ed.). (2013). *The real problem solvers: Social entrepreneurs in America*. Stanford Business Books.

Wei-Skillern, J., Austin, J. E., Leonard, H., & Stevenson, H. (2007). *Entrepreneurship in the social sector*. Sage.

Chapter 23

Iran's Woman Life Freedom Movement: How Leadership Emerged

Keyhan Shams and Trisha Gott

Staley School of Leadership, Kansas State University, USA

Abstract

On September 16, 2022, Mahsa a 22-year-old Kurdish girl was killed in Tehran by so-called morality police due to wearing her hijab improperly. After that, thousands of Iranians, led mainly by Gen Z women, poured into the streets protesting the Islamic Republic's police actions. Named after the protesters' main rally cry, the Woman, Life, Freedom (WLF) movement swept across Iran very soon and covered other aspects of Iranians' frustration with the government. The rallies have been confronted with a violent crackdown by the regime, which denied all the accusations and blamed Western countries for sponsoring the protesters. In the lack of dialogic space, Iranians have created their own spaces of autonomy. Calling these spaces the third spaces of engagement, the authors shed light on the protesters' disruptive daily activities on social media as well as physical spaces as leadership activities through the lens of leadership-as-practice theory. This chapter reframes the issue of hijab as an issue of authority which WLF as a youth-led movement is challenging. Observing protesters' practices via video clips, news, photos, and social media posts, the authors give an analysis of the movement's practices based on Harro's cycle of liberation. The authors argue that while the movement made a huge breakthrough in building a public community around its main slogan, it is suffering from a lack of unity and inclusive collaborative dialogue. Finally, the authors offer suggestions for the movement's future actions.

Keywords: Women, Life, Freedom; hijab; leadership practices; cycle of liberation; Iran; youth leadership

Inclusive Leadership: Equity and Belonging in Our Communities
Building Leadership Bridges, Volume 9, 255–265
Copyright © 2023 by Emerald Publishing Limited
All rights of reproduction in any form reserved
ISSN: 2058-8801/doi:10.1108/S2058-880120230000009023

In January 1936, a policeman attacked a farmer woman in a rural area in Iran taking off her hijab by force following the unveiling law issued by "Reza Shah," Iran's King at the time. The woman escaped furtively while crying and entered a neighbor's house trying to cover her head with a tablecloth. The policeman insisted on fining her high fees. The neighbor intervened and took the case to the rural chief asking him to convince the policeman not to fine her. The officer accepted on one condition, "She must leave this house in front of us without wearing hijab ...." (Nodooshan, 1986)

On December 27, 2017, Vida a 31-year-old Iranian woman raised her white headscarf on a stick and stood silently on a utility box in Tehran's Revolution Street, one of the most crowded streets in Iran (Siamdoust, 2018). Vida got arrested immediately and released a few days later. Ten months later, Vida took her scarf off again, this time in the middle of Revolution Square holding colored balloons. This time Vida was sentenced to one-year imprisonment according to Iran's Islamic Penal Law 1996.

Introduction

Two contradictory approaches to wearing hijab in contemporary Iran are portrayed in the stories above. The incidents took place in two different Imperial and Islamic political systems with an 80-year span of time. The stories illustrate the troubles of two major groups of women in Iranian society with different views toward hijab. One group recognizes wearing hijab as a traditional, cultural, and/or religious obligation, while the other – perhaps recognizes those components but – more overtly deems the choice to wear or not to wear the hijab as a personal inviolable right. While this issue has not been played out belligerently – at least in the public sphere – both groups have historically grappled with state-imposed regulations. The Imperial state prohibited veil and chador based on the idea that modernization must include appearances as Reza Shah said, [hijab] is the enemy of progress and development (Salah, 2005, p. 118). In contrast, the Islamic system contends that hijab protects the society from corruption as Iran's supreme leader declared that for the sake of the country's development and honor, women must follow hijab rules (Khamenei, 2012, p. 33:30). Wearing hijab has been esoterically conceived either as a matter of backwardness or as a matter of progress.

Laws about hijab have continued to affect Iranians' public life. After the 1936 unveiling law, organizations and universities were discouraged to accept women with veils (Sanasarian, 1982). Consequently, many women, especially the elderly, refused to appear in public and became isolated at home; 43 years later, the Islamic Revolution happened. Less than a month after the revolution, right before International Women's Day in 1979, the revolution leader in a speech declared that women not to work in Islamic organizations naked (Khomeini, 1979). Naked to mean without a hijab, this was declared regardless of the woman's religious affiliation or beliefs. Wearing hijab was enforced a few years later, along with enforcement, protests were suppressed, and a special police division was created over time to monitor dress codes and pick up women like Vida.

During and after Vida's imprisonment, more girls repeated her practice and were named *The Girls of Revolution Street*. Their silent voices unheard until September 2022 when the silence did not just break, it reverberated around the world. On September 16, 2022, Mahsa a 22-year-old Kurdish girl was killed in Tehran by so-called morality police due to wearing her hijab improperly (Kohli, 2022).

After that, thousands of Iranians, led by Gen Z women, poured into streets protesting the Islamic Republic's police actions. Protests spread across Iran very soon and covered other aspects of Iranians' frustration with the government. Besides women's rights, quality of life and liberty also appeared in protesters' slogans such as "Woman, Life, Freedom (WLF)." The rallies have been confronted with outrageous crackdowns by the regime. The regime has named the protesters "nudity seekers" and blamed Western countries for sponsoring them. After months, the regime and protesters still hold competing approaches to resolving the conflict. Up to now, around 480 people have been killed, more than 15,000 arrested, and four deaths were through government execution (Human Rights Activists News Agency (HRANA, 2022).

Not being a problem among Iranians itself, the government role in regulation of or banning of the hijab has become such a contentious issue. It turned into a national concern that hundreds of Iranians have been isolated or seized over the last century related to the issue. Yet is the hijab really the problem?

The hijab issue in Iran needs to be reframed. We believe hijab has been used as a tool to enforce authority, and the WLF is trying to build a new discourse, a signal to the authoritarian mindset that the time has come for change. Amid the sporadic discussions about why WLF emerged, how it sustains, and where it is headed, this chapter aims to elucidate the main issue and draw a roadmap for the next steps. Using practice theory and Harro's (2000) cycle of liberation, we will reframe the hijab issue as an ontological clash in Iran's history. We conceive hijab here as a proxy for the authoritarian mentality, replacing that mentality with dialogic shared power. Reviewing the daily practices of protesters since September 2022, we argue the conflict on Iran's streets is the manifestation of a battle between objectivist (authoritarian) and practice ontologies (emerging from WLF). Accordingly, we suggest any future steps of the WLF movement should recognize and incorporate this cleavage.

Ontological Clash: Where Did WLF Emerge From?

We do not believe the issue is whether to wear a hijab or not. It is not about whether the hijab is wrong or right. Hijab, without context, is simply a thing. This is about an objective and an authoritarian mindset that has remained over the last century at the highest level of the decision-making system despite two big revolutions in 1905 and 1979. It is a mindset that depoliticizes issues to exclude people from the decision-making process (Maeseele et al., 2017). Despite being distinct in Iran's history, the two political systems (Imperial and Islamic) share an ontological perspective, effectively, "There is only one absolute reality, and I know it the best. Follow us to be saved." This mindset sometimes wore a technocratic national development hat and issued the unveiling law and sometimes theocratic religious turban and enforced hijab law.

Now, in the third decade of the 21st century, this mindset is being jolted. Iran's current movement is not about a group of girls wanting to take off their hijab. It is majorly about inclusion in decision-making as its updated slogan says: WLF; Man, Fatherland, Prosperity. This movement rejects the binaries and seeks to build space for a new discourse, for a new mode of wielding and sharing power – this space is the in-between and effectively represents a new ontology that is emerging.

Iran's current movement shows a critical perspective toward the existing dominant socialization approach. For over four decades, the Islamic arm of the political system subjugated the republic side. Since the religious side has been the driver of this system, a citizen may confront a variety of paradoxes: "Women have freedom," BUT they must wear hijab; they can't be president; they are not considered equal to men in receiving atonement and inheritance. You may have freedom of speech BUT not freedom after speech. These paradoxes have led to the pursuit (and we would argue) development of a third discourse that bubbled over in September 2022.

Existing approaches outlined by the paradoxes above might have worked in 20th-century Iran when more people identified as religious and traditional. Today, the new generation represents more tenuous ties to traditions in comparison to generations past. According to a survey conducted by Gamaan research foundation in 2020, 68% of Iranians support the exclusion of religious prescriptions from the state law and 72% oppose the mandatory hijab. Over time, the ideological, political views, and mindsets of upcoming generations have shifted, and as they try to build their new way forward, the clash starts.

The new generation has a different ontological perspective toward the world. They do not perceive reality as independent from themselves. They perceive it as immanent, embodied, doing, and practicing. They dwell on their activities right at the time (Crotty, 1998; Dreyfus, 1991; Heidegger, 1962). Past, present, and future happen simultaneously for them in the process of becoming (Mead, 1964; Simpson et al., 2018). Hence, they are continually constructing and updating their identities (Bauman, 2005). Perhaps their relationships are purely determined by who the other is as an individual and not by their traditional role, authority, or position in society (Elchardus, 2009; Giddens, 1994). That is why Giddens (1994) argued in a post-traditional society "Getting along with the other depends on an attribution of integrity … The pure relationship sustains through the open discussion of policy issues, issues of mutual involvement and responsibility" (p. 118). This new generation more than ever requires dialogic spaces like Tam's (2019) communicative space, Uhl-Bien and Arena's (2017) adaptive space, and Quick's (2017) enabling space in which mutual tolerance can happen through public discussion. The new generation demands a shift from a religious ideological mode of control to dialogic democracy where the "self" is valued (Elchardus, 2009; Giddens, 1994).

Spaces of Negotiation: What Is Happening in Iran's Streets?

The biggest problem is that the time-objective obstinate Islamic Republic system does not notice this ontological clash. This authoritarian willful blindness has been documented in Iran's officials' views such as the supreme leader's speeches during the protests. He is on record frequently alleging that the protesters were duped by Western governments and claimed that the so-called generation gap topic fits intellectual gatherings. The reality is otherwise (Khamenei, 2022, p. 17:48). To put it plainly, this issue is all in our heads. The system rejects responsibility for problems, does not show integrity, and does not open public discussions. This is against the new generation's aforementioned ontological expectations. But aligns with what is known about authoritarian actors. A 2019 paper from Homolar and Scholz summarized authoritarian leadership as emphasizing obedience, conformity (to include both oneness and sameness), and with advancing practices of, "moral absolutism, intolerance and punitiveness towards dissidents and deviants, [and] racial and ethnic prejudice" (p. 358; Feldman & Stenner, 1997; Stenner, 2009). Consequently, Mahsa's death exposed the youth's clandestine abhorrence as their perceptions of the world were denied callously.

Therefore, with the lack of dialogic spaces, liminal spaces were created virtually and physically. People, mostly young women, started to disrupt the regime's so-called religious regulations by showing disobedient behaviors on streets and social media (dancing, singing, burning scarves, cutting their hair, tossing Shia turbans, etc.) as a tactic to amplify and document their dissent (Simis-Wilkinson & Hopke, 2019). These behaviors spread like tree roots spontaneously and contagiously in horizontal directions (Iran Studies Group, 2022). They occupied physical spaces like streets, public squares, small alleys, and house roofs without being planned. They engage(d) in a new mode of participation, which Hunt et al. (2019) define as an alternative, resistive, and transgressive practice. As a result, spaces of autonomy and flow emerged (Castells, 2000, 2012).

Nnaemeka (2004) writes about this as the "third space of engagement." A space undefined where women build a negotiated feminism in situ with cultural, political, economic, and other realities of power. In her words,

> The third space is not the either/or location of stability; it is both/ and space where borderless territory and free movement authorize the capacity to simultaneously theorize practice, practice theory, and allow the mediation of policy. The third space, which allows for the coexistence, interconnection, and interaction of thought, dialogue, planning, and action …. (p. 360)

The work in Iran included a practice to open a third space given the specific historical, cultural, and political realities of the region. Renegotiating this space included removal of those borders (spaces) and the simultaneous development of new spaces. Practices of negotiation included things like women's faces being protected, blurred out, and hidden in videos. Renegotiating this practice emerged once a woman had been arrested by the state. Once her name, identity, and practices of protest became known, she may have continued to be filmed, but now her face was included. The perceived power of the state detaining this woman is reclaimed as she renegotiated how to show up in her practices of protest. Other negotiating practices include a Kurdish mother singing an improvisational narrative song at her killed son's grave or a sister cutting her hair under her scarf to honor his murdered brother as an ancient Persian mourning act. Coordination of these practices is loosely held and understood by those outside of the network. These practices leverage the precarious freedoms that exist in mind only. As such, do these practices lead anywhere?

Liberating Practices of the Movement

Iran's current movement shows nascent signs of a detraditionalization process and liberation cycle (Giddens, 1994; Harro, 2000). Overlaid with the understanding of Leadership-as-Practice (LAP) theory, the daily, in situ, and unheroic practices of Iranians and their on-the-hoof practical coping activities exist throughout Harro's (2000) liberation cycle (Chia, 2004; Chia & Holt, 2006; Raelin, 2016). In the following paragraphs, we demonstrate how the WLF practices and liberation are intertwined.

Current Practices

Phase 1: Waking Up
When a society starts perceiving itself in a new way compared to its past, through interpersonal transformation, the process of liberation commences (Harro, 2000). Harro (2000) said, in this phase, "a change [happens] in the core of people about what [they] believe about [themselves]. This may be the result of a critical incident or a long slow evolutionary process that shifts our worldviews" (p. 619). In Iran, this phase resulted from an evolutionary process through which people prepared to rise. Women led this moment of cognitive dissonance following the murder of Mahsa. But this work began earlier.

Moments of dissonance have existed for Iranians for generations, especially after the 1979 revolution. Perhaps the women's protest on March 7, 1979, student protests in 1999, the Green Movement in 2009, Vida's practice in 2017, and the 2019 bloody November protests were part of this evolutionary process that led to the critical incident of Mahsa's death. These moments of dissonance are antecedents nestled in generations specifically, but the impact somehow connects across generations.

Although it might be the result of an evolutionary process, WLF embodies the qualities of a real wake-up. It is plural and fast-spreading with a radical-critical approach toward the political system. Its nonreligious nature is reflected in its symbolic actions such as burning scarves and tossing Shia turbans. The age (the average age of arrested protesters is 15 (HRANA, 2022), scale (160 cities nationally – all 31 provinces (HRANA, 2022), and globally), and scope (various forms of discontent: social, economic, environmental, and political (Mohaddesi, 2022)) of the movement are idiosyncratic. The movement is leaderful in that the work of the next move is shared, not held by one power.

Phase 2: Reaching Out
In this phase, transition from intrapersonal to interpersonal liberation happens. Instead of being reticent in the face of disagreement, we may express our new views and voice our disagreements (Harro, 2000). We have observed practices in

which people are exposing themselves to a wider range of differences. Specifically, there are women who wear the hijab for religious reasons that stepped forward to support those women without. Embodying practice, videos show women in hijab braid the hair of women without, signaling shared community among groups and practices. Other videos show men and women holding each other's hands, making human chains and shouting injustice together. There are videos in which women wearing a burqa (of southeastern communities) shouting WLF. Also, Kurdish and Baluch religious-ethnic leaders, for the first time, publicly recognized the banned religious groups' rights in their speeches. Actresses' unveiling, female singers' and painters' artworks, and Iranian shopkeepers' strikes in solidarity with the movement are tentacles of reaching-out practices.

Phase 3: Building Community
Practices emerged from this movement include the public building of community. Harro (2000) counted two steps for this phase: "dialoguing with people who are like us ... and people who are different from us" (p. 622). In these practices of leadership, space has been made for men, Sexual and gender minorities (SGM) groups, ethnic minority groups (e.g., Kurd and Baluch), and religious marginalized groups (e.g., Bahai and Dervishes) to join and name the injustice publicly. The marginalized groups might have had internal dialogues but now are able to reach out to each other through the engaged spaces. This is seen in demonstrations and international conferences outside of Iran like WLF panels at the Munich Security Conference and Georgetown Institute in February 2023 or joint declarations of different unions inside Iran. For instance, in Iranians' biggest demonstration in Berlin, in October 2022, SGM activists, Kurdish and Baluch activists, 1980s execution, and flight PS752 plaintiffs jointly participated and spoke.

The Way Forward: Recommendations to the Movement

The WLF movement has made huge progress in launching the liberation cycle. We believe the "public community building" is a unique breakthrough achieved partially by the movement. Iranians' practices fulfilled three of the nonviolent campaign factors that Welch (2019) described: civic disruption, tactical innovations, and winning support in the international community. However, it still lacks unity and inclusivity, and this negatively affects the persistence of the movement's nonviolent practices more than outside suppression (Chenoweth & Stephan, 2013). Authentic inclusive dialogue as the prerequisite for the next phases of the liberation cycle (coalescing, creating change, and maintaining) is missing (Fig. 23.1).

Moreover, we assume successful change and liberation cannot be achieved merely by improvised in situ daily practices in the first three phases of the cycle. As Raelin and Robinson (2022) said, "... movements may start out as dispersed social activities, be they around ... especially political causes, but they can morph into more organized activities that in some cases give rise to aggregate effects" (p. 8). This conscious agency is of great importance especially when WLF encounters breakdown moments (Heidegger, 1962) such as the disappointments after the violent crackdowns and harsh punishments on protesters like arrests, imprisonments, and executions.

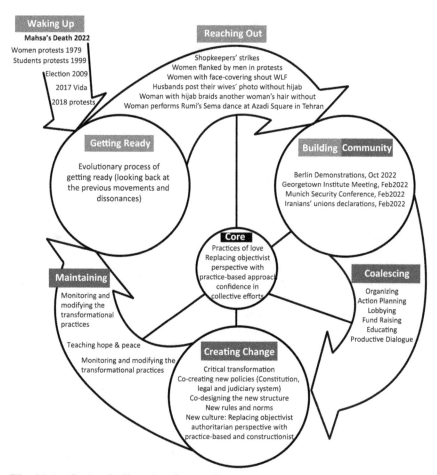

Fig. 23.1   Cycle of Liberation for WLF Movement. *Source*: Adapted from Harro (2000).

The key to surviving breakdown moments is awareness. WLF needs more deliberate, purposeful, and organized actions in its move toward the next phases of the cycle. Raelin (2020) suggested two types of awareness in LAP: explicit (deliberately getting out of the challenge) and thematic (detaching from the practical situation to reflect). We argue this awareness in a social change movement like WLF requires collective and collaborative agency (Raelin et al., 2018). In the following paragraphs, we try to propose deliberate collective practices that can be organized according to the next three phases of Harro's (2000) liberation cycle.

Phase 4: Coalescing
This phase requires minimizing different groups' conflicts and building allies (Harro, 2000). The Iranian opposition groups and protesters should build coalitions to gain more power and encourage other groups of the public to join. Harro (2000) stated that

organizing, planning actions, lobbying, fundraising, and educating are the practices of the coalescing phase. To do so, different groups involved in the movement (unions, social activists, parties, ethnic-minority groups, SGM, religious-minority groups, etc.) can embrace the engaged spaces created on the streets and turn them into inclusive *communitas* where others join and productive, collaborative, and purposeful dialogue results (Pöyhönen, 2018). According to Harro (2000), "if good dialogue has taken place and the coalitions are as inclusive of every perspective as possible, systemic change becomes the logical outcome rather than the unlikely or unattainable goal" (p. 624). Actors should make sure no one has left behind in their national dialogue; ethnic groups (Baluch, Kurds, Arabs, Azeris, etc.); religious groups (Muslim denominations, Zoroastrians, Bahai, Dervishes, Christians, Jewish, etc.); and SGM as well as different age, political, and civil society groups.

Phase 5: Creating Change
Creating change requires the coalition power built in the previous phase. The engaged spaces are shared platforms for unleashing the power by critical transformation, reconstructing the structure, and co-defining new policies (Ospina & Foldy, 2015). Using that power and having a critical analysis of the existing oppressive system, the movement in this phase embarks on creating a new culture that reflects the collective identity. Harro (2000) defined creating a collective identity as "creating new assumptions, new structures, new roles, and new rules consistent with a more socially just and equitable philosophy" (p. 623). In practice, this can manifest in a new constitution, legal, and judiciary system.

Phase 6: Maintaining
Maintaining the change after the critical transformation requires daily practices and good intent. As Harro (2000) said, "Change needs to be strengthened, monitored, and integrated into the ritual of daily life" (p. 624). The actors should be careful not to fall into the trap of the objectivist worldview which has dominated Iranian society over history. They should take a practice or experimental approach and believe everything is prone to change, and modification is possible through dialogue and working together. In this phase, teaching hope and peace is one of the main practices (Harro, 2000).

Summary

Women have been at the core of building this collective movement. Vida, the rural woman, and the thousands, and millions of others have collectively been working to build a movement, to build a new practice and new place to do that practice – a third space to engage. The completion of this space, following the liberation cycle and perhaps building upon it, requires wrestling with the ontological clash between authority, republic, and emerging practices. Power and control must also be understood as shifting away from tradition and toward a new way of negotiating space. This way includes renegotiating and planning for diverse identities. Future work can build upon understanding this movement and advance understanding of how others may build on WLF.

References

Bauman, Z. (2005). *Liquid life*. Polity Press.

Castells, M. (2000). *The rise of the network society*. Blackwell Publishers.

Castells, M. (2012). *Networks of outrage and hope: Social movements in the Internet age*. Polity.

Chenoweth, E., & Stephan, M. (2013). *Why civil resistance works: The strategic logic of nonviolent conflict*. Columbia University Press.

Chia, R. (2004). Strategy-as-practice: Reflections on the research agenda. *European Management Review*, *1*, 29–34. https://doi.org/10.1057/palgrave.emr.1500012

Chia, R., & Holt, R. (2006). Strategy as practical coping: A Heideggerian perspective. *Organization Studies*, *27*(5), 635–655. https://doi.org/10.1177/0170840606064102

Crotty, M. (1998). *The foundations of social research: Meaning and perspective in the research process*. Sage Publications.

Dreyfus, H. L. (1991). *Being-in-the-world*. MIT Press.

Elchardus, M. (2009). Self-control as social control: The emergence of symbolic society. *Poetics*, *37*(2), 146–161. https://doi.org/10.1016/j.poetic.2009.01.001

Feldman, S., & Stenner, K. (1997). Perceived threat and authoritarianism. *Political Psychology*, *18*(4), 741–770. https://doi.org/10.1111/0162-895X.00077

Giddens, A. (1994). *Beyond left and right: The future of radical politics*. Stanford University Press.

Harro, B. (2000). The cycle of liberation. In M. Adams, W. J. Blumenfeld, R. Castañeda, H. W. Hackman, M. L. Peters, & X. Zúñiga (Eds.), *Readings for diversity and social justice* (pp. 463–469). Routledge.

Heidegger, M. (1962). *Being and time*. Blackwell.

Homolar, A., & Scholz, R. (2019). The power of Trump-speak: Populist crisis narratives and ontological security. *Cambridge Review of International Affairs*, *32*(3), 344–364. https://doi.org/10.1080/09557571.2019.1575796

Human Rights Activists News Agency (HRANA). (2022). *Detailed report of 82 days of nationwide protests in Iran (first 82 days)*. https://www.hra-news.org/wp-content/uploads/2022/12/Mahsa-Amini-82-Days-Protest-HRA.pdf

Hunt, K., Paliewics, N., & Endres, D. (2019). The radical potential of public participation processes: Using indecorous voice and resistance to expand the scope of public participation. In K. Hunt, G. Walker, & S. Depoe (Eds.), *Breaking boundaries: Innovative practices in environmental communication and public participation* (pp. 149–172). SUNY Press.

Iran Studies Group. (2022). *Kalbodshenasi Naaramihaye Shahrivar* [The anatomy of September riots]. *National Security Watch*, *126*, 43–54.

Khamenei, A. (2012, May 12). *The effects of women's hijab on the afterlife and Iran's progress* [Speech audio recording]. The Official Website of the Office for the Preservation and Publication of the Works of the Grand Ayatollah Sayyid Ali Khamenei. https://farsi.khamenei.ir/speech-content?id=19808

Khamenei, A. (2022, November 26). *Basij visit* [Speech audio recording]. The Official Website of the Office for the Preservation and Publication of the Works of the Grand Ayatollah Sayyid Ali Khamenei. https://farsi.khamenei.ir/audio-content?id=51414

Khomeini, R. (1979, March 7). *The duties of clergy, referendum, and westernization*. Imam Khomeini Website. https://tinyurl.com/fs8jv6jj

Kohli, A. (2022, September 24). What to know about the Iranian protests over Mahsa Amini's death. *Time*. https://time.com/6216513/mahsa-amini-iran-protests-police/

Maeseele, P., Raeijmaekers, D., Van der Steen, L., Reul, R., & Paulussen, S. (2017). In Flanders Fields: De/politicization and democratic debate on a GM potato field trial controversy in news media. *Environmental Communication*, *11*(2), 166–183. https://doi.org/10.1080/17524032.2015.1094102

Mead, G. (1964). Mind, self and society. In A. Strauss (Ed.), *George Herbert Mead: On social psychology* (pp. 115–284). University of Chicago Press.

Mohaddesi, H. (2022). *Cheshmandazi nazari darbare khizeshhaye ejtemaei Iran* [A theoretical vision about Iran's social movements]. Unpublished manuscript.

Nnaemeka, O. (2004). Nego-feminism: Theorizing, practicing, and pruning Africa's way. *Signs: Journal of Women in Culture and Society*, *29*(2), 357–385. https://doi.org/10.1086/378553

Nodooshan, M. (1986). *Roozha* [*The days*]. Yazdan Press.

Ospina, S. M., & Foldy, E. (2015). Building bridges from the margins: The work of leadership in social change organizations. *Leadership Quarterly*, *21*(2), 292–307. https://doi.org/10.1016/j.leaqua.2010.01.008

Pöyhönen, S. (2018). Room for communitas: Exploring sociomaterial construction of leadership in liminal and dominant spaces. *Leadership*, *14*(5), 585–599. https://doi.org/10.1177/1742715018793746

Quick, K. S. (2017). Locating and building collective leadership and impact. *Leadership*, *13*(4), 445–471. https://doi.org/10.1177/1742715015605348

Raelin, J. (2016). Imagine there are no leaders: Reframing leadership as collective agency. *Leadership*, *12*(2), 131–158. https://doi.org/10.1177/1742715014558076

Raelin, J. A. (2020). Toward a methodology for studying leadership-as-practice. *Leadership*, *16*(4), 480–508. https://doi.org/10.1177/1742715019882831

Raelin, J. A., Kempster, S., Youngs, H., Carroll, B., & Jackson, B. (2018). Practicing leadership-as-practice in content and manner. *Leadership*, *14*(3), 371–383. https://doi.org/10.1177/1742715017752422

Raelin, J. A., & Robinson, J. L. (2022). Update of leadership-as-practice "practice theory": Featuring Joe Raelin Interviewed by Jenny Robinson. *Leadership*, *18*(5), 1–12. https://doi.org/10.1177/17427150221100594

Salah, M. (2005). *Kashfe hijab: Zaminehha, vakoneshha va payamadha* [*Unveiling: Contexts, reactions, and consequences*]. Institute for Political Studies & Research.

Sanasarian, E. (1982). *The women's rights movement in Iran: Mutiny, appeasement, and repression from 1900 to Khomeini*. Praeger.

Siamdoust, N. (2018, February 3). Why Iranian women are taking off their head scarves. *The New York Times*. https://www.nytimes.com/2018/02/03/opinion/sunday/iran-hijab-women-scarves.html

Simis-Wilkinson, M., & Hopke, J. (2019). Fracking, the Elipostog first nation, and disruptive public participation. In K. Hunt, G. Walker, & S. Depoe (Eds.), *Breaking boundaries: Innovative practices in environmental communication and public participation* (pp. 247–274). SUNY Press.

Simpson, B., Buchan, L., & Sillince, J. (2018). The performativity of leadership talk. *Leadership*, *14*(6), 644–661. https://doi.org/10.1177/1742715017710591

Stenner, K. (2009). Three kinds of "conservatism." *Psychological Inquiry*, *20*(2–3), 142–159. https://doi.org/10.1080/10478400903028615

Tam, C. (2019). Toward communicative space: A maritime agora of backrooms and thoroughfares. In K. Hunt, G. Walker, & S. Depoe (Eds.), *Breaking boundaries: Innovative practices in environmental communication and public participation* (pp. 203–226). SUNY Press.

The Group for Analyzing and Measuring Attitudes in Iran (Gamaan). (2020). *Iranians' attitudes toward religion: A 2020 survey report*. https://gamaan.org/2023/02/04/protests_survey/

Uhl-Bien, M., & Arena, M. (2017). Complexity leadership: Enabling people and organizations for adaptability. *Organizational Dynamics*, *46*(1), 9–20. https://doi.org/10.1016/j.orgdyn.2016.12.001

Welch, S. (2019). *After the protests are heard: Enacting civic engagement and social transformation*. New York University Press.

Index

Printed in the USA
CPSIA information can be obtained
at www.ICGtesting.com
JSHW011426301123
53046JS00006B/196

9 781837 974412